The Process of Psychotherapy

An Integration Of Clinical Experience And Empirical Research

John R. Thompson
Oberlin College

UNIVERSITY
PRESS OF
AMERICA

Copyright © 1987 by

University Press of America,® Inc.

4720 Boston Way
Lanham, MD 20706

Library of Congress Cataloging-in-Publication Data

Thompson, John R., 1929—
The process of psychotherapy.

Bibliography: p.
Includes indexes.
1. Psychotherapy.   I. Title. [DNLM: 1. Psychotherapy.
WM 420 T473p]
RC480.T448   1987   616.89'14   87-18415
ISBN 0-8191-6602-2 (alk. paper)
ISBN 0-8191-6603-0 (pbk. : alk. paper)

All University Press of America books are produced on acid-free
paper which exceeds the minimum standards set by the National
Historical Publication and Records Commission.

To Nona, Steve, Jim, Mike, and Merri
who shared me with my patients.

TABLE OF CONTENTS

PREFACE

For a considerable period of time, the various theories or systems of psychotherapy and their prescribed techniques were thought to be important factors mediating change in psychotherapy. There still are strong advocates of that position. But as the outcome literature grew, it became more obvious that different systems and techniques were obtaining similar outcome results. This gave more impetus to a general or common factors approach and shifted attention from systems to process. The history of our attempts in psychology to explicate the important process variables in psychotherapy is not a very promising one. Many workers in the field have now pointed to the need for a closer interplay between firsthand clinical experience and objective evaluation. There is a great need for clinical observations from experienced therapists in order to obtain a rich source of hypotheses to pursue in research on psychotherapy.

This book is written in direct response to those researchers who call for clinical observations from experienced psychotherapists. It includes material derived from my practice of psychotherapy with over three thousand patients during some twenty-eight years. I owe so very much to all my patients for what they have taught me about the process of psychotherapy. It is here I must acknowledge my gratitude to them. The material presented about patients in this book is factually accurate although names, locales, and specific identifying material is altered to protect privacy while preserving coherence.

In the spirit of attending to experiential data, and with the hope of expanding our concept of what is scientific, I attempt to explicate as clearly as possible my clinical observations on the process of psychotherapy. In particular, the goal of my thinking and writings is to explicate as fully and with as much feeling as possible those aspects of the process of psychotherapy that seem most important in effecting changes. In particular, the interpersonal relationship between therapist and patient is scrutinized and its components systematically delineated. In addition, the importance of the interaction and juxtaposition of component parts of the process of psychotherapy is emphasized. Traditional aspects of the process of psychotherapy are not limited to any one theoretical system, but are presented at a level of abstractness between existing theory and psychotherapeutic techniques.

My professional life has been divided equally between the practice of psychology and the teaching of *Abnormal Psychology* as well as *Systems of Psychotherapy*. Thus, I've had one foot in academia and one in practice - at times a precarious balance. My work cannot help but be informed by that dual experience.

The book presents the process of psychotherapy from a clinical point-of-view and integrates that view with existing empirical literature. Thus, it builds pathways between clinical work and research/scholarly investigations. In so doing, it makes a plea for an expansion of the very narrow and rigid definition of science the discipline of psychology holds. We need a science which can encompass the phenomena identified as constituting important aspects of the process of psychotherapy.

John R. Thompson
Oberlin, Ohio

CHAPTER 1

INTRODUCTION

For a number of years, I began my lectures on psychotherapy in the following way:

> My dear friends, what to do to tell you about psychotherapy in a few lectures. It is impossible! The practice of psychotherapy has been my professional life's work - an ever growing, changing, expanding, developing art. It has taken me to the depths of despair and trembling as well as to the heights of excitement and joy.
>
> Psychotherapy is an art and a process. You must be silent and listen with your heart and not just with your head. But, your heart must not get in the way of your head, and most importantly your head must not get in the way of your heart. They are yoked together like two oxen - as clumsy and as powerful as two oxen and you must always remember that clumsiness and that power.
>
> Be tender and marvel at the precious strands of emotion that form between you and another struggling human being. Do not move too quickly and wreck that tender web being spun. Do not move to slowly and let dust, decay, and brittleness infuse the web and trap both of you in a morass of decay - stale, dry decay with no warmth or smell. A rigid, ugly, useless, unfeeling world. Do not be afraid of your laughter and your tears; do not be afraid of your love and your hate.
>
> Give. Take nothing that is not out of health offered. Celebrate the "becoming," accept the ending. Live fully every moment of the therapy, but never live your life

1

there.

It was hoped that introduction would be enough to make any student leery of a simplistic description of psychotherapy. For, truly, in psychotherapy we deal with exceedingly complicated and intricate phenomenon which are not nearly as well understood as we should like. Benjamin (1984) has observed that there seems to be a tendency to develop models of psychotherapy that can be quickly understood, easily grasped, and simplisticly applied. In addition, she wrote:

> While reaching toward the goal of making a science of psychotherapy without losing touch with humanism, and while engaging in complicated clinical realities, there comes a moment of truth which has not yet been faced full (p. 25).

That "moment of truth" to which she refers is the fact that psychotherapy is an exceedingly complicated and intricate phenomenon that will require a great deal of effort and work before we have a scientifically adequate understanding of it.

The practice of psychotherapy, beginning with Sigmund Freud's "talking cure," is now some one hundred years old and the field has evolved into a state of enormous complexity. In the past thirty years there has been an explosion in the number of theories or systems of psychotherapy as well as increased attention given to brief or short-term psychotherapeutic modalities. During the last fifteen years, there has been a great increase in research on the outcome of psychotherapy. In the same period of time, the term "psychotherapy" has become much more familiar to the populace at large. However, there is still a rather poor understanding throughout the country as to just what psychotherapy is all about. And now we are finding more and more emphasis placed upon and attention given to the process of psychotherapy.

A brief examination of developments in theoretical orientations as well as an examination of outcome evaluation studies, helps make clear why the process of psychotherapy is becoming more and more important.

2

Theoretical Orientations

In the 1950's there were two major systems of psychotherapy: psychoanalytic theory and Carl Rogers' client-centered psychotherapy. And clearly at that time, psychoanalytic theory was the most dominant and influential force affecting our thinking about and practice of psychotherapy. Client-centered therapy tended to be seen as a "supportive" therapy and of lesser value. There was little doubt that the psychodynamic approach was dominate in the field of psychotherapy. Learning-oriented approaches, social learning theory and behavioral orientations were presented in the literature (Dollard & Miller, 1950; Jones, 1924; Mowrer & Mowrer, 1938; Salter, 1949; Shaw 1946, 1949; Shoben, 1949, Watson & Rayner, 1920) but they seemed to have little effect upon the psychoanalytic emphasis in psychotherapy.

Then, beginning in the mid 1960's there was a proliferation in the number of theories or systems of psychotherapy. By the mid-70's Parloff (1976) had identified more than 130 different approaches. One of the results of this rapid mushrooming of different systems of psychotherapy was a concomitant decline in the importance of psychoanalytic theory, a marked modification of that theory by the object-relations (Kernberg, 1975) and self-psychology (Kohut, 1971) advocates and a developing emphasis upon short-term and more behaviorally oriented therapies (Beck,1976; Ellis, 1962; Goldfried, 1971; Mahoney, 1974; Meichenbaum, 1977; Wolpe, 1958).

Along with the rapid growth of different systems of psychotherapy, advocates of the different "schools" or "institutes" developed rather defensive somewhat rigid and antagonistic stances to one another. There was a great deal of fighting and arguing with one another. Each new approach to psychotherapy was advanced with enthusiasm by its founders along with claims made for its success, and then attacked in varying degrees by proponents of other systems. By 1976 this antagonistic attitude even found its way into the title of a very fine book - Robert Sloane's *Psychotherapy versus behavior therapy*. The book really wasn't a "versus" at all but a good review of how psychotherapy had been studied and the development of an important idea that it is in error to take the stance of deciding between one system and another. But "versus" was very much the tenor of the times when discussing psychoanalytic and behavioral theories.

The chaos created in the field by proponents of various systems arguing and fighting with one another was further intensified by the fact the field of psychotherapy included multiple professions. In America, medicine was the field most involved in psychotherapy initially. But with the increase in the number of systems of psychotherapy, psychotherapists started coming from such diverse professions as psychology, social work, nursing, education and the ministry. In addition the locale for the practice of psychotherapy became more varied. Hospitals, private offices, outpatient clinics, residential treatment centers, community mental health centers, church offices, college counseling centers all became more and more common as locations for psychotherapeutic services. In addition to variations in locale, the field developed variations in the format of therapy. So we saw the development of group, family, play, and child therapies as well as a plethora in the late sixties and early seventies of human relations training programs.

Truly, there had been an explosion in the number of persons and professions involved in the field of psychotherapy as well as an explosion in the varieties and systems of psychotherapy. The field had a number of different and, at times, antagonistic factions. And much of the argument and debate engaged in by these different "schools" of psychotherapy had as their source very different views of just what was important in effecting change in the psychological or behavioral life of the patients. The various proponents of different systems believed the important factors mediating change in the patient during psychotherapy were to be found within their theoretical conceptualizations and/or their prescribed techniques. In part, the argument was that if their therapeutic techniques which were derived directly from their theory were effective in mediating change in psychotherapy, that was then proof of the validity of their theoretical formulations both about etiology of behaviors as well as about means to affect behavioral/attitudinal change. That this "mistake" could be made had a long history. For as Schofield (1964) pointed out, Zilboorg had said:

> The discovery (of the unconscious) was made on a
> neurotic patient, not on a psychotic; it was made by
> means of a successful therapeutic test. This was the first
> time in the history of medical psychology that a

4

therapeutic agent had led to the discovery of the cause of the illness while attacking or attempting to remove this cause. It was the first time in the history of psychopathology that the cause of illness, the symptoms generated by the cause, and the therapeutic agent revealing and removing the cause were combined in one succession of factors. It is doubtful whether the full meaning of this historical fact has as yet been properly appreciated (p. 94).

Thus, psychoanalysis had set the stage and provided a precedent for confusing treatment with an investigation of etiology. And that precedent continues down to this day, for in many respects an understanding of the behavior's etiology can be very therapeutic. But then seeing that therapeutic result as proof of the theoretical system from which the therapeutic techniques and the therapist's orientation derive is a very large and difficult step frought with many pitfalls. For the most part we have not attended to those pitfalls but rather have spent much time and energy arguing the various merits and shortcomings of one system of psychotherapy or another. And, of course, these systems (or these various theories) become and still remain the rather important way of presenting the field and of introducing students to the field of psychotherapy. Many books have been written presenting these various systems of psychotherapy and much research effort devoted to comparing the appropriateness or advantage of one over the other. Of course, at its extreme we were looking for the "one true and correct" theory and this kept us focused upon the theoretical conceptualizations and gave those conceptualizations great importance.

While there still are strong advocates for the position that the system of psychotherapy and its prescribed techniques are the important factors mediating change in psychotherapy, the strength of that position has been eroded by developments in outcome evaluation literature and in a more complete reporting by clinicians of exactly what they were doing in the psychotherapy sessions. Firstly, psychotherapy outcome evaluation literature started to make it obvious that different systems and techniques were obtaining relatively similar outcome results. We shall look at that literature and those results in a moment. And secondly, as we started to look more carefully at exactly what the clinicians were doing in the therapy hour and as clinicians became more and more willing to openly state what they were doing, we found that actual practice was not always congruent with particular theoretical frames of reference. (Klein et. al, 1969). Practicing clinicians were not strictly adhering to one or another theoretical orientation in their work. Rather they seemed to have taken contributions from a variety of orientations and focused more upon doing what "seemed to work." It was not unusual for clinicians to informally share with one another their successes and failures in therapy with different clients and different techniques. I presume that in this fashion they learned a great deal from one another. Certainly that had been my experience - it was by "staffing" patients with other therapists that I learned much about dealing with various apsects of psychotherapeutic procedures.

Very little if any of what clinicians were learning from clinicians was reflected in the formal literature. The formal literature, however, did report marked changes in clinical psychologists' theoretical orientations over the years. In 1961, 41% of the clinicians identified themselves as psychoanalytic in orientation (Kelley, 1961) whereas by 1976 only 19% so identified themselves (Garfield ,1970). By 1978, 58% identified themselves as "eclectic" (Kelly, et al. 1978). The two most common systems reported were psychoanalysis and learning theory. And the clinicians reported that the use of more than one theory was simply pragmatic. Two books on eclectic psychotherapy have now appeared (Garfield, 1980; Palmer, 1980).

As we started to look at what clinicians were actually doing, we found there was not strict adherence to one theoretical system. Furthermore clinicians' choices of systems were most frequently made on a pragmatic and not a theoretical basis. As Ricks et al. (1976) so nicely put it,

> So long as we stay out of the day to day work of psychotherapy, in the quiet of the study or library, it is easy to think of psychotherapists as exponents of competing schools. When we actually participate in psychotherapy, or observe its complexities, it loses this specious simplicity (p. 401).

Over these same years that saw a mushrooming in systems of psychotherapy and saw clinicians developing a more and more eclectic approach to the therapy they practiced, theoreticians and proponents of different schools were also attempting some integration of the various theoretical orientations. Or, at least, they were appealing to their colleagues to consider rapprochement. As early as 1936, Rosenzweig suggested three common factors for all psychotherapy: a) the therapist's personality, b) interpretations or what some might today call cognitive restructuring, and c) the idea that change in one area of a person's functioning can have a synergistic effect on other areas of the person's functioning. Dollard and Miller (1950) translated important concepts in psychoanalytic theory into learning theory terms. In addition, they suggested that common among all therapies were the therapist's interest, empathy, open approval, and being a role model. Franz Alexander (1963) took learning theory and applied it to psychoanalysis and gave us the term "corrective emotional experience" as well as impetus within the psychoanalytic movement to develop brief, time-limited psychotherapies. Lazarus (1977), a pioneer in the development of behavior therapy, called for advancement in our understanding of therapeutic intervention as opposed to the advancement of any one theory of psychotherapy. Goldfried and Davison (1976) said that "insight" is important in psychotherapy even though such a view could be seen as heretical from the behavior therapy orientation.

> While the definition of behavior therapy as deriving its techniques from the well-established body of knowledge in psychology sounds reasonable, it often does not occur that way in clinical practice. We have found instances where "insights" occur to us in the midst of clinical sessions, prompting us to react in specific ways that paid off handsomely in the therapeutic progress of our clients.... In accordance with most common definitions of behavior therapy this might be viewed as heresy. Perhaps in some way it is. Nonetheless our contact with reality is relatively veridical, and what we have observed under such instances is not terribly unique. If, in fact, some of these phenomena are reliable, even if they are not easily derived from basic principles of psychology, should we ignore them because we call ourselves behavior therapists? (p. 16).

Egan (1975), a Humanistic therapist, has maintained that certain behavioral procedures may be useful when the therapist is ready to work-out specific action programs with the client. And, Meichenbaum (1980) acknowledged that it may not always be possible for individuals to provide accurate introspective information on their cognitive processes, as those processes may not be immediately available to conscious awareness. This becomes shades of the unconscious in behaviorism which certainly must be heresy.

By now, it seems that behavior therapy dealing with more complicated problems has had to move into cognitive behavior therapy. The cognitive behavior theorists are starting to consider the possibility that some clients could lack conscious awareness for some cognitive processes and thus those theorists are moving closer to the psychoanalytic position of the unconscious. The psychoanalytic theorists have started to emphasize ego mechanisms and the process of "working through" which has moved them closer to the cognitive behavior theorists. And both the behavioral and psychoanalytic theorists are starting to emphasize the importance of relationship in therapy and thus are moving closer to the humanistic theorists' position.

I add in a hurry that much more of this integration is happening at the level of clinical practice than at a theoretical level. More and more clinicians are recognizing that their clinical observations are not always congruent with their particular theoretical frame of reference. Furthermore, it is becoming more obvious that each of the three major approaches to therapy - psychodynamic, humanistic, behavioral - have important ideas, techniques, interventions, and procedures to offer the clinician. And clinicians seem quite open to accepting that which in their experience works.

But integration at a theoretical level of these diverse systems of psychotherapy is a long way off. It may even be doomed to failure. As we start to seriously question whether or not all the answers may be found within any given school or system of psychotherapy, and as we become more certain about the psychotherapy outcome evaluation studies indicating no significant differences between the outcome of the various schools of psychotherapy, we are moved further and further from our present theories or systems of psychotherapy. Instead, we are moved closer and closer to attempts to identify common ingredients in psychotherapy and moved toward delineating variables that are mediating change in psychotherapy. Thus, it seems for awhile, at least, our theoretical conceptualizations

8

about psychotherapy might take a back seat. We will be focusing more upon process variables and outcome evaluations.

Outcome Evaluation

There has been a great increase during the last fifteen years in the rate at which evaluations on the outcome of psychotherapy have been accomplished. Certainly some credit for this increase in outcome evaluations goes to Eysenck (1952) whose controversial article generated much response and an increased attention to the field of outcome evaluation in psychotherapy. It resulted in enough attention that by the beginning of the 1970's Bergin (1971) was able to point to a number of breakthroughs in our understanding of psychotherapy and to suggest that studies of its general effectiveness were no longer necessary. He wrote,

> I believe that the present review has made it quite clear that gross tests of the effects of therapy are obsolete (p. 253).

The breakthroughs to which he referred included the fact that we no longer needed to ask the question, "Is psychotherapy effective?" Outcome research now needed to be directed toward answering the much more specific question which Paul (1967) had framed, i.e."*What* treatment, by *whom*, is most effective for *this* individual with *that* specific problem, and under *which* set of circumstances" (p. 111). There was also some evidence to indicate that psychotherapy may have deleterious effects. That was exciting in at least indicating that psychotherapy was powerful and like other discoveries in nature could have beneficial or harmful effects. A third breakthrough was the one suggesting specific therapist characteristics associated with deterioration and with improvement in therapy. Those findings were most exciting in that they opened more than ever before a host of possibilities for discovering specific change-inducing and retarding processes.

Around the same period of time in which Bergin was publishing, Strupp, Fox, and Lessler (1969) reporting on their investigations into the outcome of psychotherapy wrote:

9

Our investigation has yielded impressive evidence for individual psychotherapy on an outpatient basis, provided that patients are carefully selected and other circumstances are propitious. These results are strikingly similar to the conclusions which Berenson and Carkhuff have drawn from a careful review of the research on counseling and psychotherapy (p. 135).

An important finding in their work was that from the patients' point-of-view the disappearance of symptoms was only a minor aspect of the improvement they experienced. The most readily perceived and highly valued outcomes by patients were the changes occurring in psychotherapy on a broad front and not just symptom removal. The significant gains emphasized by most of their respondents were increased mastery not only over specific symptoms but in many areas of living. As one respondent put it:

I have learned to accept myself as I am, and I find that I rather enjoy being me; the most drastic change, in other words, has been to learn that I can live an enjoyable life without any drastic change (p. 36).

Strupp, Fox, and Lessler's respondents reported having new and modified orientations to life in general and reported altered self-images. Furthermore, those changes were apparent to close associates and had also occurred relatively rapidly once therapy got under way. Most outcome evaluation research has not been in a position to measure such global issues as life orientations and thus may not have been sensitive to major changes occurring in psychotherapy. Much research focused upon symptom removal which appears to be only a minor aspect of the benefits patients report getting from psychotherapy.

Strupp, Fox and Lessler's summary of the research on psychotherapy indicated that:

1) Therapists of very different theoretical orientations can be equally effective.

2) Therapeutic changes occur on a broad front and are independent of the therapists' theoretical positions and professional affiliations.

3) The efficacy of psychotherapy is primarily a function of a

10

central core of three facilitative conditions - a) experiential, b) didactic, and c) the role model which the therapist provides.

4) Facilitative conditions are not entities in themselves but rather present in all effective human encounters.

5) Techniques are rehabilitative when they free individuals to engage more fully in the kinds of life activities in which they would have become involved if the facilitative conditions had been present originally.

6) All interpersonal encounters may have constructive or deteriorative consequences.

7) Effective psychotherapy provides patients with a human experience opposite the experiences which led to the difficulties in the first place.

8) Effective psychotherapy aids patients to incorporate into their own life style the facilitative conditions offered in therapy.

It is readily apparent this summary was not focused upon supporting or attacking any extant theoretical system. Rather, it pointed to a consideration of facilitative conditions common to all psychotherapeutic systems and highlighted their importance both in psychotherapy and in other human encounters. The summary also pointed to additional evidence indicating that therapists' theoretical orientations were not related to therapeutic changes.

At about the same time as the Bergin and the Strupp, Fox, Lessler reports, Meltzoff and Kornreich (1970) and Luborsky, Singer and Luborsky (1975) published two reviews of psychotherapy outcome studies. Both reviews indicated there was much evidence to demonstrate the effectiveness of psychotherapy as well as to indicate that a high percentage of patients who go through any of these psychotherapies benefit from them.

Then Frank (1979) reviewed the status of outcome studies and drew the following general conclusions: 1) All forms of psycho-therapy are somewhat more effective than informal, unplanned help; 2) Except for the short-term superiority of behavior therapy for some conditions, no one therapy is significantly superior to any other; 3) Whatever the form of therapy, patients who show improvement tend to maintain it; and 4) The determinants of the success of psychotherapy seems to lie more in patient and therapist qualities and in their interaction than in the therapeutic method. He ends his article with the following words:

11

My overall conclusion is that the years of research on outcome, while they have yielded little in the way of definite and significant findings, have led to considerable advances with respect to the most fruitful questions to ask and the most appropriate methods for going about trying to answer them. Although we have not yet found many answers, we are becoming able to ask more cogent questions and to answer them in a more systematic and sophisticated fashion. This development supplies ground for hope that therapy research will make considerably more progress in the future than it has in the past (p. 315).

By the time of Frank's outcome review, it seemed rather clear that the benefits of psychotherapy in changing attitudes and behavior were well established. However, certainly not all were in agreement that the research results supported such a positive statement about psychotherapy. In particular those in academia were most skeptical and one might also say most removed from the practice and understanding of psychotherapy.

Then Smith, Glass, and Miller (1980) published an important little book entitled *The Benefits of Psychotherapy.* These three authors are above all else, research methodologists and statisticians who work in the field of evalution. They approached the work on this book primarily because of their interest in abstract problems of social science methodology and only secondarily because of any interest in psychotherapy. The diversity, size, and the widely varied character of the psychotherapy outcome evaluation literature was exactly the kind of data that appealed to them and their methodology. All controlled studies of the effectiveness of any form of psychotherapy from 1900 to 1977 formed the population of interest for their project and they sampled 75% of this population and 25% of the school-counseling studies for a total of 475 studies. Only after getting into their work did they realize the "hornets nest" into which they had walked. The "hornets nest" was, of course, that mutually damaging "psychotherapy vs. behavior therapy" battle that was waged so vehemently and on the basis of such little data. Smith, Glass, and Miller worked hard not to add to this internecine war by carefully specifying a distinction between research and evaluation and by carefully adhering to scientific methodology in their evaluation work.

They directed much attention to the distinction between research and evalution because the failure to appreciate that difference had led to so much derogatory commentary on the psychotherapy-outcome literature. They suggest we ought to be using the term "psychotherapy outcome evaluation". For the goal of an evaluative inquiry is the determination of the worth of a thing. Evaluation does not have as its goal explanation. And yet, too frequently reseachers were hoping to find in their results some support for "explanations." This was particularly true of the battle between the behaviorists and the nonbehaviorists both of whom were attempting to use evaluation outcome studies as proof of their respective explanations of psychotherapy. It was again the old problem of arguing therapeutic results are proof of the theoretical system from which the techniques and therapist's orientation derive while ignoring the many pitfalls in taking that step.

We are just approaching the point in psychology where we can attempt some scientific study of the determinants of psycho-therapeutic effectiveness. But as the reader shall see while proceeding through this book, I believe we are still a long way from any fruitful scientific understanding (as opposed to evaluation) of psychotherapy. And the reason for that is we are dealing in psychotherapy with variables quite foreign and unknown to science.

But, certainly psychotherapy is not beyond evaluation and that is just what Smith, Glass and Miller (1980) did. The conclusions and implications of this major work reviewing the controlled studies on the effectiveness of psychotherapy are quite devastating to any who would argue psychotherapy is not effective. There is little doubt now that the question, "Does psychotherapy work?" has been answered to the satisfaction of all but the most extreme skeptic. Furthermore, a most surprising conclusion of these authors is that psychotherapy is no less effective than drug therapy in the treatment of serious psychological disorders. They preface their conclusions and implications of their analyses with this statement:

> We have skulked behind the figures and tables for eight chapters, unseen movers pulling strings that animate the formulas and statistics, operationalizing complex ideas and concepts, wrapped in the passive voice of positivism,

13

invisible attendants to the engine of science grinding and bumping its way from hypotheses to facts to conclusions. We think too highly of our own work to disparage it now. It is not all whim and idiosyncrasy. Within reasonable limits of accuracy, it can be replicated by anyone who can read and calculate with intelligence (and to whom God has granted great perseverance). But when the work reaches the point where one justifiably asks what it all means to the world, whether it is any thing more than a book after all, then the authors can no longer responsibly hide behind the incognito of the numbers and tables (p. 181).

There are four major conclusions to this massive review. Firstly, psychotherapy is consistently beneficial and is so in many different ways. They found its benefits to be on par with other expensive and ambitious interventions such as schooling and medicine. In their words,

The parity of psychotherapy with other institutions of human improvement is insured not only by its research record of consistent benefits but also by its unique contribution. Psychotherapy is *primus inter pares* for the benefits it bestows upon the inner life of its clients (p. 184).

Secondly, the different kinds of psychotherapy do not produce different types or degrees of benefits but rather all psychotherapies are equally effective. Thus, no school of psychotherapy can claim that research proves its effects are superior. Thirdly, whether psychotherapy is conducted by group, individually, for short or long periods of time, by experienced or novice therapists makes very little difference in how beneficial it is. Fourthly, psychotherapy is no less effective than drug therapy in treating the serious psychological disorders.

It is rather amazing how different reviews of psychotherapy outcome evaluation studies are starting to come to quite similar final conclusions. Certainly one of those conclusions is that psychotherapy is effective. Smith, Glass and Miller (1980) wrote that conclusion quite strongly:

The results show unequivocally that psychotherapy is effective (p. 124).

The allegation by critics of psychotherapy - that poor quality research methods account for the positive outcomes observed - can now be laid to rest. The degree of experimental rigor employed by the researcher was *positively* related to the size of effect produced (p. 126).

Yet in spite of each qualification, and if only the most cautious and conservative estimate is made, the benefits of psychotherapy remain impressive (p. 126).

As important as these conclusions are, they are probably of little surprise to most clinicans who for a good long time suspected that was so. It may be of some solace to the more scientifically inclined. And it certainly should help those who can only believe something is true if it is empirically demonstrable.

The general conclusions of the outcome evaluation literature, however, have some very important implications for all who practice psychotherapy and for any systematic attempt to understand why psychotherapy is so effective. The conclusion that all forms of psychotherapy are effective and that the different types of psychotherapy do not produce different degrees of benefit forces us to examine much more carefully what all these systems of psychotherapy may have in common. We are being led to a general factors position as a more appropriate way for understanding the benefits of psychotherapy and thus not being encouraged to continue a focus upon any specific theoretical therapeutic approach. We are starting to have to ask ourselves the questions, "What are the fundamental elements of psychotherapy?" "What is common to all psychotherapies that might help account for the benefits we see? " "What variables are most effective in mediating the changes observed in psychotherapy?" And as we have seen, we should not be in any hurry to turn to our theories for the answers. Rather, we need to examine what may be in common across therapies. And that means we must start to more systematically attend to the process of psychotherapy.

Common Elements

We are at that point in the development of our ideas about psychotherapy where we know that no one theoretical orientation can provide us all the answers. We are also at that point in our knowledge about the outcome effects of psychotherapy, that we need to start identifying what variables in common across orientations and what practices in common for all psychotherapists may be leading to the benefits of psychotherapy. Thus, it is not in theory, systems, or techniques that we might most profitably look for our answers; but rather in process.

I, of course, am not alone in taking this position. Others have said it earlier and better. Strupp (1982) wrote:

> Since the search for "special" ingredients has proven rather unproductive, we are confronted with the strong possibility that the preponderant weight of therapeutic change is borne by psychological forces that are shared by the various therapeutic approaches despite the fact that different languages and concepts are being used (p. ix).

Goldfried (1980) writing about a rapproachement through common clinical strategies said:

> *To the extent that clinicians of varying orientations are able to arrive at a common set of strategies, it is likely that what emerges will consist of robust phenomena, as they have managed to survive the distortions imposed by the therapists' varying theoretical biases* (p. 996).

Furthermore, Goldfried gives us some hints as to where to look for these common clinical strategies. He points out it is unlikely we can ever reach common ground at the theoretical or philosophical level. Furthermore, to look at the "lowest" level, i.e. the therapeutic techniques, might reveal only trivial points of similarity. He suggests that we might find meaningful consensus if we focus at a level of abstraction somewhere between theory and technique. He calls this

16

level the one of "clinical strategies." And in that same work, he gives two examples of such strategies. Those strategies are providing the patient with corrective experiences, and offering the patient direct feedback.

I suggest that the process of psychotherapy might be close to what Goldfried calls "clinical strategies." Furthermore, I believe that a focus upon the process of psychotherapy will make more evident the general factor or factors common to all psychotherapies. It is in the area of process of psychotherapy that we focus upon the similarities that may exist among various approaches instead of the differences. It is in the area of process that we focus upon those psychological forces that are shared by the different therapeutic approaches despite the various languages and concepts theorists use. It is in the area of process that we may find some possibilities for ordering and clarifying what are vital and active "elements" common to all psychotherapies. Identifying the active "elements" common to all psychotherapies would certainly be a substantial boon to the advancement of our knowledge about psychotherapy.

This search for and/or attention to what may be common amongst the various psychotherapeutic approaches is certainly not a new development. As already noted, in 1936 Rosenzweig suggested some common factors for all psychotherapy. But what is new is an expanding interest in and firmer conviction that we must turn to an investigation of common strategies or elements in psychotherapy if we are going to make progress in understanding the effective variables of the change process. Thus, we have probably started to show more interest in finding out exactly what the therapist does in psychotherapy and less interest in what the theory or system says the therapist does.

Furthermore, as we have been more and more willing to ask patients their opinion about what has been most helpful or beneficial in their psychotherapy; we have again and again found the theoretical system of the therapy to be of little importance. Rather, from the patients' point-of-view, relationship aspects of the therapy seem to be most important. Certainly relationship is a common element to all psychotherapies.

As we have started to move away from theories in attempts to understand what variables are important in mediating change in psychotherapy, and as we move more toward investigating "clinical strategies," "common ingredients," or what I am here calling

17

"process;" it has also become more and more apparent that we need to know what the practicing clinician is actually doing.

CHAPTER 2

PSYCHOTHERAPY AND SCIENCE

Clinicians and Scientists

For a good many years now, practicing clinicians have been seeing patients in hospitals, outpatient clinics, community mental health centers, private practice offices and a host of other locales. Gross (1978) has estimated that in America more than seven million persons engage in psychotherapy every year and pay over two billion dollars for the therapy. Thus, literally thousands of psychotherapists over the years have seen millions of persons. And a recent federal survey (Turkington, 1984) indicates that one in five men and women, in equal proportions, suffer from some form of mental disorder. So, there is every reason to expect this activity of psychotherapists seeing millions of patients will continue. And yet, very little of the information obtained over the years by the process of doing psychotherapy finds its way into the research literature on psychotherapy.

Unfortunately much of the "clinical" literature is never read by the academicians or researchers. Such works as Sheldon Kopp's *Guru* (1971), *If you meet the Buddha on the road, kill him* (1972),*The naked therapist* (1972), *The hanged man* (1974); Peter Runkel's *The law unto themselves* (1970); Hilde Bruch's *Learning psychotherapy: Rationale and ground rules* (1976); Fabrikant et al.'s *To enjoy is to live: psychotherapy explained.* (1977); Kapelovitz's *To love and to work: A demonstration and discussion of psychotherapy* (1976); and the journal *VOICES* never find their way into the academic and research libraries.

The researchers and clinicians approach the field of

psychotherapy from very different vantage points and are individually rewarded for quite different endeavors. The academicians are payed for and expected to do research. They exist in an environment of "publish or perish" which only recognizes a rather limited range of scientific and/or scholarly work in the field of psychology. Above all the reseacher must have significant results in order to get published. Furthermore, it is important to get published in refereed journals of good scientific quality. All of this has been designed to assure quality and rigor in research investigations and reporting. But it has also served to severely constrict the area of inquiry for legitimate investigation. Unfortunately, as our science is presently defined, much of the field of psychotherapy was and is an area not readily amenable to rigorous scientific investigation. From time to time pleas have been made to our graduate schools to broaden their conceptualization of what constitutes research and to provide a more meaningful integration of clinical and research experience. Henry (1984) has most recently urged and outlined a system devised for creating meaningful interchange between the scientist and the practitioner. But, for the most part such requests have gone unheeded.

The clinicians are payed for diagnostic and therapeutic skills and exist in an environment which expects they will be effective in helping persons deal with specific kinds of hurts and difficulties. Clinicians generally are not expected to do research nor are they usually paid for it. The service demands in our society are relatively high and the amount of time, effort, and thought necessary for doing research is seldom available to clinicians. Since World War II, the practice of psychology and particularly of psychotherapy has increased expotentially and there have been difficulties in managing such growth. But this burgeoning growth in the practice of psychology is not reflected by any such rapid growth in research on psychotherapy or on applied psychology. The clinicians and academicians have gone down different roads at different speeds. They have developed different interests and have failed to see what interests they have in common.

For the past twenty years, I have divided my daily professional life so half the day was spent as a clinician and half the day as an academician. I personally have found that rather difficult. The difficulty is enhanced by the fact that at undergraduate institutions clinical psychology traditionally has little or no place in the curriculum. But what I feel most sharply is the difference between the academicians' and the clinicians' approaches to questions. For the most part since researchers do not practice and practitioners do not do research it becomes difficult for them to appreciate one another's perspective. Frequently from the clinician's standpoint the research done is seen as irrelevant to the issue of practice. And, from the academician's standpoint the clinicians' contributions to the literature are seen as scientifically unacceptable (Barlow, 1981). Both seem to be caught at the extreme corner of their two positions and there is little chance for them to come to a better understanding. Furthermore, as Henry (1984) has pointed out, the gap between the scientist and the professional has probably been widened by graduate programs which conceptualize and insist upon research procedures that are not only impractical for the practicing clinician but also produce results of little relevance to daily clinical work. As he points out, this gap is widened by researchers who believe that empirical research guides clinical practice. But as Strupp (1969) and Blanton (1962) have indicated, scientific research generally follows practice.

At its extreme, clinicians are saying researchers aren't helpful and researchers are saying clinicians don't know what they are doing. I do think there are more examples in the written literature of researchers being insensitive and even unkind to clinicians then there are of clinicians being unkind or insensitive to researchers. A good example of the former is the following quote from Truax and Mitchell's (1971) review of therapist interpersonal skills in relation to process and outcome:

> The implications for the practitioner are relatively straightforward.
> First, the odds are two out of three that he is spending his energy, commitment, and care for mankind wastefully; he is either ineffective or harmful. Two out of three of his colleagues, he can be quite certain, are ineffective or harmful (p. 340).

Calling people ineffective or harmful who conscientiously and with the best professional knowledge available attempt to understand and help modify unwanted behaviors, attitudes, feelings, and beliefs is pretty unkind. Then doing so on the basis of the meager evidence and studies these authors cite is making a generalization far beyond

21

what their data support. And, of course, the statement gives no credence or recognition whatsoever to the clinical literature suggesting practictioner effectiveness. It is exactly the kind of statement which has such a ring of bias that it makes clinicians reluctant to consider what the researchers are trying to say about psychotherapy.

Neither clinicians nor researchers seem to be in a position to face the great limitations and deficiencies in scientific technology for studying very complex phenomenon like psychotherapy. The scientific status of personality assessment in general is poor and controversial. If you add to that the practical difficulties in designing adequately controlled studies of psychotherapy, you start to get some appreciation for the difficulties any researcher has in working in the area of psychotherapy. Bergin (1972) wrote it most personally and succinctly:

> A second important learning experience for me was the realization that traditional experimental designs and inferential statistics have little relevance to the study of clinical problems in the currently primitive state of therapeutic technologies. Most of the methodological sophistication I learned as a graduate student and postdoctoral fellow and which is constantly reinforced by the criteria of major journal editors is too precise, too demanding of controls, too far advanced for most studies of clinical intervention (p. 452).

Bergin points to what may well be important differences between clinicians and researchers - differences that ultimately rest upon assumptions about the philosophy of science. Colby's (1962) discussion of psychotherapy and science takes us even closer to those differences.

> Psychotherapy is...a practical art, a craft like agriculture or medicine or wine-making in which an artisan relies on an incomplete, fragmentary body of knowledge and empirically established rules traditionally passed on from master to apprentice. The artisan ... looks to science for help, not to make him an applied scientist - which cannot be done anyway - but to *elucidate acute*

22

difficulties in the art. He wants help with failures, with troubles, with lapses from the expected. When called upon for help, a scientist in turn realizes *he* cannot (since life is short and art is long) develop a tested explanatory theory accounting for every event in a practical art, nor is it even necessary. His repertoire of scientific procedures is highly limited relative to the number of questions which can be asked about any subject matter. If a scientist is to contribute to a problem he must be able to formulate a *decidable* question about it. By "decidable" I mean a question which is worded in such a way that there are only two possible and incompatible answers, yes and no. Guided by the artisan, a scientist must select a certain crucial problem in the art and judge whether the problem is ready for and accessible to a systematic inquiry using currently available procedures. A scientist hopes to reduce the degree of empiricism in the art by finding that some acute problem in it can be solved through understanding the underlying explanatory principle. Other problems in the art will continue to be managed by the artisan using judgment, intuition, and personal skills (p. 95).

Here we see that judgment, intuition, personal skill - the application of the art - is honored and has its place. Equally so honored is the contribution of the scientist. And the respective orientations of and contributions we can expect from the practictioner and the scientist are roughly delineated.

The Philosophy of Science

Perhaps one of the first things any beginning clinician notices is that there are phenomena extant in their practice not noted or covered by the theories they have studied in their graduate work. Most clinicians beginning with their internship complain about the lack of integration between what they are learning in the internship practicum setting and what they are taught in the lecture hall. That this is not a new phenomenon is probably exemplified by the

23

following quote taken from Freud's (1893) obituary of Charcot.

> On one occasion, a small group of us, all students from abroad, brought up on German academic psychology, were trying his patience with doubts about his clinical innovations. "But that can't be true," one of us objected, "it contradicts the Young-Helmholtz theory." He did not reply "so much the worse for the theory," "the clinical facts come first," or words to that effect, but he did say something which made a great impression on us: "*La theorie, c'est bon, ma ca n'emp^eche d'exister*" (Theory is good but it doesn't prevent things from existing) (p. 13).

Undoubtedly those who supervise beginning clinicians in their internships hear very similar complaints from their students, i.e. "but that can't be true, it contradicts such and such's theory." Well, it is very important to remember that theory is good but it doesn't prevent things from existing. And of course, some of the things our theories do not prevent from existing are emotions, consciousness, mind, will, love, and close interpersonal relationships.

Lewis (1981) has nicely pointed out that Freud formulated his theories about "ideas" and not about "emotions" in order to make them more congruent with a rational system. As Bettelheim (1983) pointed out it may not have been Freud but rather his English translator who attempted to make Freud's system a more "scientific" or "rational sounding" one - a system that dealt with ideas and not emotion. However, Lewis goes on in her book to develop the thesis that emotion and not ideas are the basis of mental illness. With psychology's present emphasis on cognition we continue our avoidance of emotion and try to keep our conceptualizations in the framework of ideas and rationality. In fact, many are trying very hard to tie emotion to cognition. Zajonc (1980) is the only one who seems to be objecting to that.

As presently conceptualized in psychology, science seems unable to deal with consciousness and emotions. Likewise it has great difficulty dealing with dyadic social interactions. And, of course, any behavioral scientist becomes almost apoplectic if asked to deal with the unconscious. And yet, consciousness, emotions, dyadic social interactions, and the concept of the unconscious might very well be concepts necessary to describe the essence of psychotherapy. At least I think we shall see that from a clinical point of view consciousness, emotions, and the dyadic social interaction are very important aspects of the process of psychotherapy. It may well be then that we will have to develop a metaphysics of human behavior that can deal with such concepts as consciousness, emotion, and dyadic social interactions.

Science, we are taught, rests on the premise that to be "real" things must be predictable, repeatable, and measurable. Thus, physical things seem much more real to us than psychic, spiritual, or artistic things. "Consciousness," "emotion," "will," "mind," and "love" generally are not regarded as acceptable descriptions of reality. They are terms used by literary artists but not by scientists. And yet, experiences with biofeedback, attention to what the Eastern world's Yogas have been doing, and continuing developments in the psychology of medicine are all starting to tell us that the "mind" controls the body in remarkable ways and that "pictures-in-the-mind" affect physical reality.

It seems that physics and chemistry are modifying their ideas of science much faster than is psychology. The former disciplines have reduced the linear cause-effect type of science to only one part of a much larger view of science. Early on psychology tried to become more and more like physics and chemistry. Behaviorism eschewed consciousness and insisted the concept was not needed to explain human behavior. All of this happened even though Oppenheimer (1956) pleaded with psychology to develop its own science that could deal with psychology's own unique problems. For me, there is dramatic irony in the fact that now physicists are the ones modifying the science and saying that consciousness must be taken into account in any experiment.

What is most basic, most personal, and at the same time most universal may well be beyond the ordinary use of words, beyond intellect. The realm of art, poetry, religion, myth is not one of rational language but of expressive, inexplicable symbols, images, metaphors, paradoxes and myths. Even in America, there is more to life than material things and progress. There is also meaning - an awareness of what is of value and importance! And, meaning may be an essential part of the process of psychotherapy but not amenable to scientific investigation by current methodologies. Just because it cannot be investigated by current scientific methodologies need not negate its particular importance and value in affecting behavioral and attitudinal change in human beings. Most human beings easily report that consciousness, imagery, fantasy, thinking, feeling goes on "within" them. And yet, science in psychology seems reluctant and unable to approach some understanding of these concepts. It is especially ironic that the behavior therapists are the ones who have gotten us into the bind of having to investigate imagery. They have included it as a critical element in much of their therapy (desensitization, relaxation, implosive). Yet the behaviorally oriented scientific psychologists have no way to research or even define imagery. As Lewis Mumford (1967) wrote:

> To dismiss the most central fact of man's being because it is inner and subjective is to make the hugest subjective falsification possible - one that leaves out the really critical half of man's nature. For without that underlying subjective flux, as experienced in floating imagery, dreams, bodily impulses, formative ideas, projections, and symbols, the world that is open to human experience can be neither decribed nor rationally understood (p. 75-76).

As one student expressed it when Carl Rogers' philosophy was explained to him, "I see, it's not that we're locked up inside ourselves and can't get out, it's that we're locked outside ourselves and we can't get back in." I believe Bettelheim (1983) would probably agree with this student's observation. For that author eloquently points out how Freud's ideas have to be an anathema to any scientist concerned only with what is on the "outside." He writes:

> Psychological research and teaching in American universities are either behaviorally, cognitively, or physiologically oriented and concentrate almost exclusively on what can be measured or observed from the outside; introspection plays no part. American psychology has become all analysis - to the complete neglect of the psyche, or soul (p. 19).

Furthermore, he also points out how American psychoanalysis has been so badly misled by attempts to make what is basically an introspective psychology into a behavioral one - into something we can observe from the outside, really feel no part of, and act as though it has nothing to do with us personally. Probably Bettelheim's most telling point is in the following statement:

> With the mistranslation of Freud's thoughts to make them fit better into a behavioristic frame of reference - a frame of reference completely alien to psychoanalysis - it is understandable that in the English-speaking world his concepts were not only examined in this light but found wanting. If behavioristic studies could prove Freud right, his would no longer be an introspective psychology that tries to elucidate the darkest recesses of the soul - the forces least accessible to our observation. Behaviorism concentrates on what can be seen from the outside, what can be studied objectively by an uninvolved observer, what can be replicated and assigned numerical values. Psycholanalysis is concerned with what is unique to a person's life - with his unique life history, which makes him different from all other people - and it is an approach diametrically opposed to behaviorism (p. 108).

Here he made it very clear that the material, concepts, ideas, theories with which psychoanalysis deals cannot and should not be investigated via the methodologies of behaviorism. Freud had said the same thing somewhat differently and earlier, and Bettelheim quotes him:

> In the chapter of *An Outline of Psychoanalysis* entitled "Psychical Qualities," Freud wrote, "The starting-point for this investigation is provided by a fact without parallel, which defies all explanation or description - the fact of consciousness. Nevertheless, if anyone speaks of consciousness, we know immediately and from our most personal experience what is meant by it." To this statement he appended a footnote that neither the text nor the context required: "One extreme line of thought, such as the doctrine of behaviorism which originated in

27

America, believes it possible to construct a psychology which disregards this fundamental fact!" (p. 79-80).

In our development of a scientific inquiry into psychotherapy, it may help to remember the Greek philosophers' arguments about "saving the phenomena." Thus, we should not overlook phenomena when they fail to conform to our theoretical presuppositions. It is important to remember that theoretical notions and research findings do not encompass *all* of clinical reality. To "save the phenomena" we must not overlook the experience and wisdom of the practicing clinician. However, it is incumbent upon clinicians to attempt to explicate as fully and articulately as possible the nature of and insights into aspects of process of psychotherapy. Our knowledge will then be rooted in clinical observation. At that point the researcher may have valid subject material to which research methodological sophistication can be applied and/or developed. Thus, the argument is that we must not limit our observations, experiences, and concepts to some old existing notions about science. Rather, science must take responsibility for developing means of investigating phenomena which are relatively easily identified, reported, and experienced by a wide range of observers. I submit consciousness, mind, will, emotion, fantasy, love are all some of the phenomena widely experienced and observed with which a linear cause-effect science seems unable to deal. It is a serious error to require clinicians when writing about their observations and experiences in psychotherapy to do so within the confines of what psychology considers to be scientific. It is also a mistake to discount what practicioners write with the easy phrase, "That certainly isn't scientific." I believe our discipline will be better served by requiring science to expand in order to deal with the phenomena clinicians see rather than insisting clinicians' perceptions be constricted to fit an extremely narrow and less and less adequate metaphysics.

Fortunately, we are thinking human beings and can develop other views of science. Manicas and Secord (1983) have recently pointed out that a Copernican Revolution has taken place in the philosophy of science which has profound implications for the social sciences. The rather standard view of science included logical empiricism in which the test of truth of a hypothesis was a "correspondence" between theory and data. Hypotheses were to be tested against the "facts" and "facts" could come from a theory-neutral data base.

Individual behaviors are seen by psychologists under this standard view of science as a function of a multiple set of variables and the task is to identify those variables which account for the greatest amount of variance. This is the Humean regularity conception of cause.

The alternative to this standard view of science that is now available has been called *the realist theory of science* (Bhaskar, 1975) or *transcendental realism* (Bhaskar, 1979). Here the scientific laws do not reflect regular concommitance between events as is true for the standard view of science. Instead, laws are about the causal properties of structures that exist and operate in the world. The essential concept here is that living organisms have certain active powers or capacities that must be recognized and described. Then, the next step is to specify what structures in the organism's nature account for that power or capacity. The positivists would aim at establishing functional relationships between variables and that is the core of their science. The realist view however has causal mechanisms as the core of its science. Furthermore, the realist theory can sharply distinquish between the task of the clinician and that of the researcher. The latter practices science by creating at least partially closed systems. This has worked quite well for the physical sciences where the difference between the action of material objects in the laboratory and outside of it are not nearly as radical as is true for psychology or the social sciences. Thus, as Secord (1983) has said:

> ...the upshot is that experimental psychologists have no warrant for extending their results to *behaviors* outside of the laboratory. They can, however, as noted earlier, legitimately assume that *capacities* demonstrated in the laboratory potentially extend to the everyday world (p. 9).

The clinician uses the discoveries of science; but in order to effect change in the everyday world, must bring to bear a great deal of knowledge that extends beyond science. In doing that, the clinician relies upon ordinary descriptions of behavior and experience, and upon descriptions which include individuals' accounts of their behavior. As Secord (1983) wrote:

29

At the same time, it is important to recognize that this type of application, as in, say, psychotherapy, takes the behavioral scientist far afield, compared to laboratory research. But it is worth emphasizing that there *is* no way of bridging the gap; the chasm is there because that's the way the world is. The applied scientist must be *more than a scientist*, he or she must have considerable knowledge and experience relevant to the application, and must draw upon biographical, historical, and contextual knowledge if the application is to be effective. This is true because of the nature of our world, and not because of the immaturity or wrongheadedness of social science (p. 11).

The "realist" view can accomodate the fact that psychotherapy does not occur in a vacuum and that determinants outside of the therapy hour can have important effects. Furthermore those therapies that have posed the most problems for researchers are the *Humanistic* and *Existential* theories. They are conceptualized in ways that resist application of the scientific method as defined by positivism. But they may well be more amenable to investigation by the "realist" view. Because clinicians do have to be more than scientists, and in so doing rely upon ordinary descriptions of behavior and their experiential data, it is little wonder they can feel fallible and uncertain. It is also little wonder that experimental psychologists can sometimes unkindly express their opinion that clinicians are doing little more than applying some common sense and are not involved in "science" at all. The *realist theory of science* or *transcendental realism* holds that application cannot be a wholly scientific procedure. Because of the radical openness of social phenomena, in contrast to the closed system phenomena of the physical sciences, the behavioral sciences are only partly applicable to real world problems. Thus, application cannot be a wholly scientific procedure. The basic scientific knowledge which clincians have must be augmented by their competent human judgment.

Weimer (1980) has also called attention to the issue of the philosophy of science as it relates to psychotherapy. In a magnificent beginning to his article, he writes:

Taking an attitude similar to the missionary bringing

"the true religion" to the heathen, the philosopher or methodologist has often preached the gospel of "true scientific method" to the heathen clinician, pontificating in favor of adequate research design and inveighing against devils such as introspection, intuition, empathy, and the N of 1 in order to bring what are assumed to be methodological sinners to the salvation of respectable scientific conduct (p. 369).

He then goes on to suggest that for those of us who work in complex domains such as the psychological and social "sciences," *rational constructivism* may well have failed us and that what constitutes scientific understanding in complex domains is vastly different from what we have been taught to desire. Referring to the work of F.A. Hayek (1978), he points out that science cannot be a search for laws but instead theoretical science should be concerned with *patterns of regularity*, i.e. explaining abstract, underlying principles rather than laws governing particulars.

Weimer (1980) strongly argues that the traditional philosphy and methodology of research available to clinicians leads to ignoring anything which cannot be easily quantified, to a reliance upon statistical instead of theoretical understanding, and to proposing a *scientistic methodolatry.* He uses Hayek's (1952) definition of scientism which is:

...an attitude which is decidedly unscientific in the true sense of the word, since it involves a mechanical and uncritical application of habits of thought to fields different from those in which they have been formed. The scientistic as opposed to the scientific view is not an unprejudiced but a very prejudiced approach which, before it has considered its subject, claims to know what is the most appropriate way of investigating it (p. 15-16).

With this definition, Weimer believes that much of what is said to be a "rigorous" and "exact science" of psychology is nothing more than a confusion of scientism for science.

Now, the implications of Weimer's position for psychotherapy is found in the primacy of the abstract where the centrality of the "tacit dimensions" are emphasized. As Maxwell and Maxwell (1980) point

31

out, Freud's "free-floating attention," Reik's "listening with the third ear." and Rogers' "empathic understanding" are effective ways in which the tacit dimension of knowledge are activated and given some free reign. It is not at all unusual in psychotherapy for the patient and/or the therapist to "learn," "come-to-realize," or finally "understand" some principle or generalization that has been a rule for the behavior. The behavior finally has "meaning!" The therapist and patient were not consciously aware of this "rule" or "generalization" or "meaning" for the behavior and they did not come to the realization of its existence by a logical, rational process. Rather, it is tacit knowledge or what the clinician might call "insight." And that "insight" is frequently irrational, illogical but it still has *great* meaning!

My own experience as a clinician suggests that psychotherapy cannot be a wholly scientific procedure. It also suggests that any clinician also serves as a scientist and uses the scientific method. The essence of the scientific method used by the clinician includes 1) observation, 2) inference, and 3) verification. The clinician starts with a problem and observes what happens in the interaction between therapist and patient. The skill and ability to observe and the powers of observation are very important for any clinician. As Freud (1905 [1901]) expressed it:

> He that has eyes to see and ears to hear may convince himself that no mortal can keep a secret. If his lips are silent, he chatters with his fingertips, betrayal oozes out of him at every pore (p. 77).

It is this careful observation of the patient that gives the clinician a great deal of data and that forces the next step which is inference. The clinician starts to formulate hypotheses about what is happening, about what is being observed. As soon as clinicians ask, "What accounts for this event?" they are involved in theory, assumptions, inferences. The next step involves checking the validity of those inferences against the reality of further observations. In this fashion, clinicians develop some of their knowledge about patients as well as some of their tacit understanding of human behavior.

Clinician's Contribution

As noted in the last section, Henry (1984), Bergin (1972), and Colby (1962) all point to limitations science places upon our ability to conceptualize and investigate much of what we deal with in psychotherapy. I do not believe we can adequately consider or investigate the process of psychotherapy without expanding our notions of the scientific method.

At this point in the development of our attempts to understand the phenomena of psychotherapy, many workers in the field are pointing to the need for a closer interplay between first hand clinical experience and objective evaluation. (Barlow, 1980; Goldstein, 1968; Klein & Gurman, 1981; Lazarus & Davison, 1971; Shaffer & Lazarus, 1952; Strupp, 1968).

Goldfried & Padawer (1982) directly state that need:

> ...there currently exists a great need for gathering clinical observations from experienced therapists, who, as "problem finders," can offer us a very rich source of hypotheses to pursue in our research on psychotherapy (p. 32).

Goldfried (1980) had earlier said that a systematic and objective study of the therapeutic change process is needed to advance our body of knowledge. Furthermore, he stressed that in our attempts to get there, it would be a great mistake to ignore what has been unsystematically observed by many. The clinical observations can offer a starting point for and supplement to other research approaches.

It is becoming more and more apparent that the actual clinical functioning of the experienced therapist should be the point at which future research efforts begin. Early on Maslow (1966) argued that firsthand experience with a phenomenon was necessary before carrying out research or involving ourselves in abstractions. He was insisting on a place in knowledge and in science for experiential data.

Much earlier Shaffer and Lazarus (1952) had pointed to the importance of clinical practice and the insights gained there for generating meaningful research hypotheses. They wrote:

> We obtain most of our hypotheses from direct contact

33

with people who are adjusting or having difficulty in making adjustments. In psychotherapy and in attempts at personality evaluation in the clinic, as we see important samples of human behavior, we are led to hypotheses about personality mechanisms. This is the stuff that clinical research begins with.... it is important to recognize that the two sources of ultimate knowledge - the clinic and the experimental laboratory - are indispensable to each other (p. 67).

And finally, Strupp (1968) has so nicely and directly expressed the rift between psychotherapists and researchers as well as the unfortunate effects that has on the development of our knowledge about psychotherapy. He called for a closer collaboration between psychotherapists and researchers and in his own life has lived that request. He wrote:

Personally, I don't think it is possible to do meaningful research on any aspect of psychotherapy without extensive first-hand experience as a therapist or patient; on the other hand, one can practice the art of psychotherapy without being aware of the principles one is employing. Ideally, the researcher should approach the phenomena of psychotherapy with a clinicial attitude, and the therapist should have a critical and inquiring mind (p. 31-32).

It is to this call for specific information from clinicians about their firsthand clinical experience that I am pleased to respond and which has formed the reason for this book. Here I report the thoughts, feelings, experiences that have been mine as I've been involved in the process of psychotherapy with over 3000 patients during some twenty-eight years. In the spirit of attending to experiential data, and with the hope of expanding our concept of what is scientific, I attempt to explicate as clearly as possible my clinical observations on the process of psychotherapy. The emphasis will be upon explicating as carefully as possible aspects of the process of psychotherapy which appear most important to me in changing disordered behavior and modifying self-esteem.

The settings for my practice have included a U.S. Army Mental

Hygiene Clinic, a psychiatric hospital, psychiatric ward of a General Medical and Surgical hospital, outpatient clinics, a college psychological service and private practice. The bulk of that practice has been in individual psychotherapy and the content of this book refers directly to individual psychotherapy. In my experience, the process of group and family psychotherapy certainly have some similarities to the process of individual psychotherapy. But both are sufficiently complex and different to merit consideration in their own right. Thus, I think it misguided and quite inaccurate to assume that what I'm saying about the process of psychotherapy will apply equally well to group and family therapy. I wish my remarks and analyses to be kept solely to the process of individual psychotherapy. My theoretical orientation has been a psychodynamic one and I have found the concepts of ego defense mechanisms and the unconscious quite helpful. My formal education was in the field of psychology and in a department where there was a strong emphasis upon learning theory and upon Carl Rogers' client-centered therapy. I completed a two-year internship in settings that were strongly psychoanalytic in orientation and predominantly Freudian within that orientation. As one might well imagine, Dollard and Miller's (1950) book *Personality and Psychotherapy* was of great interest to me and certainly of some help as I attempted to integrate my formal education in learning theory and my internship learnings in psychoanalysis. Carl Rogers' writings always made good intuitive sense to me and there was never any great conflict integrating them into both the learning and psychoanalytic theories. It seemed to me that much of Rogers' writings were equally applicable to learning and psychoanalytic theory and they nicely informed both theories regarding the importance of specific factors in the interpersonal relationship between therapist and patient as well as having a basic optimistic philosophy about the importance, beauty and development of human beings. I am basically optimistic and Rogers' view of human nature at base being progressive and good is much more "true" for me than Freud's more pessimistic view of the human condition. Learning theory was always of great help to me in understanding how persons may develop some of their repressions, symptoms, fears as well as of help in understanding a variety of ways to extinquish, modify, or change those behaviors. Thus, for me, learning theory as well as Rogers' emphasis upon self-concept helped inform psychoanalysis. Now since that time, psychoanalysis has itself moved from Freud's emphasis

35

upon Oedipus and sexual conflicts to include aspects of learning theory and Rogers' client-centered therapy. Self psychology and Object Relations psychology - the writings of Kernberg (1975), Kohut (1971, 1977), and Blanck and Blanck (1974) - are all excellent examples of psychoanalytic theory expanding to include contributions from self-concept and learning theory. And I found that psychoanalytic theory nicely informed learning theory. The psychoanalytic theory helped identify and/or pinpoint important or crucial areas in the development of the individual - it helped focus one's attention upon specific areas or phases in the individual's adjustment and helped identify what may well be some of the most important "learning periods" in a person's life. Then, for me, psychoanalytic theory with its postulate of an unconscious allowed for the conceptualization of learnings for which persons were not consciously aware but which nevertheless would have an affect upon their behavior.

Initially in my practice I paid a great deal of attention to theoretical conceptualizations. They were certainly the "figure" in the therapy I did and the patient-therapist relationship was "ground" or the backdrop. Over the years, I have found myself focusing more and more upon patient-therapist relationship issues for they so nicely informed the theoretical considerations. In many ways the theoretical conceptualizations are best left to the patient. If I have patience, then generally my patient will tell/show me the etiology of his/her disorder and will explicate it fully and precisely giving it the individuality and emotion that is the patient's in leiu of the sterility and generality that is the theory's.

Of course, my giving less attention to theory could also be a result of the fact that the theoretical conceptualizations have become so familiar to me and are second nature now. They are certainly part of my therapeutic identity. In addition, with more years of practice I find myself not needing to know quite so much about the patient anymore nor having any pressing need to "be right." It is not that theoretical conceptualizations are no longer important or that I think they are of little value or use in psychotherapy. That is not at all true. It is that I no longer see them as the total answer - the final "truth." At this point they are much too intellectual to contain a preponderance of the truth. And my experience has taught me that while the theoretical conceptualizations are important, they are of little therapeutic value separate and apart from the interpersonal relationship issues in psychotherapy. So it is to those relationship-feeling-affect issues in psychotherapy that I find myself giving much more attention now than to the theoretical conceptualizations *per se*. Of course, in psychoanalytic theory itself there has been this shift to a focus upon relationship issues. So much so that one could say Langs (1976) has almost made a fetish of attention to the interactions between therapist and patient.

Now it may also be important in understanding my theoretical orientation to acknowledge my lack of interest in behavior therapy and cognitive behavior therapy. It is not that I have simply ignored them. Given my formal preparation in learning theory and the fact my master thesis was done in the area of cognition I had good exposure to scientific foundations in learning and cognition. When Wolpe (1958) was first published, some of my colleagues and I read him and started to utilize his therapeutic procedures particularly in the treatment of phobic disorders. Then in the late 1960's and early 1970's a number of works on the practice of behavior therapy became available as well as a plethora of professional continuing education workshops. I read the books, attended some of the workshops and thought it important to know and understand this new area in psychotherapy. But I always found the practice of behavior therapy boring. For the most part, there were never any surprises in the sessions and it seemed possible to go about my work in a rather technical, precise fashion. Certainly the relationship with the patient was not emphasized. Of course, it was important to maintain some rapport and motivation enough to continue the therapy. But that was done relatively easily and I never had much of a sense of having to commit myself rather fully and personally to the patient and/or the therapy. The commitment instead seemed to be to the importance of the therapeutic techniques being used and their congruence with the theory from which they grew. I think the therapy "worked" quite well. By that I mean, symptoms did in fact change, abate, disappear. The patients' reported feeling better and pleased with their results. The therapy was, for the most part, short-term with very specific and limited goals. But, as I said above, I found it boring. The therapy just seemed to me to lack an intensity and depth and affect and cognition to which I had become accustomed. I missed the interpersonal relationship with the patient. But most of all I missed learning how and why the patients had developed the attitudes, values, behaviors and symptoms so very evident in their personalities.

I do truly experience joy and exhilaration when the pieces of any human being's life start to fit into place and reveal that person's struggles with the "slings and arrows of outrageous fortune" - that fortune which resulted in the learnings, beliefs, hurts, fears, behaviors, choices, patterns, symptoms of their current existence. At that moment, when those "secrets" are revealed, I fully appreciate the beauty, pathos, dignity, God-like quality of every human being. Then is when I feel privy to those strong forces in every person to continue to survive, to endure, and to live through the outrageous indignities visited upon the basic nature of human beings.

Having said the above, it should be obvious I am in no position to evaluate behavior therapies. Nor do I have any great need to do so. My being bored with behavior therapy is certainly much more a function of my needs and personality quirks than a function of anything necessarily inherent in behavior therapy *per se.* But it certainly does mean that my experience with the process of psychotherapy might not be at all related to the processes found in behavior and/or behavioral cognitive therapies. I simply can't speak to that for my experience with those therapies is much too limited. Thus, my experience and these writings on the process of psychotherapy are limited to dynamically oriented individual psychotherapy.

Further, my clinical practice has been for the most part with adults and adolescents. I have had minimal experience with children and minimal experience with a geriatric population. Within the adult and adolescent population however, I have had a broad exposure to males, females, homosexuals, Blacks, Whites, and diagnostic categories from the psychoses to adolescent adjustment disorders.

And lastly, while speaking about my experience as a psychotherapist it also seems important to recognize that in addition to changes in the importance of various aspects of my theoretical orientation over the years, there have also been significant changes in the person I am. Karen Horney (1937) pointed out that life itself can be an effective psychotherapy. In addition to the formal psychotherapy I've had, my own life and the lives of those most significant and closest to me have brought me experiences which required I grow and expand and deal with my own particular idiosyncracies. Two life experiences have been most important in helping me to grow, develop and know more about my "self". One was a gift and the other an outrage. The gift was my wife's own growth, development, and wisdom. She grew to be a feminist and risked everything precious to her for the ordination of women to the priesthood in the Episcopal Church. In doing that, the gift she gave me was the ability to see my own sexism. The outrage was our youngest son at 17 years of age being diagnosed as having Hodgkins disease. That experience required me to examine my strong needs for control and to eventually be able to laugh at my inane attempts to be like a god. Becker's (1973) excellent book *The denial of death* was an accurate statment of where I had lived my life. The book's meaning now makes fine sense to me.

These changes, or additions, or expansions or developments in "me" over the years certainly have been reflected in my practice of psychotherapy. The person I was and am becomes a part of the psychotherapeutic experience. It has and will play a role in the therapeutic relationship with patients. I think I am a much better therapist today than I was years ago. In fact, reviewing cases while working on this book became a matter of embarrassment at times. I seemed so naive, cocksure, and competent as a beginning psychotherapist. I was so much into my head and theoretical conceptualizations and unknowingly worked so hard to avoid my feelings and fears of inferiority and inadequacy. I wish I could go back to some of those patients and do a better job of therapy this time.

I am aware of how highly suspect science must hold anyone's writing from their own experience. Furthermore, my task is complicated even further by the fact that any psychotherapist who becomes a participant observer is subject to the principle of indeterminacy, since it is impossible to make observations about the patient-therapist relationship without altering that relationship and perhaps in important ways. Also, since I am relatively convinced that therapy must be an emotional experience, writing about its process cannot be solely an intellectual-rational activity. It must admit of some subjectivity and emotion and it must include attempts to analyze emotion - a term that has continually given science headaches. All this, of course, makes my task quite difficult. For the task is to be able to express subtle, vague, emotional feelings, intuitions, hunches without also incurring the title of "quack" or "guru." Nevertheless, if we are to have our knowledge informed by the phenomena of clinical reality it becomes important to attempt a systematic explication of what the clinical practioner has observed over the years of practice.

CHAPTER 3

PROCESS OF PSYCHOTHERAPY

Rosenzweig (1936) was one of the first to suggest common factors for all psychotherapy. He prefaced his short and enjoyable article with the wonderful Alice in Wonderland quote; "At last the Dodo said, '*Everybody* has won, and *all* must have prizes.'" It was a fine way to say all psychotherapies were having their successes. And since they were all having success, there must be something common to all - something in every psychotherapy that would be leading to these "successes." In the article, he pointed to three common factors: a) the therapist's personality, b) interpretations or the fact that all therapists had some formally consistent doctrine from which they operated, and c) the idea that change in one area of a person's functioning can have a synergistic effect on other areas of the person's functioning.

I suppose it is not too unlikely that alternative formulations of a problem would each have some element of the "truth" in it. Since the personality is interdependent in its organization, affecting one aspect of the personality with whatever element of the "truth" one's conceptualization may have, will then also tend to modify the whole personality. In this sense, Rosenzweig's second and third factor were interdependent in their effect upon "success" in psychotherapy. However, the first factor (therapist's personality) tended to be conceptualized as an element in its own right and as something common and important to all psychotherapies.

From Rosenzweig until the 1970's not much attention was given to identifying or researching factors which might be common to all psychotherapies. It was a time of focusing much more upon particular theoretical systems of psychotherapy. There were many intellectual comparisons of the pros and cons of various systems of psychotherapy as well as the development of many new theories or

41

systems of psychotherapy. Practicioners, many of whom had been trained in the psychoanalytic tradition, were dissatisfied with their attempts to help a number of patients. Out of that dissatisfaction they developed different ways, forms, or techniques in approaching and dealing with patients. And these developments were not just capricious or trial-and-error. Thought was given to what might be important in providing psychotherapy to a given patient. That thought, along with the clinician's experience in doing the psychotherapy, helped form the base for the development of new systems or theories of psychotherapy (Rosen & Stern, 1983; Ellis, 1983; Lowen & Koltuv, 1983; Satir & Brothers, 1983, Fagan & Greaves, 1983). The focus very much was upon systems or theories of psychotherapy and not upon attempting to examine what the various psychotherapies might have in common. During this period, when systems of psychotherapy were mushrooming, very little was written about what the systems had in common. Garfield's (1957) textbook on clinical psychology was an exception. In it he suggested the importance of a number of common features in psychotherapy and included such things as 1) a sympathetic nonmoralizing therapist, 2) an emotional and supporting relationship, 3) catharsis, and 4) interpretation or the opportunity to gain understanding of one's problems.

Then in the 1970's more attention was given to noting what similarities there may be - what is common among - our various theories and/or systems of psychotherapy. Frank (1961, 1973) emphasized expectations and persuasion as elements common to all therapies. When writing about healing he said:

> All [methods of healing] involve a healer on whom the patient depends for help and who holds out hope of relief. The patient's expectations are aroused by the healer's personal attributes, by his culturally determined healing role, or, typically, by both (Frank 1973, p. 76).

Here he made the role of the psychotherapist and the expectations of the patient rather pivotal aspects of psychotherapeutic success and these two elements were certainly common to all psychotherapies.

Strupp (1973a) becoming increasingly skeptical about the therapeutic efficacy of the specific therapeutic techniques employed by varied theories of psychotherapy finally wrote:

I have become more strongly impressed with the therapeutic effects of such nonspecific factors as faith, trust, hope, and favorable expectations of therapeutic change that any good psychotherapist inevitably engenders in his patients (p. 23).

Then that same year Strupp (1973b) completed a work dealing with what he saw as the basic ingredients in psychotherapy. A major focus of that work was the relationship between therapist and patient. Part of that relationship was conceptualized as "helpful" where the therapist was respectful, understanding, polite, and confident he or she could could help. Part of that relationship was conceptualized as "powerful" where the therapist could influence the patient through (1) persuasion, (2) encouragement of honesty and self-scrutiny, (3) interpretation, (4) role modeling, and (5) manipulation of rewards. Thus, the relationship he wrote about had strong affective components to it. He wrote about it as containing "loving" aspects and referred to it as an "emotionally charged affectional relationship" (p. 6). He emphasized in this article the extent to which a psychotherapy relationship was patterned after a parent-child relationship.

Then Garfield (1974), seventeen years after his first work suggesting common features in psychotherapy, wrote specifically on what he saw as the therapeutic variables in all psychotherapies. He identified these three major areas as common to all psychotherapies: l) patient expectancies, 2) the therapeutic relationship, and 3) the role of explanation. Patient expectancies included the clarity of the patient's perception of his or her problem and of how psychotherapy may help as well as the patient's expectation of help and the degree of hope. The therapeutic relationship included Garfield's earlier identified sympathetic, nonmoralizing healer, an emotional and supporting relationship, and Truax's and Carkhuff's (1967) accurate empathy, warmth, and genuineness or congruence. Explanation included such phenomena as insight, understanding, and naming one's difficulties. Garfield saw the latter as being reassuring or therapeutic for patients regardless of the explanation given.

Next, Raimy (1975) pointed out that very disparate theories of psychotherapy still treated all patients as rational, thinking persons. In this regard, all psychotherapies agreed that the patients' conditions were related to their expectations and beliefs about the world and their place in that world. Thus, understanding was seen to be a common as well as a therapeutic variable in all psychotherapies.

Appelbaum (1978) in focusing upon pathways to change in psychoanalysis also listed what could be called common ingredients. Not surprisingly, insight is first on his list. This, of course, corresponds to what others have called "explanation" or what Raimy has called expectations and beliefs. The therapeutic relationship was another variable Appelbaum saw as a pathway to change. This variable included the fact that psychotherapy provided the patient with a "new," improved nurturing environment in which to grow. In addition the patient could internalize the cooperative, understanding partner (therapist) which then allowed the patient to engage in self-analysis and guidance. Lastly, the importance of the interpersonal relationship included the fact that the patient had someone to whom to turn instead of having to be alone. In Applebaum's words:

> Independent of the content of the analytic hours, this primordial image of a helper, someone to live for and with, someone to work out one's difficulties on, directs outward and makes workable what otherwise might be the circular, festering conundrum of neurosis (p. 148).

The concept of "expectations" are also in Applebaum's writings although they are listed under the headings of "suggestion" and "shift to activity". There he talks about the fact that with the help of the therapist, the patient is offered the hope of changing. The patient then backs up that hope with the intention to bring about the change. That intention is exemplified by the expenditure of time, effort, and money on the therapy and by the patient starting to act upon his/her new found knowledge.

In addition to these three rather common ingredients in psychotherapy (explanation, therapeutic relationship, expectancies), Applebaum identifies two other major categories which have not been particularly noted and/or highlighted by others looking at what is common in all psychotherapies. The two Applebaum identifies are "corrective emotional experience" and "emotional" release. Emotional release seems to be close to what Garfield (1957) called "catharsis." The "corrective emotional experience," of course, comes directly from the psychoanalytic conceptualizations. Its meaning may well be included in Raimy's (1975) writings about understanding, Garfield's (1974) conception of explanation and maybe even Strupp's (1973a, 1973b) use of interpretation of unconscious material.

Some of those writing about the role of understanding, explanation, insight as a factor in psychotherapeutic effectiveness included in their conceptualization the idea that the patient acts upon that new knowledge, understanding, insight and does so in such a fashion as to modify old, erroneous, harmful or no-longer useful attitudes and behaviors. That is, whereas the psychoanalytic writers have made a distinction between insight (understanding, explanation) and corrective emotional experiences (believing, feeling, acting differently as a result of insight); other writers have tended to use only one term (understanding, explanation, interpretation) to represent the entire process of re-conceptualizing one's view-of-the-world and then acting on that new view in such a way as to change the pathological or neurotic or not-so-useful attitudes and behaviors. Whether or not we have one or two terms to identify these aspects of the psychotherapeutic process is probably of little consequence at this moment. However, I lean toward the use of two terms if only because it may force us into a more thorough analysis of the various components of "understanding," " insight," " explanation" and how those components effect and/or interact with therapy and life experiences to bring about new ways of behaving in significant life encounters.

Lastly, Applebaum briefly and only speculatively raises another variable which may be common to all psychotherapies. He speculates that the psychotherapeutic process results in an altered state of consciousness and that that altered state could well enhance capacities for change. In my experience this variable he identifies is not noted by any others writing in this field. He raises a very intriguing possibility. While his writings suggest this altered state of consciousness as perhaps important for the client, I also wonder if it can't at the same time be a variable important for and active in the therapist. Certainly Freud's "evenly hovering attention" has some self-hypnotic elements to it. In any event our Western society at large and the discipline of psychology in particular are not at all favorably disposed to considering altered states of consciousness. In psychology, hypnosis has tended to be classified along with para-psychology, ESP, and meditation as fringe, rather lunatic, anti-intellectual and anti-scientific nonsense and fads. In the Western world we tend to fear altered states of consciousness (except those obtained by alcohol or nicotine), see them as dangerous if not downright evil, and are admonished to stop daydreaming, to be realistic, and to keep our "feet-on-the-ground." So, we certainly have not had either within the society or within the professional discipline a climate which would permit a fair consideration of the role of altered states of mind in psychotherapy or elsewhere for that matter. Nor, of course, have we been in any position to investigate or research altered states of mind. However, hypnotherapy and hypnoanalysis have gained more acceptance recently and certainly the importance of relaxation and imagery in behavior therapy as well as the developing interest in biofeedback and medical psychology may well force us to a more careful and less prejudiced consideration of altered states of consciousness. But certainly at this time, altered states of consciousness are not seen as one of the variables common to all psychotherapies and Applebaum's suggestion remains speculative and intriguing.

In 1980 Brady, Davison, Dewald, Egan, Fadiman, Frank, Gill, Hoffman, Kempler, Lazarus, Raimy, Rotter, and Strupp (1980) (all prominent therapists) were asked to share their views on the effective principles of psychotherapy. They were asked to do this from the vantage point of their own experience as clinicians. Again, three major areas were identified although this time "expectations" was not one of the three. Explanation, therapeutic relationship, and corrective experiences were the three areas. While the majority of therapists found all three of these variables to be of some importance in their clinical work, there certainly are differences among them as to the importance they place on any one of these three variables. Also, there was marked variability among the therapists in definitions for these variables as well as in the extent to which these variables were considered effective. For example, in response to the question "To what extent does offering patients/clients feedback on their thinking, emotions, and behavior facilitate therapeutic change?" - a question dealing with the varible of explanation - Brady said, "...I do not find it a major treatment strategy" (p.164). Dewald said, "Interpretation or other forms of feedback alone do not create change. Change occurs as the result of how the patient responds to and uses the feedback offered by the analyst"(p.164). Egan said, "If new experiences constitute the 'machinery' of behavioral change, then feedback is the oil that keeps it running" (164). Lazarus said,

46

"Feedback alone, without providing alternate (more adaptive) reactions or responses is limited" (p. 167). And Raimy said, "Verbal feedback that graphically encapsulates a client's misconception about himself or his relationships is for me the 'therapeutic act' *par excellence*"(p.167). So, we see the role of understanding and explanation is viewed all the way from being a therapeutic act *par excellence* to not being a major therapeutic strategy at all.

In response to the question dealing with the role of the therapist-patient relationship in effecting change in psychotherapy; Brady said,"There is no question that qualitative aspects of the relationship can greatly influence the course of therapy for good or bad" (p.169). Davison said, "This aspect of therapy is of the utmost importance" (p.171). Dewald indicated he saw it as crucial to the entire therapeutic process. Egan regarded it as too often over played and Fadiman saw it as "...a mix of blessings and impediments" (p.171). For Frank it is "...the cornerstone of all psychotherapy" (p.171). For Gill and Hoffman it is "...the central consideration in the process of change" (p.172), and for Strupp it is "crucial for therapeutic change" (p.175). In general, the therapeutic relationship was another variable seen by a goodly number of these clinicians as important to the change process. Two major aspects of the relationship seems to have been emphasized. One includes the importance of a caring, trustworthy, and confident therapist. The other emphasizes the importance of the relationship as a place in which the patient can obtain new awareness, perspective, and ways of relating. So, in that sense, the relationship is also tied to or interrelated with "corrective emotional experiences."

In the third area, which I labeled "corrective experiences," there was very good agreement among these experts as to the importance of that variable for successful therapy. They were asked this question, "What is the role played by new experiences provided to the patient/client facilitating change?" Brady said, "I regard new experiences...as critical to favorable change" (p.157). Davison said, "I have absolutely no doubt that this factor is absolutely crucial for therapeutic change and that, indeed, it cuts across all therapy orientations" (p.157). Dewald said, "In psychoanalysis and psychoanalytic psychotherapy, new experience plays a crucial role in facilitating change" (p.158). Egan said, "I believe that new experiences are critical in facilitating change"(p.158). Fadiman's answer was, "Without new experiences, there is no change" (p.159).

47

For Frank "...all psychotherapy is a new experience..."(p.159). Gill & Merton said, "There is little doubt that the therapist's personality and his manner of relating can often provide the patient with a new and beneficial interpersonal experience" (p.160). For Kempler "...new experiences are our essential aspect of changing"(p.160). Lazarus said, "By definition, without 'new experiences' there can be no change"(p.161). For Raimy "Almost everthing I do in therapy consists of trying to provide the client with new experiences..."(p.161). Rotter said, "If one accepts the idea that a new thought is a new experience, then of course, all change follows from new experience" (p.162); and Strupp said, "Thus the essence of psychotherapy is interpersonal learning, a new significant experience (*Erlebnis*) that, if all goes well, modifies basic aspects of the patient's patterns of relatedness in ways that are called therapeutic"(p.163).

A summary of what these clincians have said from their own experience suggests that "new experiences" are very important if not crucial for the therapeutic change process. Now as noted, I have called this area "corrective experiences" whereas the question specified "new" experiences. I am assuming that therapists in answering this question had in mind "new" experiences which were corrective of old habits, learnings, expectations. I do not think these therapists were just thinking of "new" experiences *per se* as being necessarily therapeutic and in fact the question specified "experiences provided to...facilitating change." Seldom, anymore, would the patient be advised to take a trip to the mountains, a vacation by the seashore, or a Carribean cruise as a way of resolving depression, anxiety, phobias, sexual dysfunctions, interpersonal relationship turmoils. Nor would we generally encourage patients to go out and seek new experiences of any kind in any place and believe that alone would necessarily be therapeutic. All of this is not to say that trips, vacations, cruises, new experiences of all kinds can't be therapeutic. Given the right conditions, any or all of these "new" experiences could be therapeutic. But those "conditions" would help dictate what may or may not be "corrective experiences" and thus psychotherapeutic. For me, the category "new experiences" includes the concept of corrective emotional and intellectual experiences. And, as noted earlier, it is also related to and interdependent with the concepts of explanation, interpretation, and insight.

Thus, it starts to appear that in different ways and with a limited number of terms as well as with varied emphases therapists from diverse orientations and practices are pointing to four major areas in which there is some commonality among different therapeutic systems. Those four major areas can be classified under the headings: 1) Expectations, 2) Therapeutic Relationship, 3) Explanations, and 4) Corrective Experiences. Furthermore, I submit that these headings might well be at a level of abstractness between theory and technique. For the most part each of these headings will have a definition in the different systems of psychotherapy at both the theoretical and the technique level. Also, each of the theories will give different weight to the importance of these variables in affecting change in psychotherapy. But, as we more carefully examine the process of psychotherapy, it may become even clearer what role these four relatively common ingredients of psychotherapy may play in affecting change and at what points in the psychotherapy one or the other of these variables becomes of paramount importance. Furthermore, as we more carefully examine the process of psychotherapy, we may be able to define these terms more explicitly and in greater detail . At this point, all four of them are relatively general terms and furthermore we talk about them as though they were separate, independent variables or aspects of the process of psychotherapy.

However, the process of psychotherapy is a unity - an entire whole which is only arbitrarily divided into categories. Such division is our way of attempting to understand complex phenomena. And it is of some importance that many persons from varied theoretical orientations are reporting some very similar generalized abstractions about what are the most important aspects of the psychotherapy process.

My Experience of the Process of Psychotherapy

My view of the important variables in the process of psychotherapy is not too different from what the literature has indicated as important variables. In my experience the 1) dyadic interaction or therapeutic relationship, 2) interpretation, insight, understanding, and 3) corrective experience are all very important parts of the psychotherapy process.

As we summarize large bodies of literature and experience we should carefully note whether or not the terms or language used is equally understood and/or similarly defined. The words "therapeutic relationship," "interpretation," "insight," "understanding," "corrective experience" probably do not accurately convey all of the meaning and complexities I feel and understand when I use those terms. The reader and I will simply have to accept the present limitations of words and space-in-which-to-place-the-words. It will take the major portion of this book to explicate and attempt to make clear and understandable what I mean by the three areas identified above - "therapeutic relationship," "interpretation/ insight/ understanding," and "corrective experience." But we have to begin at some point. There has to be a place at which we start to build a vocabulary and an experience together. That mutual experience will hopefully allow us to understand one another and permit us to view a third phenomenon from a similar base or platform and thus be able to comprehend what it is we are "seeing". But that cannot be done simply, easily, and in haste. It will take time for us to build the frame in which we can better view the phenomenon I'm attempting to explicate.

Three Variables.

There is a chapter in this book which deals with "interpretation/insight/understanding," and another chapter dealing with the concept of "corrective experience." However, the area of "dyadic interaction or therapeutic relationship" is sufficiently complex and mulifaceted that I have broken it into component parts. Thus, there are three chapters that deal with this variable in the process of psychotherapy. The very next chapter discusses the therapeutic relationship, which certainly includes some of those common variables Garfield (1957) identified as well as some of the variables Rogers (1951, 1957, 1961) postulated as so important and that Truax and Carkhuff (1967) helped confirm. In addition that chapter contains a section on what I've chosen to identify as the interpersonal relationship in psychotherapy. I thus attempt a distinction between what may well be aspects of the dyadic interaction between patient and therapist that are commonly seen as being therapeutic (and which in my experience are very important parts of the psychotherapy process); and aspects of the dyadic interaction that are part of the realistic, socio-culturally based personal relationship between the therapist and the patient. Then the chapter on transference and the one on countertransference deal with two other important but nevertheless different aspects of the therapeutic relationship.

I hope it will be helpful to have this multifaceted approach to the concept of "therapeutic interpersonal relationship." In my experience, the dyadic interaction or what I am calling the "therapeutic interpersonal relationship" is extremely important in the process of psychotherapy. And, almost all psychotherapy theorists give some importance to the nature of the relationship between the therapist and patient. But it is well past the time when we can continue to speak and write about the therapeutic relationship as though it were one concept, or had a generally agreed upon definition. Different theorists may well agree that the therapeutic relationship is important but have great disagreements over precisely what they mean by the term "therapeutic relationship." In the hope of speaking most accurately about the process of psychotherapy, I attempt to define different aspects of the "therapeutic interpersonal relationship" and the role they may or may not play in the process of psychotherapy.

Therapeutic Alliance

Now in addition to the variables of relationship, interpretation, and corrective experience; the literature also identifed "expectations" as a common variable. I have not identified "expectations" as one of the variables I've found to be important in the process of psychotherapy. Nor did the prominent therapists in Brady's (1980) report speak about expectations as an important part of therapy. But they were also not asked any question that could reasonably be expected to elicit their experience with patients' expectations in psychotherapy. Certainly others (Garfield, 1974, Applebaum, 1978) have considered it a variable common to all psychotherapies and of importance in effecting change. Frank (1961, 1973) has considered it to be one of the most important variables accounting for success in psychotherapy. As I review my experience as a psychotherapist, it seems to me that the issue of "expectancies" has played a role in the process of psychotherapy but I have not systematically or even consciously conceptualized it as a separate variable. I have not given

51

it a predominant place in my thinking about the process of psychotherapy. Rather, it seems I may well have subsumed it under two other headings: "therapeutic alliance" and "counter-transference."

As I consider what happens when I first see the patient and we have our first session together, I do not think I am consciously attending to the patient's expectations. But I am very carefully and attentively listening to and observing this other human being. In addition to the content of the patient's talk, I am also keenly aware of the patient's affect, demeanor, voice tone, attitude, posture, facial expressions, body movements. I am attempting to feel-sense-see-understand-comprehend-know as much as I possibly can about where that person *is* at the very moment I am talking-interacting with him or her. And in doing all of that I suppose I do respond to some patient expectations. However, I cannot say that I am consciously aware of them - or that I have conceptualized psychotherapy or the process of psychotherapy as including the patient's expectations. Rather, I am most keenly aware of attempting to "meet" this other person on their ground, of attempting to understand how they see/feel this moment, of assuming the "internal frame of reference" (Roger's 1951) so that I might be as fully with that person during the session as possible. Now in doing that, I am confident that I'm hearing and responding to patient expectations. But that is certainly not all that I am doing and I'm not at all sure it is the most important thing I am doing. What I think I am doing is twofold: I'm starting to understand what problems this individual may have so that I can know whether or not this is something with which I feel prepared to deal, and I'm beginning to work on the development of a therapeutic alliance.

As I begin to develop a therapeutic alliance, I pay considerable attention to the patient's expectations for psychotherapy. For it is in working on the development of therapeutic alliance that I'm listening for the patient's commitment to, fears about, wishes, desires, and hopes for psychotherapy. Furthermore, in some cases, as psychotherapy progresses it becomes necessary again to focus upon the therapeutic alliance. Patients may come up against some particularly strong internal and personal resistances and start to question the whole process and use of psychotherapy. Or, patients may find that the problem which brought them to psychotherapy is now relatively well resolved and they are feeling much better. But, they now more fully and consciously realize they have another much greater problem with which to deal, and they have some reluctance to start on the "new" problem. In both of these situations, I would find myself again focusing upon therapeutic alliance and that would include aspects of patients' expectations. But again, I would not see the expectations as being solely important. Their importance would be the place they may hold in helping or hindering the development of a therapeutic alliance. Thus, I find the concept of "therapeutic alliance" a much more encompassing and useful one for identifying one variable that make up the process of psychotherapy than the concept of "expectations."

Most of the people who have written about the importance of expectations in psychotherapy have limited their concerns to the patient's expectations. I think the therapist's expectations may also play a rather important role in the process of psychotherapy. But again, I don't find myself attracted to developing a category labeled "expectations" for conceptualizing the process of psychotherapy. Rather, I think the therapist's expectations become part of the interpersonal relationship in psychotherapy and/or part of countertransference in the process of psychotherapy.

So, I have not found it useful or important to identify and/or included expectancies as a separate function in the process of psychotherapy. Nevertheless, I do not think I discount its importance. It is only that I place it within what I see as broader or more encompassing functions.

We now have the following terms to represent different parts of the process of psychotherapy: 1) The Therapeutic Relationship, which I divide into four component parts. 2) Therapeutic Alliance. 3) Interpretation, Insight, Understanding. 4) Corrective Experience. In my practice I have noted two other identifiable and important parts to the process of psychotherapy. One is what I have called "Material Flow," and the other is "Termination" or ending the psychotherapy. Then, in addition to these six variables, I also suggest one principle as being important - i.e. a principle about the interrelatedness and interdependencies among these six process variables.

Before expanding on the principle of interrelatedness, we shall briefly consider what is meant by "Material Flow" and "Termination."

53

Material Flow.

Briefly, the term "material flow" refers to the observation that the content and affect from one session to the next in a series of psychotherapy sessions seem highly interrelated and connected to one another. It is almost as though the patient "works" his/her therapy for the hour. Then one week later they continue as though there had not been seven days, or 168 hours between sessions. There is, thus, a flow of the material with which they are dealing in the therapy from one session to the next. It seems to me this flow becomes even more obvious when the patient is seen more frequently than one-time-per-week.

In attempts to highlight and identify "material flow," I summarize each session in one or two sentences immediately after the session ends. I ask myself, "What did he/she say to me today?" and then attempt to answer that question in one or two sentences. In this fashion, I noticed that statements from one session ran into and made sense with statements from sessions next to it. I could see the "progress" or change in the material from session to session. It is as though I could see the problem being "worked on" and "worked-out." Thus it is generally not a surprise when the "topic" is changed. For the "material flow" readily prepares one to "know" when a problem is coming to an end.

Another way in which I have been able to see the importance of "material flow" in the process of psychotherapy is related to changes the patient reports in his or her behavior with significant other persons. It is not unusual for patients to report in the therapy hour some changes in behavior with significant persons in their world outside of therapy. By doing so, patients are already, without any therapist's overt prompting, trying out new found insights and expanding the range of interactions with persons outside the therapeutic relationship. Certainly this is an important part of the corrective emotional experience, but it is also a part of the "material flow." When the patient moves out into the environment with other people in significantly different ways, I take that as evidence that the therapy-work is "working" or is significant. (I must parenthetically add that patients can go about trying out new behaviors in the outside world in such a fashion as to constitute a resistance to therapy. So it is not just trying out new behaviors outside of psychotherapy that can be a sign of growth and change. Rather, the manner in which those behaviors are attempted and the underlying motivations for so acting are crucial.)

Once patients successfully accomplish interacting with others in their environment on the basis of the insight, understanding, and experience they obtained in therapy; then new and additional material will start to surface in the psychotherapy sessions. The material will start to flow again, perhaps in a different direction or on a different topic. It is as though the patient is now "done" with one issue or one facet of the issue with which he or she was dealing and is now free to move on to the next emerging issues, i.e. to what next occurs in his or her process. It is also here, that I find it so very important to follow the patient's leads - something I think should be done almost all of the time anyway. I think that if we don't take our cue from the patient's process, we will miss seeing the depth, beauty and uniqueness of that particular human being.

The following case vignette contains examples of "material flow." It does so in terms of how one session tends to lead into the next session, in terms of how a series of sessions will be focused upon one "issue," and in terms of how new behaviors with significant others outside of therapy bespeaks a change in the therapy material.

Joseph a 26 year old male seeks psychotherapy out of a rather strong sense of feeling out of place alot, on the outskirts of things, not involved and feeling inadequate, inferior, deprived. He was seen three times a week for some 45 sessions. This vignette is taken from the 6th to the 15th session, a period of 3 1/2 weeks in his therapy. Following are the one-two sentence summaries for those sessions:

#6: I realize I can lead my life anyway I want. I've been feeling more anger.

#7: I'm late and quiet today and fear confrontation.

#8: There is another character in me, angry and evil and destructive, but also very vulnerable if expressed or shown.

#9: I dreamed I tamed a wolf (the female part of me) enough to have it lie with me. The cub (my little boy) ran away.

#10: I don't trust authority (you) and can't share with them because they have/will betray me.

#11: I show you a part of me - the crazy, self-punishing, self-castigating part that says I'm no good and am bad and must make amends.

#12: I told Mary [his girlfriend with whom he lived] of a part of me. Therapy is stretching. It's scary and I have some resistance.

55

#13: I have been angry this week. Mary hasn't seen that side of me before.

#14: I can't remember an important dream. You start to pin me down but I'm afraid of being touched and touching.

#15: I could dream of being violent with father, some aesthetic sexuality with mother, and a baby drowning.

In these few sessions, Joseph moves from tentatively showing me that he can feel anger (session #6) and is not quite sure how or what to do with it other than come late and be quiet and fear confrontation (session #7) to being more explicit about an angry-evil-destructive part of him (session #8). Then in session #9, with a dream, tells me that he would permit me to approach the tender, sensitive part of him (the female represented in his dream as interpreted by him as a wolf) but the cub (the little boy in him) would still run away from me. In session #10 he is reminded by himself that he doesn't trust authority and fears he will be betrayed by them. What was there to do with this material but personalize it? Both he and I knew he was talking about us. It was however, the first time in his life he had directly said these feelings and beliefs to any "authority" figure. Evidently there was some corrective emotional experience for him in this session of stating his feelings and me taking his lead to personalize and own that it is our relationship, in part, he is talking about. For, the ending of that session was an agreement for both of us to push even harder in therapy. And then in session #11 he can show an important, significant part of himself well-hidden from those with whom he has relationships.

Then we see in the next two sessions that he shares part of himself with his girlfriend, Mary. And he is telling me about that in the therapy hour as well as the fact that he feels therapy is stretching him personally and pulling him to abstract feelings he can't define but of which he is afraid. Small wonder then that in the next session he reports having had an "important" dream which of course he can't remember and is afraid of being touched or touching, i.e. connectedness. So in his verbal and non-verbal language, he is signaling a change in the content, manner, affective tone, of the therapy sessions. The process is being worked-out. It is as though he has done what he needs to do in order now to be in the position of approaching his most important issues, which are feeling out of place alot, on the outskirts of things, not involved or in other words a lack of connectedness. Of course, he did not consciously plan this whole approach - this sequence of sessions #6 to #14 - nor did I, his therapist. How would I know that was where he was going until he got there. All I could know was that something was happening - the process of psychotherapy was occurring, there was a sequence, relatedness, "flow" of material. As he gained some security and corrective emotional experiences within the psychotherapy sessions, he was able to try out sharing some new behaviors with significant others outside the therapy hour. And then in the 15th session he tells us (both me and himself) what his important dreams are all about: anger with father, sex with mother, and being "drowned" as a baby. Well, those are nice Oedipul themes and for the next 15 to 18 sessions, relationships/feelings with and about father and his own sexuality *vis a vis* those relationships/feelings are the "material flow" of therapy.

A simile for this concept of "material flow" would be watching somebody work on a piece of needlepoint. You notice that they have begun to work in the reds of a rose in the lower half of the piece. And session after session you see the "rose" start to become more obvious, take shape, have color and shading. At first they are slow in doing the work and it seems they only add to the needlepoint pattern when in the hour therapy session. Then one day you notice that a great deal of work has been done on the "rose". It is obvious they were working on it outside of therapy - and, in fact, they may tell you exactly when and how they did so. Now, they point out, there is only a little bit left to do on that "rose" and they may ask your advice as to how they have done on this "rose," i.e. they may ask for some reassurance. But they also point to where they want to start work next - on a green leaf!

You can see I enjoy watching patients do their "needlepoint" and thus take part in their "material flow." I consider it an important and crucial part of the process of psychotherapy. Chapter 9 deals with this aspect of the process of psychotherapy.

Termination

The sixth variable I identify for the process of psychotherapy is "termination." It is a subject not regularly covered by therapists in their writings and certainly not one identified by those looking for communality among the various systems of psychotherapy. Yet, in my experience it is an important aspect of the process of psychotherapy and one which takes some skill and knowledge in order to accomplish a successful and effective end to psychotherapy. Chapter 11 deals with this variable.

Interrelatedness.

Now that these six variables have been listed and identified as though they were separate and discrete parts of the process of psychotherapy, it becomes important to emphasize their interrelatedness and interdependencies. This principle for the process of psychotherapy - that the variables are interrelated and the process forms a whole - has not been emphasized in the research or clinicial literature. In actual practice the clinician cannot so easily separate and discriminate between these various components of the process of psychotherapy, as is done in this book. Generally, even in one session, the clinician finds that first one aspect of process is important (alliance) only to then be replaced by another aspect of process (perhaps relationship). These variables in the process of psychotherapy fluctuate in importance during the therapy and perhaps even within one session of psychotherapy. For example, it is generally assumed that the therapeutic alliance is a variable important in the process of therapy within the first few sessions, i.e. only until the therapeutic alliance is established. That is not necessarily the case. Certainly the first sessions are ones in which the development of a therapeutic alliance becomes important. But it is also not unusual that therapeutic alliance could assume importance at some later point in therapy during periods of resistance or at times of moving to new levels of analysis. The therapist would then be required to again focus upon therapeutic alliance factors in the psychotherapeutic process.

In addition to the importance of these different parts of psychotherapy varying from session to session or even within one session, there is also the fact that these parts or identified variables of the process of psychotherapy are interactive. We may have a combination of variables at any one time which is therapeutic, whereas one or two or three of the variables alone would never result in a therapeutic process. When a helpful, meaningful interpretation is made in one session, that experience becomes part of the

58

"therapeutic interpersonal relationship" between patient and therapist. It also may become part of the "therapeutic alliance." It simply cannot *stand* as just an experience in and within the realm of "interpretation, insight, understanding" alone. Rather it interacts and combines with other variables in the process. Furthermore, if that interpretation was helpful, meaningful and of use to the patient, and affected the alliance and "therapeutic interpersonal relationship" positively, the next time an interpretation is made it is probably more likely to be considered. For then it is made in the context of a strengthened alliance and a relationship that includes experiences of helpful interpretations.

I know I'm struggling with attempts to make this clearer. The image that comes to my mind is making bread. Flour is going to be a major ingredient. But we will also need yeast to enable the flour to rise. In addition some liquid (perhaps milk). But if the milk is too warm, it may kill the yeast and the flour will just sit there a soggy lump. Furthermore some may like shortening and salt in their bread. And finally, we need some heat at the right time and in the exact amount and for a specified period of time to bake the bread. Tell me, what is most important in making the bread? And are its ingredients (milk, flour, salt, yeast, shortening, heat) anything different or more once they are combined in a specific and understandable order? It is the interaction between and combination among these various elements or ingredients that makes the bread. Likewise, the process of psychotherapy requires a much more complex but perhaps as carefully measured interaction and combination of elements as that attended to in the production of bread.

In part, it is knowing about and understanding the interaction and combination of the elements of the process of psychotherapy that is the art of psychotherapy - or that may more accurately be called a portion of the therapist's professional judgment. In any one session, the therapist is not only attending to the material being discussed and presented, but is also continually feeling/assessing varied aspects of the therapeutic relationship, alliance, transference, and counter-transference issues. And the therapist's interventions, statements, questions, or interpretations are made in light of how, in that therapist's professional judgment, the various elements of the process of psychotherapy are juxtaposed.

In an attempt to more fully explain what I mean by the

importance of the interaction between and combination among the elements or variables of the process of psychotherapy, the following vignette is offered. John was a young, 19 year old white male, very bright and handsome. Others saw him as a very "together" man who was fun-loving, well-accepted, and quite accomplished. His initial contacts with me were for a "one-time-advice-session only." He made an appointment with me in the school's Psychological Services, made it clear this was to be only a one-time session, and wanted some advice on handling a present interpersonal relationship problem. Seven months later, he again makes a similar appointment and again on an issue of a present interpersonal relationship problem and again was clear about it being a one-time only session. Certainly there are many students who come to a school's counseling service for help in handling some interpersonal relationship problem and one session is frequently all that is necessary. But in this case, there were some differences which suggested to me there was more pain, hurt, fear and many more repressed, underlying issues to be dealt with than is true for the majority of students coming for "advice" on handling some interpersonal relationship problem. Some of those differences included the fact that John demonstrated very little upset or affect connected with the "problems" he was having with the present relationship. In addition my approach to his request was to engage in problem solving techniques but he seemed little interested in that and it was obvious those suggested approaches and/or solutions were of little interest to him (which, of course, made me think that we weren't dealing with the problem). Then, what history I obtained from him indicated that he never knew his biological father although that man had until most recently lived in the same country as John. Lastly, he made it very clear we were to only have one session. By now, the reader may have guessed that his relationship problems were ones in which he lost interest whenever the relationship got serious.

Three months later he is ready for psychotherapy. This time he is upset and obviously in emotional distress when he calls for an appointment. Over the phone, he asks for advice on how to handle the present upsetting interpersonal relationship problem, but it is a weak request and he really is asking "What shall I do?" He can accept my professional advice to go into psychotherapy and makes an appointment with my secretary for a time to start seeing me. In this "first" session the work, or really contact, from the two earlier appointments helped at least moderate some of his anxieties about me and how I may interact with him. I wonder what this "first" session would have been like without those two earlier contacts and some contacts with him on campus in more social and informal settings? But it seemed he was ready to work in this "first" session and could state the insight that he had avoided-escaped some of his feelings by binge eating and sex. He gives a rather remarkable history and some clear dynamics centering around the lack of relationship with his father - who was divorced from his mother when John was 9 months old. Even though his father lived in the same country as John, he never knew him, he had no pictures of his father, no contact with his father's parents - John's grandparents. He'd had a series of "step-fathers," and got along with none of them.

Now, in this session it became quite obvious that a therapeutic alliance was only barely beginning to form - was quite tentative and could easily be destroyed. I "guessed" that one of the first transference issues would be related to whatever feelings he had for father and his "step-fathers" and that even in this very session I could not escape being in some sense perceived as a father-figure who would "hurt"or "leave" him. I also realized that we had some form of "relationship" on the basis of our two earlier contacts and our informal contacts on campus. That relationship was a positive one and probably an important reason he now approached me for psychotherapy. My own feelings about this "first" session included a sense of excitement about working with him, an enjoyable curiosity about how this history he presents has affected him, an optimism about his ability to really deal with what turned out to be (although I didn't know it at the time) a lifetime of crap, and a desire to do a very good job of therapy with this man. It seemed to me that on the face of it his problems were so very obvious and his ego strength such that he could make excellent progress in psychotherapy.

It was patently obvious in this "first" session that John had problems/feelings centering around the father-figure. It certainly would have been "appropriate" to ask him in that session how he felt about the fact his father and mother were divorced when he was 9 months old and he has never seen or heard from his father since. And I'm confident, John would have given an answer to that question. An answer, but not the one he could give if that question were asked in a different context. The juxtaposition of the variables in the process of psychotherapy in this "first" session included our

61

positive interpersonal relationship, God knows what transference feelings from his earlier father-step-father experiences, and a barely forming therapeutic alliance. If I had asked the question, I think he would have given me a polite and appropriate answer that would have masked from both of us his true feelings. So before asking that question, I would like to have a "platform" upon which both he and I can stand and that we both sense is relatively secure -i.e. I would like to have more of a sense that he and I had established a therapeutic alliance - that we both were really committed to this business of psychotherapy as a way of helping him resolve some of his problems. Furthermore, I needed to know more about the nature of our "therapeutic interpersonal relationship." I've indicated I thought it had many positive features. But what he had told me about his father and step-fathers, made me wonder what was in the transference relationship. So, I waited and did not ask the question. I waited for a time when there was more therapeutic alliance, where I felt more confident about the transference relationship, and also for a time when both of us had more experience "feeling" in the sessions than had been possible in this "first" session where much time had been devoted to obtaining history.

Generally within some three sessions I find that the therapeutic alliance is relatively well formed. Such was not the case for me and John. But by the fifth session there seemed to be some alliance established and the sessions in between had revealed some of his "emotional position" or transference feelings in therapy. He a) feared that his anger would destroy relationships, b) felt penetrated by inquiry into his past, c) was not sure he would really be accepted by people, d) started to realize that he had lots of feelings about his father, and e) believed that "fucking-up" relationships was better than falling in love and then having people leave.

By the fifth session, we had established some base of a therapeutic alliance, our "therapeutic interpersonal relationship" was and had remained a relatively positive one, the emotions he was experiencing included fearing he ruined relationships, would not be accepted and that I would leave him. The material of the fifth session was presented in such a fashion that there were no intense feelings shown on his part or felt on mine. But the data or content of the material was clear. He was talking about mother and father and avoiding facing the fear/feeling/guilt associated with his parents. In that "environment" or that juxtaposition of the variables of the process of

62

psychotherapy and within the context of the material in the fifth session; I asked him, "What is it like to be a human being whose father leaves you and whose mother beats you?" He smiles and fights the feelings - he knows he can't cry and yet some of it is there welling-up in him. He says, with his smile starting to fade on his face and great control washing over his body and making it very tight, "I'll have to have absolute trust in you to show that."

Now, I submit he would have given a quite different answer to that question had it been "appropriately" asked in the first session. The juxtaposition of process variables was quite different by the fifth session than it was in the first. And that juxtaposition in the fifth session permitted an answer that made it patently obvious to him and to me how strong, deep, and vital his feelings were about his position in life as a child with his parents. The answer also indicated the fine strength and ability he had in contacting and dealing with me. There was no inequality at that moment, no higher doctor-lower patient relationship. He was not saying, "I won't share my feelings with you." He was not saying, "Here are my feelings, take care of me doctor." He was saying "I have to have some strong trust in you to share those kinds of feelings."

And that kind of a response, one which helps make more obvious to him the strength and pain of some of his feelings - the source of those feelings, and the vitality of our "therapeutic interpersonal relationship" - was in part dependent upon the particular juxtaposition of the variables in the process of psychotherapy. It is the interaction between and combination among these vital common elements or variables in the process that are important determinants of the course and effectiveness of the therapy. Thus, any analysis or study of the process of psychotherapy must attend to all the elements or variables in that process. This is really saying nothing more than that psychotherapy *is* a process composed of those vital elements common to all psychotherapies - an ongoing, changing, dynamic, fluid juxtaposition of interrelated and interdependent factors. Life *is* a process -it continues from one point to another, is related to and builds upon what has gone before, anticipates what is to come in the future, and creates something new in the present. In any process the variables are interrelated and interdependent. And they are interrelated in such a fashion as to create a new whole. Malone (1981) said it so very well:

63

Experience has dimensions. When persons experience
they think, they feel, and they behave. The dimensions
of experience can be described as cognitive, affective,
and behavioral. There can be little doubt that when an
experience is fully experiential, all three of these
dimensions are fully present, and so integrated that
none of the particular dimensions are separated out in
the consciousness of the person experiencing. You
think, feel, and behave as one. You think your feelings,
feel your thinkings, think your behavings, behave your
feelings, feel your behavings, and behave your thinkings
(p. 87).

Thus, to study the process of psychotherapy, we artificially divide
the "whole" into some component parts. We do this in an attempt to
better understand the effectiveness and significance of the many
things we are doing/feeling/ thinking in the therapy. But we should
be careful to remember that our division of process into common
elements or variables is artificial and that the interrelatedness and
interdependency of these variables is crucial to the process of
psychotherapy.

Most simplisticly put, I visualize individual psychotherapy as two
magnets placed on a table. The magnets' poles face one another but
they are placed on the table far enough apart so they aren't
completely pulled to one another - they form an elipse with space
between the two horeshoes. When we look at the two magnets on
the table we see the magnets, the table, and little more. But if we
cover those magnets with paper and randomly throw iron filings onto
that paper, we will see those filings reveal a pattern. The iron filings
do not just take a random shape. Rather, they reveal the
electromagnetic forces between the two magnets. They give us a
clear picture of the strong forces operating in the space between
those two "bodies."

Similarly, in psychotherapy when two people sit down and face
one another there are "forces" in that field between them, or as Kurt
Lewin (1951) so aptly put it years ago "lifespace" including those two
persons. And yet for the most part, persons in this society are not
formally trained to observe and/or identify those forces in that
lifespace. In our pragmatism and behaviorism, we are much more
likely to attend to the shape, color, appearance of the two "magnets"

instead of to the "vibes-in-the-air" between these two people. We should be careful whenever we operationalize any of the variables in the process of psychotherapy to not become so attracted to their shape, color, form, and substance that we fail to see the "forces" created by their juxtapositions. And in doing psychotherapy, it is the therapist's task to be informed about the forces created by the juxtaposition of process variables and that exist then in the lifespace between therapist and patient. For in that lifespace the forces in the process of psychotherapy are carried out. And it is in those forces that the effective elements of psychotherapy exist and that what is common to all psychotherapy will be found.

And the names of some of those forces are "support," "trust," "hope," "caring," "love," and "souls-meeting." They are powerful forces capable of changing attitudes, beliefs, ideas, goals, motives and behavior. They are complex forces whose structures and functions are difficult for us to comprehend. We think they are elusive since we don't understand how we help create and/or destroy them. But they come about through the process of psychotherapy and are the result of the interrelatedness and interdependencies of the vital common elements or variables of the process.

Additional Aspects of Process.

At this point we have six concepts or variables and one principle by which to begin to conceptualize the process of psychotherapy. As we attempt to find ways to simplify and explicate what is meant by the "process of psychotherapy," it is important that we not lose sight of the very complex phenomena with which we are attempting to deal. Our six "simple" terms and one principle can mislead us if we do not keep in mind that the process of psychotherapy is multi-staged, has variables that are interdependent and interactive and involves transactions between two persons who are in varying degrees embedded in the process itself. There is no reason why in any one session or in analyzing any one case we shouldn't see elements of the process of psychotherapy all intertwined together in that one session or case. There is also no reason why any one statement a patient or therapist makes in a session can't be multidetermined. I am sure the human mind is quite capable of handling/juggling/understanding all these intertwined and interrelated elements at once. It is only the

65

"analyzing mind" that has to and/or wants things in such neat compartments. But we must remember the damage we may do to our understanding of the process of psychotherapy when we insist upon putting it into neat compartments.

In addition to the complexities of interdependent and interactive variables, the process of psychotherapy is also some form of an educational-learning process. It includes learnings which help extinquish old habits or behaviors as well as learning new ways of behaving. This learning differs from what we generally consider to be education in that its focus is upon unconscious learnings and/or affective-emotional learnings. In this way, psychotherapy is an education-learning aimed at the most important meaningful values and beliefs in our own individual unique life. But most of our experience with education focuses upon a cognitive process with little affect and/or emotion involved. So one might say that traditional education deals with cognitive-emotional facets of persons' experiences whereas psychotherapy deals with emotional-cognitive facets of persons' experiences. Furthermore, it seems that what has been learned in the patient's affective-emotional sphere in the service of containing anxieties or securing some adjustment is highly resistant to extinction. Thus, while extinquishing old behaviors and learning new ways of behaving in psychotherapy sound as though they should directly relate to existing learning theories, in fact there is not such a direct relationship for the kind of extinction and re-learning involved in psychotherapy. And certainly part of the reason for that may be that in psychotherapy we are generally dealing with material at the core or center of the person's existence. That is, we are dealing with emotions-cognitions that are central to much of what the person feels and believes. We are dealing with issues around which the patient has centered or formed a significant aspect of his or her life. Thus, it is not like learning algebra, or physics, or a foreign language. It is not even like learning economics, political science or psychology. In essence, the learning involved in psychotherapy is *not* an academic learning. It is very far removed from that. It might better be called an emotional learning. Thus, our attempts to directly apply learning theory and principles to the process of psychotherapy are doomed either to failure or to being relegated to a very small number of behaviors unless ways are found to include unconscious and emotional learnings.

Lastly, the process of psychotherapy is one that is pervaded by emotional involvement. Neither partner in this process engages in alliance, relationship, interpretation, corrective experience, the flow of material being discussed-felt-seen-examined, and termination without a considerable amount of emotional involvement. Traditionally in the psychotherapy literature, much of this emotional involvement has been discussed under the headings of "transference" and "countertransference" and couched in words designed to strip it of its emotional flavor and power. The major portion of the emotional involvement in which both patient and therapist are invested and that develops as a result of the therapeutic process has not been well explicated.

Most persons probably have little difficulty realizing that the patient has considerable emotional investment in the process of psychotherapy. In fact, I am inclined to believe that most persons over-estimate the patient's emotional involvement in psychotherapy. I think that initially most patients are quite reluctant to invest much emotion into the therapy process. Certainly they come to the first session anxious and afraid, perhaps somewhat embarrassed and ashamed. They are hurting and they do want help. But generally the desire is for help at no great emotional cost. In fact, the fear of what psychotherapy may cost emotionally is sometimes a deterrent to seeking treatment. It is with the development of the therapeutic alliance, that the patient's emotional investment in the process of psychotherapy really begins. And from that point on, he or she has considerable and varying emotional investments.

The therapist's emotional investment in the process of psychotherapy is generally not readily identified by most persons except to say, "How can you stand listening to problems all day long?" While most people have little difficulty seeing the patient as making a considerable emotional investment in the process of psychotherapy, they are not inclined to see the therapist as also making a considerable emotional investment. And yet there is no other profession which requires its practicioners to make such a considerable emotional investment over such an extended period of time and to understand the nature and effect of that investment as does the profession of psychotherapy. After all, the psychotherapists' speciality is emotion and it is emotion that is the crux of so much psychopathology. How does one deal with "emotion" unemotionally? After all, a great many of our patients' problems have to do with their inabilities to *care* or to *love*. How does one teach care and love without caring and loving? And certainly emotion, caring, and loving are not part of the *technique* of psychotherapy. Technique is something one learns, has a considerable degree of control over, can use or not use at will, and generally has with it little or no emotional or affective state. The precise application of techniques is done by technicians. For the most part, the work of dentists and surgeons are good examples of the application of techniques in attempts to ameliorate problems. But I submit that psychotherapists in being most successful cannot be primarily technicians. They have to care and love - they must have a deep commitment to their patient and their work. Care and love are not "something" we can at will turn on or off. Nor are care and love something we can successfully fake. We can help to create the conditions in which care and love can exist and perhaps even flourish. And I suppose we can equally well create conditions which are designed to prevent the occurrence of care and love. But the emotion itself is not something over which we have immediate, direct, and complete control. And yet as I have already said, care and love are extremely important forces in the psychotherapy process.

The character of the psychiatrist as developed by Peter Shaffer (1974) in the play "Equus" has examples of that caring and loving. Dr. Dysart certainly would not be typified as a "do-gooder", nor is his role portrayed as the loving, caring doctor who just can't do enough for his patient. There is a sense in which he is rather selfish, not particularly motivated to take the patient (Alan) at all, and definitely caught-up in his own middle age crises. But at the end of the play Dysart has a soliloquy filled with his pain - the pain of not being able to do enough for Alan, of not really knowing how to help him, and of facing the limitations of his profession. At the end of the soliloquy, which is the end of the play, we find these lines:

> In an ultimate sense I cannot know what I do in this place - yet I do ultimate things. Essentially I cannot know what I do - yet I do essential things. Irreversible, terminal things. I stand in the dark with a pick in my hand, striking at heads! I need - more desperately than my children need me - a way of seeing in the dark. What way is this? *What dark is this?*...I cannot call it ordained of God: I can't get that far. I will however pay

it so much homage. There is now, in my mouth, this
sharp chain. And it never comes out (p. 106).

The care and love he has for Alan and the struggle to do even more
than he can do to help him comes through clearly in the soliloquy.
And the very last lines indicate the "price" he has paid for his
emotional involvement with Alan - for Equus' bit is now the sharp
chain in his mouth.

The process of psychotherapy is certainly not something at this
stage in the development of our science or of our own thinking that
we are going to be able to define in terms of precise concepts or
easily understandable techniques. As Helen Lewis (1981) so aptly
pointed out Freud had suggested the term *Seelsorger* for an analyst.
Seelsorger literally means "curer of souls." I think that is an apt term
for what we as psychotherapists are about. Thus, in the process of
psychotherapy there is a "meeting of souls." Psychotherapy
conceptualized in that fashion will certainly have some "souls" throw
up their hands in horror and ultimate disgust. Part of that horror
and disgust is because psychotherapy so conceptualized seems
impossible to ever understand or research from a scientific point-of-
view. I do not believe that at all needs to be the case. But I do think
that conceptualizing the psychotherapist as a "curer of souls" helps
bring home to all of us the extremely complex multi-faceted nature of
the process we now are going to try and understand.

CHAPTER 4

PSYCHOTHERAPY AND RELATIONSHIP

Certainly it is trite and a truism to say that all psychotherapy involves an interpersonal relationship. I come to the office at the beginning of the day and find that my two o'clock hour is filled with a new patient - somebody I have not yet met and do not know. I find myself wondering about the person and start to look over the appointment information sheet. I'm interested in whether this "new" person is male, female, young, middle-aged, old, married, single. Is there any indication of why the appointment was made and/or if the person had psychotherapy before? Already I am starting to have some feelings about this "new" person. Certainly with the scanty information I have about the person; my feelings are based upon my own needs, fantasied expectations, and existing circumstances and not upon realities attendant to the two o'clock patient's being. But the point is, already I am starting to think and feel about another human being and to start to set or manufacture some of the first strands in the interpersonal relationship between the two of us. Over the years, my feelings about this two o'clock patient have run the gamut all the way from being rather excited and pleased to "meet" a new patient, looking forward to the formation of a new therapeutic relationship and what it may produce to feeling put upon, angry my two-o-clock time was filled because I had already planned doing something else with it.

At two o'clock I go to meet my new patient, introduce myself and invite her into my office. I am already "sizing" her-up and she also is starting to have some feelings and thoughts about me. We are two human beings who until this moment had never met. There are a series of societal rubrics we follow which include being pleasant and cordial with one another, showing her where we meet, inviting her to sit. Further, those rubrics say I am to be the "doctor" and she the "patient." She is to tell me her "problems" and I am to be "helpful."

71

Already we are starting to relate to one another and as time goes on in this two o'clock hour many feelings and ideas about one another will come up.

So that there is a relationship between therapist and patient is a simple given. I think no one will argue that fact any more than they would argue the fact that there is a relationship between patient and physician, between client and attorney, between employee and employeer, between fellow workers or colleagues. The existence of an interpersonal relationship between therapist and patient is denied by no one working or writing in the field. The question is not, "Is there an interpersonal relationship?" The answer to that is a simple, "Yes." The question is whether or not that relationship is of any importance to the process of psychotherapy.

Importance of Relationship

I. In Everyday Life.

Perhaps one place to begin considering the importance of relationship to the psychotherapeutic process is to focus upon the importance and/or role relationship plays in our everyday life. In particular, we might note how we feel and what we do in times of crisis or great stress - those times when we feel the burden of the universe crashing in upon us. I think most of us turn to some other human being at such moments - to family members, close friends, persons upon whom we might lean or depend. We look for someone from whom we might garner support, nurturance, and affirmation. We look for someone to help us so we do not have to "walk the road" alone.

Rainer Maria Rilke (1980) captures some of that need, and more, in these lines:

> "Man of the people and my friend, you have not kept
> your word...You promised me light and consolation, but
> here you show us only night and suffering." I reply:
> "Man of the people and my friend, listen to a little story.
> Two lonely souls meet in the world. One of them begins
> to utter lamentations, imploring the stranger for
> comfort. And the stranger, bending toward the

petitioner, whispers gently: 'It is night for me too.'"
"Is that not consolation?" (p. 54).

And indeed, is it not consolation? For aren't we upheld, affirmed, strengthened when we make meaningful contact with another human being who has been through and/or experiences what we are experiencing? Somehow knowing that for others it is night too, strengthens and affirms us and enables us to continue on, feeling better about ourselves, and realizing that we too can live through this night.

And I would suggest that it is not only in pain, grief, darkness, and despair that we seek contact, sharing, and relationship with another. I believe it is also true in excitement, happiness and great joy. Again, we want to share our excitement, happiness and joy with another human being. We want to tell them how happy we are and we want them to join us in celebration. How difficult, unsatisfying (I'm inclined to say unnatural) it is to celebrate great happiness and joy all alone. To tell my joy only to the walls, the furniture, the floor, the windows would be frustrating, depressing, unfulfilling. Sharing it with my dog would certainly be better, except she can't really understand why I'm so happy. She's just happy I'm happy. I really need another human being who can genuinely understand my joy and accept it as a gift and celebrate with me.

And isn't the bonding, connecting, touching, seeing, hearing, of loved ones extremely important and self enhancing to us? It is their remarks to and about us that have much greater impact upon us than the exact same remarks made by a person with whom we don't share a loving bond. The opinions, perceptions, and values of those emotionally close to us have a much greater effect and impact upon us than do exactly the same opinions, perceptions, and values of persons whom we don't know or to whom we aren't close. And won't every one of us take quite differently a penetrating, unflattering critique of ourselves from someone whom we know loves us than if that same comment comes from a stranger or from one with whom we don't have a loving bond? It is from those with whom we are close and with whom we have a strong interpersonal relationship that we are more likely to learn - to whom we are more likely to listen - and from whom we are more likely to take advice. For it is not only that they "know" us better than others do; but it is also that they are a friend, that they love us, and thus also have our interests at heart. We have a "relationship" with them - which is to say we know a great deal about them and their interests, biases and motivations. And we experience a comradeship, a sisterhood, a bonding together and an upholding and supporting of one another. That is, we feel we "belong" and this gives us support and freedom as well, of course, as responsibility and obligation.

Anna Perrott Rose (1954) writes about the life of a young Latvian boy displaced by the second World War. Because of the war's and life's exigencies the boy was close to being, if not, psychotic. She adopts this boy and the book is an account of their life together. The entire book is a testimony to the importance of relationship in everyday life and of Anna Rose's astuteness in giving this young boy a loving and suppportive relationship. I highlight one example from her account and that has to do with getting this boy to learn English. He had been in America for a considerable period of time, had been in a number of foster homes and attended both private and public school systems. Yet, he was most deficient in his learning of English. He balked at learning to read and persisted in his refusal for a number of years.

When he was in the seventh grade, his adopted mother's sister gave a birthday party for her twin boys. She made it explicit that they were just having family for the party and no one else. This Latvian boy felt he could not go because it was just for family. His adopted mother exclaimed, "Well, *you're* family!" He was amazed at this statement and then delighted to find it was true. And he eventually told her, "Now this thing I will tell you. I have real home now and I am family. Now I am happy. Now I will learn your English for you and now I will read." (p. 159). And he did.

This anecdote serves as a good example for what most of us have experienced at one time or another in our life. That is, the feeling of bonding, belonging with and to someone and how that makes us feel accepted and wanted as well as enables us to commit ourselves to certain responsibilities. Bonding, belonging and acceptance can change our minds and modify our motivations. Relationships in everyday life provide examples of how one gets to the mind by going through the heart.

Our own experience should tell us that relationship has much to say about our ability to hear, understand, or receive something from another person. Relationship will affect how motivated we may be to complete a particular task or accomplish some set goal. Relationship affects how we feel interacting with or in the presence of the other person. Part of our psychological nature includes a need for relationship. In the early years of life that need is most clearly seen in bonding with and dependent ties to parental figures - no matter how inept they are at parenting. Adolescence and its turmoil is made even more traumatic by the need for peer acceptance and emotional relationships separate and apart from the family. And in old age, when we may find ourselves again alone, we still seem inclined to bond together with our peers. Community centers throughout America are filled with two age groups: adolescents looking for relationship and older people looking for companionship.

Lastly, perhaps the easiest place to see the importance of relationship in everyday life is when you or a close member of your family is seriously ill and in the hospital. The support and nurturing we need and can get from others at that time is remarkable. The other's touch, a few words, the look in their eyes all help to convey the sense of support, understanding, a being-with-you and upholding you through this trauma. It helps one feel not alone, perhaps able then to carry on, and it can prevent a giving up in total despair. Relationship upholds our self-esteem and affirms our personhood.

The reader can add from his or her own experience additional examples of the importance of relationship in everyday life. Focusing upon what effects relationships may have had in our own experience is important and helps us better understand what is meant by the term; but it does not address the issue of how important relationship may or may not be in psychotherapy.

II. In Psychotherapy

Joanne Greenberg's *I Never Promised You a Rose Garden* (1964) was an extremely popular book on college campuses near the end of the 60's and the beginning of the 70's. Not since Clifford Beer's *Mind That Found Itself* (1921) was an account of a serious psychopathological condition so popular. Greenberg's book was published as a novel. Only later did it become apparent that this work of fiction was based upon the author's own life and that her psychotherapist had been Frieda Fromm-Reichmann. Among college students, the book's popularity included the fact it dealt with the disorder of schizophrenia in a peer. But they were also attracted to the nature of the interpersonal relationship, described in that book, between the patient and therapist. At an age of extreme sensitivity and vulnerability, these college students seemed particularly drawn to what they rightly saw as the therapist's humanistic, respectful, therapeutic, and sensitive approach to the patient. In part, they saw it as a rather unexpected aspect of the "doctor-patient" interaction. It was not in tune with their stereotypes of, and, in some cases, experiences with psychotherapists. The novel nicely captured some aspects of the interpersonal relationship between patient and therapist and highlighted the fact that therapists are mostly responsible for formulating and maintaining effective interpersonal relationships in psychotherapy.

Bruch (1974) informs us that it was Fromm-Reichmann's custom at the end of therapy to review with her patients what they felt had been most helpful and significant in their psychotherapy. It was from Bruch then that we learn what Joanne Greenberg had considered most important in her work with Fromm-Reichmann.

> Years later, as treatment approached successful termination, Fromm-Reichmann, as was her custom, reviewed with her patient what she herself had considered most helpful and significant for the recovery. I report it here as I heard it from Fromm-Reichman. When questioned the girl said, "You shouldn't ask, doctor. It was the WE experience...don't you remember, doctor, the first day, when I said, you will take away my gut pain, you will take away my trances and you will take away my food, and *what will I have then?*...Don't you remember what you said...you did *not* say 'I will take it away'...You said, 'You come and tell me about all of this - that tells me that you do not want it. What I hear is that you want *us* to free you from them.' I tell you, doctor, that word *us* did the trick. Here was somebody who did not think she could cure me, or do it for me, but who said, 'We'll do it together'" (p. 17).

This vignette nicely highlights the importance of the interpersonal relationship in psychotherapy. In, through, around, and in addition to being the doctor; Fromm-Reichman was also another human being touching, understanding, and committing herself to working *with* Joanne for Joanne's eventual good. There was an equality between patient and therapist. Fromm-Reichmann knew that while she had expert knowledge of psychopathology and human behavior in general, her patient had specific and unique knowledge of her own psychopathology and behavior. Both "experts" were needed in order to do successful psychotherapy. And both seemed to know that neither one alone could effect the cure.

For a long time, it has been recognized that a relationship between two people and involving some verbal behavior was common to all forms of psychotherapy. Over twenty years ago Ford and Urban (1963) wrote:

> Individual verbal psychotherapy appears to have four major elements. First, it involves two people in interaction. The interaction is highly confidential. The patient is required to discuss himself in an intimate fashion...Second, the mode of interaction is usually limited to the verbal realm... Third, the interaction is relatively prolonged.... Fourth, this relationship has as its definite and agreed purpose, changes in the behavior of one of the participants (p. 16).

In 1969 Strupp, Fox, and Lessler published their quite ambitious attempts to study the psychotherapy experience from the patient's point-of-view. They found [as have Sloane et al. (1977) more recently] that from the patient's point-of-view the relationship between patient and therapist was of great importance to the outcome of psychotherapy. In these author's words:

> Irrespective of variations in the form of therapy and other considerations, the emergence of a "warmth" factor was particularly noteworthy. It permeated all ratings and assessments - those of patients as well as therapists. We concluded that a sense of mutual trust was unquestionably a *sine qua non* for successful psychotherapy; in its absence, little of positive value was accomplished (p. 17).

It is probably fair to say that most contemporary theorists stress the importance of relationship as a fundamental aspect of all forms of psychotherapy. As we saw in Chapter 3, there remain differences regarding the extent to which relationship is important in psychotherapy and perhaps differences regarding the nature of therapeutic relationships. But almost all theorists assign it some role in the psychotherapeutic process.

Perhaps those who have assigned it a least important role in the process of psychotherapy are the behavior therapists. Certainly the early work on behavior modification might relegate relationship to rapport or a harmonious connection between therapist and patient. The cognitive and behavior therapy theorists have principles of learning and reinforcement contingencies as the most important variables in modifying patient's behavior and relationship is of much less importance. In fact, those theorists are only slowly and reluctantly coming to examine the importance of the relationship in psychotherapy. For the most part, they have seen relationship as important only in its functions of rapport, modeling, increasing client expectations for improvement, and effecting client's self-efficacy expectations. They have not even said much about the role that relationship could play as a reinforcer (Morris, & Magrath, 1983; Arnkoff, 1983).

Recently, however, even the behavior therapists have been discovering some of the important aspects of relationship in the psychotherapeutic process. Klein, et al. (1969) reported behavior therapists use the therapeutic relationship and clinical judgment in their work with patients even though their theoretical formulations may not include such phenomena. As Klein *et. al.* observed:

>...much of what they did was what any clinician does in dealing with patients, and they did it by second nature, so to speak (p. 264).

Sloane, Staples, Whipple, and Cristol (1977) conducted a very important study which found that patients in behavior therapy placed a high emphasis upon the patient-therapist relationship. In fact, it seemed that patients placed much more emphasis upon that relationship than did the behavior therapists. This suggests the behavior therapists may be overlooking an important variable in their treatment process. Certainly evidence is accumulating to show the importance of relationship factors in the behavior therapies (Kazdin & Wilcoxon, 1976; Alexander, et al., 1976; DeVoge & Beck, 1978;

Ford, 1978; Jacobson & Margolin, 1979).

Hokanson (1983) has recently and cogently summarized the behavior therapists' dilemna with relationship in the following way:

> Many of the behavioral therapies indeed seem to work with clinical patients, but when current-day researchers try to investigate *why* they work, they come up with some disturbing results. It appears that the successes are not readily explained by the basic principles upon which the therapies were originally designed. Rather, the research results suggest that the success of these treatments is affected, to a large degree, by such non-behavioral factors as (1) clients' beliefs about the effectiveness of therapy; (2) broad changes in clients' self-concepts and feelings of mastery; (3) clients' motivations to adhere to a treatment program; and (4) certain emotional aspects of the therapist-client relationship. What an embarrassment! (p. 165).

It may even be that the behavior therapists, whose theories said little or nothing about the therapeutic relationship, will be those whose research starts to reveal the particular importance of relationship in psychotherapeutic practice. If that does happen, it would not only be ironic but also a testimonial to people's willingness to change cherished positions given scientific evidence.

At the opposite extreme from the behavior therapists are the humanistic theorists who tend to conceptualize the therapeutic relationship as one of the most cogent and crucial parts of the psychotherapeutic process. In between these extremes lay the largest bulk of theorists who combine or blend in various fashions both relationship, cognitive, affective, and technique variables. It is this middle group who probably have the most influence upon present thinking and practice of psychotherapy. We no longer tend to view the relationship in psychotherapy as simply some form of rapport, for it is probably much more complicated than that. Nor do we any longer tend to view the relationship as simply a friendship. For while having a good friend is certainly helpful, most psychotherapists would not consider a good friend to be enough to modify many of the behaviors and problems patients bring to the psychotherapy hour.

Most theories of psychotherapy see the therapeutic relationship as having considerable importance in the process of psychotherapy. And in recent years, the nature of the interpersonal relationship between therapist and patient has come in for a great deal of attention (Applebaum, 1978; Brady, et al., 1980; Frank, 1961,1976; Garfield, 1980; Horwitz, 1974; Luborsky, Singer, & Luborsky, 1975; Marmor, 1976; Patterson, 1967; Prochaska, 1979; Sloane, 1969; Strupp, 1973,1976). In fact many have suggested that relationship is the vehicle by which change occurs (Jacobs, 1978; Kempler, 1973; Polster & Polster, 1973; Yontef, 1976; Zinker, 1977).

Malan's (1976a, 1976b) findings suggest that psychotherapy outcome is related to relationship and is best when both patient and therapist are willing to become *deeply involved.* In his second work, he contends that patient-therapist interactions give emotional understanding and significant meaning to the focused interpretations. He uses the term *successful dynamic interaction* to talk about the importance of the relationship between patient and therapist.

A year after Malan's work was published, Johnson and Matross (1977) wrote specifically on the interpersonal influence in psychotherapy. They describe the process of influence in psychotherapy as being more a function of the therapeutic interpersonal relationship than of characteristics in the patient or the therapist. Two years later, Frank (1979) reviewed the status of outcome studies and concluded that more of the determinants of therapy success lie in the personal qualities of patient and therapist and in their interaction than in the therapeutic method used. Most recently, Strupp (1982), in a foreword to Goldfried's book on converging themes in psychotherapy, wrote:

> I believe that we have made a certain amount of progress in coming to grips with the pertinent factors whose understanding must be refined in the future. There has also been a greater appreciation that the answers are not likely to be found in the "techniques" favored by a given "theoretical orientation," but rather that therapeutic change is embedded in the matrix of the *transactions* between a particular patient (client) and a particular therapist (p. ix).

At this point, I think there is little doubt that the interpersonal relationship between patient and therapist is critical for doing effective psychotherapy. Certainly reviewers of the empirical work on this question are unanimous in their opinion that the relationship is critical (Gurman, 1977; Lambert, et al., 1978; Mitchell, Bozarth & Krauft, 1977; Parloff, Waskow & Wolfe, 1978). And a recent book (Lambert, 1983) has as its central thesis the proposition that positive personality changes are related to positive patient-therapist relationships.

More and more investigators of the psychotherapeutic process are coming to similar conclusions. In different ways and from a variety of approaches they are pointing to the interpersonal relationship between patient and therapist as an area whose complexities must be better understood and whose effect upon behavioral change may be considerable.

We now turn to a brief consideration of the complexities involved in patient therapist interpersonal relationships and then to an extended attempt to conceptualize the components of positive patient-therapist relationships.

Complexity of Relationship

Until rather recently, scientists, theorists, practitioners only paid minimal attention to the complexities involved in interpersonal interactions between patients and therapists. Attention would be devoted to one or two variables such as the transference, or the working alliance, empathy, or unconditional positive regard. And through recourse to such concepts, we spoke about and researched the interpersonal relationships between patients and therapists. Thus we started with simple methods and with circumscribed conceptualizations in attempts to understand different aspects of the therapeutic interpersonal relationship. This approach was probably a necessary first step. But is is only a first step, and it has kept us from facing the enormous difficulties involved in conceptualizing let alone comprehending the complexities of therapeutic interpersonal relationships. I propose it is to our advantage as a profession and science to now attempt more systematic explications of the interpersonal interactions between patients and therapists with particular attention given to the interactive nature of the various components in those relationships.

My own experience has left me relatively convinced that the process of psychotherapy must be understood in terms of the interactions between therapists and patients. Psychotherapy is an interactive process whose foundation is an interpersonal relationship. Just as a foundation for a building does not make an entire house or building, so this "foundation" for the interactive process is not the totality of psychotherapy.

Permit for a moment a small but hopefully useful simile. A house or building cannot be constructed without a foundation. Furthermore, the nature of the foundation will have much to say about the eventual shape and stability of the final structure. There also comes a time in building when the foundation really becomes forgotten, or ignored for the most part, or in Gestalt terms has become "ground." It is the wall, roof, turret or particular artistic pattern one is constructing that is predominate in one's mind, is focused upon, or in Gestalt terms is "figure." As construction progresses, there may come a time when we focus upon the foundation again - when for a time it becomes "figure." For example, we may be ready to add some particularly heavy trusses to the structure. But before starting that work, we again check the foundation. Is it still holding well? Are there any signs it would give way under the added stress we propose to place upon it? For a time foundation again becomes "figure" and the building becomes "ground." Or we may discover that we need to add an entire room or wing to our building - space not originally planned. We need to decide whether that weight can be added to the existing foundation or whether we will have to construct an additional foundation. And if the latter case holds, we will need to determine if we have space in which to place additional foundation. If so, we will need to determine how or in what fashion we may be able to tie-into the existing foundation. And so in the building process there are times when we will attend to foundation and know that it will have much to say about what can be built and how it will be built. Other times in the building process we will essentially ignore foundation - knowing it is firm and sufficient - and focus our attention and labors upon completing the planned structure.

What I am attempting to say by this simple simile is that the interpersonal relationship between patient and therapist is like a foundation or a platform upon which all the rest of the psychotherapy takes place. And the nature of that interpersonal

82

relationship between patient and therapist will, in large part, determine what can or cannot be accomplished in the psychotherapy. For this foundation or platform, which both patient and therapist mount each session, is the place in which positive and negative transferences play their active role in psychotherapy. Upon this platform is built the therapeutic alliance. And from that alliance, along with transference, countertransference, the therapist's knowledge and skill as well as the patient's expert knowledge of him or herself comes insight and corrective emotional experiences.

The interpersonal relationship between patient and therapist, which is a foundation or platform in psychotherapy, is also something that comes in and out of importance and/or awareness during the course of the psychotherapy. That is, at one time it will be "figure" and at another time "ground." It is not unusual that we may go from session to session in psychotherapy paying little or no particular attention to the foundation - to the interpersonal relationship. A session today may well be a continuation of what was being dealt with in the preceding session. And the next session a few days from now an extension of the material dealt with in the last and prior sessions. This process of "working through" can take place for a considerable period of time with little or no attention given to the foundation upon which patient and therapist are standing - to their interpersonal relationship. Or a number of things could happen to bring our attention back to the foundation - the relationship. Resisting the therapy, countertransference issues, completing a working-through process, dealing with termination are all situations which refocus our attention once more upon the interpersonal relationship and make it "figure" for the psychotherapeutic work. Also, the nature of the interpersonal relationship between therapist and patient will help to determine what material can be dealt with and in what fashion and with what depth. In many respects then, the interpersonal relationship between patient and therapist may fit the simile of a foundation for a building.

As a result of my clinical experience, I am relatively convinced that the interpersonal relationship between therapist and patient contains emotional forces that are crucial for explaining the powerful effects of psychotherapy upon attitudes, feelings, self-esteem, self-acceptance, and behavior. And, as the reader has already discovered, I consider the process of psychotherapy to be closely tied to the interpersonal relationship between patient and therapist. But this is not to say that the process of psychotherapy and the interpersonal relationship between patient and therapist are one and the same thing. Stressing the importance of the interpersonal relationship and seeing it as crucial to the process of psychotherapy, does not mean that is all there is to psychotherapy. For psychotherapy requires much more than relationship. It is also dependent upon the psychotherapist's technical skills, theoretical orientation, diagnostic acumen as well as upon the patient's wishes, desires, and goals.

In reading the literature on relationship in psychotherapy, I have found the concept poorly defined and used in different ways by different authors and researchers. Some talk about a "therapeutic relationship," others about a "working alliance," others about "empathy, genuineness, non-possessive warmth," others about an "interpersonal relationship," and still others about a "normalizing objective approach." All schools of psychotherapy are in agreement that a "positive" relationship between patient and therapist is necessary for effective psychotherapy. But what is "positive" and what is "relationship" are left relatively vague and imprecise in definition. Frequently the interpersonal relationship between patient and therapist is presented as though it were only one relatively monolithic and undifferentiated variable.

I submit that the relationship between patient and therapist is a many faceted, multi-determined set of complex interactive relationships each one of which is composed of a number of emotional variables. It is not just *one* relationship but a number of relationships. And, those relationships are interactive with one another.

This many faceted, multi-determined nature of the relationship in psychotherapy may be why it has been so difficult to define. It also may be why we have used so many different words in our attempts to convey the meaning of the interpersonal relationship in psychotherapy. It probably is also the reason it is so very difficult to do any systematic research on interpersonal relationships in psychotherapy. And yet we must find ways to better understand, more accurately conceptualize, and systematically research the interpersonal relationship forces that exist between patient and therapist. For it is in these many faceted, multi-determined, interactive interpersonal relationships between patient and therapist that the foundations are set for the creation of those healing emotional forces in the lifespace between the patient and the therapist.

And in attending to relationship, it will also be important to bear in mind that not only are the variables within the interpersonal relationship interactive; but that interpersonal relationship is also interactive with other important components of the psychotherapeutic process. When we start to come to grips with the implications of having to deal with a relatively large number of highly interdependent forces (variables) in order to "explain" psychotherapeutic process, we will start to realize what an immensely complicated process psychotherapy is. I do not believe we are at all close to that point in our science were we can meaningfully make relatively simple statements about or identify a few general principles for the process of psychotherapy. Any simple statements we may make are all on the "wrong" side of complexity. First we must go through and understand the complexities involved in the process of psychotherapy and then we will be in a position to make the simple statements. But then, those simple statements will be on the "other" side of complexity. At this time we are not even close to such important simplicity; we may be much closer to the place where we can see the obscure complexities.

It certainly is not enough to say that the interpersonal relationship between therapist and patient is a many faceted, multi-determined, set of complex interactive relationships. While that is a sentence talking about complexity, it is still a simple statement. We must also identify those sets of interactive relationships that make-up the total relationship. And that is exactly what this chapter attempts to do. While attempts are made to identify the many faceted sets of complex interactive relationships that make-up the *one* total relationship; it is important to keep in mind that the parameters identified (and then called by different names) merge, intertwine, interact with one another in multitudinous combinations to form one fabric. It is that *one* fabric, that *one* relationship to which patient and therapist respond and through which they interact to create and complete the process of psychotherapy to which we now turn.

Therapeutic Interpersonal Relationship

I choose to use the term "therapeutic interpersonal relationship" to identify the *one* relationship - this one fabric, which is the

85

amalgam of all the other relationships constituting the interaction between patient and therapist. Furthermore, I conceptualize this "therapeutic interpersonal relationship" as being composed of the interaction among and between the following relationships: a) the interpersonal relationship, b) the therapeutic relationship, and aspects of the c) therapeutic alliance, d) transference, e) countertransference, and f) corrective emotional experience.

The reader will identify some of these variables as ones more traditionally found under the rubric of process variables in psychotherapy than the rubric of interpersonal relationship. I refer particularly to "alliance," "transference," "countertransference," and "corrective emotional experiences." However, they are included under the "therapeutic interpersonal relationship" because, in my experience, portions of each of these process variables directly affect the therapist-patient relationship. Thus, I see them as playing an important role *both* in the process of psychotherapy and in determining the nature of the "therapeutic interpersonal relationship."

There are three other varibles I consider important in the process of psychotherapy not included under the concept of the "therapeutic interpersonal relationship." Those three are 1) "insight/ understanding/ interpretation/ conceptualization," 2) the "working-through" or material flow in psychotherapy, and 3) termination. I can certainly see the first of these three as having some impact upon the "therapeutic interpersonal relationship." But I believe that impact to be minimal and thus do not include "insight" under the rubric of relationship. I have difficulty seeing "material flow" and termination as significantly contributing to the "therapeutic interpersonal relationship." I see them more clearly as part of process *per se* than of the "therapeutic interpersonal relationship." However, again that is not to say that process variables and interpersonal interaction variables aren't interactive. I believe they are. And how the material in the process of psychotherapy will flow and how therapy will be terminated is highly dependent upon the "therapeutic interpersonal relationship" and that relationship will, in part, be dependent upon the nature of the material dealt with and how easy or difficult it is for the patient and the therapist to permit, encourage, or allow the flow of material and/or the termination of psychotherapy. Again, we face the highly interrelated and intertwined nature of factors involved in the very complex phenomena of psychotherapy.

Before turning to a consideration of the "interpersonal relationship" and of the "therapeutic relationship", let us briefly define the four other variables posited as playing some role in forming the "therapeutic interpersonal relationship." Those variables are aspects of the "therapeutic alliance," "transference," "countertransference," and "corrective emotional experience." There are separate chapters in this book for each one of those variables.

"Therapeutic alliance" refers to those interactions between the patient and therapist that, in Freud's words, "make of the patient a collaborator" (Breuer & Freud, 1893-95 p. 282). It includes those healthy, realistic aspects of the patient-therapist relationship whereby the two parties influence one another in such a way as to arrive at common therapeutic goals. In addition, it includes indications by both parties that they are making mature committments to systematically working toward those goals.

"Transference" refers to those aspects of the relationship between patient and therapist in which the patient has displaced affects from significant persons in his or her life onto the therapist. These are not feelings and expectations based on the reality of the relationship between the therapist and patient. Rather, they are feelings and expectations from the patient's past. They are based on the experiences with or perceptions that the patient had of significant persons in his or her life. Those feelings and expectations are now displaced upon the person of the therapist in the here and now.

By the term "countertransference," I refer to those aspects of the relationship between the patient and therapist in which the therapist has displaced affects from significant persons in his or her life onto the person of the patient. Again, these are not feelings and expectations based on the reality of the relationship between the therapist and patient. In addition, this term refers to those specific feelings, fears, and confusions the therapist may experience when the patient is dealing with material in the psychotherapeutic process which is conflictual for the therapist.

I use the term "corrective emotional experience" in very much the same sense that Alexander & French (1946) used it when they first put it forth. However, as the reader will see in the chapter dealing with this variable in the process of psychotherapy, I believe that definition also includes a great deal of phenomena that have gone by different names, i.e. "behavioral rehearsal," "risk taking," "role playing" - all of which meet the criteria of the original term. The term "corrective emotional experience" refers to all those aspects of the psychotherapeutic process which provide the patient with emotional experiences which help "correct" earlier distortions, beliefs, feelings, expectations. Obviously all such experiences do not occur within the therapy sessions; and, in fact, it is probably necessary for successful therapy that such experiences occur outside of the psychotherapy hour and on a rather broad scale. But some of those experiences do occur within the psychotherapy hour and occur with the person of the therapist. It is those "corrective emotional experiences" which occur with the person of the therapist that are then part of the "therapeutic interpersonal relationship." The following is a very simple example. Assume that my early life experiences taught me that authority figures never listened to me, to my ideas or my feelings. My subsequent experiences with authority figures either confirmed or could be distorted to help confirm and finally solidify that expectation or belief. Then upon meeting and being with my psychotherapist (an authority figure), I would expect not to be listened to and could be extremely adept at detecting the slightest indication of not being heard. Now, if my therapist is well skilled in the practice of the therapeutic relationship, I could find it more and more difficult to continue to maintain my expectation that this authority figure will not listen to me. In fact, I could start to have an experience in the relationship with my therapist that has emotional concomittants with it telling me that this authority figure is not only listening to me, but wants to hear me and *unbelievably* wants to understand me. I start to have a "corrective emotional experience" and because it occurs in the psychotherapeutic hour and with the person of the therapist, that experience becomes part of my relationship with the therapist and thus part of the "therapeutic interpersonal relationship."

Now as simple as this example is, or perhaps because it is so simple, we can also see how these relationship(s) variables are interactive and how they along with process variables form a whole fabric called psychotherapy. To stay with the simple example: If indeed I truly expect authority will not listen to me, and I then have this experience (or experiences with my therapist) that authority does listen; I might start to feel some relief, some gratefulness this is happening, some strong appreciation for my therapist and an increased sense of being able to do some significant therapy work. These feelings then become part of the "therapeutic alliance" helping to further solidify my collaboration with the therapist. But those feelings now affecting the "therapeutic alliance" came out of the "therapeutic relationship" (discussed below) and a "corrective emotional experience." Furthermore, with this more solid "therapeutic alliance," I will probably be in a better position to have other "corrective emotional experiences" with my therapist further increasing my trust and willingness to risk dealing with even more difficult problems than those I've raised so far. And so these relationship(s) variables start to interact with and build upon one another forming the complex matrix I've called the "therapeutic interpersonal relationship."

To take this simple example further, it is not unexpected that I would have some pretty strong feelings as a result of the belief and experience that authority figures will not listen to me. I suspect I would be very angry with authority figures. However, since this was a lesson learned very early in life, I couldn't be sure it wasn't my fault authority never listened. Thus, I may have some vague guilt feelings associated with authority and my feelings of anger. Furthermore, let's assume that when I found myself angry about not being listened to and expressed that anger; I was rather severely rebuked. Thus, I learned to do something else with my anger than show it - perhaps distort and misdirect it. Now, of course, these feelings of anger and guilt can be displaced from the persons who were my original authority figures to the person of my therapist (the present authority figure). Thus I could find myself angry with my therapist but also expecting to be rebuked for that anger and not sure that I don't deserve that rebuke. These feelings are then part of the "tranference" relationship(s) in the "therapeutic interpersonal relationship." Now, those feelings of anger and guilt added to the feelings and experiences that are part of the "therapeutic alliance" and part of the "corrective emotional experience" start to leave me rather confused and upset. My "world" is not so ordered and understandable anymore. On the one hand are my feelings of gratitude and relief and being pulled to a closer collaboration with my therapist. But those feelings are also in juxtaposition with the "transference" feelings of anger and guilt. I start to feel that there is something upsetting about these sessions with my therapist. So I start to complain that I'm feeling worse. I may even suggest it is my therapist's fault - the therapist is making matters worse for me instead of helping me. And when I express that concern, the therapist says, "And how do you feel about that?" I realize what I feel and I want to say, "Mad as hell!"

To continue this simple example depicting the fabric of psychotherapy, it is highly unlikely that my reason for coming to therapy was because authority figures don't listen to me or because I had difficulty expressing my anger. Those aspects of my psychology are probably not so cogently available to my consciousness. Rather, most people come to therapy out of a few rather common symptoms - anxiety, depression, frustration, and the inability to concentrate being predominant ones. It wouldn't be unrealistic to say I came to therapy because I was more depressed than usual. It may have gotten to the point where I wasn't even sure I could get up and go to work in the morning. Lets say it all seemed to start back a few months ago, about the time I was transferred to another department at work. As it turned out my "new" boss was a person who listened to no employee and whose supervisory philosophy was one of using negative reinforcement as an incentive instead of the philosophy of positive reinforcement that my former boss had used. But, as is true for all of us who have our "neuroses" or "special life distortions," we don't want to have to change our minds. So consciously I could see no relationship between the "new" boss and my symptom of depression. Probably within the first session my therapist had a very good idea about what dynamics were important in my case. But the therapist would have been a fool to give me an intellectual discourse upon the nature of my problems in that first session where neither therapist or I had developed any platform (relationship) upon which to stand and through which to deal with this material. Furthermore, if the therapist had given me a correct and complete psychodynamic diagnosis of my difficulty in that first hour, I could so easily have interpreted it to fit with my firm conviction that authority never really listens to me. The therapist would then have been involved with me in weaving a canvas upon which both of us could bounce around forever without accomplishing anything more than working up a sweat, becoming exhausted and confirming what I already believed. Instead of a platform from which both of us may examine my view of reality, we would have had a trampoline upon which to bounce up and down.

Hopefully, this simple example will help us remember the

90

complexities involved in the many faceted, multi-determined set of complex interactive variables constituting the process of psychotherapy. Also, as we now turn to a consideration of the "interpersonal relationship," and the "therapeutic relationship" this simple example may remind us that we are involved in an arbitrary dissection of the "therapeutic interpersonal relationship."

A. Interpersonal Relationship.

As already noted, six factors are posited as being important in the formation of the *one* "therapeutic interpersonal relationship." The "interpersonal relationship" is one of those six variables. Under this term, I include all of those aspects of the dyadic interaction that are based upon the real personal relationship between patient and therapist. As Anna Freud (1954) so correctly wrote:

> ...so far as the patient has a healthy personality, his real relationship to the analyst is never wholly submerged. With due respect to the necessary strictest handling and interpretation of the transference, I feel still that we should leave room somewhere for the realization that analyst and patient are also two real people, of equal adult status, in a real personal relationship to each other (p. 618).

Her father, without ever writing about it or expanding upon it also recognized the importance of the "real" relationship. In *Analysis Terminable and Interminable* he wrote:

> ...not every good relation between an analyst and his subject during and after analysis was to be regarded as a transference; there were also friendly relations which were based on reality and which proved to be viable (Freud, 1937, p. 222).

The patient and the therapist are two people in a relationship with one another. The nature of that "real" personal relationship is dependent on a number of factors including such things as age, sex, race, education, vocation, socio-economic status, and perhaps religious and political affiliations. We might expect the personal relationship between a therapist and a patient who is a professional and has a developmental and cultural background similar to the therapist's to be somewhat different than the personal relationship between a therapist and a patient who is a laborer, has little formal education, and a developmental and cultural background quite different from the therapist's. But, in any event, the real relationship certainly includes the fact that one of the people in the dyad is identified as a patient and the other is identified as a therapist. Thus, the personal relationship takes on characteristics of other professional-client relationships.

The "real" personal relationship includes a realization of the individual differences between the two persons in the dyad as well as a recognition of the responsibilities the relationship entails and the limitations that are placed upon it. The therapist is expected to maintain a professional attitude, to keep confidential the material shared, to be available and ready to work at the time agreed upon, and not to impose upon the relationship or assume entitlement to any special perquisites because of it. The patient is expected to be at the office at the agreed time, to pay the bill regularly, to also not impose upon the relationship or assume entitlement to any special perquisites because of it.

In many respects, this personal relationship between patient and therapist has much in common with other personal relationships where openness and acceptance are expected and where one person has agreed to do what he or she can to help another person. It is also a relationship which builds over time and thus may take on some additional characteristics. For over a period of time, the patient has the opportunity to get to know the therapist much better. Certainly it is obvious that the psychotherapy situation itself is one in which the therapist will learn and know a great deal more about the patient than vice versa. But the person of the therapist does not completely allude or escape the patient. Therapists' waiting rooms, decor of their offices, the way they dress, their particular mannerisms, the fashion in which they interact with the secretary or receptionist or a colleague - that, and much more, is available for patients to see and is some of the evidence used in forming their realistic view of the therapist as another human being.

My experience has been that many patients are extremely perceptive about the person of the therapist. And out of their love for us, they tell us a great deal about ourselves and help us become even better psychotherapists. Furthermore, it is only over time and through various experiences with us that the patient is then able to trust us. Trust is never something that comes at the beginning of a relationship. It is something that develops over time and only then if there is reason for it. For trust to develop, we have to have some kind of personal relationship with the other. And I suppose it may be that we will only deeply trust those whom we realize care for and/or really love us.

Now the "interpersonal relationship" in and of itself is not necessarily the crucial or most therapeutically determining factor in the psychotherapy work. But, it certainly can aid and assist in or detract from and impede that work. In particular, I believe it will play a rather major role in the formation of the therapeutic alliance. After all, when we are going to collaborate with someone, what we know and how we feel about that other person has a great deal to say about the nature and subtle ramifications of our collaboration. Furthermore, the therapeutic alliance is one of the first tasks in most psychotherapeutic endeavors. Thus, its formation, while certainly effected by and dependent upon "therapeutic relationship" variables, is perhaps initially overly determined by "interpersonal relationship" variables. For the "interpersonal relationship" may be what is most readily available to the patient in the initial stages of psychotherapy and is then what the patient must most fully rely upon in forming collaboration.

Let me now provide some examples of the significant role "interpersonal relationship" can play in the psychotherapeutic process. The examples go from the general to the very specific.

I first became acutely aware of the importance and role of "interpersonal relationships" in psychotherapy after moving from a large metropolitan area to a liberal arts college in a very small, rural, and isolated town. In the metropolitan area my patients and I seldom if ever saw one another except in the psychotherapy office. I could attend plays, concerts, other cultural and recreational events and go about the necessary shopping and commerce seldom seeing or being seen by my patients. In essence, they had access to very little information about me. But at the liberal arts college, where I both taught and practiced, my patients had relatively easy access to a great deal of information about me. In the first place, a large portion of my patients came from the student population all of whom had easy access to much more information about me than is typically available in the consultation room or from its personnel. In addition, it was usual for me to see and be seen by patients at plays, concerts, movies and while shopping in the town stores. Furthermore the town was very small, rather provincial, and dependent upon the college as a major employer. Thus, there was a strong injection of vocational politics into social interactions with the resultant maintenance of an active "grapevine." Through this "grapevine" additional information, accurate and inaccurate, was available on many members of this community including me, its first clinical psychologist.

My formal training and clinical experience had emphasized the importance of the therapist being a *tabla rasa* upon which the patient could project and transfer feelings. I was concerned that the reality of who I was being so readily available and at times unavoidable might compromise or make more difficult my psychotherapeutic work. But I soon learned that patients have a great deal to say about their therapy even though they may not explicate that knowledge and even though that knowledge may not all be conscious.

I found patients tended to divide themselves into a couple of groups. One group wanted no contact with me outside of the consultation room, wished not to be recognized or to recognize me should we pass one another on campus or in town, and if both of us happened to attend the same public meeting they would leave. I also discovered that for the most part this group was not interested in hearing about me from other sources. They would not seek-out students in my classes to ask them questions about what kind of professor I was; they would avoid coming to any public presentations I gave on campus or in town; and they were not inclined to go out of their way to tell others they were seeing me in therapy.

The second group were people who went out of their way to say hello to me on campus or in town, wanted to introduce their friends to me, and felt slighted and ignored if I failed to recognize them on campus or in meetings at which both of us happened to be present. They were interested in and wanted to attend the public present- ations I made in town and on campus. And they made no secret about their psychotherapeutic relationship with me and enjoyed hearing other patients' and students' opinions of me.

At first I thought the differences between these groups might be directly related to differences in comfort being identified as patients. I initially thought persons in the first group might have felt more shame, embarrassment, and guilt about having "a problem" than did persons in the second group. However, I came to realize that was not so. On the whole, those persons who avoided a relationship with me outside of the consultation environs were persons who were dealing much more in their psychotherapy with transference and early developmental material than were those persons who actively sought a relationship outside of therapy. That is, the persons in the first group were dealing more with what one might call "neurotic" or repressed or unconscious material than were the persons in the second group. I and my patients were somehow modifying the nature of our "interpersonal relationship" to accomodate the work that was to be done in the therapy. Somehow they and I, perhaps at an unconscious level, knew that to be most effective in dealing with repressed and unconscious material it was necessary to have a "therapeutic interpersonal relationship" which maximized the chances for transference and projection. And to do that our "interpersonal relationship" was restricted and built mainly upon material available only in the consultation room and its environs. The second group were people who, for the most part, had what were rather usual adolescent adjustment reaction problems. Their therapy was generally not of long duration, it focused much more upon current, here-and-now issues, and they seemed to need and appreciate the understanding and opinion of an older person. In addition, they were basically psychologically healthy individuals struggling with dependent-independent conflicts and with establishing adult-adult relationships with their parents. A psychotherapeutic relationship which had an emphasis upon the "interpersonal relationship" between us proved to be "just-what-the-doctor-ordered." They, emerging into their own adulthood, needed the experience of relating more personally to an adult. But, it is important to note that just any adult probably would not have sufficed. They needed an adult skilled in "therapeutic relationship" and in understanding ways in which adolescents will perpetuate and prolong dependence and child-adult relationships. Nevertheless, it was obvious they also wanted and needed a different kind of "interpersonal relationship" than did patients who fell into the first group.

A second example of the "interpersonal relationship" in psychotherapy comes from my work with a relatively young man who had a very long history of serious psychopathology and had been treated by a series of analysts and therapists since childhood. His symptoms at the time I saw him focused around very obsessive-compulsive needs for order, cleanliness, and perfection. We had been successfully working for a period of time and he had made some rather good gains on his own personal growth and development as well as experiencing some abatement of his symptomatology. We had reached a plateau in therapy and were just about ready to start on a further and difficult working through of some of his fears, conflicts, and problems. As he looked at me in one of the sessions, I immediately realized he was seeing "me" - not the doctor, not his therapist, not a person upon whom he was placing a great deal of transferred affect. He was seeing the "person" I was. He looked at me, and with a bit of a smile on his face and the shaking of his head from side to side he said, "I don't know if this will ever work. An optimistic Christian and a pessimistic Jew!" I could have hugged him! He really saw me and he told me who I was. He also knew himself on that count and through those words I knew he was saying, "I can't believe we've already accomplished what we have accomplished and I'm getting ready to go on with more work with you. But I'll be damned if I can figure out why it should work at all and it might not." His statement was very much part of our "interpersonal relationship" - it recognized the individuals we were, the respect we had for one another, and the task in which both of us were mutually engaged.

The next example comes from my work with a man who had some of what Frankl (1963) would identify as existential neurotic conflicts as well as tenacious conflicts centering around a fear of success. He was quite ambivalent about starting any psychotherapy but finally made a sufficient committment to begin. He presented and talked about what seemed to be psychologically significant and important material. However it was done in such a way that he kept psychological distance - he was not permitting himself to be fully involved in the material, in the therapy, or with me. Then there were a series of four session in the first two of which he started to deal with some feelings about and relations of intimacy with males and with the paranoid feelings that emerged. In the process of work with that material he seemed to be able to deal with my personalizing what he was saying. The third session of this series he canceled and in the fourth session he was very angry with me. We worked this some but neither one of us really understood it. He felt he couldn't trust me and I did what I could to interpret the relationship between intimacy and paranoid feelings - to point out that when he gets close to a person he finds some way to stop the involvement. But by the end of the session I simply felt the intensity of his resistance and had many questions about the reality of his upset. Later that day he telephoned me and apologized for the way he behaved in the session. I let him know there was no need for an apology and I very much felt that was true. In my own feelings, I did not notice any desire for an apology, I did not feel that I had been personally attacked or unfairly maligned or used. I also felt, but did not express, a real closeness to him for calling - a sense of how it was a courageous and considerate thing he was doing. Among other things, I also responded in a "doctory" fashion and told him we could talk about it in our next session.

That "session" came much sooner than he or I anticipated. For that evening his girlfriend, with whom he was quite close but with whom he also had started to develop some feelings of being restricted and possessed, had died from what appeared to be an overdose of drugs. He had a friend call asking me if I would come to him. At the time of that call, I realized that most of me stopped being his therapist. I was just another human being who could feel for, be scared for, ache for another human being. What could I do but just be the person I was? There was no way under these circumstances to be his psychotherapist.

At midnight I was driving to where he lived and wondering what I could really do to be of any help. When he saw me, he came up to me with tears streaming down his face and open and vulnerable in his body language said, "Can you believe this?" We had talked at some length in his therapy about his problem with and fear of being left and abandoned - particularly by women. No! My God I couldn't believe it! I put out my arms to hold and embrace him and he falls into them. Then he relaxes and I feel the whole weight of his body falling onto me and into my arms. I have to work to hold him up and it is obvious he needs to be held - to know there is someplace/somebody who will simply let him collapse and do nothing. I am glad to be that place/body - I guess I'm useful after all. (My, what therapist hasn't wondered about that!) He was so open and so hurting and very much in touch with his feelings. After having a goodly share of his hurt, he could get angry about such injustice and unfairness in the world - throw things about the room, curse, and in time let me know he no longer needed me there. I don't know what my being there really meant to him - although I do know it was important. But I do know that my being there taught me a good deal about him. I gained a fine sense of how much he needed his own head and the chance to pursue his own bent. He felt too many adults were pulling him one way or another. And that lesson certainly became part of his therapy.

Our next session was not for a week as he went to his friend's funeral. When he returned to therapy, he talked about the fact he got good support from friends (male and female) and could now see that males could be close and loving. His therapy from that point on included involvement. What we had gone through together certainly was part of our "interpersonal relationship." There were no more questions about trusting. The experience became part of our "therapeutic interpersonal relationship."

As Fagan (1971) wrote:

> The therapist needs to know from inside himself when his presence is the most important contribution he can make to the health process, and when his response as one human being to another is more important than any therapeutic busywork (p. 102).

It is not always an easy distinction to make, this one Fagan talks about. But I think there are times when we can only be the person we are - when we cannot "work" and thus be "on" with our therapeutic skills. In fact, there are times when our therapeutic skills would be an anathema. Can you think of many things worse than my interpreting to this man as he sinks into my arms and upon my body that, "You need to be held and to know that there is someplace and somebody who will just let you collapse." As I image it now, I see him taking back his strength, standing on his feet, looking me in the eye, and saying "Go to hell you son-of-a-bitch" as he walks off. And he would be right. If I can't at that moment of enormous sorrow, anger, hurt, bewilderment, confusion in his life just be the human I am created to be; then why in the world should he collaborate with me in attempts to get his important life straightened out?

The last example comes from my work with a man who had already partially related his symptom of keeping undue psychological distance in his interpersonal relationships to unresolved sexual issues.

His psychotherapy was not a difficult one. He was very well motivated, and rapidly established a therapeutic alliance. He readily became involved in a productive "working through" phase of psychotherapy which was augmented by the use of hypnotherapy. In my experience, the use of hypnotherapy seems to make the "therapeutic interpersonal relationship" much more intense and close. His therapy also was one in which there was a minimum, if any, focus upon the "interpersonal relationship." We were really dealing with a few residual conflicts and he probably fell into that group of patients with whom there was no personal relationship outside of the consultation office. Exactly half way through his therapy (which lasted for a total of 18 sessions) he indicated he had been invited to attend a weekend retreat - a retreat he already knew I was scheduled to attend. We spent a portion of one session dealing with the meaning/ramifications of us both being at that retreat. I wanted the freedom to be fully myself on the retreat, which meant aspects of the person I was would become much more obvious to him. I told him these things along with the fact I couldn't be his "therapist" on the retreat. It was left to him to decide whether or not he wished to attend.

As it happened, we both attended the weekend retreat. It proved to be an important and beneficial experience for us and for his psychotherapy. The most significant session of the psychotherapy series occurred right after this retreat. In part that was because the experiences at the retreat taught him not to fear males and not to just emulate or imitate someone else. At the retreat he found there were value issues upon which he and I legitimately disagreed. And what was so beautiful about that experience is it taught him not to look someplace else for his Buddha (Kopp, 1972). It was inside himself and he didn't need to be or try to be what others are or say he should be. He only had to know and be himself. He found great strength in that realization - strength enough to not have to agree with and/or attempt to emulate or model me. The weekend experience taught me the importance of being my human self fully and openly and the healing that is in that honesty, as well as the acceptance that is there for that.

These aspects of the "interpersonal relationship," which developed as a result of a rather intense weekend together, became an important part of our "therapeutic interpersonal relationship." It made the remainder of the therapy work even easier. He

99

immediately started to deal with his feelings about and relationship with his own father. He felt relatively secure in his relationship with me and thus could more readily identify and make evident those times when he felt angry with me. It is as though I had become a "full" person for him and in that process his dependent/ narcissistic needs for me to be omnipotent and thus solve his problems were thwarted. But they were thwarted at a time in his life when he no longer needed to hang onto the belief that there is an all-knowing one who will make the world safe and good for you. He was then able to get on with the business of analyzing his feelings/ fears/ problems in collaboration with a person whom he respected, trusted, and knew rather well.

Now the above are given as examples of how the "interpersonal relationship" plays a constructive role in the total "therapeutic interpersonal relationship." They are not given with the intent of saying this is how therapy should be conducted, nor to say that one should focus upon or develop the "interpersonal relationship" in psychotherapy. As I said at the outset of this section, there are times when it is important for therapy that the person of the therapist encroach as little as possible into the therapy. This is not to say that the therapist should "hide" the person he or she is, and I discuss therapist's honesty at much more length under the heading of "therapeutic relationship". But, I do believe it is very important the psychotherapist *be* the person he or she is. That does not mean psychotherapists should insist on being seen as the persons they are by patients or that psychotherapists impose the persons they are upon patients.

1. Dual Relationships

Now before leaving this section on "interpersonal relationships," it is important to briefly discuss the problem of dual relationships - situations where the psychotherapist may have another relationship with the patient in addition to that of therapist. For it is in the area of "interpersonal relationship" that any dual relationship the therapist may have with the patient is centered and from which it will then have its impact upon the "therapeutic interpersonal relationship."

As a general rule, I believe dual relationships can so compound the "therapeutic interpersonal relationship" as to make

100

psychotherapeutic work ineffective, destructive, or at best confusing. In the dyadic interaction between psychotherapist and patient, it is the psychotherapist's responsibility to understand, explicate, and conceptualize the "therapeutic interpersonal relationship." The psychotherapist is expected to be the expert in understanding interpersonal interactions and relationships. When a psychotherapist has a dual relationship with the patient, keeping tract of the nature of the "interpersonal relationship" as well as the total "therapeutic interpersonal relationship" can become much too difficult a task. Strupp (1973) has nicely pointed out how important it is to understand the relationship in therapy.

> ...the goal of scrutinizing the interpersonal relationship between therapist and patient demands that the field be kept as "clean" as possible in order to evaluate the respective contributions of patient and therapist. If the therapist fails to impose controls over himself and his communications, this goal is almost impossible to achieve (p. 47).

A psychotherapist attempting to be a therapist for his or her own spouse is probably the most cogent example of a dual relationship which could lead to great confusion and a destructive psychotherapuetic outcome. The nature of the relationship between married persons - or persons committed to sharing their lives together - is so complex, intense, and poorly understood that it would result in the "interpersonal relationship" being so powerful as to overwhelm most of the other variables comprising the "therapeutic interpersonal relationship." Since the relationship between two married persons is extraordinarily complex and extremely personally involving, it is highly unlikely any psychotherapist who attempts to do therapy with his or her spouse could adequately understand, explicate, or conceptualize the "therapeutic interpersonal relationship." In no therapy session could these two people escape the fact that they are married. Thus, what happens or is said in the psychotherapeutic session becomes part of their marriage and their marriage starts to become part of the psychotherapy. It seems to me, if one thinks about this for a moment, there would then never be any way of identifying the temporal boundaries of the psychotherapeutic encounter.

101

The very same things I've just said would also apply for the dual relationship of parent and therapist, i.e. a person attempting to be a psychotherapist for his or her own child. Again, I think the nature of the interpersonal relationship between parent and child is much too complex and intense to be added to the variables involved in developing a "therapeutic interpersonal relationship."

Now these examples might be nothing more than belaboring the obvious. I think most psychotherapists readily agree it is inadvisable, unethical, impossible or highly inappropriate to attempt any psychotherapy with a spouse or with your own child. I would say you shouldn't even attempt any diagnosis of your spouse or children. Attempts to diagnose or be psychotherapeutic with one's spouse or children can so easily grow out of the therapist's own defensive needs. I, at least, have found it sufficiently difficult just to be a spouse and a parent. To add to the complexity of those relationships that of psychotherapist or diagnostician is too difficult. This does not mean, of course, that my knowledge of psychology and of the nature of human behavior is completely set aside and has no part in my loving and parenting life. I think that would be impossible. And if not, it would be asinine. But that knowledge and understanding is only one very small part of my relationship and in no way does it threaten to become an overriding or overwhelming aspect of my major relationship with my spouse and children. In fact, if it was an overriding or overwhelming aspect of that relationship, then I'd say the relationship was so constricted and weak and without substance as to be of little or no significance. But conversely, the relationship with spouse and/or children is sufficiently complex and intense as to override or overwhelm all the therapist and/or patient may do to have a "therapeutic interpersonal relationship."

It is when we get into less obvious examples of dual relationships that there may be more disagreement among psychotherapists as to the appropriateness or lack thereof of combining the psychotherapist's role with that of another. In my own situation, the most common dual relationship issue stemmed from the fact that I both taught and practiced in the same community. Thus, there were times that persons in my class would come to me for psychotherapy and vice versa. Generally I found such dual relationship too confusing. In the case of students in my class who sought to see me for psychotherapy, I would work with them so we gained some understanding of why it was important we not engage in a

102

psychotherapeutic relationship. I would assist their efforts to make contact with another psychotherapist with whom they wouldn't have a dual relationship and with whom they could work. In the case of persons whom I was presently seeing for psychotherapy who also wanted to take my class, it was generally possible to have them wait until the psychotherapy was completed before taking the class.

I have had no particular difficulty working with persons in a student-teacher relationship with whom I've earlier had a therapist-patient relationship. I do understand, however, that this situation is one which has led to some of the most difficult ethical and conflict-of-interest cases to come before the American Psychological Association's ethical concerns committee. In my experience the student-teacher relationship has been enhanced by the earlier patient-therapist relationship. After all, there are communalities between education and psychotherapy in terms of what makes for good learning. Perhaps most teachers intuitively understand the importance of relationship for education and realize no one learns from somebody who doesn't care for them. But it is also true I have been careful about the kinds of student-teacher relationships I agreed to after having seen someone in psychotherapy. I would not care to be in the position of making subjective judgments about their acceptance or rejection into important courses or programs. In fact it has been common practice for those of us involved in selecting students for the college's peer counselor program to exempt ourselves from discussion and vote on any persons applying with whom we have had or are having a psychotherapeutic relationship.

I also have had no particular difficulty working with persons in a therapist-patient relationship with whom I've earlier had a student-teacher relationship. So, former students who have come to me for psychotherapy have not posed the same problem as have current students. In fact, those former students who came to me for therapy generally had seen our student-teacher relationship as a good one, or placed it in a rather favorable light. Their expectations were that I would be a good psychotherapist, and those positive aspects of our "interpersonal relationship" usually enhanced the therapeutic alliance.

Another common dual relationship problem for most staff in college psychological services is related to the fact that since they have a position and a title within the institution and since the institution pays their salary, their relationship with the student-

103

patient may also include loyalties and responsibilities to the institution. Halleck (1971) nicely refuted the myth of political neutrality in psychiatry and has given us many examples of how psychotherapy can become political. If students have to have a "psychological" reason for being assigned a single room in a dormitory, for getting permission to live off-campus, for being excused from eating in the college dining halls, then you can be sure the more assertive, active-aggressive and persistent ones will obtain such "psychological" excuses. And in the process of doing it, the therapist will be placed in a dual relationship position. The "interpersonal relationship" between therapist and patient in that instance could be one in which the patient is more interested in the therapist's institutional affiliation and institutional power than in the therapist's therapeutic acumen. Obviously under such circumstances little psychotherapy will take place.

A third common dual relationship problem that can occur when dealing with a college population is related to the fact that most of the patients are adolescents and unable to pay for their psychotherapy. Thus, they make recourse to their parents to fund the treatment. Now in addition to dealing with the adolescent's feelings about this dependence upon and need for some family resources, such a situation can also place the therapist in the position of having a relationship with the parents. So in addition to being the adolescent's therapist, you could also be the parent's employee. This is not the place to discuss different ways of handling such dual relationships in attempts to maximize therapeutic effectiveness. However, over the years I have been impressed with the courage parents have shown and the trust they have placed in their son's or daughter's ability to select and work with a psychotherapist. That courage and trust are demonstrated for me when month after month parents receive only a bill and send only a check. Nothing but bills and checks pass between us. I also, by the way, am grateful to these parents for by such minimal relating they have made the "therapeutic interpersonal relationship" between me and their offspring much easier and possible. At the end of therapy, I generally thank the parents for their courage and cooperation. In response to that thanks, one parent kindly told me it wasn't so much courage that prompted remaining in the background but the perception that if he intervened both his son and I would have wisely closed the door on him.

These examples certainly do not exhaust the dual relationships possible in psychotherapy. The profession has not given the kind of systematic attention and consideration that is actually needed to the importance of the effect of dual relationships upon the "interpersonal relationship" in psychotherapy. I was hard pressed to find adequate research references and citations on this issue. And yet, I think the "popular" notions of psychotherapy and other kinds of helping relationships would have us believe that dual relationships are not at all uncommon or out of the question. Ministers frequently find themselves in complicated relationships: counselor to a parishioner who is sister to the minister's bishop and the wife of a member of the church board that openly disagrees with the minister's policies on many issues. How is that for making a complicated and probably impossible relationship tangle in which to do any psychotherapy? Probation officers frequently juggle dual relationships. On the one hand their relationship with the parolee is defined as a helping one where they want to understand and help the parolee make an adequate adjustment to society. On the other hand, their relationship with the parolee is one of watchdog and referee - making sure the parolee does not behave in such a fashion as to break parole and be returned to prison. Nurses are another example of persons in the helping relationship who generally have to deal with dual relationships. On the one hand they have a relationship with and responsibility to the physician and on the other a relationship with and responsibility to the patient. One might think such a dual relationship would not be conflictual - after all the nurse and doctor are all engaged in the same goal. But the means to that goal differ greatly, and I'm sure you would find most nursing services readily identifying this dual relationship as problematic and generally frustrating.

Obviously these last examples are not taken from the psychotherapeutic situation *per se* and some might say they have nothing to do with the practice of psychotherapy. But hopefully they serve the purpose of pointing out how dual relationships can complicate and confuse the patient-therapist "interpersonal relationship." The reader interested in a further discussion of the interpersonal relationship in psychotherapeutic work is referred to Greenson (1971,1972).

We now turn our attention to the "therapeutic relationship" and the factors of which it is composed.

B. Therapeutic Relationship.

Under the heading of "therapeutic relationship" I include those aspects of the "therapeutic interpersonal relationship" that are now relatively well-established as important characteristics of all helping relationships. I am referring to the variables of non-possessive warmth, empathy, and what has gone by the name of honesty, congruence, authenticity, or genuineness. They are the variables that compose the "therapeutic relationship," and I consider them fundamental to successful treatment. Furthermore, their implementation is almost exclusively the responsibility of the psychotherapist. Perlman (1979) writing about relationship said:

> The usual words used to describe a "meaningful" relationship as well as a "working" or "therapeutic" relationship - all "good" in the sense of being gratifying and growth promoting - are warmth, loving, caring, acceptance, responsiveness, empathy, genuineness, attentiveness, concern, support, understanding (p. 29).

The variables of loving and caring, both powerful and intense emotions, will be considered in the next section. In part, they grow out of the "therapeutic relationship" in the context of the other relationship variables in the "therapeutic interpersonal relationship." But all of the other terms Perlman uses are aspects of what I call the "therapeutic relationship" and I believe can be subsumed under the three major categories of non-possessive warmth, empathy, and genuineness.

Perhaps a brief word needs to be said explaining why I include these variables under the rubric of "relationship." For it is possible to present nonpossessive warmth, empathy, and genuineness as psychotherapeutic skills or even as therapeutic techniques specific to particular theories of psychotherapy. In both instances, they could be presented quite separate and apart from relationship. However, I believe that these particular characteristics of the psychotherapist's personality and behavior tend to merge with and become part of the "therapeutic interpersonal relationship." They are most clearly perceived by patients as charcteristics of the therapist's personality and of the relationship between the two of them. Perhaps with the exception of empathy, patients do not perceive or feel these characteristics of the interaction as psychotherapeutic techniques or therapeutic skills learned in the process of becoming a psychotherapist. Indeed, at times the patient comes to think that the therapist is a warm, accepting, understanding, honest person. And, of course, in many respects most therapists are such persons. However, there is no need for the patient to precisely demarcate aspects of the therapist's personality which are traits most predominate and characteristic of him or her in the psychotherapy hour from those most characteristic of him or her in life outside the consultation room. In fact, it may be to the patient's benefit not to make such distinctions until near the end of therapy. Then in the termination phase, if it has not happened before, the patient does make such distinctions and realizes consciously what was probably known unconsciously, i.e. the psychotherapist in his or her interactions with others in the world is not always so warm and understanding and accepting.

Lastly, and most importantly for placing these characteristics under the rubric of relationship is the fact that the therapist cannot just "practice" these techniques or "put-them-on" for the psychotherapeutic hour and then lay them aside. For these are not only skills and sensitivities which can be learned, but they are also philosophical positions and value choices that are personal and become part of the psychotherapist's internal and overt life. To begin with, even before their professional education, many psychotherapists are relatively convinced of the importance of each person and committed to being of assistance and help to them. Then as they work with patients, therapists are reinforced for their personal characteristics of nonpossessive warmth, empathy, and genuineness. These qualities become more and more a part of their personality. In the psychotherapist's everyday life we may not see these qualities evidenced to the extent they are in the psychotherapeutic hour. But we may see them as more obvious characteristics of psychotherapists' personalities than they are as obvious characteristics of engineers', chemists', physicians' personalities. It is probably not in the quality of these characteristics that psychotherapists differ in and out of the consultation room, but in the quantity of them. They are, or in my opinion should be, in abundance in the psychotherapeutic hour. And above all, they are not something that can be "put-on" or "taken-off"

107

like a stethescope or a white lab coat as we go in or out of the office. Or tell me, how can anyone "put on" genuineness? If it is "put-on," it can't be genuine. Thus, one cannot just "act" these important characteristics of the "therapeutic relationship." In actuality they become part of the person of the therapist. Thus, it should not be surprising that patients perceive these characteristics as part of the therapist's personality. For in reality, they do become part of the therapist's personality.

It just seems to me that there are so many reasons for placing these variables under the rubric of relationship that it is inappropriate to see them simply as skills and/or techniques. Furthermore I think they should never be taught as something separate and apart from the psychotherapist's own personality, attitudes, and value system.

Beginning with publications in the early 1950's, Carl Rogers called our attention to the importance of these variables of relationship in the psychotherapeutic process. He placed the variables within a theoretical formulation and included them as necessary conditions for successful psychotherapy. It was his work that gave us such terms as "non-possessive warmth," "empathy," and "honesty," "genuineness," "authenticity" (Rogers, 1951,1957,1959,1961). The research investigations focusing upon these characteristics of therapist-patient relationships began with Whitehorn and Betz (1954). They certainly included work by Rogers and his students who continuously and carefully examined their own clinical work and conducted some of the first empirical research on these variables (Rogers & Dymond, 1964; Rogers, 1967). Others (Hiler, 1958; Carson & Heine, 1962; Baum, et al., 1966) added to that research literature and by the beginning of the 1970's, Truax and Mitchell (1971) could review enough studies to suggest that these variables were generally typical of successful psychotherapists.

By the mid '70's Truax & Carkhuff (1976) published a guide for teaching effective counseling and psychotherapy skills. They placed a great deal of emphasis upon the importance of the therapist variables originally hypothesized by Carl Rogers. In the next two years, there were three major articles reviewing research on these therapist variables. Mitchell, Bozarth, and Krauft (1977) reappraised the therapeutic effectiveness of nonpossessive warmth, empathy, and genuineness. Their work was followed the next year by Parloff,

108

Waskow, and Wolfe's (1978) review and by Bergin & Lambert's (1978) review of the research on these variables and their relation to process and outcome. These reviews clearly indicated that nonpossessive warmth, empathy, and genuineness were fundamental to successful long-term psychotherapy.

Today there is fairly consistent agreement among psychotherapists and counselors that these variables are at least desirable if not necessary conditions for successful counseling and psychotherapy. They are those aspects of the helping relationship most frequently taught to paraprofessionals and to volunteer workers in community clinics and telephone hotlines. The empirical research literature generally supports the position that these variables of psychotherapists' personalities or of their relationship with patients are important to the process and outcome of psychotherapy.

Furthermore, it seems rather clear that these variables are almost exclusively the contribution of the psychotherapist. (A variable in the "therapeutic interpersonal relationship" almost exclusively the contribution of the patient is transference.) Truax and Mitchell's (1971) review provided some empirical evidence for the view that "therapeutic relationship" variables are the therapist's responsibility. In their words:

> Putting together these several studies focusing upon the question of who is causing the levels of conditions in interviewing, counseling, or psychotherapy, the evidence is both uniform and strong in indicating that in both therapeutic and informational interviewers it is the interviewer, not the patient, who determines what the level of accurate empathy and genuineness shall be. Furthermore, considering nonpossessive warmth, the findings from therapy interviews indicate that the different therapists offer different levels of warmth, and that patients in general have little affect on the level of warmth offered (p. 325).

More than any of the other variables in the "therapeutic interpersonal relationship", it is these in the "therapeutic relationship" *per se* that are most crucial for helping to create conditions which permit and encourage patients to openly describe, discuss, and examine problems, feelings, attitudes, and beliefs. They are instrumental in forming a "space" in which both members of the dyad have room to learn about and understand with some depth and detail the patient's world, perceptions, and experiences. It is not only the patient who benefits from having this "space," but also the therapist. For it is in this "space" that the therapist learns so very much about the structure and development of psychopathology; is privy to the unfolding of layers of defensiveness; and experiences moments of ironic/ pathetic/ joyous understanding of the patient's behaviors, attitudes, positions, and beliefs. It is in this "space" (created in part by these "therapeutic relationship" variables) that both parties finally understand some of the patient's behaviors and attitudes - seeing how they were important and necessary at one time but are now no longer useful and may even be hurtful. And in the process of this happening, the therapist gains an understanding of this other person - an understanding which is beyond any theoretical or intellectual analysis of "the problem." And that kind of understanding only increases the therapist's adherence to these "therapeutic relationship" variables. It also assists to develop the feelings of caring and loving the therapist has for the patient and the patient for the therapist. For by the process of psychotherapy and in the "space" created by "therapeutic relationship," we can receive an understanding with depth and fullness which permits us to sense the struggles, strengths, dignity, and greatness inherent in persons. Perlman (1979) speaks about this "space" created by the "therapeutic relationship" as an island:

> A relationship formed for the purpose of helping a "learner" provides a safety island, a place and person with whom one can risk making mistakes without fear of ridicule or censure, where corrections and directions are given with concern for the person's own individual pace and capacity, where glad recognition is given for trying, even if the effort falls short of the intent (p. 91).

In this quote, she does not speak of what the therapist gets from the "therapeutic relationship." But she does point to the relationship's centrality in creating the psychological "space" and to the conditions whereby the process of psychotherapy may unfold and in which the patient has optimal chances for self revelation and exploration.

The "therapeutic relationship" is a crucial aspect of the "therapeutic interpersonal relationship." Let us now consider each one of the three major categories comprising the "therapeutic relationship."

I. Non-Possessive Warmth:

A) Definition

Raush and Bordin (1957) were among the first to attempt a theoretical analysis of the components of warmth in a psycho-therapeutic setting. The therapist's spontaneity, commitment, and effort to understand were all conceptualized as part of "warmth." Much later, Truax and Mitchell's (1971) research indicated that both the intensity and intimacy of a relationship were strongly related with warmth. Also Strupp, et al. (1969) had found that when patient's viewed their own psychotherapy, the "warmth" factor was particularly noteworthy and it included a sense of having the therapist's respect. While it may not seem appropriate to the theory of behavior therapy, these qualities of nonpossessive warmth are just as important to patients in behavior therapy as to patients in other forms of psychotherapy (Ryan & Gizynski, 1971; Sloane, et al., 1975; Ford, 1978).

In an attempt to understand what is meant by nonpossessive warmth, let us begin with a dictionary definition. The adjective "possessive" refers to ownership, to a rather excessive or characteristic desire to possess - to have as one's property. It also can refer to a jealousy at the personal independence of another or to anyone else having an influence on the other. The noun "warmth" refers to a quality or state of gentle heat. Its meaning also includes a liveliness of feelings, emotions, or sympathies and affection or kindliness. Common parlance certainly has used "warm" and "cold" to describe people's personal characteristics or attitudes. We have all heard the phrase, "He's a cold fish." It is commonly applied to persons from whom we have received no sense of accepting contact or recognition of our individuality and who also seem to emit no "warmth" or compassionate emotion. "She's such a warm person" is

111

a statement we've heard and probably used to describe someone from whom we received acceptance, respect, and who made us feel most welcome and wanted. Furthermore, my choice of gender for these common parlance examples is not without meaning. I suggest it is more usual for us to find "warm" women and "cold" men than vice versa.

Thus, nonpossessive warmth refers to a condition in which the therapist experiences and in some degree manifests a liking, affection, respect for and interest in the patient *without* a desire to have that person believe and/or behave in any specific way or a desire to have that patient be or become anything in particular for the therapist. It includes an unconditional acceptance of the other's personhood and has with it a nonjudgmental attitude with an emphasis upon nonblaming. It includes characteristics associated to those situations in which we say/feel we have been "warmly received." Thus nonpossessive warmth refers to a condition in which the patient experiences being accepted, made to feel comfortable, unhurried, and has the other's respect and full attention. Furthermore, it is my experience that nonpossessive warmth is a particularly active and powerful force in the first sessions with a patient. For then is when some of the foundation stones will be set for the relationship between therapist and patient. Initially being respected, not judged, accepted, liked and having another human being genuinely attempt to understand us seems to be most helpful if not necessary in our moving toward self revelation and examination. Ford's (1978) research has indicated that judgments by patients about therapist-patient relationship were made early in therapy and served as a basis for continuing or dropping out of therapy. Many studies (Shapiro, 1974; Rosenzweig & Folman, 1974; Baekeland & Lundwall,1975; Shapiro et al., 1976; Strupp & Hadley, 1979) have indicated that dropping out of therapy and/or unsuccessful therapeutic outcomes are related in patients' minds to not being respected, liked, or taken seriously by their therapists. Doherty (1971) suggested, and Fehrenbach & O'Leary (1982) have some data to help confirm the idea, that clinicians' treatment decisions are significantly influenced by how personally attractive the therapist finds the patient. The data on this subject is quite limited and does not hold for a range of treatment contexts. Nevertheless, I think it is not unlikely that we will find it quite possible to have higher levels of nonpossessive

112

warmth with those patients whom we also find personally attractive. It may also be that the liking, affection, attraction to the patient is a rather fast and immediate event - one that we therapists make relatively rapidly upon meeting the patient and do so unconsciously - or at least without an analysis of why we find this or that patient so attractive.

In reviewing my own experience, I find that those patients to whom I'm initially most personally attracted and with whom I can easily maintain an attitude of nonpossessive warmth are persons who are quite intellectually bright, fast thinkers, relatively open in their feelings, at ease with introspection, not ambivalent about wanting help, and seem to perceive me as one who can be of help. Obviously these characteristics are ones that probably make my task as a psychotherapist much easier. In fact, they may come close to describing any psychotherapist's "dream" patient. Patients with whom I do not find myself intially attracted can best be described as excessively intellectual, well defended and cautious about making any personal statements, rather rigid and forceful in their belief systems but inclined to keep what they think to themselves. With these patients I have to more consciously attend to issues of nonpossessive warmth.

Certainly in these two examples I have described persons who are at opposite poles in their abilities to form interpersonal relationships with anyone, let alone with a psychotherapist. I have long been aware that I enjoy and need close interpersonal relationships. Thus, I find persons who also enjoy and are at ease with close interpersonal relationships much more attractive and personally stimulating. But in addition, I think that there is some hesitation on my part to too readily "give myself" or commit myself to helping someone about whom I'm not sure - perhaps not sure I can help or at a deeper level not sure I can trust.

Now in describing the differences in my response to these two hypothetical persons, I kept referring to my "initial" attraction. That was on purpose and refers to the fact that once therapy is underway nonpossessive warmth and my conscious awareness of liking and being attracted to the patient is much more even across patients. The differences initially noted are no longer so prevalent. I think this is because once therapy is underway, reality factors have a chance to play their role. Thus I learn much more about my patient. Obviously some of that learning helps modify my earlier countertransference feelings. Also many other aspects of the "therapeutic interpersonal relationship" now come into play, not the least of which are the patient's transference feelings and my abilities to empathically relate to the patient's life. The "work" we are doing in the psychotherapy process is pulling me closer to the patient, helps modify any ambivalence or reluctance I may have had to get involved, and generally enhances my "liking" of the patient. At the same time, the "work" of psychotherapy is probably modifying the patient's behaviors in such a fashion that I will start to find the patient even more attractive and likeable.

Maintaining a position of nonpossessive warmth is not always particularly easy. One of the crucial aspects of a helping relationship in Carl Rogers' (1951) theory is the therapist's attitude and philosophical orientation. That attitude and orientation is both a significant and a scientifically observable fact. The attitude Rogers stresses as basic is one that accepts the significance and worth of every human being. To hold it, the therapist must see the patient as an important, significant, worthwhile human being capable of taking part in the solution to his or her problems. Now that may sound as though it is relatively easy to do, but our American society encourages judgment and categorization of persons. So, instead of acceptance, we are much more inclined to judge. Furthermore, it is not enough just to avoid judging. Rogers (1951) was clear that nonpossessive warmth could not be a point of view held at the verbal level, but our behavior was crucial in reflecting that attitude.

> If we do hold this point of view at the verbal level, to what extent is it operationally evident at the behavioral level? Do we tend to treat individuals as persons of worth, or do we subtly devalue them by our attitudes and behavior? Is our philosophy one in which respect for the individual is uppermost? Do we respect his capacity and his right to self-direction, or do we basically believe that his life would be best guided by us? To what extent do we have a need and a desire to dominate others? Are we willing for the individual to select and choose his own values, or are our actions guided by the conviction (usually unspoken) that he would be happiest

114

if he permitted us to select for him his values and standards and goals? (p. 20).

Beginning students generally have more difficulty understanding and risking accepting the position of nonpossessive warmth than they do with any of the other variables in the "therapeutic relationship." One of the problems students regularly raise is the fear that unconditional acceptance or a nonjudgmental stance will only condone all the person's behavior. It is the argument that "silence gives consent" and by unconditional acceptance you give patients permission to continue in their "unacceptable" behaviors and beliefs. Such words so frequently used by students indicate they haven't come close to considering the possibility that the other person's behaviors and/or beliefs *are* quite acceptable.

The other common criticism or misperception students have about nonpossessive warmth is seeing it as constituting nothing more than a passive, "laissez faire" attitude - an attitude in which the therapist does not really care what the patient believes or does. This is not at all the case! Passivity and lack of interest could only be perceived by the patient for what it really is - rejection. It is not that the therapist does not care what the patient believes or does, it is that the therapist does not judge what the patient believes or does. The therapist does not assign blame or apply a judgment of right or wrong to the patient's behavior and/or belief. With nonpossessive warmth there is a realization on the therapist's part that judgmental attention to what the patient does and/or believes is of little consequence in either altering that behavior and belief or in helping that other important, significant human being solve his or her own problem. And lastly, there are so many other things we therapists must attend to and to which we must direct our attention, and energies during the psychotherapeutic hour; that it is simply counter-productive and much too draining to engage in the business of being a judge. This is not to say that many patients don't want a judge or at least will act as though they do.

B) Judgment

A few words need to be said about judgment as it can be an unfortunate restraint upon nonposessive warmth. People always seem to be judging other people. Instead of being taught to listen to and understand another human being, we are taught to evaluate and judge whether or not what they have to say and/or how they behave is right or wrong. The American society with its Judeo-Christian and puritanical heritage seems to emphasizes judgment. No place does this seem clearer to me than in a discussion of religion between two persons who are opposite and fundamentalist in their beliefs. In such discussion, I find there is generally little warmth, almost no understanding and/or appreciation for one another's personal religious position, and a great desire to "possess" or have that other person embrace your beliefs. It is almost as though neither party dare entertain any ideas or feelings that might contradict what they already believe. They do not want to be in the position of the King in the play *Anna and the King of Siam* who found "confusion in conclusions I concluded long ago." And so they stay involved in judging one another as they systematically increase the decibel level of their own verbal arguments in the hope that loudness itself might penetrate the other's resistance.

Now it may be that initially our training to judge is unavoidable. At least theoretically the early infant's mental development has very limited categories for moral judgments (Kohlberg, 1981). The development of some superego functions could occur at a time when stage one reasoning is most predominant and thus the world would be divided into those behaviors and attitudes that will give us reward or incur punishment from our parents. Things are then "good" or "bad," "right" or "wrong" and judgments are necessary. This is certainly not the place for a discussion of how our rather judgmental societal attitude may develop or of the adequacy of existing theories of moral development. But hopefully the present very limited discussion does highlight how unique a nonjudgmental relationship may be for persons in this society. Furthermore, it helps to highlight the fact that psychotherapists must go against much early and, unfortunately at times, later training in order to develop characteristics of non-possessive warmth and thus enhance the "therapeutic relationship." In addition to the fact that a nonjudmental attitude may be a rarity in our society, we also probably only give lip-service to the idea that persons are of equal worth. Our behaviors generally betray the social-class consciousness that is in our hearts. We easily equate individual human worth with

116

material wealth. For the most part, we have not escaped "blaming the victim" - a concept Ryan (1971) so nicely explicated. As a society, we tend to believe that poor people bring it upon themselves and really aren't as important and as significant as the corporate presidents. Our attitudes toward persons who drive up in Rolls Royce or Cadillac limousines are quite different than attitudes we hold toward "bag ladies" or transients we see walking the city streets. As much as we might want to say we see both persons as equally important, significant, worthwhile human beings; we probably are inclined to see the former as more significant and worthwhile than the latter.

Since these teachings from our society might well be counter to the attitudes and philosophy necessary for a successful "therapeutic relationship," we can see that psychotherapists must have various means available for monitoring and assessing their feelings and behaviors with and toward the patient. Psychotherapists have to be able to know to what extent they may be providing nonpossessive warmth session after session with patient after patient. And most importantly, they must be sensitive to those instances in which they find it difficult and maybe impossible to maintain the position of nonpossessive warmth with a patient. Certainly, there are scales available for measuring nonpossessive warmth (Truax, 1962). The audio and video taping of sessions and their review by oneself and/or with others is certainly another way therapists may check on the extent to which they are providing the most viable "therapeutic relationship" for patients. I have also found it useful to utilize various questionnaire forms for patient feedback - obtaining from them estimates of both interpersonal relationship factors in their psychotherapy as well as satisfaction and outcome estimates. Most importantly I find that my own philosophical orientation must be periodically examined and I have to seriously ask myself how I feel and what I believe about any particular patient.

C) Summary

I'm relatively convinced we will not give others what we ourselves do not already have. Thus, we cannot give others non-judgmental liking, affection, and respect if we have not received and/or do not have those things for ourselves. An empirical relationship between

117

self-regard and the regard one holds for others has already been demonstrated (Fey, 1955; Kanfer & Marston, 1963). In addition, we can now point to a number of studies suggesting that the therapist's psychological health may also be a variable affecting the success of treatment. For it seems that psychotherapists who are themselves psychologically disturbed may effect deterioration in their patients (Parloff, Waskow, & Wolfe, 1978; Bergin & Lambert, 1978). Thus, to make a contribution to the "therapeutic relationship," it seems important the therapist have good self-esteem and be psychologically healthy. We have already said that the responsibility for establishing a viable "therapeutic relationship" is almost exclusively the psychotherapist's task. We only expect the therapist to hold nonpossessive warmth for the patient. We do not require patients to have nonpossessive warmth for their psychotherapists. And being realistic, we also know there are strong forces in ourselves and in our society negating the maintenance of an attitude of nonpossessive warmth. So, obviously, there are going to be times when we fail to provide it. But, hopefully we are able to tend toward and habitually maintain sufficient nonpossessive warmth in the psychotherapeutic hour to provide the patient with a unique, non-judgmental, accepting relationship - a relationship that is an important factor in developing a viable "therapeutic relationship" and thus a viable "therapeutic interpersonal relationship."

II. Empathy

A) Example

Empathy has had and continues to have many definitions, probably none of which are fully adequate. It has long been regarded as an important component of effective psychotherapy - we know that it exists but are not at all sure how to define it. The lack of precise definition is not a matter of attempting to be elusive or ambiguous. Rather, the phenomenon to which the term refers is not readily identified as a common experience in our everyday interpersonal interactions and does not neatly fit into the realm of either the cognitive, the affective, or the conative. For me the experience of empathically understanding another human being has a strong affective component - it gives me "goosebumps!" There is with it an insight experience, a sense of really understanding how that other person feels - but understanding that feeling in the context of all the beauty and pathos and complexity of that other person's world. It is seeing and understanding in a very deep and clear and unambiguous way one small aspect of that other person's life. And it is conative in that it includes a striving and desire on my part to understand the intricacies of this other person's world. In addition, somehow or other the "I", the "me", the "person-I-am" who is doing that seeing and understanding is not even there. For the moment I don't even know how "I" feel about the understanding, the insight - this "honored sharing." Somehow or other, the person I am, the experiences I have had are not part of that understanding. In fact, if I attempt to relate my own experiences to what I am hearing from the patient, I generally will not succeed in having an empathic understanding. Thus, for me, empathy seems to be something more than just a conscious process. It is related to Freud's (1924) attitude of "equally hovering attention" and Reik's (1949) listening with the third ear. It is as though the patient's unconscious is speaking in some way to my unconscious. I then consciously experience it as a clear, obvious, "right-on" event full of understanding. And there is with that understanding a feeling of quiet joy, thankfulness, and some awe. The words which the feelings seem to say are, "Oh, my God I see it!" Furthermore there is with it no great compulsion to tell the patient I understand. I do not experience it at all as something "I" have accomplished. "I" am not even there! And, while there is no great compulsion to tell the patient I understand, there is also the sense that words can spontaneously come out of my mouth saying the feeling and understanding conveyed by the empathic experience. The words do not seem to be said for any purpose, they just cannot help being said. And furthermore, once the words are said there is nothing more that needs to be done. The empathic understanding seems to require nothing more. It is experienced as a rather full, complete understanding of one small aspect or fraction of the other's life and it would be impossible with words to convey the fullness of that experience. Furthermore, it does not seem necessary to do anything with or about that understanding.

This is in direct contrast to an intellectual understanding. With intellectual understanding, I find myself wanting to focus the patient's attention on some aspect of the material revealed by that intellectual understanding. I want to do "something" with it and "help" the patient see and understand its meaning and importance. Furthermore, the feeling associated with an intellectual understanding is quite different. It is a feeling of excitement, and a sense of "maybe-we-have-found-something." But, there is no genuine awe with it nor that secure peace which tells both patient and me "this is the truth."

Hokanson (1983) provides us with a case by which it may be possible for us to experience both intellectual understanding and empathy. In this case, the patient comes to therapy because she experiences temper outbursts toward her daughter. Even though she resolves to control herself, she still finds that in a day or so something rather inconsequential will trigger an outburst. She is married, a college graduate, presently a housewife and the mother of three. In therapy she is precise, unemotional, and businesslike. She knows that she is a very logical person and it is difficult for her to deal at a "feeling level." In the middle of the second session she says:

> But I seem to be stuck. If anything, my outbursts have been getting worse for a number of years now. It's frustrating.....You know, a thought just popped into my head. It doesn't fit in anyplace, but since you want me to describe such random thoughts, here it is. Lisa is my husband's favorite among the children. I don't see where that has anything to do with the situation, but there it is. As I think I told you earlier, my husband, Herb, is very understanding during my little episodes. And he's generally a very easygoing person .. ...He works as the office manager in the _____Company, which I'm sure you know is one of the biggest firms in the city. I think they have something like five hundred employees in the home office alone, and I saw in yesterday's paper that they may even be taking over the ____ Company....Well, where was I? I, er, how should I say it, I can't seem to get the knack of what I'm supposed to do (p. 272).

120

Here we start to have some intellectual understanding. It includes a realization that somehow or other her temper outbursts toward Lisa are tied with the fact this child is her husband's favorite. We also "understand" she had to distract herself from any further thought about the possible relationship between Lisa, her husband, and her outbursts by talking about where her husband works. Later on in the same session she says:

> Sometimes I wish he [husband] would be more firm with me generally...or at least control me when I'm having an outburst towards Lisa. But he just seems incapable of it...or maybe these temper tantrums of mine catch us all unawares. They happen so fast nobody can control them....It's me who has got to control myself (p. 273).

The therapist's response is certainly an empathic one.

> Right now your feelings about it maybe go in several directions. "Why doesn't he control me when I act that way? But, they happen so quickly, he can't be blamed....(p. 273).

And, as is so frequently true when we respond empathically it seems to help or give the patient permission to continue and go even further into and with the material.

> No! It's clearly illogical to blame him. It's my responsibility. I'm the one doing it to Lisa. He can't be expected to get inside my head and prevent these outbursts before they occur.

> Therapist: And if I sense your feelings right now, it's kind of, indignation, saying, "Hey wait a minute, Herb can't be blamed for these temper outbursts."

> That's right. I'm the one who is responsible [Pause]. I don't know, when I talk about it like this, or even think about it by myself, I feel kind of, I don't know what you'd call it...unresolved, or something. I get the feeling

121

that there are other things going on, underneath. It's disturbing. I get upset with myself when I can't figure things out logically....What do you think? I see that our time is just about up (p. 274).

Here we intellectually understand that she is starting to sense there may be something significant to this relationship between Lisa, her husband and her temper outbursts - that what is of real consequence is "underneath" and not yet apparent or clear. I certainly can't be sure what her feelings are about what she has said. But from the words alone I'd be inclined to respond, "You sense that there may be other things going on underneath and that's a little scary and disturbing."

Then in the fourth session, this patient tells us a good deal about her past life. She relates this history without affect or strong feeling. But even as you read the transcript it will be difficult to avoid having your own feelings about what is being said. Some of what we start to feel/understand as we hear this material will be part of an empathic understanding.

[The client proceeds with a very bland, unemotional account of her history. Throughout this fairly lenthy narrative her very precise, intellectual, and emotionless approach does not change.]

I was born in Belgium. My parents were Jewish, pretty orthodox, and they were both professional people. Doctors. They were both on the staff at _____ Hospital. I had one younger sister, two years younger than me. You know, the one who is now living in Arizona. We were a very close-knit family. I can remember my parents in those early years as being absolutely wonderful. The house was always filled with affection. They gave us a great deal of time. Everyone was close to one another ....It's hard to describe. How should I say it? Those early years just seemed brimming with affection [Pause].

I was young, five or six, when the war broke out. I don't think I even noticed it really, to tell the truth. Oh, I suppose I must have noticed a general increase in

122

tension. My parents had to work long hours, and so forth, but I think they were so protective, and at ease with us girls, that we didn't realize what was going on. A short time after the Germans occupied, it happened. I remember I was standing at the front window. I was six. A covered truck stopped in front of our house, and men in uniform jumped out. I really didn't know what was happening, but my parents were wild. In a matter of seconds my parents had my sister and I at the back door, and they sent us across the alley to our neighbor's house. It all happened so fast. The next thing I knew my sister and I were looking out the neighbor's window, and the soldiers were dragging my parents to the truck. Naturally we didn't understand about concentration camps as children, but I think I somehow realized - perhaps from the reactions of our neighbors - that we would never see our parents again (p. 279).

Doesn't this transcript start to make you "perk-up," give you some feelings and perhaps the beginning of an emotional understanding? Her therapist's commentary probably reflects our own feelings at hearing this story. "All the unspeakable agonies of the holocaust enveloped me. Even more, the image of a six-year-old child, seeing her parents being dragged off to their deaths, gripped me with grief and anxiety. How terror-stricken she must have been at the time. Absolute, stark, childlike terror" (p. 279). This therapist certainly has an empathic understanding - it is almost as though she were there viewing the patient as a terror-stricken six-year-old. The therapist was "in-touch-with" and empathically understanding feelings that the patient herself could only now hold in the unconscious.

As I read this patient's words I saw her world cruelly, immediately, incomprehensibly turn from a very idyllic, happy childhood - where she was loved and with loving people - into one of horrendous loss with no means or way of recognizing that loss or saying goodbye. And furthermore, it was a "world" I was completely unprepared to hear. I had no preparation for it. I did not expect it. I had not been brought to that place with her. Until this moment, I did not know this was part of her "world."

The patient, however, relates this story as though she were talking

123

about an uneventful trip to the grocery market. Her therapist noted the patient showed no signs of terror, anxiety, or grief. And so the empathic understanding here is the sad and deep realization of how very traumatic and terrible this experience was/is for her - how the horror, fear, rage of it all is too much to approach or get close to - how for so long she has had to keep the strong, hurtful affect associated with this unfair, unjust, outrageous fortune from touching her. I think I would have done just what her therapist did, say nothing. The "spontaneous" voice in me is saying, "My God, what a terrible thing for a six year old to face."

The importance of the empathic response is that it identifies, clarifies, and brings to life a vital and substantive part of that other human being's existence. We really start to "know" that other person. For example, in the present case I am no longer concerned, or worried about her temper outbursts with Lisa. I don't even want to understand them right now. That would be an intellectual exercise of little or no consequence. Here, right in the therapy office, right in this moment between these two people (therapist and patient) LIVES what is of consequence, LIVES what has never been put to rest. And in large part, the reason it LIVES in this session is that through empathy it has been brought to life. From the patient's demeanor, behavior, and vocal intonations we gather she is not consciously aware of the strong feelings associated with this episode. But, the patient has now pointed the way to that "room" in her life in which those forces live and unconsciously determine her behavior. Are you there with her? Do you feel the terror and anxiety under her calm and logical exterior? Does her remark in the second session, "I get the feeling there are other things going on, underneath," now make even more sense? Do you feel some hope that we really may get to what's going on?

In this fourth session, she continues to explain that she and her sister were smuggled from neighbor to friend to relative and eventually ended in England as refugee's. There they were adopted by an elderly couple of the English upper class who showered both girls with love and support. The girls lived there for nine years and during that time grew to love these "parents" very much. Then, quite unexpectedly they received a letter from their parents who had survived the holocaust, were living in America and desperately searching for their daughters. Within a matter of days these two girls

124

left the old couple, who had been their parents for nine years, and went to America and to their "biological and first-six-year" parents. The patient never again saw her "other" parents - this elderly couple.

Does the reader have any feelings about these events? Can you be in "her world" - be a small girl of six who is scared and confused and hurting terribly and eventually goes to England. Then have another happy, loving home, where you are protected and wanted and enjoyed and have fun with your life. Then choose between loves and lives and livings done with adults from zero to six and loves and lives and livings done with adults from six to sixteen. But really no choice. Just pack-up and leave. And *again,* no time to say goodbye or to put-to-rest what the end of living with loving and giving by other human beings means. Do you start to have some empathic understanding? And the intellectual understanding, of course, includes the knowledge that this patient's "problem" is going to have something to do with separation from loved ones.

As we shall soon see, like most intellectual understanding or knowledge, it lacks the kind of precision, exactness, depth and truth that gives a patina and shine only obtained through empathic understanding - or an understanding that has both the head and the heart locked together in it - the genuine article!

In the seventh session she starts to take us even more into her world and to be there in it at the same time. By that I mean, she starts to add (or tell us about) the other pieces in this important tapestry of her life and she does so with affect. Now gone is the controlled, logical, unemotional protective core. She is even more of herself with "us" now. Do you feel honored? Are you appreciative? I am! It is an old and rare jewel she is uncovering for us and for herself. In the seventh session she is talking about a boy, a man who was in law school and whom she loved and who loved her.

> And what's more, the relationship was getting stronger
> and stronger. I didn't think it was possible, but it
> was....We had been going together for seven or eight
> months, and then, out of the blue, he said it was all over.
> I thought he was joking. No signs, no warning. Just
> finished....Oh, I don't know, he said we were too serious,
> you know. He wasn't ready to settle down, that sort of
> thing. It, it was, was all over....I really went off the deep

end. It was too much for me. Everything within me shut down. I become deeply depressed...and stayed that way, it seems, for a long time. Two months, three, I don't know. But then I slowly started to come out of it, and some new emotions took over...I came out of it very angry - at him, at men in general, I guess, at the whole world. And I also remember, very vividly, that I made a solemn promise to myself never to again let my feelings go out to anyone. I couldn't tolerate that sort of thing happening to me again. I didn't think I could survive another loss like that [starts to weep] (p. 283).

And now can't you feel her strength - her resolve to put an end to this world that gives her loves only to abruptly, unexpectedly, and with no warning whatsoever take them away from her? This is three times within eighteen years. It is certainly enough! There is no way she will put up with anymore of it. She tells us, "I didn't think I could survive another loss like that." It is a telling statement, for it implies that she knows she can survive another such loss.

In the eighth session she feels changes taking place within her, and two excerpts from that session indicate those changes and the insight she has obtained into her condition through the process of psychotherapy.

I'm not sure how to explain it, but I can feel some changes taking place within me. Right now I'm calmer than I've been in a long time. I've become much better with Lisa. I haven't had an outburst in over a week, and not many before that.....But at the same time I feel some deeper things, I just get vague, what should I call them, premonitions, of darker issues that I have to deal with [Laughs]. The curious workings of the feminine mind (p. 284).

I can't refrain from adding, it is not the curious workings of the feminine mind, but of the human mind. And by the tenth session she is able to identify what is much closer to the "real" problem.

[Very serious and determined]: You know, the real

126

problems in my life are not between me and Lisa. They're between Herb and me. I've been hiding from that fact for months, years even, but there it is. Whatever these problems are with me and Herb, I've been taking them out on Lisa. Sort of diverting my anger and frustration onto her - his favorite, remember? I'm afraid I've led us both down a blind alley in therapy....I need to start exploring my marriage...but I sense that it will be a hard thing to do (p. 285).

Buy the sixteenth session the full realization of what psychodynamics have been operating in her life comes to the patient and to us. I have badly compressed this case and do not want to leave the reader with the mistaken notion that this patient's fine progress in therapy and the events of this sixteenth session were due only to empathy. That is simply not true. She had a skilled therapist who in addition to sensitively and correctly conceptualizing the psychodynamics in this situation was also knowledgeable about transference phenomena and its management. Following are the excerpts from the sixteenth session that I think allow us opportunity for empathic understanding in depth.

Therapist: I can't help feeling that your emotions right now are touching on deep things in your past.

Client: [Long pause; weeping subsides] I haven't really looked at it that way. I'm just so caught up in my feelings right now [Pause]. I had the same intensity of feelings toward the first boy I was in love with - the law student....And I suffered so much afterwards - I nearly died - that I made a promise to myself never to feel that way toward anyone again....That was so many years ago, I thought I had gotten over it.

Therapist: But now you're...

Client: Now I'm wondering if I really did get over it....I knew when I started going with Herb that it wasn't the same. I didn't have the same intensity or depth of

127

feeling with him....I thought it was more mature...that affection would grow...but, but [Starts weeping uncontrollably] as I look back at ten years of marriage now, I know I never once let myself go...never once gave my feelings to him....Oh, my God! What a waste!...Ten years of marriage down the drain....And it wasn't Herb's fault - the poor, sweet, tolerant guy - it was mine. I was too scared to give him the feelings that rightfully belong to him....It was safer, the way I made it happen....Oh, my God! Herb, what have I done to you...and the children?

Therapist: Those fears, and the hurt, must have really been profound.

Client: [Getting very agitated again]: Well, I couldn't risk letting my feelings go. After the breakup, when I was eighteen, I knew I'd be destroyed if I let myself love someone again, and, and...if they left me again [Crying].

Therapist: Being left again...

Client [Crying suddenly stops. The same frozen expression as in the first session of therapy comes over her face. And then it melts into a look of absolute anguish and terror. She wails desperately: Mamma! Mamma, ahhh, eeeah! Pappa! No. Come back....Mamma, ahhh, argh [Convulses in tears for long period]. Those bastards. Those filthy, Nazi bastards!...They took them away. Left me alone [Shivering]. Why me? I could have gone with them. Holy God, why did they leave me? [Long pause]. Is it any wonder I can't love anyone - can't let my feelings go?...I can feel it freezing over now....Oh, Mamma, Poppi...Herb.

Therapist: You've faced it. The agony at the bottom of the pit.

Client [Exhaused, withdrawn]: Yes. That's it....What

128

filth. Excrement [Long pause]. How can people do that to fellow human beings? I'll never fathom it. Never get over it [Pause]. You know, I can see myself, in my mind's eye...the little girl in the window [Embittered, distant]...the filth of the world burying any tenderness and love she might have been capable of.

Therapist: But...

Client: No, it's okay. Don't say anything. I'll be all right [Bitterly]... Just sit with me for a while and let me pull myself together [More emphatically]....I'm going to be all right...I need to talk to Herb...(pp. 289-290).

And now we (patient and therapist) see/feel/understand what for so long has directed the most important part of her life. And it is not intellectual and it is not just all emotional. It is, as her therapist empathically put it, "The agony at the bottom of the pit." And the patient's answer quietly confirms this "truth." There is nothing for the therapist to say and the patient's wisdom informs the therapist, "Don't say anything....Just sit with me...."

B) Definition

Let us now try to more accurately define "empathy." It seems to have come from the German expression *einfuhlung* which referred to a process of aesthetic appreciation - to a process whereby the observer of an art work would lose self-awareness and go into, become one with the object of attention (Jackson, 1975). Rosalind Dymond (1949), a pioneer in attempts to measure empathy, defined it as "the imaginative transposing of oneself into the thinking, feeling, and acting of another and so structuring the world as he does" (p. 127). Rogers (1957) said empathy was, "To sense the client's private world as if it were your own, but without ever losing the 'as if' quality - - this is empathy, and this seems essential to therapy. To sense the client's anger, fear, or confusion as if it were your own, yet without your own anger, fear, or confusion getting bound up in it, is the condition we are endeavoring to describe" (p. 99). Katz (1963) placed an emphasis upon the affective aspects of empathy. "When

129

we experience empathy, we feel as if we were experiencing someone else's feelings as our own. We see, we respond, and we understand as if we were, in fact, the other person" (p. 3). The cognitive therapists have seen empathy as "step [ping] into the patient's world and see [ing] and experience life the way the patient does" (Beck, et al., 1979, p. 47). Carkhuff, Pierce and Cannon (1977) see it as the process of "crawling inside another person's skin and seeing the world through her eyes" (p. 65).

There have also been attempts to described different types of empathy. Stotland, Sherman, and Shaver (1971) described four types - three of which I think have nothing to do with empathy and the fourth sounds like sympathy. Bebout (1974) relying upon data from group therapy settings described three types of empathy. I admit to having difficulty following his definitions. Katz (1963) attempts to describe the empathic process as having four phases, and Truax and Carkhuff (1967) developed a scale to measure different degrees of empathy. Their definition of a high level of accurate empathy is as follows:

> The message "I am with you" is unmistakingly clear - the therapist's remarks fit perfectly with the client's mood and content. His responses not only indicate his sensitive understanding of the obvious feelings, but also serve to clarify and expand the client's awareness of his own feelings or experiences. Such empathy is communicated by both the language used and all the voice qualities, which unerringly reflect the therapist's seriousness and depth of feeling. The therapist's intent concentration upon the client keeps him continuously aware of the client's shifting emotional content so that he can shift his own responses to correct for language or content errors when he temporarily loses touch and is not "with" the client (p. 46).

Certainly all of the definitions we have considered include the goal of obtaining an accurate understanding of another person, of sensitively and continually being "with" that other person, and of losing or avoiding or setting aside self-awareness during that process. Jackson (1975) has provided a composite definition of empathy which

130

effectively consolidates many perspectives and is probably our best definition. According to Jackson, one empathizes when:

> one senses the other's private world as if it were his own, but without ever losing the "as if" quality; he sees, feels, responds, and understands as if he were, in fact, the other person. The process is both subjective and objective. It requires subjective involvement in another's world but without ever losing a sense of separateness or detachment. Empathy is convergent (feeling into) rather than parallel (feeling along with). To become the other, to assume his depression, or to become depressed would not be empathy. Empathy involves both intellectual and emotional experiences and it requires both intellectual and emotional energy. It also requires a degree of commitment to the other. Furthermore, empathy includes more than perceiving and experiencing another's world. It also involves the accurate communication of that perception to the other. For empathy to affect the relationship, the other must know he is being understood (p. 14).

So, by this term "empathy," we mean a form of understanding that contains a sensitivity to and awareness of the patient's feelings without an emotional identification which would entail the therapist experiencing those same feelings. It is the essence of seeing the world completely from the patient's point-of-view or frame-of-reference and knowing the feelings that accompany that perception but without experiencing the intensity of those affects the patient experiences.

C) Implementation

While the term is difficult to describe, its implementation is even more difficult. For its implementation requires the therapist to forget him or herself as much as possible - to set that "self" aside with all its desires, ideas, and experiences and to enter as fully as possible this other person's world of feelings and personal meanings and experiences. Not only do we have to be able to set aside our own biases and percepts, but we have to attempt to so enter that other person's private world that we lose all desire to evaluate and judge. That is extremely difficult to do since we have all been taught from infancy to judge and evaluate what another person says. Higher education prides itself on helping us develop our abilities to "think critically" not our abilities to understand another person. To have another person really understand us with some depth and completeness, is generally not part of our common experience. In fact, it is a much more common experience to have persons too quickly say they understand us and too rapidly assume we are both on the same "wave length." Part of what annoys us when somebody says, "Oh, I understand!" is that we realize they don't understand, they don't wish to understand, and their statement is an attempt to get us to stop talking about our position. It is my contention therapists should never make the mistake of saying, "I understand!"

Now, in addition to losing the desire to evaluate and judge in order to implement empathy, we also have to enter that other person's world of meanings in as sensitive a fashion as possible. We must be able to enter and move about in that other person's world in such a fashion as to not trample the meanings and values so very important to that person. This is saying that the therapist continually remains aware of the dignity, importance, significance of this other person even though that therapist is also "lost" in listening to and being with that patient. And lastly, there are times we fear empathically understanding another human being. Part of that fear may be related to the realization that to really understand another human being may require us to change. After all, truths we learn as psychotherapists can also be truths about ourselves and our own worlds. Such truths may affect our values, beliefs, and what we think are permanent conclusions about existence and about what should be. It is the old axiom that warns us to be careful in our learning - we may learn more than we want to know.

Entering thoroughly, completely and empathically into another's frame-of-reference is a rare, but from my point of view, beautiful experience. Once it is done sufficiently, you realize the strength, wisdom, ability, pain, and healing powers that other human being had and has. With that realization, it is then possible to see with what excellence and ingenuity his or her life has been lived. At that point you have no difficulty answering the patient's question, "What would you do if you were in my shoes?" There is only one answer to such a question. The answer is, "I would do exactly what you have done."

D) Results

Now the results of empathic understanding for the process of psychotherapy are considerable. First, with its implementation within the framework of the "therapeutic relationship;" the psychotherapists obtains a much clearer, fuller, richer, and uniquely accurate understanding of the patient's psychodynamics than is available by any other means. This is not to say that there aren't a number of ways to determine and understand the psychodynamics in any given case. There certainly are many ways, including psychological testing. And these other ways are important and legitimate means for understanding our patient's psychodynamics and problems. But there are none that give such a rich, complete, and "personal" understanding as does empathy. I have never been misled by empathy. What I have learned about a patient as a result of empathic understanding has never led me astray. I have frequently been misled by my clinical judgment, by my theoretical conceptualizations of cases, and also misled by psychological test results.

Another result of empathy is that is seems to encourage and permit the patient to expand upon, make more complete, the material for psychotherapeutic consideration. And in so doing, the patient greatly enhances the positive effects of the psychotherapy process. After the therapist makes an empathic response, it is not unusual for the patient to then expand even further upon and to go more into depth with the material. Certainly the case cited above is an example. In the sixteenth session the therapist's statement, "I can't help feeling that your emotions right now are touching on deep things in your past," appears to have set in motion a series of associations, feelings, memories in the patient that lead to what is most significant and crucial in her psychological life. I think most of us have had the experience of being really understood on some personal issue by another human being. And frequently when that happens we want to say more, we are eager to expand further, we are excited about the idea that here is another human being that can "see" it as we do. We want to "share" more with that person! Now,

133

of course, in the process of doing just that - of sharing more with this other person - we also learn a great deal about what we think, feel, and believe. We learn where we are confused and unsure. That process helps us sort out what is "true" and what is still hazy.

And that is certainly another result of empathy - patients get to hear and more intimately experience themselves. It is not only that for the first time in their life somebody has insisted upon and wanted to understand them, but that they are also given permission to carefully listen to themselves and to openly examine their ideas, feelings, and memories. The empathic understanding allows an open and nonjudgmental examination of any of our ideas and feelings. It never requires that we be right or wrong - it only recognizes that we are and have been! And in this sense, empathy interacts and is intertwined with the nonpossessive warmth of the "therapeutic relationship" - one variable reinforcing and enhancing the other to make, with a third strand of genuineness, a fabric called the "therapeutic relationship."

And a last and probably most important result of empathy is that it enhances closeness, alliance, the "therapeutic relationship" and thus the "therapeutic interpersonal relationship." The experience for both patient and therapist is one of being brought closer together. It is one of two human beings on the face of this planet earth working together in harness and in harmony for the benefit of psychic freedom - or in words that Bettelheim (1983) indicates Freud might use, for the "souls freedom."

Ginott (1980) writing about her own experience following the death of her husband tells us of the importance of empathy:

> Like most widows I was flooded with advice. I was encouraged to keep busy, to work, to meet people, to make a new life, to be strong, courageous and hopeful - and not to cry and feel sad.
>
> I found all advice irritating. I resented it. I did not need anyone to tell me what to do, what to feel or how to behave. What I did not know was how to make myself feel better. Advice talked to my head, not to my pain; it by passed the suffering I felt.
>
> What was helpful?
>
> Words that touched my heart; that reflected to me the

134

way I felt, that made me feel comforted and understood. "How lonely and painful it must be for you! What effort it must take just to get up every morning! How bereaved you must be! How difficult it must be for you to go on without this man whom you loved and respected so much! It is not an easy time for you!" My heart was bleeding and what I needed was an emotional bandage (p. 78).

There is nothing like being understood, and particularly being understood for those issues which touch us so deeply or for which we may have a sense of much shame or guilt or importance. Empathic understanding gives us strength to face and deal with our troublesome issues as well as the hope that we have a "soul mate" to help us overcome the history which burdens and oppresses us. And in the experience of empathy the two persons involved are brought much closer together. I purposely have said "the two persons" even though the bulk of the discussion on empathy has indicated it is the therapist's responsibility and doing. In many respects that certainly is true. But we must also remember that the patient has been willing to return to a time and place in their life where honesty and openness about their real feelings and beliefs was possible - generally a time in early childhood before we learned that society doesn't want honesty and is not interested in our needs and desires or understandings. Empathy is part of what helps to create that environment of acceptance and freedom to be whatever-we-are-at-the-moment and to openly show and state it without having to pay the price of rejection or alienation or disgust or hostility, or degradation. You see, part of the reasons these prices are always paid is that we don't understand fully. I'm sure some "objective scientist" could have carefully observed the patient that Hokanson (1983) has so thoughtfully given us, and indicated to her that she didn't really give herself to her husband and children - that she "should love them more." Just like the advice given to Ginott - Keep busy, work, meet people, make a new life! People who really think they know are sometimes so ignorant! And, of course, they are correct - Hokanson's patient did not give herself to her husband. But those who are so correct do not understand! So there is an enormous difference between the "truth" and "understanding" or between what is "accurate" and the "truth." Never take a "truth" out of context or strip it of its affect. In empathic understanding we are encouraging the "truth" that has with it deep understanding.

This empathic understanding leads to closeness between the persons involved (therapist and patient) and markedly enhances the "therapeutic interpersonal relationship." Perlman (1979) has devoted an entire chapter to the thesis that "vital, heartfelt relationships arise out of emotionally charged experiences that are felt in depth, expressed, received, and resonated to by another" (p. 45). In the situation of and around empathic understandings both patient and therapist are involved in emotionally charged experiences shared and resonated to by another person. Have you not been left with some feelings about the "case" that Hokanson so thoughtfully gave us? Are you not pulled to that marvelous woman?

The two people involved in an empathic understanding are recognizing and sharing a very important and significant force - one with great emotional consequences - in the life of one of the members of the dyad. That sharing helps form closeness and relationship. That helps build ties between those two persons - ties that are made of the fabric of "real truth" and nonjudgmental understanding. And in our attempts to make our way in life there is nothing like having someone along who does not judge, who works to understand how we see the world and reflects that understanding, and who helps (through empathy) to lead us to the truths and feelings we are attempting to avoid - who helps lead us to our own soul!

III. Genuineness

This third aspect of the "therapeutic relationship" has been referred to in the literature as "honesty," "authenticity," "congruence," and most frequently now as "genuineness." The concept was initially proposed by Rogers (1957) and in his definition he said:

> ...the therapist should be, within the confines of this relationship, a congruent, genuine, integrated person...within the relationship he is freely and deeply himself, with his actual experience accurately

represented by his awareness of himself (p. 97).

It is a concept not easy to describe and even more difficult to implement and maintain. Yet, like non-possessive warmth and empathy it also seems to be of considerable importance in assuring successful psychotherapy. Genuineness requires that the therapist develop an ability to be sensitive to and aware of his or her own feelings and attitudes during the process of psychotherapy. And this ability to be aware of your own feelings and attitudes is "couched" in the very same space and at the same moment that you have set-yourself-aside and are working to understand the world through your patient's frame-of-reference. It almost sounds as though we are asking an impossible task, i.e. that therapists forget themselves completely and also that therapists be aware of their feelings and attitudes so they may respond in a congruent and genuine fashion. It is not impossible as long as one accepts the fact that no one is ever going to do all of this perfectly. Now it is not only that therapists have to be aware of their own feelings and attitudes but also sufficiently accepting of them to allow them to show. For genuineness requires that the therapist's feelings, behaviors, and statements be congruent. If they are not congruent, the communications to the patient will contain contradictory messages. In this sense then, "genuineness" is not a matter of responding consistently from one time to another; although that could happen. It is a matter of responding congruently at any one moment - of having feelings, behaviors, and words in harmony. Therapists, or all who work in a helping relationships with other human beings, have to learn that it is safe to be transparently real and have to continually work at being genuine.

Carl Rogers (1961) talking about himself wrote:

> It does not help to act calm and pleasant when actually I am angry and critical. It does not help to act as though I know the answers when I do not. It does not help to act as though I were a loving person if actually, at the moment, I am hostile. It does not help for me to act as though I were full of assurance, if actually I am frightened and unsure. Even on a very simple level I have found that this statement seems to hold. It does

137

not help for me to act as though I were well when I feel ill.

What I am saying here, put in another way, is that I have not found it to be helpful or effective in my relationships with other people to try to maintain a facade, to act in one way on the surface when I am experiencing something quite different underneath. It does not, I believe, make me helpful in my attempts to build up constructive relationships with other individuals. I would want to make it clear that while I feel I have learned this to be true, I have by no means adequately profited from it. In fact, it seems to me that most of the mistakes I make in personal relationships, most of the times in which I fail to be of help to other individuals, can be accounted for in terms of the fact that I have, for some defensive reason, behaved in one way at a surface level, while in reality my feelings run in a contrary direction (p. 16-17).

Thus, genuineness requires the therapist to be "real" in the encounter with the patient - to work to negate defensiveness and any phoniness. Most importantly, it negates hiding behind a professional facade. And you can be sure there are patients who want therapists to maintain a professional facade and want to avoid seeing/feeling therapists as "real" persons. On more than one occasion, I have had a patient look at me and say "You're not supposed to have any feelings, that's not professional." On further exploration, it generally becomes obvious that they are saying my feelings for and about them are upsetting to them. They don't want me to like or dislike them. My having genuine feelings about them helps pull them into a human relationship and they wish to solve their problems of being a human being with other humans on the face of the earth by recourse to a computer or a robot. That is they wish to solve human problems without recourse to human relationships and feelings.

Now, having said this much I believe it important to add that genuineness does not mean I am preoccupied with or think I have to engage in a great deal of self-disclosure with my patients. Having my feelings, behaviors, and words congruent when interacting with the patient does not mean that I have to share all of my feelings, ideas, and attitudes with the patient. For the most part I do not believe our patients are that much interested in our ideas, attitudes, feelings, and problems. After all, there is little reason for them to be interested. It is their life they are focusing upon and about which they wish to do something. The therapist's life is really of little consequence except as it helps or hinders the therapeutic process.

Genuineness does not mean the therapist *has* to self-disclose. There is nothing in self-disclosure in and of itself that means it will be therapeutic. For the therapist can self-disclose out of needs to avoid dealing with some issues the patient wishes to raise, or out of narcissistic problems, or out of some abortive attempt to have a personal relationship instead of a "therapeutic relationship" with the patient. Genuineness is related to self-disclosure in the sense that the therapist should be at ease with who he or she is and be willing and able to disclose that "self" to others. It does not mean they *have* to disclose their "self."

Orlinsky and Howard (1978) reviewed twenty studies of therapy genuineness and found fairly consistent results. Six of the studies had null or marginally mixed results, fourteen of the studies found a significant positive relationship between genuineness and psychotherapeutic outcome. In their words:

> Cumulatively, these studies seem to warrant the conclusion that therapist genuineness is at least innocuous, is generally predictive of good outcome, and at most may indeed be a causal element in promoting client improvement (p. 307).

Earlier, Truax and Mitchell (1971) in reviewing the research in this area certainly came to a similar conclusion, i.e. a significant positive relationship between genuineness and psychotherapeutic outcome. However, they most correctly indicated that it was the absence of phoniness and defensiveness that contributed to improved therapeutic outcome. Thus, genuineness *per se* was not so crucial. Rather the lack of genuineness was important and mitigated positive therapy results. They suggested that instead of the term "genuineness," we find some negative term to identify the condition of phoniness and defensiveness.

A number of studies suggest that psychological disorders in

psychotherapists lead to poorer treatment results. Thus psycho-pathology might be that negative term. Vandenbos and Karon (1971) derived a pathogenesis score from TAT responses and found the patients of therapists with high pathogenesis scores functioned at a lower level six months after therapy than patients treated by healthier therapists. Garfield and Bergin (1971) found that therapists with elevated MMPI scores had less therapeutic success with patients than therapists with less ominous MMPI scores. Parloff, Waskow, and Wolfe (1978) in a review article point to studies indicating that the better the therapists' adjustment the more useful they may be to their patients. Bergin and Lambert (1978) also indicate that there are a growing number of studies supporting the idea that pathogenic therapists may inhibit therapeutic success and even lead to client deterioration.

However, I do not think pathogenesis is the same thing as lack of genuineness. Pathology entails a great deal more than just defensiveness and perhaps phoniness. But it can include those two characteristics and in that sense has something to say about the genuineness variable of the "therapeutic relationship." Pathology however will also include a great deal of unconscious learnings. In my conceptualization of the process of psychotherapy, those unconscious learnings would become part of the countertransference phenomenon. So pathology in the psychotherapist (and whom among us does not have some?) can have a deterimental effect upon at least two aspects of the "therapeutic interpersonal relationship" - one on the variable of genuineness and the second on countertransference.

There probably are a number of reasons why this variable of genuineness is important in forming effective "therapeutic relationships." For one thing, the lack of genuineness will at best confuse patients. Most of us have had the experience of sensing or thinking that someone close to us is upset or irritated by something. We ask them, "What is the matter? Is something wrong?" They immediately answer, "No, everything is fine, why do you ask?" Only later do we find out that they were indeed upset and irritated. But at the moment we asked "what is wrong?" and were told "everything is fine," we experienced a momentary confusion. Their words told us they were not upset but obviously something made us think or feel they were upset. So such an experience tends to confuse us and we

140

are then inclined to mistrust our own perceptions and experience. We may start to think we have badly misperceived the situation. If we don't have a great deal of trust in our own abilities to begin with (which most of our patients don't), we can become even more confused and concerned about our abilities to perceive and understand others. When we eventually find our perceptions of these others were accurate, we have additional questions. We wonder if they purposely misled us or if they themselves weren't even aware of how they felt. Their defensiveness or lack of congruence or lack of genuineness put a small barrier in our relationship with them. We are not sure we can trust them to be honest with us or even with themselves. And that kind of mistrust and confusion in the context of psychotherapy becomes part of the "therapeutic relationship."

In addition, if therapists can't work at and have some success with being genuine; they provide patients with poor role models. Patients identifying and modeling themselves after such therapists would learn defensiveness and phoniness.

But I think even more crucial is the fact that in the process of psychotherapy the therapist and patient are really engaged in a pursuit of the "truth" - certainly the "truth" about the patient. If we are really looking for the "truth" then we can't be involved in the activities of deception, deceit, defensiveness and dishonesty. They all are exquisitely designed to mislead, confuse, and obfuscate. Thus, if the therapist is serious about wanting to help the patient find his or her "truths," genuineness in the relationship becomes an important element in the process of psychotherapy.

Genuineness means that we are honest with ourselves, which is a first step in any relationship with another human being. And genuineness means that we will be open and honest in our participation in the relationship with the other. We cannot pretend to be interested in or pretend to want the best for that other person. Pretending means only that we shall remain untouched and on the outside of the relationship. It teaches the patient what he or she may have already learned very, very well - i.e. act the part and don't get involved. And in the process of pretending we never feel the freedom of openness and honesty or experience the "truth" to which that freedom leads. Genuineness means that we are working to be honest with ourselves. We are asking the patient to do that and we are willing to do the same hard work. Genuineness means that we

141

want to avoid defensiveness and that we care about relationship and understanding.

Defensiveness and phoniness will always negate relationship, because if we cannot be who we are then the other person has no one with whom to relate. To authentically relate to another human being we must as fully as possible experience ourselves so they can experience us. I cannot relate to an image or an idea or a fabrication or some superficial, societal imposed notion of what a human being is. Let me meet the person and they me. We breathe, we sweat, we cry, we fear! Both of us know that we have in common the fact that each one of us has hopes and dreams, fears and desires, frustrations and secrets, guilts and shames, loves and hates. We are both two-legged animals on the face of this planet who really have no sense of what this creation is all about. And both of us are thinking beings trying our best to find our own individual unique ways.

Many years ago Lewis (1956) wrote a charming little novel entitled *Till We Have Faces*. It was the story of a Greek queen who wanted to do her gods' will but legitimately complained that if the gods wanted their will done why didn't they meet her face to face and tell her their desires. She decided that upon her death she would put this charge to the Gods - if they wanted her to do their will, why didn't they meet her face to face? When her death arrives, she learns a "truth" that prevents her from putting the charge. The "truth" is, how can the gods meet us face to face until we have a face?" Indeed! Not only how can the gods meet us face to face until we have a face - until we put aside all the deceptions, deceits, nonsense we think we are and honestly present ourselves - but how can our patients meet us (and we them) until both of us become more and more the persons we are? Until we have faces, there are no meetings!

And if we have our "face" in that therapy session with our patient - - if we work to be genuine, then we can know that our intentions with that other human being are not to judge, evaluate, coherce, force, or to require that other person to become something for us. We can then know that our intentions as a therapist with this patient are to understand, discover, support, and just sit quietly with that other struggling soul on the face of this earth.

As Paul (1978) so accurately wrote:

The paramount lesson our patient has to learn is that we

142

mean never to advise him, judge him, valuate, scold, exonerate, and the rest. And it's obviously insufficient for us simply to have told him of that intention (p. 249).

Of course, we can't just tell him or her of that intention. They have to see and feel it and that happens when we as therapists can fairly adequately implement genuineness and the other two variables that constitute the "therapeutic relationship."

Summary

There may have been a time in the development of our ideas about psychotherapy when these three variables (non-possessive warmth, empathy, genuineness) were thought to be both necessary and sufficient conditions for effective psychotherapy. However, at this point there is a growing conviction that while these variables are important they are not the end-all and be-all of psychotherapy. Mitchell, Bozarth, and Krauft (1977) in their review of the research on these variables reached such a conclusion:

> The recent evidence, although equivocal, does seem to suggest that empathy, warmth, and genuineness are related in some way to client change but that their potency and generalizability are not as great as once thought (p. 481).

And Parloff, Waskow, and Wolfe (1978) in a later review come to a similar conclusion about the importance of these three variables to the outcome of psychotherapy.

> The associations found are modest and suggest that a more complex association exists between outcome and therapist "skills" than originally hypothesized (p. 251).

For me, part of that "more complex assocation" is contained in and described by the words of "caring," "love," and "souls meeting." It is to those concepts in the context of the total "therapeutic interpersonal relationship" that we now turn.

143

Caring, Loving, Souls Meeting

Now we come to what is probably the core or the essence of the "therapeutic interpersonal relationship" - i.e. caring, loving, and souls meeting! The "interpersonal relationship," the "therapeutic relationship," and the relationship contributions of alliance, transference, countertransference, and corrective emotional experience ultimately coalesce into caring, loving, and souls meeting.

Maybe it is presumptious of me to write it this way. Certainly the words "caring," "loving," "souls meeting" are going to upset most hard nosed scientists and perhaps deter them from any further consideration of what I may have to say. Furthermore, in our society those words connote a soft, mushy, imprecise, touchy-feely, effeminate, and perhaps even superficial or hypocritical state. Caring, loving, and souls meeting are the work of clergy and gurus, of women and mothers. But men and certainly logical, rational, clear-thinking, hard-nosed scientists wouldn't be caught dead playing with such concepts.

Admittedly these concepts are scientifically difficult to deal with particularly if we insist on remaining with a metaphysics of logical positivism. I think they are also terms which denote processes and affective states with which males in the American society are most uneasy. For the most part, men have chosen to deny, ignore, degrade, and rarely speak about the processes and affective states these terms identify. Furthermore, the responsibility for inculcating and nurturing these processes has been assigned to women. (Anything assigned to women in a sexist society certainly means its not important.) Lastly, we have in our society so many misconceptions about love that my using the term incurs the risk of adding to confusions instead of clarifying matters. The reader is referred to Peck's (1978) excellent work in identifying some of those misconceptions. By caring and loving I do not mean dependency or falling-in-love or romantic love or sexuality. It seems to me that much too frequently caring and loving are equated only with sexuality, which means we completely overlook their major characteristics of respect and admiration for another person along with a strong desire for that other person's welfare.

In any event, I find it impossible to talk about the process of psychotherapy and particular the importance of the "therapeutic interpersonal relationship" without recourse to the concepts of caring, loving, and souls meeting. For it is the affective state identified by those terms which I believe provides the strong glue or healing stance or psychological condition which permits the "work" of psychotherapy to take place and makes that "work" a meaningful and healing activity. I think our patients know they can't learn what is crucial and important for them from anyone who does not really care for them. As John Dewey (1934) put it:

> Craftsmanship to be artistic in the final sense must be loving; it must care deeply for the subject matter upon which skill is exercised (p. 47-48).

The therapist loving the patient is a sign of that commitment and deep caring "for the subject matter upon which [his or her] skill is exercised." And as Fabrikant (1977) has pointed out:

> It [psychotherapy] is a science and discipline by virtue of training and an art by virtue of the therapist's person and sensitivities (p. 7).

It is the "art" aspect of psychotherapy that calls for caring and love and souls meeting in order to do excellent psychotherapeutic work. As is the case whenever we deal with the complexities of an art form, precise definitions and unambiguous examples are difficult to come by. This is, of course, the reason that learning any art form requires an apprenticeship. One must work closely, even intimately, with a master in the hopes of learning to see and do what he or she sees and does. The internship in clinical psychology, the residency in psychiatry and the practicum in social work are forms of apprenticeships - of learning from other masters what they see and do. But it is, of course, not enough to say caring, loving, and souls meeting are all part of the art form. Since I use the terms, it is also incumbent upon me to attempt to explicate as carefully as possible what I mean by them and why I see them as so very important to the process of psychotherapy. It is that task to which I now turn.

1. Unique Relationship

Our everyday interpersonal interactions with one another do not readily admit to the uniqueness found in a "therapeutic interpersonal relationship." In that sense the relationship in therapy is a rather rare experience for most people. Certainly some aspects of the relationship in therapy are related to and part of important relationships we have with others in our life. Openness, acceptance, understanding are all characteristics that might describe a number of interpersonal relationships we have with others. But I think it rare when that openness includes genuineness; acceptance includes unconditional positive regard; and understanding includes empathy. Or probably a large number of people could say they have interpersonal relationships which include intimate, warm, emotionally absorbing involvement. But I think it quite rare when the relationship includes those characteristics (which it does in psychotherapy) but does not make requests or demands for reciprocity (which it does in our usual relationships.) And while those who have had exceptionally good parenting can recall being affirmed for who they are and encouraged to independence, those characteristics are not particularly dominant in the majority of our day-to-day interpersonal interactions. Yet, in the psychotherapeutic relationship those two characteristics are omnipresent.

And not only are all these characteristics (openness, acceptance, understanding, intimacy, warmth, emotional involvement, affirmation and encouragement to independence) important aspects of the "therapeutic interpersonal relationship," they exist in a situation where the therapist is quite neutral save for the desire to strive toward "health." That is, they exist in a situation where the other person in the relationship (the therapist) is making very, very few demands upon the relationship. Generally there are only two demands: that the patient keep the appointment and pay the bill on time. Furthermore, all the above characteristics of the relationship exist fairly independently of the patient's response or contributions. Whereas, to maintain the above characteristics in our usual day-to-day interpersonal relationships, it is incumbent upon us to consider the other person's needs, desires, personality characteristics and quirks. As the old saw has it, a person's friendship must be kept in

146

constant repair. Thus there is a mutuality, a give and take, to our usual or regular interpersonal relationships. That need to attend to the relationship, to "repair" the nature of the ties between us and the significant other, is *not* part of the patient's task in the "therapeutic interpersonal relationship."

In this last sense then, the "therapeutic interpersonal relationship" may be unique. For it is a relationship in which one member of the dyad (the patient) need not consciously attend to how he or she is affecting the other member of the dyad (the therapist) but will nevertheless experience an emotional bonding with, an acceptance and understanding from that other person as well as self-affirmation and an encouragement to autonomy. Paul (1978), has construed the therapeutic process in terms of ego-autonomy which emphasizes the importance of encouraging autonomy. He points out that a psychotherapeutic relationship permits a much freer exercise of our autonomy than that possible in our usual interpersonal relationships where the results of our autonomous expressions can have so many implications for the relationship.

The non-evaluative attitude on the therapist's part along with unconditional positive regard, is a form of therapeutic objectivity. This therapeutic objectivity, however, exists in the context of an intimate, warm, accepting, understanding relationship. Thus, this objectivity does not have the characteristics of being cold, aloof, formal, uninvolved, unfeeling, or autocratic. It is an objectivity born out of the fact that the therapist's life is not lived with or for the patient's life. The therapist's life is certainly with and for the patient's life, but it is not *lived* with and for the patient's life. The therapist is keenly living every moment with the patient, but he or she is not living their life *with* the patient. So it is a relationship replete with characteristics of caring and loving but also one in which those strong, important and essential aspects of our human existence are not making demands upon patients to do anything other than know and become as fully as possible the persons they are.

In many respects then the "therapeutic interpersonal relationship" is a very unique kind of interpersonal relationship. It has many of the positive aspects of caring and loving - upholding and supporting us, encouraging and affirming us, accepting and bonding with us - without the demands, requirements, or loss of ego-autonomy that most caring and loving relationships entail. And it is unique in its consistency. When meeting with our therapist it is essentially the same open, accepting, understanding, warm, intimate, emotional involvement that we experienced the session before and the one before that. And for fifty minutes at a time, we the patient, remain the center of attention; the recipient of a caring, loving, understanding relationship in which no demands are placed upon us to reciprocate. (It is truly rare when in some fifty minutes of personal interaction with another human being, we are not required to reciprocate, show some interest in and understanding of that other person.) It is a relationship in which another human being is working very hard to know and understand us as much as possible, and does so without making any moral or value judgment until we are ready to evenly choose for ourselves. The therapist is truly interested in and excited about us discovering the "truth" in ourselves but in no way hurries us or imposes his or her own "truths" upon us. There is a slowness and pacing that negates hurrying and sees it as counterproductive and misleading. In the fifty minute hour, it seems as though we have all the time in the world to sit and feel and think and be about whatever it is we are at that moment. And all during the session, the therapist is attentively with us and serves as a depth-sounder: letting us know when we may have *hit* upon something deep within us; letting us know when we seem to be in very shallow and safe water and, in fact, may be about to hang-up on some sandbar and be going no place at all.

I am a sailor and the simile I make is meaningful to me. I hope it can help convey to the reader the consistent, dependable, important assistance the therapist can be in this relationship with the patient and how because of the relationship the therapy work is accomplished.

The therapist is not a raucous depth sounder insisting we attend to it. Rather, he or she is a simple reminder - somebody who suggests, "Something seems to be there if you wish to attend to it." You see, the wise psychotherapist knows patients will attend to *it* when they want to and also knows patients sail in particular waters for a purpose. So at one time the patient may chose to ignore or not attend to what the depth sounder detected. But when that patient insists on sailing back and forth over the same water and always picking up the same "substance" with their depth sounder; eventually it becomes "kosher" for the therapist to say, "Why do you continue over and over to come back to this place only to ignore it? Let us not ignore the fact you keep coming back here over and over again. Let us go slower this time and see if we can identify anything about the 'substance' - how large it may be, its shape, how it is lying on the bottom. What do you think it may be? Let's investigate it a bit." And these words are said in the context of the "therapeutic interpersonal relationship" and said with genuine feelings of care and love.

2. Care and Love

What does it mean to care for and love the patient? I can only share with you my experience and what other psychotherapists have told me about their experiences. For me, the sense of caring starts rather early in my contact with the patient. In the first place, I'm very interested in getting to know this other human being whom I've just met. And as patients start to tell me something about themselves and why they have come for psychotherapy, I start to care for them in the sense of wanting to do the very best I can to understand and be of help to them. Then, imperceptively and gradually that caring generally changes to a deeper and more encompassing attitude of loving. It is clear to me that part of what brings about this change is my growing understanding of and fuller knowing about that other person. It is as though I initially care about this other person but don't really know who she or he is. It is, in part, out of the caring that I'm listening carefully, striving to meet-know-understand-see this other human being. And when that process successfully results in a revelation of some aspects of the other person's essence, love starts. At that moment of revelation I am humbled and awed by the majesty of the truth revealed. Seeing the person behind his or her masks, or generally the person hidden in their unconscious, gives me a sense of being honored and of feeling love and respect for the majesty and beauty of that other human being. And that love then makes easy the responsibility of helping that other person come to see, feel, love, and not fear the "hidden" aspects of their true self.

Peck (1978) gives us a nice example of what I am trying to describe. It was because of listening to a slip of the tongue that he could "know" part of the essence of the patient for whom he cared and could love.

149

Perhaps the most touching slip of the tongue in my experience was made by a young woman on her initial visit with me. I knew her parents to be distant and insensitive individuals who had raised her with a great deal of propriety but an absence of affection or genuine caring. She presented herself to me as an unusually mature, self-confident, liberated and independent woman of the world who sought treatment from me because, she explained, "I am sort of at loose ends for the moment, with time on my hands, and I thought that a little bit of psychoanalysis might contribute to my intellectual development." Inquiring as to why she was at loose ends at the moment, I learned that she had just dropped out of college because she was five months pregnant. She did not want to get married. She vaguely thought she might put the baby up for adoption following its delivery and then proceed to Europe for further education. I asked her if she had informed the father of the baby, whom she had not seen for four months, of her pregnancy. "Yes," she said, "I did drop him a little note to let him know that our relationship was the product of a child." Meaning to say that a child was the product of their relationship, she had instead told me that underneath her mask of a woman of the world she was a hungry little girl, starved for affection, who had gotten pregnant in a desperate attempt to obtain mothering by becoming herself a mother. I did not confront her with her slip, because she was not at all ready to accept her dependency needs or experience them as being safe to have. Nonetheless, *the slip was helpful to her by helping me be aware that the person really seeing me was a frightened young child who needed to be met with protective gentleness and the simplest, almost physical kind of nurture possible for a long time to come* (p. 250, italics mine).

For me, that is a good example of seeing the person behind the masks. It effects me in such a way as to enhance the feeling of love and I submit that it has effected Peck similarly. For the words I've underlined in what he has written reflect that caring and love. It is out of his caring and love that he will now meet this person with "protective gentleness and the simplest, almost physical kind of nuture possible for a long time to come." And it is that love that will help heal!

I do not think this kind of response to revelation is unusual. I believe most psychotherapists have experienced it on a number of occasions.

A 26 year old artist, at his girlfriend's urging, sought psychotherapy with me. He reported feeling on the "outskirts of things and having problems getting involved." He seemed to be a very open, likeable, handsome man who had managed quite well and quite independently to make his way in the world. In most respects I think people would describe him as a capable, competent, very likeable, independent and secure man. He certainly initially impressed me that way with the one reservation that he felt he stayed on the "outskirts of things." However, by the fourth session I very much started to realize how scared, hurt, defensive, and angry the "little boy in him" was. And this revelation included the fact that he had tried to repress and forget - to shove away from himself - this hurting, scared, angry kid. He, of course, had good reason to be a hurting, scared, defensive, angry child. His father had been in his life on only two occasions, and both times for only two years. The first time the father was around was from this patient's birth until his second year of life. The second time was when the patient at age 9 years went to live with father. That lasted for only two years and then the patient was sent to boarding school. It seemed on both occasions father was incapable of "fathering." Mother was a driven, forceful, rather nervous high strung professional person who had succeeded in a male's world and who had for the most part turned over the "mothering" of this child to an extended family group. As therapy progressed, the patient realized he had "forgotten" a great deal of his past, particularly the feelings. He had no memory at all of his seventh grade year. He correctly saw himself as someone who easily assimilated to his environment and he felt it was very much up to him to keep himself and his "world" together. Now, how can you not help but love that "little boy?" A hurt, scared, defensive little boy trying to hold his "world" together. And in that love how can

151

you not help but know that this is what must be healed? And certainly you have some idea as to how to help a defensive, scared, hurt, angry boy. You have to first establish a relationship with him - a relationship in which you work very hard to prove to him you will not do what others have already done to him. And if you are going to constructively respond to that "little boy," you must be prepared for disciplined commitment. And it is out of seeing and meeting and knowing that "little boy" - sensing that "little boy's" loneliness and struggle to be heard and felt and attended to - that you can easily love and care for this man's welfare and make that disciplined commitment necessary for the psychotherapy. And it is in large part the various juxtaposed components of the "therapeutic interpersonal relationship" that have opened the doors to this patient's psyche and have given the therapist the eyes to see and the ears to hear the patient's soul.

The next and last example I give of caring turning into love comes from my work with a 20 year old college sophomore. I had seen him for some twenty-four sessions before he revealed a tender and sensitive part of himself - that part of his true essence which had been so badly bruised and thus had to be protected. He was a pleasant, rather quiet and intelligent man who was so thoughtful and precise in his thinking and verbalizations that at times he seemed strained. He appeared rather sad and unhappy and listed three reasons for seeking psychotherapy: 1) problems being motivated for his school work, 2) problems with his family where they were not close, and 3) feeling depressed since the tenth grade. For the first fifteen sessions we move rather slowly, somewhat methodically, and intellectually. He talks about important material but it is without much affect-involvement except for some of the issues centering around his relationship with his father. Furthermore, during all these sessions it is obvious to me that he resists getting too close to others and, of course, to me. The message seems to be not to get too close to him. And in caring for him and because of some love for him, it was possible for me (a contact freak) not to push for relationship. I did have an understanding of how rigid, practical, passive-aggressively controlling and emotionally non-giving his father was. And I had some understanding of how frustrating and at times upsetting that was to his son, my patient. Realizing part of the transference would require I be seen as he saw father, it was easier

152

for me to hold back and out of caring with understanding have patience. With the end of the school term, this period of the therapy came to a close. Both of us felt some gains had been made. Specifically he felt therapy had been important in that he now had hope of leaving some of his old ways and of building on closeness and communicating with others. I realized that at that time in his life to admit how important a relationship with another might be to him was not an easy or uneventful task.

In the fall he writes asking to continue his therapy and in the letter refers to me as, "you (sic) acquaintance from the summer months." I took this to mean a step toward relationship even though the "slip of the pen" indicated the anxiety he had surrounding that event. Nine sessions later he revealed a hurt, bruised person inside this polite, considerate, thoughtful, intelligent man. He was talking about the great difficulty he had writing a paper for one of his courses and the suicide thoughts associated with the fear of failure. He was expressing much more anger in this session along with the view that the world was a hostile place designed to make it difficult for him and to degrade him. I also heard hurt with that perception and pointed out to him my sense of the hurt along with the fact that he felt put down, not listened to, and also felt others are motivated to degrade and humilate him. And then, the revelation! He had said it much earlier and probably many times before this session, but now I could see and feel it. His father and his three brothers (all older) had continually, systematically, regularly, but thank goodness not successfully, degraded, ignored, refused to listen to or consider this man's desires, wishes, ideas, hopes, ambitions, fears or questions. He was a member of a family in which all of the males seemed to be competing for the number one slot and he was low man on the totem pole. At that moment I could understand how people had really hurt him (probably not intentionally at all) and how he didn't expect men would have his interests or needs at heart. Furthermore, as I sensed and perceived those hurts I also realized that by allowing me to see this part of himself he was taking a great risk. He risked that I wouldn't be one more male degrading, ignoring, and pushing-him-down. So he risked being open to more hurt and rejection. The health in him had pushed him to risk being "blacked-and-blued" again. What he had revealed was not clear to him at all and I did not try to point it out to him or interpret it. There are times (probably

153

many of them) when it is important to be silent. I was just in awe and so thankful for this revelation. And in the next session he talked about being confused by our last session and not sure at all what was going on. Now tell me, what is *not* to admire and respect and LOVE there? Don't you want to put your arms around him and hug him and tell him you love him and tell him to hang-in-there because we will get through this tunnel yet?

And so, what is this caring and loving which I say results from the coalesence of all the factors constituting the "therapeutic interpersonal relationship?" It is knowing in part and with some certainty the ground upon which our patients are based and from which they operate. This knowing is not just an intellectual experience but more precisely an insight experience. It is an empathic understanding of some depth and completeness. The caring and loving also means biding your time and waiting until the patient can relate to you. It is seeing and sensing their hurt and pain and yet knowing you can only do so much - you can only take those steps with them they will permit. It is knowing there is no sense to rant and rave and insist they take the next step, for the empathic understanding tells you why they can't do that yet and the caring and loving give you patience. Caring and loving is being grateful that you are in a place and at a time in which you can see and hear a part of the essence of this other human being. And loving them is sensing and knowing how much depth and greatness there is in them as well as feeling better about them than they may feel about themselves. Loving is really hearing that other person! And, loving is really understanding that other person! And in addition to the hearing and the understanding, it is accepting that other person. Love is not betraying the trust patients place in you when they put themselves "on-the-line" and risk showing you their souls.

Love also includes seeing the strength, integrity, and lack of hypocrisy in this other person - the patient. It is seeing beyond their pathology and conflict to what is most important - their strengths and capabilities. Look at the strengths and capabilities the persons in the above examples had to have in order to continue on with their lives - to grow and develop and make the very most they could of themselves despite the enormous pain and hurts they had to bury, contain, suppress, and repress. And loving is seeing those strengths and capacities. But most importantly, the perceiving of such

154

strengths and capacities can't be a false hope or a Pollyanna put-on. By that I mean it can't be a countertransference hope. It has to be based in reality. You have to see and feel it. Love also is seeing how patients have cut themselves off from themselves, and how they have isolated or crippled themselves. And it is being appreciative for what they have shared with you. Generally quietly and secretively they have let you in on a magnificent truth about themselves - something about their real nature which they have hidden from others and themselves for such a long, long time. And love is appreciative for that sharing with you and with themselves.

It is fun loving patients because it is so rewarding. The reward is in being able to see how uniquely powerful, capable, ingenious and whole universes human beings are - in a way the god of their own world. And when you *see* that, it is exciting and a bit awesome. Perhaps it is good to be somewhat in awe of our patients for it reminds us of their and our own greatness.

Love is tenderly, gently, forcefully urging patients back to their health and wholeness - to parts of themselves they have run from, are scared of, or have not attended to. Love calls them back to see who they are.

However, the therapist must also be careful and not overwhelm the patient with love. When I say that love is a core and healing force in psychotherapy, that is not to say that love and it alone - love with nothing else or love in great abundance and overflowing - is all that is needed. It is important to remember that a part, if not a major part, of patients' problems can be an inability to accept or tolerate or respond to love. Frequently our patients have problems with allowing affection and loving. In so many cases love, or what they have taken for love, has resulted in pain and hurt. So, they try to do without love or closeness or at least with only a semblance of it. At times in psychotherapy it becomes rather obvious that patients both want and fear love. Somehow or other love was distorted or betrayed or led to great pain in their lives. It is not that they had no love, although for those persons who manifest psychopathic character disorders it does seem as though no cell in their body ever experienced love - they seem to have no experiential understanding of that concept. But, most of our patients have experienced love and its healing and its joys. But, they have also frequently experienced its distortions, its use to control, and its ability to hurt. They do not

155

want to experience that confusion and pain all over again.

Thus, it becomes important for therapists to titrate how their love is shown and expressed so as not to overwhelm patients or give them more than they can handle at any one time. I had been seeing a man with an extremely traumatic childhood, who harbored multiple and severe psychological problems, and engaged in a great deal of acting out and paranoid ideation. He continually had problems with the police, drank to excess, and required recurrent hospitalizations. Nevertheless, over a seven month period he had been relatively regular in two times per week appointments for psychotherapy. As is so characteristic of persons with borderline disorders, he had never asked me anything about myself or given any verbal indication that he saw me as anything other than "the doctor." Then he came in for one of his regular sessions and took his usual place in the office. But atypically he was very quiet with his head and eyes cast down on the carpet, he looked hurting and lost and handed me a letter. Even though he was not looking at me and even though physically he was pulled into himself, I did not feel he was withdrawing from me or trying to create psychological distance between us. He was very much "with me." I read the proffered letter. It was from his insurance company and informed him his benefits for the year had expired and that future years' benefits for his psychological condition were markedly curtailed. I knew his financial situation was very tight, he was living with his mother, and he had few resources. After reading the letter, I attended to what I was feeling. Then I said to him, "David, you and I have worked too hard too long to let our work go down the drain because of some insurance company. We will just find some way to continue." His response to this was to sit up, come out of his funk and start talking about some event of the past day or so. I was perplexed for it was as though he hadn't heard my response. I reiterated what I had said. Again, he started to talk about some other seemingly innocuous event of the past day or so. I reiterated again and added, "Didn't you hear me?" At this point he hurriedly and rather forcefully said, "I heard you, I just can't stand to hear you care!"

I think all of us know there are times when it is important to titrate how our love is shown and expressed! Love seems to be a very powerful force. I'm tempted to say it is *always* a part of the healing, the changing, the "becoming" that we've done in psychotherapy. I know we need a great deal more scientific, theoretical and research attention to the role of this variable in the process of psychotherapy. It would be an interesting study to see what psychotherapy with a complete absence of love would or would not accomplish. And by accomplishing something with psychotherapy, I am not referring to just changing behaviors. We all know human behavior can be changed without love. Any person sufficiently and appropriately punished for a specific behavior will stop showing that behavior in situations likely to incur such punishment. For me, psychotherapy accomplishments should also include changed feelings, attitudes, perceptions, and a freeing of spirit and soul. I'm not sure that can come about without caring and love.

Lastly, I find that the loving of patients is something that lasts. By that I mean it is not only during the course of the psychotherapeutic hour that I'm wanting the "best" for patients - wanting to find ways for them to see/find/feel themselves and gain freedom to grow and expand and be. It is between sessions I'm thinking of them, also. It is knowing that in the coming week they are going to risk something new with another person and wondering how that is going. And after the psychotherapy is over, something can remind me of the patient and I wonder if the world is going well for him or her. I'm always glad to hear from former patients - a letter, a postcard, something that tells me about their life. It is a continuing interest I have and an abiding wish that they obtain their destiny.

Now, before leaving this section I should, of course, point out that the idea of love being important for successful psychotherapy is not new with me. Bettelheim (1983) in the cover sheet to his recent book quotes Freud in a letter to Jung:

> Psychoanalysis is in essence a cure through love.

And Strupp (1973) has written:

> In the final analysis, the patient relinquishes his resistance out of love for the therapist; he goes through the painful struggle because there is the hope that things will come out differently; he gives up his repressions because he is deeply convinced that there is a new safety and security in the relationship (p. 66).

and,

> It seems to me that the therapist has to *care*; he must
> have a deep and genuine commitment to the patient and
> a pervasive dedication to help. Without these, the
> patient could never carry through the arduous and
> painful work of therapy (p. 66).

as well as,

> ...I do not consider it possible to treat the therapeutic
> process as a *purely technical* one; unless these technical
> operations are undergirded by something else - call it
> love for one's work, or whatever - therapy must remain a
> sterile, lifeless ritual (p. 66).

and most forcefully,

> ...*in the final analysis the patient changes out of love for
> the therapist* (p. 140).

Peck (1978) also sees love as essential in psychotherapy.

> We are now able to see the essential ingredient that
> makes psychotherapy effective and successful. It is not
> "unconditional positive regard," nor is it magical words,
> techniques or postures; it is human involvement and
> struggle. It is the willingness of the therapist to extend
> himself or herself for the purpose of nurturing the
> patient's growth - willingness to go out on a limb, to
> truly involve oneself at an emotional level in the
> relationship, to actually struggle with the patient and
> with oneself. In short, the essential ingredient of
> successful deep and meaningful psychotherapy is love (p.
> 173).

So, conceptualizing love as an important ingredient for effective
psychotherapy is certainly no new idea. What may be different is the

158

emphasis I place upon it as well as seeing it directly related to and developing out of the "therapeutic interpersonal relationship."

3. Souls Meeting

Out of caring and loving the therapist is helping some of the work of therapy. And because that work is done out of caring and loving in the context of the "therapeutic interpersonal relationship" with its important characteristics of respect for the dignity, worth and importance of that other person; it has the ability to "touch" that other person emotionally and significantly - to touch them in their soul. When the soul of one human being cares about the soul of another human being, encourages that other soul to "become" and helps create a way for that to happen, then two souls meet.

By the term "soul," I do not refer to what may popularly be identified as a religious substance. I am speaking about a core or essence or the "psyche" of a person. I am referring to the innermost being in a person - that being which is, which was, and which can become. By "soul" I mean everything that person "truly" is. Soul is what is left once all the pretensions and false masks, defensive character armour, unnecessary roles, and societal impositions are washed away. I am using the term very much in the same sense that Bettelheim (1983) indicates Freud used the term. The word *Seele* refers to to a person's essence, to that which is most spiritual (not necessarily religious) and worthy in a person.

With this definition, when two souls meet we experience a rather overwhelming sense of pure truth - a moment when two see, feel, understand, or have emotional insight into the same perception. There is at that moment of souls meeting a quiet certainty of connectedness and the realization that there is "salvation" in the world. It is a realization that human beings can in fact change, grow, know and if we wish become what we are in our souls. There is a fine bonding of or weaving into relationship that occurs when souls meet. Most of us have had the experience of being deeply touched by someone who cares for us and who really knows us. In part it is the experience of absolution after confession except we see there was no need to feel badly or guilty or confess. A person is in a position to touch our soul who truly respects and admires us, does not want to hurt us, is not in competition with us, doesn't have to have something

159

personal from us, and knows how we feel.

Now much of what therapists do to encourage and enhance the "therapeutic interpersonal relationship" are the disciplined steps necessary to enable them to experience the care and love for patients. That discipline along with therapists' own personal therapies and continued self-examination helps them to know their souls - to be in touch with what is at their core or the essence of their being. Being in touch with one's soul makes that soul much more available for touching the soul of another.

And as is true for all of us, the patient's soul also needs and wants to be touched. But the patient's soul can be very afraid of being approached or touched. It may well be defended and surrounded by innumerable walls, pits, false gods, distractions - anything to keep us away from it. I believe that it is only through genuine care and love that patients finally permit us to directly and constructively touch a very small portion of their souls. However, once that touching successfully happens; it is much easier for those two souls to touch in the future.

For me the experience of "souls meeting" in the psycho-therapeutic context is a very powerful, quiet and moving enlightenment. It carries with it the realization of the beauty, graciousness, dignity, pain and greatness of that other human being. At times it is almost too much to bear and I softly cry at its beauty! It is a characteristic of mine to cry at beauty. With my patients, when our souls meet I can sense/feel/ comprehend the pain, hurt, necessity for protection that soul felt and endured as well as the strength, beauty, righteousness and perfection of that soul. The tears are a release -- they are a gift of thanksgiving. Thanksgiving for the fact this other human being has obtained some real freedom in an existence designed to crush almost any freedom as well as thanksgiving for the fact that souls are so magnificently constructed! And it is in the meeting of souls that I find my head and heart yoked together - there is a congruence that is palpable and I can sense and feel the harmony of my thoughts, feelings, and words. My words, however, never convey the full meaning of that experience anymore than they do now.

Hokanson's (1983) case of Joey serves as an example of some of what I mean by "souls meeting." Joey was a twelve-year-old-juvenile referred by the court and given the option of participating in therapy

160

or being sent to a juvenile facility. In his short life, he had been abandoned by both parents, experienced great inconsistencies in affection and discipline, had a long-term pattern of aggressive, rebellious behavior and a chronic history of social isolation from adults and peers. Purposefully and most fortunately he was assigned to a young male therapist who was street-wise and experienced with delinquent adolescents. Approximately four months after therapy was initiated, the police department some eighty miles from where Joey lived called his therapist. Joey had been picked-up in that city, no charges were pending, but he had been found wandering and disheveled in the bus terminal. After much hesitation, Joey had given the police the therapist's name and the police were concerned this runaway boy be properly supervised. Joey's therapist drove to the next town to pick him up. On the ride back this conversation took place:

> Client [Nervous and withdrawn]: What are you thinking?
>
> Therapist: I'm not sure what to think. What happened?
>
> Client: Aw, I don't know....What's the use....It's all a pile of crap.
>
> Therapist: You really seem down. Feel like talking?
>
> Client: No.
>
> Therapist: Come on, give it a try.
>
> Client: Christ! You don't give up, do you [Angry]. I stole some money, all right? I lifted it and just took off.
>
> Therapist: What the hell!
>
> Client: I knew you'd be upset.
>
> Therapist: Damn right I'm upset. Tell me about it. What happened?
>
> Client: I took about fifty bucks from the people I'm staying with. It was right there - in the bureau drawer. I just picked it up and hopped a bus.
>
> Therapist: Why did you do it? They been bugging you, or something?
>
> Client: No. They're okay, man....I don't know why I did....I just been all tensed up and everything. Needed to get away.

161

Therapist: From them?
Client: No.
Therapist: From school?
Client: No.
Therapist: From me?
Client [Long pause]: What are you going to do
    with me now? Turn me over to the judge? Send
    me away?
Therapist: What do you think I should do?
Client: If you had any sense, you'd kick me in the ass
    and send me back to the judge....That's what my old
    man would have done. That's what my uncle did
    [Starts to weep].
Therapist: Joey, I don't want to do that....I love you...like
    a son, or a kid brother, or whatever the hell you
    are. I don't want to lose you...into that jungle.
Client: [Crying]: Oh, Jesus. Do you really mean that?
    You're not just saying that?
Therapist: No, I mean it. I was hoping you could feel
    the same way.
Client: I do (p. 243).

In this small vignette we capture some of the flavor of love and
souls meeting that is so important in the process of psychotherapy. It
was not just that this therapist was wise and knew enough to respond
in an appropriate way. Or that he had a grasp of the psychodynamics
in this case and understood that Joey was testing and acting out. It is
not just that he knew and said the right things. He had caring and
loving and *felt* the right things. What was communicated was his
intense caring about and love for Joey - his wanting the world to be
good for him - his wanting to support, uphold, honor, elevate him
with all his soul. And all of this exists in the context of a relationship
with Joey which included driving eighty miles to get him, being
willing to try to understand why he did what he did, having some
empathy for his pain, hurt, confusion, anger and meeting all of that
with one force - love alone. Here was the right combination of
thinking, feeling, being, openness, hope and love for both of these
persons so that their souls met. It, of course, is no surprise that this
episode constituted a significant turning point in Joey's therapy - a

point from which he now made significant and continued psychological growth.

After having said all the above, I think it necessary to add that I do not believe the process of psychotherapy is just being caring and loving or souls meeting. Nor do I think just being caring and loving is sufficient for one to experience within the psychotherapeutic setting the event of souls meeting. I think caring and loving are very important results of an effective "therapeutic interpersonal relationship" and are in some degree necessary for effective therapeutic outcome. But they are not sufficient conditions. A great deal of skill and knowledge about psychopathology, adjustment, personality, psychotherapy and the operation and mechanisms of principles of human behavior are essential. But I will add that I think all that skill and knowledge is useless in psychotherapy unless you also have an effective "therapeutic interpersonal relationship" where caring and love can exist and where souls might meet. Again, the process of psychotherapy is a whole piece - one fabric constituting many strands all of which are effected and changed by one another so that the end result is something quite different from the individual pieces or elements of which it was originally constructed. That need not unduly upset us unless we are so obsessive-compulsive that there is never any hope we shall see or experience a simplistic wholeness to creation.

Now while the words I have used here in attempts to define what I believe is the "core" or "essence" of the "therapeutic interpersonal relationship" may be hard and difficult to "hear" and perhaps too nontraditional when applied to a process we wish to better understand and make evident and clear through scientific principles; they may not be as beyond-the-pale as a first reading or examination of them suggests. Orlinsky and Howard (1978), in reviewing the research literature pertinent to the relationship between process and outcome, have given us an empirically based description of effective psychotherapy. I submit that in intent and direction it is not at all far from what I have been discovering from clinical experience. Their words are quoted here in length.

> Effective psychotherapy, as an *interpersonal process* is distinguished most consistently by the positive quality of the bond that develops between its participants.

163

Whether it occurs in a dyadic relationship or in a primary group, the bond among participants in beneficial therapy is marked by a high degree of cohesiveness. This is shown in various ways.

There is an intense and effective investment of energy in relationship roles, evident both in the patient's self-expressive emotional attachment to the therapist (or to the group), and in the therapist's active collaboration through whichever techniques he or she feels most capable and confident in using.

A second element associated with cohesiveness of the social bond in beneficial psychotherapy is the good personal contact, the solid grounding in one another, that is made by the participants. This personal contact is characterized by mutual comfortableness and trust, a lack of defensiveness on both sides, seen in the patient's spontaneity and the therapist's genuineness; and also by a strong and sensitive rapport, a sense of being on the same wavelength, that arises through empathic resonance and reciprocal understanding.

There is finally an expansive mutual good will mobilized between participants in beneficial psychotherapy - a strong sense of affirmation that is not merely acceptance but also acceptance and encouragement of independence, that can be challenging as well as supportive out of concern and respect for the other person's basic interests and autonomy. This safe, stimulating, but supportive atmosphere balances and makes tolerable the direct expression of deeply painful, frightening, and abrasive sentiments - sentiments that might be (and probably have been) overwhelming in other, less resiliently cohesive relationships. (It is a fair guess that something akin to this is at the core of effective psychotherapy, whether one prefers to think of it in terms of "growth facilitating conditions," "positive transference" and "working through," "corrective emotional experience," "reciprocal inhibition" due to the generalized relaxing influence of the therapeutic bond, "modeling," or "positive reinforcement" for the emission of adaptive interpersonal and self-directed responses).

Effective investment of energy, good personal contact, and mutual affirmation stand out as three aspects of the cohesiveness that seems to mark the beneficial therapeutic bond (p. 317).

Perhaps these words are easier for some persons to hear than the ones I have used. But I submit, Orlinsky and Howard are talking about care, love and souls meeting.

CHAPTER 5

THERAPEUTIC ALLIANCE

In Saint-Exupery's *The Little Prince* (1943) there is a moving account of taming the fox. This children's book is the story of a little prince's travels to many planets. On earth he encounters a fox. But knowing nothing about foxes, he is surprised when the fox cannot play with him because as the fox says, "I am not tamed." The fox explains that before they can be friends, he must be tamed. "What does that mean - 'tame'?" asks the little prince. "It means to establish ties," says the fox. "To establish ties?" asks the little prince. And the fox answers, "Just that. To me you are still nothing more than a little boy who is just like a hundred thousand other little boys. And I have no need of you. And you, on your part, have no need of me. To you, I am nothing more than a fox like a hundred thousand other foxes. But if you tame me, then we shall need each other. To me, you will be unique in all the world. To you, I shall be unique in all the world..." (p. 80). And so the fox teaches the little prince some basic rules in behavior modification. The fox points out that in order for him to be tamed, the little prince must be very patient and at first keep his distance. He is to come only so close and then sit down and just be still. And he is to do that day after day for a considerable period of time, moving closer every day. The little prince obliges. Then the fox points out that it would be better if the little prince came at the same time everyday. In that way, the fox would start to anticipate his arrival, look forward to it. It wouldn't be quite as "upsetting" as having the little prince just come at unpredictable times during the day, and furthermore the fox could then prepare his heart to greet the little prince. So, the little prince obliges. And, finally the fox is tamed and he and the little prince are friends.

Then, when it comes time for the little prince to move on, the fox cries. And so the little prince indicates that since the fox will cry and be sad the taming had done him no good at all. But the fox indicates that the taming had done good and then goes on to explain how it had changed his perception of the world - for grain-fields which are the color of the little prince's hair were heretofore of no use to the fox at all. But now those fields remind him of the little prince and he will love to look at the fields and listen to the wind in the wheat. The development of a therapeutic alliance is like taming the fox. It is to establish ties, to collaborate with one another, to be unique in one another's eyes. And there is generally some pain when it comes time to part.

When patients come for psychotherapy some part of them is fearful, leery of the psychotherapist and suspicious they may be hurt - or that parts of them they hold precious, their neuroses, will die. After all, none of us have our defenses, repressions, misperceptions, or distorted attitudes for nothing. We have worked hard for them and developed and nurtured them over a considerable period of time. As any psychotherapist can testify, those defense mechanisms have served the patient well in the past and it is not at all clear to the patient that relinquishing them now would be at all wise. Symptoms generally bring patients to psychotherapy, and like all of us they want to be rid of the symptoms without having to change their minds or lose their defenses, repressions, misperceptions and distorted attitudes. The appellation "shrink" is not a complete misnomer. And, who really wants their mind shrunk?

So, if the little prince, or any psychotherapist, rushes in and attempts to hold the fox and pet the fox and in a loud voice insist on being friends, it would only result in a "sound and fury" signifying failure and reinforcing the fox's fear of little princes. That would negate therapeutic alliance! The psychotherapist must know how to tame the fox. And in that taming, the psychotherapist also holds the knowledge that at some point both he and the fox will have to feel some sadness. That is because there will be losses. There can be a loss of "parts" of the patient which served him or her well in the past. Then, the psychotherapist can be changed by such taming and thus lose "part" of him or herself. Finally, there will come a time of parting for both patient and therapist. That parting can have loss in it as we shall see in Chapter 11.

However, without the taming of the fox there is no psychotherapy. We and our patients have to interact and establish ties. As already noted in the chapter on Relationship and Psychotherapy, there has to be an openness and genuineness and movement toward self-disclosure on the part of both participants in this dyad of interaction. It is no good if the "fox" is so afraid of us that he or she will never show their face. And yet that part of the patient which is the "fox" is frequently so afraid that they haven't even fully showed their face to themselves, let alone to anyone else. It is no good if the psychotherapist is so afraid of commitment and so insistent on control that he or she won't develop the patience, engage in the necessary compromise, and risk the changes in life necessary to assure the taming - the therapeutic alliance.

As an intern working in a psychiatric hospital, I was assigned to establish a "working relationship" with a man recently admitted to the hospital who was psychotic. Part of his history included the fact that he had been subject to unpredictable beatings by his father. He would be tied to the bed and whipped with a leather strap, and these beatings would occur randomly and without provocation. To begin establishing a relationship, I met with this man daily for some fifteen to thirty minutes at a time. Within a week and a half I found no change at all in his demeanor with or attitude toward me. Nor had his behavior on the ward changed. With most patients, I generally could detect changes indicative of a developing relationship within a few days and ward personnel would have generally noticed changes in the patient's behavior. However, this man seemed totally unchanged from the day of his being admitted. I consulted with my supervisor about this predicament and he asked me, "When do you see this man?" I pointed out there was no specific time I went to the ward. During the course of the day when I found I had a half-hour or so I would go to the ward, take him to some available room and talk with him. I had no sooner gotten these words out of my mouth, when my supervisor smiled and I knew that I approached this patient as unpredictably and randomly as had his father. The only question he must have had was, "When would I unprovokedly attack and hurt him?" I was doing a lousy job of "taming the fox." Of course, after that consultation I let the patient know we would meet at the same time and the same place every day. Within less than a week after this commitment the expected changes started to come. He started to relate to me and to some extent to others as persons who might not beat him and just might have his interests at heart.

What is involved in "taming a fox" or developing a therapeutic alliance? I identify five components and they are all the psychotherapist's responsibility. Certainly the patient has some responsibilities, as does the fox. However, here we are concerned about what the psychotherapist must do. The psychotherapist must be an (a) ally with the patient, (b) stable in the sense of evidencing some consistency, (c) have a commitment to the process of psychotherapy and to the patient's welfare, (d) desire to tame the "fox" and that includes not being unduly afraid of that "fox," and (e) risk involvement with the patient and being changed by that patient.

The therapeutic alliance requires making a collaborator of the patient in the psychotherapeutic work. If two people are going to undertake any significant task together, it becomes important that both of them have a sense of being able to trust one another as well as the sense that both of them are able to contribute to the work ahead. It requires knowing that when the going gets rough neither party will give up but will give their very best to getting through those difficult times. It requires a commitment to endure and a stablity that says "I can still see reality and I am still here with you." It involves being willing to risk and hurt and change, to cry and bleed and lose sleep and want with all your soul that other person's welfare.

Ultimately it's knowing that when that fox finally trusts you, you don't really want to hurt it or do it wrong. You see you can't hate or dislike or despise the fox and still tame it. What self-respecting fox would ever permit that? What principle of psychology would ever say you could be at peace with that which you hate? So, you see for therapeutic alliance, it is no good to hate and dislike and despise the defenses, repressions, misperceptions, or distorted attitudes that have resulted in the psychopathology. Don't hate them. Make a friend of them and thank them for all they have done. For truly, they have helped "save" this patient at a time in his or her life when he or she needed that kind of salvation. It is only now that they are counterproductive, have outlived their usefulness, and are hurting the patient's life. They have had an important life and don't want to die either. So, can't we have the graciousness to bid them a decent funeral and say an appropriate eulogy and suffer the pain of their loss?

The world is not simply divided into the good and the bad, and we are not the gods who shall make the judgments of what is evil and righteous. Therapeutic alliance means that the patient and the therapist will work together to decide what can and should be for the patient. It respects that both of the particiants in that dyad have

170

strength and power, both are right and have an accurate perception of individual "realities" on their side.

The simile of "taming the fox" is not too far off if we remember that it is the "fox" or the patient who fears they have the most to lose in this taming. The fox fears for his life whereas the little prince just wanted to play with somebody. Foxes, I think, instinctually fear people. People don't think a fox will take their life. There is a big difference there. Psychotherapists should be sensitive to how much their patients are risking. Again, psychotherapists must remember the appellation "shrink" and thus remember their patient's fears.

Clinical Experience

My clinical experience has been that within three sessions a therapeutic alliance appropriate for conducting psychotherapy is generally formed. There have been a few cases in which that alliance seemed to be there within the first session. However, that is rather infrequent and almost all such cases in my experience have had a positive psychotherapeutic experience earlier. Many more cases have taken longer than three sessions before I had a decent sense that a relatively firm and useful therapeutic alliance was in operation. Not infrequently the initial therapeutic alliances are reserved ones. By that I mean the patient was willing to attend to and work on some aspects of his or her psychological life but still reserved the option to avoid other important aspects of their psychological adjustment. Also, sometimes the alliance was a reserved one in the sense that I was still "suspect." While at the moment they had some understanding that I may not be like they had found other persons in their life, there was still some reservation. The "fox" had started to trust but still held in abeyance the well-learned lessons that people will hurt you.

From my clinical perspective the development of the therapeutic alliance and the point of shift into that alliance is as follows: Generally the first session begins with what can probably best be described as a rather stereotyped interpersonal relationship overweighted with "doctor-patient" ways of interacting. I may begin by asking, "How can I help you?" or "Where shall we begin?" or "Perhaps you can tell me why you made the appointment." So, generally the first business is getting as detailed an explanation as possible of the symptoms or reasons for making the appointment. I listen very carefully to the symptoms and the reason for the appointment and without being at all judgmental attempt to determine in as much detail as possible the precipitants for the symptoms, the circumstances surrounding their development and the reasons for finally deciding to see a psychotherapist. Once I have a decent sense how the patient is experiencing distress on a conscious level (the symptoms), I ask permission to get some history. Generally patients are most cooperative and relieved to be asked questions about their history. The history is quite thorough, pointed but not inappropriate, not prolonged but perhaps from the patient's point of view disconnected. Again, I'm listening and observing intently. Every pause, hesitation, shift in the chair, cough, swallow, eye-blink is noticed. (Psychotherapists can't be accused of not being interested in what seems trivial). It is not just with words but with their demeanor, their actions, and various and sundry cells of their bodies that our patients tell us what is hurting them. I think that within the first few sessions patients tell us rather precisely about their psychodynamics. They frequently do it in camouflage or in some obtuse language - for the "health" in them wants us to know but they aren't yet in a therapeutic alliance so a protective part of them would still hide their fear. So near the end of the first session, I have some general idea of what are important, if not crucial, issues in the patient's life - some general understanding of the psychodynamics operating and a better sense of what is necessary in order to start to effect a therapeutic alliance. Almost always this is an intellectual understanding, it amounts to very tentative hypotheses, and I realize I don't really understand at all. Certainly it is not an understanding in depth with a patina and shine that give it true life and meaning. But it is a decent intellectual exercise and generally serves as a very rough road map pointing to directions needing further inquiry. Near the end of the first session, it is generally possible to make some broad interpretations - i.e. to indicate what areas seem problematic and ones the patient might want to further explore. For the most part, these are things the patient already knows although may not have verbalized. They are tantamount to the apocryphal story of the little boy who was asked what the psychiatrist did. He said, "Oh, he tells you what you already know about yourself only you didn't know you knew."

This stating of what areas or feelings or issues seem to be

important and might be worth pursuing is a first step in identifying what therapist and patient might work on or attend to together - it identifies reasons for which making an alliance is worthwhile. Furthermore, in this first session the patient is starting to experience some aspects of the uniqueness of the therapist-patient relationship. That is, the patient is starting to experience some non-possessive warmth, unconditional positive regard, genuineness, and perhaps a bit of empathy. Some of the initial fears of being found "crazy," laughed at, degraded, maligned, or judged inferior hopefully have not happened. It is also in the first session that I deal with the issue of whether or not the patient may wish to pursue this "problem" in psychotherapy (given that in my opinion it is an appropriate way to approach the problem). The cost of therapy, possible times for sessions, and the fact that both of us have to see if we think we can constructively work together are also discussed. I generally suggest to patients that within three or four sessions, they will have a sense of whether or not I am the kind of person with whom they think they may be able to work and that I also would then have a better sense of whether or not I felt I could be of help to them.

What I have outlined as generally happening in the first session includes these components of therapeutic alliance: 1) patients are accepted and taken at where they are, 2) some initial steps are made to help determine where they want to go, 3) the therapist starts to generate tentative hypotheses about where they need to go in order to adequately deal with their problem, and 4) some general hypotheses are posited regarding what the therapist may do to help them get there.

Of course, all of the foregoing is predicated on the assumption that the issue the patient is to deal with is not something that is resolved within a session or two or three. Certainly there are plenty of cases that come to college counseling services, and a host of other settings, that are handled quite adequately in a few sessions. Should psychological services be more readily available to the population at large, I think we would find a great many patients helped within a very few sessions. Certainly some of the work of the Kaiser Permanente Foundation and reported by Cummings and Follete (1976) suggests that this would be the case. The marked increase throughout our country in the use of brief psychotherapy techniques also suggests that it is not at all impossible to achieve some substantial psychotherapeutic goals in a few number of sessions.

In the second session, patients generally give some indication they have seriously thought about the problem area identified in the first session. Perhaps they share some dream or some experience of the past week which reinforces the cogency of the problem they have identified and indicates they are already starting to think/feel about its meanings. A not uncommon scenario is as follows: To my question in the first session "Give me an example of a time in your life when you were good and angry;" the patient might have replied, "That's a funny question, I never considered anger good." Or after some reflection, the patient may say, "I can't think of any situation." Near the last quarter of the first session, I would suggest to the patient that it appears as though anger may be a problem for them. Generally they have no difficulty concurring with that conclusion and say something to the effect they think that is probably true but have never really given it much thought. Then in the second session, it is not unlikely they may report having noticed that there were times during the past week when it was most appropriate to feel anger and it surprised them to note they weren't angry but in fact tended to feel depressed or irritated with themselves. Generally not a great deal of work would be done in the second session with this problem other than reinforcing its cogency. The second session stays at a rather pleasant and somewhat intellectual and superficial level except for the fact that there are generally ample opportunities for empathic understanding - i.e. the patient and I start to try to understand at a feeling level some of what they have heretofore dealt with intellectually or by avoidance or fear or suppression. It is here that patients are first introduced to some of the real work of psychotherapy. It is here they start to learn the psychotherapist has no fast or easy or glib answers for their problem and that neither one of us really understands with enough completeness just what is actually involved in the problem. It is here that patients are first introduced to the necessity for slowly and carefully examining what they really believe and feel about important or conflictual issues in their lives. Furthermore, they may start to experience some abatement of anxiety and some sense of relief based on an emerging realization that they have taken a constructive step toward dealing with some of their problems. That is not to say they feel their problems are now solved or that they have finally found that authority or guru who will solve their problems. Rather it seems to be more an expanding hope that solutions to their problems can be

174

found and that they will have a significant and major role in shaping and determining that solution. At first blush, to those not initiated in the process of psychotherapy, this may seem to be a disappointment. For one might think that what patients really want is some "expert" to solve their problems for them. But on further thought, who among us wants our destiny, happiness, values, beliefs, needs and life choices determined by some "expert?" I don't think we do. Anyway, the reality of the matter is that "experts" can't determine those matters for us anyway, so we don't have to worry about it.

Thus, by the second session, patient and therapist may be more clearly defining the first and second components of therapeutic alliance (where the patient is and wants to go) as well as adding the dimension of indicating how psychotherapy may work - what we will be doing together in our sessions. The patient is starting to learn there are no fast, easy answers given by some "expert" and that systematically and purposefully working together might well lead to understanding, answers and relief.

Then, generally by the third session (sometimes the fourth or the fifth), there are perceptible shifts indicative of the development of a therapeutic alliance significant enough to assure some intensive psychotherapeutic work. Three of the major signs of that shift are 1) a decrease in the superficial and pleasant manner in which material is presented for consideration; (2) an obvious increase in the amount of affect felt and shown with the material of the session; and (3) sometimes direct but more often tangential remarks or indications of fear or anxiety about the possible consequences of continuing along the road our work together seems to be taking us.

Examples of these shifts are found in the early sessions of the twenty year old college sophomore described in the care and love section of the preceeding chapter. In the first session this man is controlled and pleasant and rather straightforward in presenting the three problems upon which he wishes to work. He does it almost as though our work would be an academic exercise. In that session, however, he can accept the interpretation that it is hard for him to be in touch with his feelings. In the second session he indicates that he wishes to start with the problem that is the least "personal," i.e. his school work. Near the end of that session, I suggest he might wish to keep a journal while he is in therapy. His response is that he has wanted to keep a journal but is fearful of others reading it and of

175

what it may reveal about him. In the third session, he begins with wondering if it isn't just the place he is in that may be making him feel unhappy. It doesn't take him long, however, to shift from trying to find some easy and external source for his difficulties and start to show and express some of his deep hurt. He admits that at times he can cry because he feels so worthless and incapable. And in that third session he is showing his turmoil, his sadness and his desire to keep all that hurt just to himself. The session leads him to explain how he can't show that hurt to his folks and particularly to his father. Then he can say that he is very angry with his father, but he says it without any demonstrable affect. Thus, in three sessions he has moved from a rather intellectual and pleasant but business-like approach to his problems to the point where he shows a bit more affect and reports emotional turmoil. At the same time he is narrowing the focus of his therapeutic considerations to more manageable and personal material. That along with his closing statements in the third session are all indicative of the emerging therapeutic alliance. It is near the end of the third session that he starts to have his concern about where therapy will take him. For me the concern was a way of saying he already unconsciously knew that the direction in which therapy was carrying him would take him into his feelings and particularly feelings of strong anger for some family members. While the verbalization of his concern was a mild form of resistance, it was not said with the implication that he refused going down that road and would have nothing to do with it. Rather, it had more a flavor of "I don't think I like where this is going to lead but I wonder where it will go." It is as though he was caught in and/or tugged toward an experience that at some level he could recognize as important. Furthermore, it was stated in such a fashion as to indicate he already knew therapy had done something to him and he wasn't sure he liked it or wanted what it was doing.

Another example of the shift toward therapeutic alliance comes from a patient who as an adolescent had some psychotherapy. I was her second therapist. She was a bright, articulate, open person who presented herself as rather sure and capable and "at home" with emotional matters. Her reason for seeking psychotherapy this time was that she repeatedly found herself making friends with women who would then become involved with a boyfriend turning the relationship into a threesome in which she would feel pushed out. In the second session she is initially rather anxious and uncomfortable (not the poised, confident person of the first session) and she focused upon her discomfort with men. She could point out that she distrusted them, felt she wouldn't be treated well or respected by them, and wouldn't be really loved. While this material was not presented matter-of-factly, there was little affect associated with describing these attitudes and seemingly no desire to go into depth with any one of them. Then in the third session she points out, that within the past week, she had come to realize how very much she is afraid of men and also how very uncomfortable she can feel around her father. This time it is not just a listing of attitudes about men but a statement of insight into something not fully recognized earlier and a sharing and realization that was accompanied with much affect and discomfort. I did not think it wise to personalize this material as it seemed scary enough for her to realize these things about herself and her father without also confronting the fact they existed in our relationship together. At the end of the session, she gives me her journal to read. I accepted this as a sign of her wanting to form a therapeutic alliance - to show herself to me but not have to deal immediately with my reaction. Then in the fourth session she is very much into a therapy relationship - she recognizes her fear of the male's seductiveness and accepts the interpretation that the two of us (a male and a female) are forming a relationship. She recognizes feeling embarrassed and confused with that situation. Not only for her was there a rapid shift from the first session into a therapeutic alliance but there was also by the third and fourth session the evidence of developing transference feelings. The therapy was well underway.

The essence of these perceptible shifts is that the issues of the patient's present psychological existence and where she wants to go are fairly well identified, at least for the moment. And patients start to experience and feel some of the anxiety and pain attendant to self-examination and perhaps get ready to risk the prospect of some changes. These steps are indications patients are starting to trust that their therapist will be a constant and stable ally.

In addition to these more detectable shifts, there are subtle variations in the patients' mannerisms which are suggestive of the development of a bonding with the person of the therapist. Patients start to "settle down" and begin to touch upon the edges of hurtful, scary, uncharted feelings. There is a greater openness on their part although it seems almost unwanted by them and is couched in some ambivalence. It is as though they find themselves momentarily rooted in feeling what they have attempted to avoid - it has happened almost against their will but they are not unhappy with that experience. It is as though against their will they have revealed to themselves and to another human being something avoided for a long time. And for my part, it is during this time (when therapeutic alliance is first starting to form and solidify) that I find it necessary to carefully empathize. For it is as though I realize they are showing some very precious tender parts of themselves which neither they nor I yet understand, and which neither they nor I can be sure we want to see. Thus I sense I must be "careful" in responding so as not to trample upon values and feelings and beliefs that may be so very important to them. In addition, frequently the material of the session indicates what transference material may now be coming to the fore.

So, in addition to the "interpersonal relationship" the therapist may have with the patient and in addition to the emerging development of the "therapeutic relationship" (which along with the patient's needs and desires is starting to produce a therapeutic alliance), we also have added to this interplay of developing emotional strands between patient and therapist some transference elements. Before patients are fully committed to therapy, they start to experience some of therapy's nature and its effects. However, like the fox being tamed, they are still not sure they won't be hurt. So, the therapist must not move too rapidly because the fox is still leery and easily frightened. What the fox has to experience is that being this close to another human being is not unduly upsetting and, in fact, may be a relief. It is here that therapists' skills in "therapeutic relationship" and understanding psychodynamics and transference phenomena are crucial. It is here that therapists' abilities to "listen with the third ear" and their intuitive sense of how to move or be still, reach out or pull back are important. Now after having said all that, I hasten to add that psychotherapy is not at all like doing surgery. A mistake here and there need not be disastrous. I have made plenty of mistakes in psychotherapy and in the development of the therapeutic alliance. I wince when I think of some of them and am eternally grateful for patients' willingness to endure and forgive my insensitivities. After all, foxes also have a lot to say about whether or not they will be tamed.

To get a better understanding of some of these subtle variations in patients' mannerisms suggestive of the development of bonding, it may help to think of the everyday experience of meeting someone and developing a friendship. Initially there is a pleasantness and superficiality about our interactions and conversations with one another. We, in fact, generally work to avoid any unpleasantries or discussion of topics that might be controversial. We are also generally attentive to cues we get from that other person which help tell us whether or not he or she wants a friendship, is interested in spending more time with us and getting to know us. As the friendship develops we become more relaxed in one another's presence - our body stance reflects that lessened tension - and we are involved in fewer pretensions. The way our friend looks at us, greets us, how our eyes meet, and our attentiiveness to one another's moods are all different once we are friends. Those subtle variations in our demeanor bespeak our bonding. There will still be some things we remain hesitant to discuss and/or share. When we hesitantly risk some sharing, aren't there again subtle but perceptible cues that signal that change? We become quieter, more serious, carefully look at that other person's eyes or face before we decide whether or not this is the person and the time and place for such sharing. Or perhaps we are sufficiently anxious and scared that we look down, or look away but still have to share something even though we are trembling inside and so anxious we can't be aware of our friend's initial response. Well, people in psychotherapy aren't any different than people in the street. The same kind of feelings, fears, and risking is involved in any situation where we are undertaking an intimate interpersonal relationship. We would expect to see the same kind of verbal and bodily cues associated with the process of establishing relationship whether it was in or out of psychotherapy. Now I am not saying that relationships in and out of psychotherapy are the same at all. I've already indicated that the "therapeutic interpersonal relationship" is a unique experience. What I am saying is that human beings have limited and predictable ways of expressing and showing signs of bonding, liking, attraction, and love. Those signs will be the same in and out of psychotherapy.

Research Results

There now is decent empirical evidence showing that psychotherapists in both outpatient and inpatient settings form conceptualizations and perceptions of patients within one or two sessions (Bishop, Sharf, & Adkins, 1975; Brown, 1970; Meehl, 1960; Rosenzweig & Hartford, 1972; Shader, Kellam, & Durell, 1967). Furthermore, there is evidence indicating that the development of "liking" between therapist and patient is also rapidly established - again within one to three sessions of psychotherapy (Fehrenback & O'Leary; 1982; Ford, 1978; Saltzman, Luetgert, Roth, Creaser & Howard, 1976; Wills, 1982). Certainly, as already indicated, my own clinical experience is quite in agreement with these findings. Nevertheless, I still find it difficult to believe. Even after years of clinicial experience, I am still amazed and delighted at how rapidly therapeutic alliance can develop. It is almost as though the fox was desperately wanting to be tamed; and, of course, in Saint-Exupery's (1943) little story it was. Certainly our everyday experiences in forming perceptions of and relationships with other people do not suggest that bonding and intimate relationships are so rapidly established. We certainly need to know a great deal more about the structure of early psychotherapeutic sessions and about the reasons why the initial processes of psychotherapy result in such rapid conceptualizations and emotional ties. In the conclusion to his book, Wills (1982) writes:

> All of the work reported in this volume supports the proposition that therapeutic relationships develop quite rapidly. Fehrenback and O'Leary (Chapter 2) found that therapists' perceptions of clients are essentially formed during the first contact, and a number of crucial client judgments, including the decision to continue or drop out from therapy, liking for the therapist, and expectation about the probable value of treatment, are largely formulated during the first two to three sessions of therapy (Wills, Chapter 17). This formulation suggests that further research should shift to intensive investigation of the early stages of relationship development to learn more about the determinants of clients' initial reactions to therapy and the rapid belief, expectation, and self-efficacy changes that probably occur during the first interview session and shortly thereafter (p. 486).

It is to a further consideration of these early stages of psychotherapy and what has been called therapeutic alliance, to which we now turn in an attempt to identify specific characteristics that might account for such a rapid development of perceptions and liking. In undertaking this task, I am indebted to Fisher & Nadler (1982) for their work in summarizing some of the literature from social psychology on conditions associated with giving and receiving aid as well as their identification of four categories useful in conceptualizing that literature. They discuss characteristics associated with giving and receiving aid by recourse to the areas of: 1) donor characteristics, 2) aid characteristics, 3) recipient characteristics, and 4) content characteristics. Using this four part division, an attempt is made to identify various aspects of the early psychotherapeutic sessions that lead to such rapid development of some form of therapeutic alliance.

Donor Characteristics: The literature in social psychology suggests that people will generally respond better to help when the helper is an ally and someone they like and respect. Such helpers and their aid are more favorably evaluated by helpees. In addition such helpers engender feelings of obligation and increased reciprocity in the helpees. Zimbardo, Ebbesen, & Malach, (1977) have indicated that more likable and less aloof therapists hold patients better than do less likable and more aloof therapists. Likability and aloofness will be aspects of the "interpersonal relationship" between therapist and patient from the moment of the first meeting. Also, from the very first session, the patient will experience some aspects of the "therapeutic relationship." In particular, psychotherapists' characteristics of non-possessive warmth, unconditional positive regard, non-judgmental attitudes, and genuine desires and attempts to understand the patient will probably be some of the most unique, and perhaps unexpected, characteristics of the relationship that patients experience quite soon in therapy sessions. They are aspects of relationship that are not part of most persons' everyday experiences. It is probably more likely patients expect to receive judgment and advice rather than acceptance and empathy. It is also likely patients will fear having to reveal things about themselves or being caught in contradictions or lies. Of course those things will probably happen. Most of us in psychotherapy reveal things about ourselves we didn't think we wanted to reveal and most of us get caught in contradictions or an untruth. But the important issue here in terms of donor characteristics is that the psychotherapists' motives are not to make the patients reveal that which they do not want revealed or to catch them in contradictions or untruths. The psychotherapists' motives are simply to understand along with the patient and as completely as possible what the patient is seeing and feeling. I had begun treatment with a man who was hospitalized for a severe depression and some psychotic confusion. When obtaining his history in the initial session, I asked if there had been any deaths in his family. He answered "No" quite easily and straightforwardly. Then in the next session while talking about some other events in his life he said, "Then, after my brother died...." I interrupted him, was quite surprised and said, "Just a moment, I'm confused. When I asked you the other day if any members of the family had died, you said no. But now you say your brother died?" His immediate response was, "Oh, I guess I must have just forgotten." It, of course, was no big surprise to find out that the nature of his brother's death (which happened when they were both children) was such that this patient felt directly responsible for it, had never told anyone else what he knew about the circumstances of the accident that killed his brother, and had contained and nurtured his guilt as well as worked extremely hard to never again be angry with anyone lest that anger result in the tragedy he had experienced with his brother. He did not feel my question was something "catching him in a lie" nor, of course, was that my motive. The motive was to understand and not to judge.

The orientation and attitudes of the "therapeutic relationship" help the patient see the psychotherapist as an ally. Of course, that is just what the therapist is and wants to be - an ally with the patient. If psychotherapists think of themselves as doing something *for* their patients that would tend to negate therapeutic alliance. Allies do things *with* one another; they collaborate, cooperate and have mutual interests and needs. Hopefully the psychotherapist is the patient's ally not out of any altruistic needs to "do good" but rather because being an ally is the choice which most satisfies the psychotherapist. In the process of collaboration and cooperation, and generally well within the first or second session, the psychotherapist and patient will reach some agreement upon how they will go about their work together and what that work will be. It includes decisions about what problem or problems will be addressed, when and how frequently to meet, deciding on the fee and method of payment, and agreements on how *we* shall proceed in the therapy hour. Those agreements, as they would with any ally, frequently include explanations of why it is in both parties' best interests to proceed in a certain fashion for the process of psychotherapy.

A good example of the importance of the patient understanding the reasons for some of the procedures used during psychotherapy is given by Greenson (1965) in a classical article on the working alliance. A young man entered analysis with Greenson after two and one-half years with an analyst in another city. In one of the first hours on the couch, the patient took out a cigarette and lit it. When Greenson asked what he was feeling when he decided to light the cigarette, the patient petulantly indicated he knew he wasn't supposed to smoke as his other analyst didn't allow it and he expected Greenson would forbid it too. When pressed further for what feelings, sensations, thoughts were going on in him at the moment he decided to light the cigarette; the patient indicated he had become somewhat frightened and wanted to hide his anxiety. Greenson could then explain that it was better for such feelings to be stated in words rather than in actions as he could then more precisely understand what was going on. At that point, the patient could realize he was not being forbidden to smoke, only that it would be more helpful to the process of analysis if he expressed himself in words and feelings. I submit that "explanation" is an example of the therapist being an ally, whereas forbidding smoking with no explanation is an example of the therapist being an authority figure.

Now while the patient's liking and respect for the psychotherapist is of some importance in the development of therapeutic alliance, I believe it is the therapist's fulfillment of the role of "ally" that is the most cogent variable of all the donor characteristics listed here in attempts to explain why a therapeutic alliance can start to form so rapidly. It is the psychotherapist's enduring commitment to working with the patient as an ally and an ally that has the patient's welfare at heart, that gives the patient security to try out new ways of behaving and strength to risk seeing the world from a new perspective. It would seem that psychotherapy is an aid-giving process which most favorably meets requirements characteristic of donors who maximize recipients' acceptance of that aid as well as engendering recipients' feelings of obligation and reciprocity.

Aid Charcteristics: Here the literature indicates that positive reactions to receiving help are generally associated with receiving large amounts of help, of high quality and which are appropriate to one's needs. Negative responses to help are more likely to occur when aid requires restricting important freedoms or decreasing rewards for successful outcome. I have not found patients worried that psychotherapy may restrict some of their important freedoms. More frequently the worry is that psychotherapy will reduce some of their inhibitions and thus lead to too much freedom. It is not unusual to find some patients initially apprehensive that their employer, or perhaps some family members, will find out they are in psychotherapy resulting in a possible decrease in rewards from those persons. This is not altogether an unrealistic fear. If patients have to consistently take time off work to meet therapy appointments, some explanation has to be made to the employer. Also, when third-party payments are involved, it is possible that employees in the company's personnel office administering group health insurance policies can identify which employees are using health benefits for psychotherapy. Unfortunately some employers could view the necessity and/or desire for psychotherapy as indication that the employee is unstable, weak, abnormal and untrustworthy. The fact the employee is in psychotherapy could temporarily jeopardize his or her chances for vocational advancements and rewards, and that could be a considerable cost to pay for the psychotherapy. The relationship the patient has with certain family members could be one in which loss of status, prestige, and ego could occur should others know of the psychotherapy. I must add, however, patients' reservations of employers or relatives finding out they are in psychotherapy are generally short-lived. As patients start to experience the positive characteristics of the psychotherapy, they frequently gain the security and strength to deal with others' unrealistic perceptions of what it means to be in or have had psychotherapy.

I believe that what one gets in psychotherapy generally meets the positive characteristics of a large amount of help of high quality, and directly appropriate to one's needs. Patients start to experience this "help" from psychotherapy almost immediately. Some researchers have noted marked symptomatic relief from a single session (Frank, 1963; Smith & Glass, 1977) and others report it to have occurred in less than five sessions (Rosenthal & Frank, 1958; Uhlenhuth & Duncan, 1968). It seems to me that two conditions might account for the experience of immediate relief: 1) the concomittants of the decision to begin therapy, and 2) the experience of finding another person willing and able to help with the problem.

184

The first condition is related to the fact that within the first session patients have somewhat resolved and acted upon an important decision as well as reduced a great deal of ambivalence about psychotherapy. Patients do not inconsiderately make the decision to seek psychotherapy. They have generally vacillated and wondered about it for some time. Part of their concern has included just which therapist to see among a number who may be available. It is not without some fear and trepidation and pushed by the pain and discomfort of their symptoms or condition that they finally take the step of making an appointment. It might be very good if we could see patients at the time, or at least in the same day, they made the appointment. For then we would probably learn a great deal more about the turmoil and discomfort that predicated their decision for therapy as well as being able to circumvent some of the ambivalence about and intellectualization of their discomfort that arises as a result of having to wait for a week or two before being seen. In any regard, the first session does stand for the fact that now they have actually taken an important step toward seeking help. Thus, there is some relief in knowing that they have actually done something very concrete and appropriate toward dealing with the problem. While they cannot be at all sure that this will ultimately be a helpful step, at least they have the relief of knowing they are no longer attempting to deny or hold in abeyance attending to the problem. I suppose that one could say because they have taken this first step, engaged in the task of seeking a psychotherapist, made an appointment, and invested thought, time, emotion and money in the first session; they have started to resolve some cognitive dissonance. That may be so. But I submit it is experienced by the patient as relief. Some important indecisiveness is now "off their shoulders." Also, patients are most likely within the first session to resolve some ambivalences about psychotherapy. Fears that their "mind" will be read, that they will be degraded and humiliated, that they are hopeless and helpless, that they will be found to be quite psychologically disturbed and insane and thus shunned are all generally disconfirmed. The fear that they are somehow weak and pathetic or miserable and complaining is also not supported. They do not lose their dignity, they are not made an object for diagnosis and dissection, and they *are* invited to form a partnership with a professional who thinks they are capable of making significant gains in the solution to their problems. Is that not relief? Is that not a large amount of help to receive within one hour? How many hours or days or weeks have they used in attempts to make some progress on resolving their difficulties? How many people have they talked to, talked with, hinted at in attempts to find some relief for what is bothering them? I submit that most patients have spent considerable time, energy, and money in attempts to resolve their difficulties before ever coming to the psychotherapist's ofice. And then within one hour of psychotherapy some of their ambivalences are dispelled, they are given some help and probably considerable hope. I submit all of this is of considerable value in giving the patient realistic relief - and it can occur in varying degrees within the first session.

The second condition accounting for the experience of considerable and immediate relief is related to the "therapeutic relationship." For with the beginning of therapy and the "therapeutic relationship," patients start to realize that there is a human being who really wants to listen to and understand them. They start to experience some of the unique characteristics of the "therapeutic interpersonal relationship." Thus, they may begin to realize they need to listen to themselves - something they have really not been encouraged to do - as well as begin to realize there is somebody who will help them look in directions they may have never seriously considered before or may have unconsciously or fearfully avoided. For the most part as we share our problems with others they are more likely to give us advice than to help us listen to ourselves. Perhaps the patient fears that the psychotherapist "doctor" will be the same way - just give advice that is not particularly useful, appropriate, or indicative of any depth of understanding of their dilemma. After all, giving advice is generally easy to do and usually doesn't cost the advice giver anything. Giving advice can be an inconsiderate way of telling people they aren't worth bothering with or worth much commitment toward helping. But instead of advice giving, what the patient frequently experiences in that first session is the realization that it is important to listen to themselves and that it is not too fearful or forbidden or impossibly anxiety producing to look at things that heretofore they and others around them assiduously avoided. The therapist thinks those things are important, and of course the patient knows they are but feared examining them. As already noted, it is not unusual for me in the first session and after taking a history to tell the patient that it looks as though there may be some conflicts or problems or difficulties in

186

this area or that one or with this person or that experience. And generally the patient's response is one of some fright and anxiety - it is as though the patient feared I would say it as well as hoped I would say it. That initial and temporary fright is then generally followed by evidence of relief, and the patient says something to the effect of, "Yes, I think that's so." With that statement, the patient and I have started to form an alliance for now both of us know in which area we may begin to work.

Being able to identify and talk about that which we fear with another human being who is not judging but listening, who wants to understand and helps us listen to ourselves as well as assists us to look in new directions at those issues, conflicts, and life experiences we have feared to face and discuss - all of that is, I submit, receiving a large amount of help appropriate to our needs. Thus, it is not surprising that patients frequently feel relief *and* hope within one or two sessions of psychotherapy. Psychotherapy is a unique experience designed to directly and immediately address the patients' concerns and does so in a way which indicates patients are worthwile, significant, important human beings. I tell you that makes me feel good when I am the patient. I think it makes other human beings feel good when they are the patient. And, of course, the psychotherapist is not just putting on or giving an image of hope, interest, and belief that the patient is worthwhile and important. It is a genuine orientation and attitude. If it is faked, I think that would be disastrous. Therapists who want to fake it should hurry into their own psychotherapy.

Now, in addition to patients finding that therapists do want to listen to and understand them, they also discover that they can't put therapists into the same bind others have accepted. That is, patients find it difficult to continue to "act out" their neuroses with therapists. Like most of us, patients are quite adept at getting others to fulfill their expectations. If patients are convinced others will eventually leave them, or authority will be inconsiderate and inflexible, or men will be crude and sexually preoccupied, or women will be controlling and manipulative they will have succeeded in surrounding themselves with persons to reinforce and confirm those beliefs. Their therapist is to be no exception. In fact, frequently their therapist is to be the "test case." While it is in the area of transference and the psychoanalytic understanding of transference neurosis that these issues become most predominant, they nevertheless play some role in

187

the therapeutic alliance and come under the rubric of aid characterisitics. For in the initial encounter and early contacts with the therapist, patients start to realize the therapist is not fulfilling their expectations. "Not to worry," patients will make massive and prolonged attempts to prove that this human being (the therapist) is exactly like other significant persons in their life. But the fact that the therapist does not initially and readily conform to patient expectations is both a surprise and a challenge. The surprise embodies the hope for patients that finally they will be rid of their gross misperception - a hope that is mainly unconscious at such an early stage of therapy. The challenge is in finally proving once again, even with a recalcitrant subject like the therapist, that their predominate view of humanity is most correct and not to be abandoned. This facet of the dynamics between patients and therapists, which can operate early in psychotherapy, is both a relief (at an unconscious level) and a challenge that can keep patients in psychotherapy and add to the therapeutic alliance. For patients, at some level, can now hope that their perception of the world (as being filled with persons unconcerned about them and their needs) is in error. At the same time patients can be attracted to remaining in therapy for a little while with the expectation that they will be able to prove the therapist is exactly like others whom they feel have made life so miserable for them.

So, it seems that while some of the characteristics of psychotherapy might increase negative responses in recipients (decreasing rewards) the amount as well as the nature, quality, and appropriateness of help received early on in psychotherapy easily fit the requirements of positive aid characteristics.

Recipient Characteristics: The research here indicates that persons with high self-esteem and high need states are predisposed to respond more negatively to help. Fisher and Nadler (1982) point out that *threat to self-esteem* models (Fisher et al., 1982; Gergen & Gergen, 1974) might appropriately be applied in determining how patients differentially respond to accepting psychotherapy. *Threat to self-esteem* models posit that the self-related consequences of receiving aid determine how recipients will respond to the help. Furthermore, these models assume help contains both self-supportive and self-threatening aspects.

One of the self-threatening aspects of seeking psychotherapy may be loss of self-esteem. In my experience, patients differ greatly in the extent to which they initially see psychotherapy as a threat to their self-esteem. There are probably some persons who see it as such a threat that they never enter a psychotherapist's office. The Protestant Ethic, which sees independence as a virtue and achievements as signs of salvation, is an active part of the American society. Probably most persons first contemplating psychotherapy experience some loss of self-esteem. That is partially reflected by ambivalence about psychotherapy, as well as by the fact that most patients are "forced" into psychotherapy by symptoms that have become unbearable rather than out of an understanding of how life's exigencies have shackled and harmed them. Szasz (1960) has suggested that our view of psychological disorders as mental illnesses is a myth created to overcome some of the results of the Protestant Ethic and our Puritan heritage which tied these psychological problems in living to evil and sin. One of the characteristics of the age of witchcraft was a belief that persons succumbed to the forces of the evil one and carried out the devil's wishes of their own free will. This certainly carried free will to its preposterous conclusion and is the epitome of what Ryan (1971) has called "blaming the victim." Remnants of these aspects of witchcraft are still with us today. We still shun, fear, and avoid persons who are seriously psychologically disturbed and are inclined to see them as causing or having brought upon themselves their own problems. And unfortunately, seriously psychologically disturbed persons are frequently not seen as human beings. We don't call them witches anymore or burn them at stakes, but it has only been in the past thirty years that we've moved to a more humane treatment of persons seriously disturbed, and that shift is by no means complete. We still harbor institutions in which persons are not treated humanely and the nation's "street people" remain living testimony to our reluctance to provide adequate help to disturbed persons who happen to be poor.

So, I take it almost as a given that any patient entering psychotherapy for the first time will have struggled to some extent with feelings of loss of self-esteem. Some of their fear and apprehension on this score has been settled by the time they call for and keep the first appointment. For taking that step alone indicates some courage to risk self-devaluation. Then almost immediately in the first session, most psychotherapists are perceptive of and sensitive to any remarks from or signs in the patient indicative of their feelings about starting psychotherapy and how this is related to their self-

189

image. After all, if you are going to tame a fox, you have to get to know some things about that fox and particularly about what may scare that fox. And so, immediately in psychotherapy the therapist is sensitive to self-esteem needs and hopefully does not have needs to degrade and demean people.

Then, if we look at the important attributes of the "therapeutic relationship," it immediately becomes obvious that the psychotherapist enhances and supports the patient's self-esteem. Suppose for a moment that psychotherapists spoke, acted, and behaved in a fashion characteristically opposite from that identified in the "therapeutic relationship." Then we would do what we could to demean this other person, to be smug, authoritarian, aloof, and indulgent. In a word, we would do what we could to encourage even greater loss of self-esteem. Does anyone need a research study to tell them such a psychotherapist would soon have no patients except those with great masochistic needs?

All of the above is only to say that patients' self-esteem needs will be important in the development of the therapeutic alliance and that patients who have high self-esteem needs may require a little more attention and work to eventually form a therapeutic alliance. But, the psychotherapeutic situation is masterfully conceived to deal with issues of self-esteem. Smith, Glass, & Miller (1980) have called it, *"primus inter pares* for the benefits it bestows upon the inner life of its clients" (p. 184). In my experience I have not found differences in self-esteem needs to be a particularly important variable in predicting patients' abilities to form a therapeutic alliance. Some may require a little more attention to self-esteem issues than others, but I have not experienced high self-esteem in patients as necessarily resulting in a negativity to psychotherapeutic help.

As for the research results indicating high need state related to negativity to assistance, I don't know what to say. Part of my problem is in attempting to define what is meant by high need state when applied to patients seeking psychotherapy. Frequently the determination of patients' high need state for psychotherapy is done external to them. Others may frequently perceive a person as in a high need state for psychotherapy when the person him or herself doesn't feel that to be the case at all. What we are dealing with then is not the patient's need state but those of relatives or persons close to and involved with the one whom they identify as "the patient." In addition to the problem of who determines the need state, there is also the problem of how it is determined. I suppose it would be possible to equate severity of diagnosis with need state. In that event we would expect persons with psychoses to evidence more negativity to the help of psychotherapy than those with adjustment disorders. I suppose, there is a sense in which one could say that is true. I think few would disagree with the general statement that persons with psychotic disorders are more difficult to treat psycho-therapeutically than those with adjustment disorders. I think it is probably also true that it may be more difficult to establish a therapeutic alliance with persons who have psychotic disorders than with persons who have adjustment disorders. In that case then, high need state could be said to be related to a less favorable attitude toward the help of psychotherapy.

However, I am not sure high need state for psychotherapy or even the severity of the psychological disorder are the most useful concepts to attend to when attempting to identify recipient characteristics for those seeking the help of psychotherapy. Instead, I would suggest that it is the patient's ability to form personal relationships with anyone that is the most crucial psychotherapy recipient characteristic determining the ease and/or difficulty with which therapeutic alliance will be established.

Persons who have been unable to form close or meaningful personal relationships with others in their life will also present special problems when it comes to forming the therapeutic alliance and "therapeutic interpersonal relationship" necessary for successful long-term psychotherapy. Individuals whose personalities are essentially narcissistic or psychopathic as well as persons with borderline conditions are good examples of patients for whom the development of therapeutic alliance is difficult and at times perhaps impossible. Persons with severe psychotic disorders, particularly those with paranoid features in their disorder are examples of patients who require much time and careful attention in order to form therapeutic alliance. To return to our simile of "taming the fox," one might say that these persons are the foxes who have never been tamed by anyone or who have had very threatening, harmful, injurious, ruinious experiences in their interactions with others who have attemped to tame them. The example earlier in this chapter of the man whose father unpredictably and randomly strapped him to the bed and beat him is a case in point. His experiences with other human beings in his life taught him to fear letting anyone close to him. I think that in the not too distant future, we will have a great deal more data indicating that persons who manifest some of the more severe psychological disorders have early histories indicative of much more personal violence, abuse, and degradation than do persons without such disorders. Carmen, Rieker, and Mills (1984) found that 43% of a sample of 188 psychiatric patients had been assaulted, raped or subjected to child abuse, incest or marital violence. Fifty-three percent of the female and twenty-three percent of the male population they studied had suffered some form of severe violence. Traditionally we have not asked patients for any history of violence, but with this kind of data it becomes incumbent upon psychotherapists to be more attentive to these possible aspects of their patients' histories. And this study focused only upon physical violence. It is much more difficult to define and document psychological violence. But I submit psychological violence could be just as devastating howbeit more hidden and undetected. Our society isn't particularly oriented toward seeing psychological violence, and we don't give much support or sympathy to those subjected to its ruinious nature. We are more inclined to say, "Forgive them, they don't know what they are doing" for persons who perpetrate psychological violence than we are for those who do physical violence. But in any event, if the fox has already been violated physically or psychologically by other human beings, then it is a fool if it is not extremely cautious as the psychotherapist attempts to tame it.

I submit it is patients' early experiences with other human beings relevant to the issue of forming personal relationships that is the most crucial recipient characteristic affecting the development of therapeutic alliance. When the majority of a person's relationships with other people have been gratifying, rewarding, enjoyable, and fulfilling; then that person is easier to "tame" for psychotherapy than when a majority of that person's relationships with others have been damaging, hurtful and injurious.

Thus, it would seem that the social psychology research on recipient characteristics does not as easily relate to the situation of receiving psychotherapeutic help as did the research results on donor and aid characteristics. However, for one of the recipient characteristics - self-esteem - psychotherapeutic help is specifically designed to attend to and affect that characteristic and in that regard is again a form of help which can enhance the recipients' acceptance.

Content Characteristics: By this term, Fisher and Nadler (1982) refer to the conditions surrounding the aid transaction. In the social psychology literature, it appears that when help can be reciprocated or the recipient allowed to remain anonymous, there is a better response to that help than when it is given in public or cannot be reciprocated. Psychotherapy is a form of help that easily meets both conditions - anonymity and reciprocity.

Reciprocity is generally assured by the fact the patient pays a reasonable fee for the professional services. For a mutually agreed upon amount of the therapist's time, temporary use of the therapist's office, and for the therapist's skill and knowledge the patient reciprocates by helping that therapist earn a living. Patients thus provide psychotherapists with the resources to feed, cloth, and shelter themselves and their families, as well as educate their children and obtain sufficient amenities to make life reasonably comfortable and enjoyable.

Now certainly in "free" clinics, or state, county, or institutionally supported psychological services, that form of reciprocity may not be so readily apparent or available. At times both the therapist and patient may have to remind themselves of the fact that the patient's taxes, or employment benefits, or school tuition, or pre-paid health fees are what is making it possible for the psychotherapist to be there and thus what reciprocates for the time in psychotherapy. But admittedly this is not always easy for either party to remember. Furthermore, when the psychotherapist's salary comes from an institution or Health Maintenance Group, there are bound to be some splitting of loyalties between patient and organization. For a number of years, I have simultaneously worked under both conditions - maintaining a private practice as well as providing services under contract to an educational institution. I have noted differences both in myself and in my patients related to these two settings. When the person with whom I'm working in psychotherapy is the same person who writes me a check or gives me money to pay for the psychotherapy, it is very clear who my patient is and for whom I'm working. And it is very clear to patients how they are reciprocating. In the institutional setting, my pay does not come directly from the patient. Instead it comes from the institution that employs me and is taken from funds it collects for student health fees. Thus, only indirectly does the patient reciprocate. Furthermore, my association with the institution entails some assumption that I will contribute to its welfare. So, in the institutional setting the manner in which I'm recompensed could create divided loyalties and make less evident the fact that patients are reciprocating for the help they receive. Certainly the debate about the effect the fee may or may not have upon the outcome of psychotherapy continues and is far from being resolved. But, in my experience, most patients in long-term psychotherapy are grateful for what has happened in that process and have genuine desires to reciprocate. I believe it is important for patients to understand that they do reciprocate and how it is done. No psychotherapy is a matter of one person doing for and giving to another without also getting something of value in return.

The second identified aspect of content characteristics important to aid receipients was anonymity. Certainly anonymity is a well institutionalized aspect of the process of psychotherapy. Many states have laws regulating the practice of psychotherapy and those laws include privileged communication for the professional relationships with clients. Even when and where such codification in law doesn't exist, practice has dictated its necessity. Part of the necessity for anonymity relates to the fact society is still inclined to stigmatize persons who seek psychotherapeutic aid. After all, public knowledge a vice-presidential candidate received treatment for depression was sufficient to rapidly terminate his candidacy and to cast suspicion upon the person who selected him as a running mate. Most patients, however, relatively rapidly become unconcerned about others knowing they are in psychotherapy. In fact, patients may take on a justifiable pride in systematically working hard to understand themselves and others. They come to realize the courage it takes for any person to risk understanding themselves in some depth.

Of course, while most patients relatively rapidly become unconcerned should some others know they are in psychotherapy; they, nevertheless, are quite justifiably concerned that the content of what they are dealing with in psychotherapy remain private. I say justifiably so since material dealt with in psychotherapy can include fears, guilts, secrets, and shames which the patient has had difficulty handling and/or accepting. No patient is about to let such concerns be a public matter. Furthermore, the material dealt with in psychotherapy is initially fragmentary, ambiguous, unclear, unformed, vague and shadowy. It is like doing sculpting. We think we know what will eventually be revealed or formed, but during the process of sculpting it is not at all clear just how this piece will finally look. And we don't particularly care to have others who know absolutely nothing about art or sculpting see our work until we are more certain about its shape, form, outcome, and how we feel about it. Likewise, the patient in psychotherapy is involved in a process whose outcome and results are not readily apparent and which take time to understand, work through and resolve. To share that therapy work with others who generally do not have the necessary education or experience to understand is simply counter-productive. Furthermore, the motivation others may have for knowing what is going on in somebody else's psychotherapy is generally suspect. And so part of the need for privacy in psychotherapy is that we are dealing with very unclear, ambiguous, obscure, partially known events and feelings and we just don't want anyone chipping away at the material with which we are struggling. In their training and experience, psychotherapists have learned how to do this "sculpting," and in the therapeutic alliance they have started to teach the patients how to do it for themselves. But others who have no understanding of or appreciation for the process of psychotherapy are best kept from tampering with what is being formed - to say nothing about those whose motivations for wanting to know what may be going on in therapy are to undercut and prevent the development of any piece of "art", "sculpture," or personality with which they do not approve.

In psychotherapy it is more than or perhaps a special form of anonymity that surrounds the aid transaction. The privacy of psychotherapy includes an exclusion of the outside world. It is as though once the office door is closed for both participants (therapist and patient) there is no other world than that which exists and is created within the four walls of the office. For me, as psychotherapist, I and my world cease to exist as I settle down to listen to and be with the patient. My phone will not ring, there are no buzzers or lights or other signals to tell me there is another world outside these walls. And should some emergency demand my secretary interrupt, it is always accompanied by some apology on his or her part for the interruption. It is as though the whole world has learned this fifty minutes is sacrosanct and I am not to be interrupted. If some noise from outside interrupts or the sound-proofing of the room I am using is inadequate, it is most disconcerting to me and I rapidly become annoyed.

As a patient, I found my psychotherapist's office walls excluded

195

the outside world as well as contained within them everything and anything I wished to say, do, or fantasize. The privacy was complete. These two worlds (the one outside and the one inside my psychotherapist's office) could not meet, touch, or converge except at my desire and command. And because of that fact, the therapist and I could experiment with a variety of possibilities or options for "the world". We could play a number of games or try on a number of costumes, scenes or sets in our attempts to determine which game or play was the most accurate representation of *my* reality. And only when I was ready to take those games, or that play or those important life revelations outside of that therapy office's walls would the drawbridge be lowered. I, the patient, was the only one who had recourse to the mechanisms of that drawbridge. I, the patient, always determined what would be taken out of that "private place" and what would be left inside. I believe it was Fritz Perls who said, and I know it was a colleague by the name of Marlin Butts who taught me, that all good psychotherapists are marvelous garbage collectors. I left lots of garbage inside my psychotherapist's office and I know lots of garbage has been left inside my office. In common with most psychotherapists, I like and know what to do with garbage. You re-process it! It teaches you what to expect and do with other persons who come to you seeking psychotherapy. Oh, maybe it is not garbage after all!

Part of the privacy of the psychotherapy office and sessions includes the fact that one does not have to have original or actual realities present in order to relive some of the traumas, fears, and conflicts of the past. The therapy hour is a private space in which the patient and therapist can manufacture and create a necessary "world" which permits re-working those life experiences which halted personal development and growth. Because this is a "private place" and because the world is excluded, patient and therapist can make of it whatever world they think is going to be most beneficial and helpful. I was treating a young man for some adjustment reaction disorder problems when he found himself quite resistant to further work and progress on his dilemmas. He immediately suggested the possibility of hypnosis as a method for helping him overcome this mild resistance. The agreement was that once hypnotized he would be instructed to go to some time or place or scene that would tell him something important about his problem. Once hypnotized and given that instruction, he found himself in his bedroom at home. He was describing the room and telling me what he was doing when all of a sudden he stiffened, seemed to be quite frightened and stopped talking. I asked him what he was doing. He explained in a hurried and breathless manner that he was pushing the chest and other furniture in the room up against his door as his mother was trying to get into the room. I told him to relax, take the furniture away and let his mother come in. He immediately responded, "No, you don't know how seductive she is." That certainly was true, I did not know he experienced his mother as extremely seductive. I reassured him by telling him to relax, slowly take the furniture away from the door, and that *we* would be able to handle his mother's seductiveness. Well, this "little world" we created inside the four walls of the therapy office was eventually helpful to this young man in dealing with some unresolved Oedipul problems.

Lastly, the privacy, or world exclusiveness, or anonymity of the psychotherapy office includes the fact that while the person of the psychotherapist is certainly actually there and interacting with the patient and is the object of many transference wishes and desires, he or she is not available for the gratification of those desires. So while the patient may wish or desire, fantasize and dream about having sex with the therapist or being taken care of by the therapist or injuring, hurting, and killing the therapist; the patient cannot actually gratify any of those desires with the person of the therapist. However, at the same time, the therapist is reliably available at the appointed time, a real human being who will accept and discuss and permit the existence of such desires without censure or judgment. Psychotherapists hopefully understand that none of these feelings or desires are really for them, but are part of the creation of a world "in private" generally useful for the work of therapy. Hopefully, psychotherapists also understand that it would be disastrous for them or their patients to act upon such fantasies. Both persons know at some level of their consciousness that the world created in the psychotherapist's office is not the world in which either one of them fully exists. Both persons can also realize it may be necessary to "pretend" this therapy-office-world exists in order to effect the resolution of long lasting and unwanted impediments to the patient's existence.

It appears to me that the nature of psychotherapy is such that it magnificently fulfills the qualifications of content characteristics associated with obtaining good responses to aid transaction.

197

Reciprocity is generally readily available. Anonymity is judiciously maintained and contains a "privacy" which is quite unusual and which permits and encourages a wide range of anonymous fantasizing.

This short review of the extent to which the process of psychotherapy meets characteristics Fisher & Nadler (1982) have identified as being important in determining aid recipients' favorable response indicates that at least for three of the four areas psychotherapeutic help contains strong positive characteristics. For *donor, aid,* and *content characteristics*; psychotherapy is a form of help meeting identified positive qualities. In the area of *recipient characteristics* it meets those qualities as far as the variable of self-esteem is concerned but there is some question as to how appropriate the variable of "high need state" may be when applied to the psychotherapuetic situation.

Perhaps then, the fact that many therapeutic alliances develop fairly rapidly within a few sessions is in some way related to the psychotherapeutic method having so many positive characteristics of aid transactions immediately and readily available to the patient. It is a form of help that judiciously attends to the recipient's self-respect and dignity; and, in fact, depends and banks upon that respect and dignity. For it was self-respect that most likely brought the patient to therapy in the first place. And the patient rapidly learns that the psychotherapist is not someone who will do something *for* the patient but rather is a professional who will use his or her skills, abilities, knowledge to do something *with* the patient.

Variety of Alliances

So far we have discussed therapeutic alliance as something that is formed or established early on in the process of psychotherapy. While there is a sense in which that is true, for you have to have some kind of alliance or agreement to work together in order to keep meeting in the psychotherapy hour, the nature or form of the alliance can change throughout therapy.

Let us go back to our beginning analogy of taming the fox. If all the fox will permit is that you may work with it to the point where you may sit fifteen feet away, then your alliance with the fox is to work to eventually reach that point. You, the therapist, will have to accept that condition of the alliance if the two of you are going to work together. You may understand and know that the fox really needs to be stroked and petted - to learn that actual contact will not harm it. However, if the fox will not *stand* for such talk, won't consider that possibility, and in fact will leave and stay away from you if you insist on such a ridiculous goal; then you will have to decide if you are or are not willing to enter into an agreement to work to the point of sitting fifteen feet away from the fox.

This is a way of saying that the therapeutic alliance is for a specific purpose. The therapist and patient must have some agreement as to that purpose. And that agreement may not necessarily and seldom is in the form of a formal contract. At times it is not even in the form of overt or specific verbalizations. It is frequently an unspoken but nevertheless an implicit agreement. There, of course, is another and simple way of saying this. You take patients where they are. You do not insist they see the world the way you see it and you work with them where they are and to the very limit of where their world will allow them to be. In my experience, not infrequently that means you do "sit fifteen feet away" or you start with what therapeutic alliance you may be able to establish in order to enable you to even get the person to consider psychotherapy.

Here is an example of meeting a patient where he is. Early in my internship and before the advent of psychotropic medications, I came upon a patient while making ward rounds in a V.A. Hospital who had just been discharged from the Navy. I found him cowering under a table in the solarium, looking very scared, confused and shaking. The nursing staff informed me he had gone there frequently since being admitted the day before and at no time seemed to be in contact with reality. I crawled under the table, sat down, introduced myself and said, "Can I help you?" He stopped shaking, looked me in the eye, evidenced some relief and gave a short smile that turned into hebephrenic laughter. There were no words and it was obvious he was going to say nothing coherent. I maintained a rather business-like approach and told him I would be back tommorow at the same time to see him. My instinct told me not to push him at this point or stay too long under that table. The next day when I came to make ward rounds he was under the same table. Only this time he was not shaking nor did he look so scared. I again crawled under the table, reintroduced myself and told him, "You will remember that yesterday I asked if I could help you and told you I would be back today at the same time." He told me his name before retreating into some hebephrenic verbiage which I couldn't understand. I stayed a little longer under the table this time and again told him I would be back tommorow at the same hour. The next day he was sitting on top of the table. By the end of the week we could agree to meet in a room off the ward - just the two of us - for fifteen minutes at a time. I really didn't know what we would do with our time together. But my unspoken therapeutic goal was to aid him in attending to what the world-at-large called "reality." He had already demonstrated some agreement with this therapeutic alliance by being at the table on the ward where I told him we would meet and being there at the time I said I'd be there. And he had slowly but nevertheless detectably increased his rational verbal interactions with me over the few days we had been meeting. One of the first things he "explained" to me in our fifteen minute sessions were his hallucinations. He saw Marlyin Monroe in the nude which pleasured him greatly, but it was always followed by the devil replete with tail and a pitchfork chasing him. At that point he would cower and duck for cover (under a table on the ward) to escape the devil's punishment. When I asked him, "Did you ever think these visions could be a figment of your imagination?" he seriously considered my question and said, "No." I told him I thought they could be and we had by then a sufficient therapuetic alliance that he could consider my words. All of that, of course, is a fancy way of saying he trusted me. In the next few "sessions" he asked if he could have a pencil and a pad of paper as he wanted to remember some of the things we talked about and he particularly wanted to know what he had to do to work his way off the locked psychiatric ward onto one of the open wards and eventually out of the hospital. Hallelujah! I could have hugged him - but that would have scared this Navy "fox." I assured him he could have pad and pencil. In our "sessions" he marked down things he felt he would forget if he didn't put them to paper. In this way, before the advent of behavior therapy or token rewards, he rapidly learned what he needed to do to "get better" and eventually work his way out of the hospital.

Now certainly some will say this man had no psychotherapy and I do not quarrel with that. However, he did have a therapeutic relationship and he developed a therapeutic alliance for some specific purposes which both he and I were able to agree upon. Within two months he came before the discharge staff of the hospital and was discharged with the understanding he would regularly go to an outpatient service in his community. I had no doubt but that he would do that. I never saw him after he left the hospital. I hope life wasn't too rough on him.

This case contains examples of a number of therapeutic alliances. They begin with his willingness to permit me under the table and then to meet me every day on the ward. He did not have to be waiting for me. He could have avoided me or he could have remained in his schizophrenic verbiage. I would not have been willing to attempt to break through that verbiage. Then he agreed to fifteen minute individual sessions off the ward and next to work toward being able to behave in such a fashion as to get off the locked and onto an open ward. The next alliance was to work toward discharge from the hospital and toward a place where he could continue to get help with his adjustment. During all that time he certainly saw and was able to use me as an ally in overcoming some of the debilitating symptoms of his disorder.

The next example is one in which the patient was initially very reluctant to make any therapeutic alliance, had strong fears of and mistrust for doctors and psychotherapists, but over a period of eight sessions is able to form an alliance for some psychotherapeutic work and move to the point where he can seriously consider entering a long-term psychotherapeutic relationship.

His initial appointment was made on an emergency basis by a close friend. The friend explained that he was very concerned about this man who was incessantly talking, not sleeping, going a "mile-a-minute" and at times becoming irrational and irritable. The friend accompanied the patient to the office for this first appointment. The patient's initial behavior was subdued and his demeanor had an air of embarrassment and shame. He immediately explained that his friend feared he may be a manic-depressive. However, without denying that may be the case for himself he continued to explain that most people just didn't understand him as he had a great many ideas and some philosophical positions that weren't popular with and even foreign to this society. I sensed, however, he was pleased his friend had made the appointment and was fearful of and embarrassed by the possibility he may have a serious psychological disorder. That possibility seemed enormously ego demeaning to him. Obviously, if I was to "tame this fox," it would be necessary to move slowly and to leave an escape path open for him should he become too scared. At the same time I was not about to enter into a complicity with him denying his disorder. For, of course, he didn't want that either or he wouldn't have agreed to the appointment with me. He was quite willing to discuss his symptoms and could state that he probably did become bizarre and manic at times. Near the end of the session he pointed out that he had been feeling better in the past day or so and thought maybe he would all right. I think part of the fear he had in seeing me was that I would find him very disturbed and insist on hospitalization. This ambivalence of wanting help and at the same time not wanting to admit any need of help was a difficult one to traverse. I suggested to him that since he was feeling better, let's see how the next two days or so went for him. I pointed out to him that if the manic feelings became too much there was a very useful medication and we could explore that possibility. There was no hesitation on his part in agreeing to such an arrangement. He said he knew about the medication, it was lithium, and if he wasn't feeling better in the next day or so he would like to talk with me about that possibility. We easily agreed to an appointment in two days time with the understanding he could call me at any point in between if he felt that it was necessary. This was a first but certainly very tenuous step in developing a therapeutic alliance. In the session two days later he reported feeling much better and he looked and sounded markedly improved. He shared with me some of his interests in spirituality and in psychic phenomenon, and indicated that he found me a "kind" man unlike his expectation which was that I would be brusque and authoritarian. I agreed with him that he did seem to be feeling much better than he had been and again suggested we give it a couple of more days and see how he feels then. In the third session he reported that he had continued to feel OK and he then took another step toward expanding our therapeutic alliance by indicating he felt he should start to focus upon relationships with and within his family. He indicated he felt it was a "Pandora's box" but maybe it would help to look at some of it. He certainly was very clear in circumscribing the nature of our work together and in indicating he wanted to carefully examine a few things and didn't want the "Pandora's box" flung wide open. By the end of the third session, an agreement was made to have a series of sessions in which we would attend to some aspects of the problems, conflicts, and feelings associated with the family. This therapeutic alliance enabled him to begin to learn something about the process of psychotherapy. That learning modified his expectations that psychotherapy would be another form of manipulation and power plays - games he and his family played for years. Furthermore, it allowed him to start to identify important and useful issues in the convoluted maze and psychopathologies of his family's history. By the time the school term was approaching an end, he decided to make room in his life for long-term psychotherapy. In essence, over the short period of time I saw him, he made a series of ever expanding therapeutic alliances to the point where he could use long-term psychotherapy as a way to deal with some of his dilemmas.

Now, one could say these really aren't therapeutic alliances. Instead what is happening is that the patient is given some support and reassurance and slowly led into making a therapeutic alliance. I would have no quarrel with that position. However, I submit you cannot give someone support and reassurance and "lead" them into psychotherapy unless they are willing to permit such support, reassurance, and direction. And by permitting it, they are in fact in alliance with you. In as much as that alliance is helpful, I call it therapeutic. Thus, I take the position that you have to start where the patient is and make an alliance with him or her at that point to do what work can be done in the parameters of that alliance. Thus, it is a therapeutic alliance and provides opportunity for making some kind of inroads or gains or determinations which could result in further alliances or, of course, could also be abortive. "Foxes" are different one from another, have different histories and different reasons for being tamed. And we can only "tame" them by starting at that point where they will permit us to begin the taming.

And now a last case example which demonstrates the development of a number of therapeutic alliances in the course of long-term psychotherapy. This was a man with a one to two year history of multiple somatic complaints including fatigue, unusual bowel movements, abdominal pain, and nausea. He had been referred to a very reputable diagnostic and treatment center in a metropolitan area and was in the process of being evaluated. He made the appointment with me because he knew I taught a course in Abnormal Psychology which had a section on psychophysiological disorders and he wanted a professional opinion about the adequacy of the center to which he had been referred. He had been referred in the work-up to one of the staff psychologists. He was both fearful and angry about that. He could verbalize his anger but not the fear.

He interpreted the referral to the psychologist as meaning. "They think all my problems are in my head." I tried to reassure him and gave him general information about the relationship between tension and somatic symptoms. I could honestly assure him he had chosen an excellent center for his diagnositic work-up and encouraged him to follow through with his psychological appointment. He had thought of calling and cancelling that appointment and reiterated his concern that he may have contracted some parasite in his travels abroad. I allowed as to how that could be but urged that the next step would be to see what the psychologists thought. I suggested we meet in ten days which would be after he had met with the diagnostic center's doctors.

Now on the face of it one could say he made this appointment in an attempt to find a way out of relating his somatic symptoms to psychological distress - attempting to find some support for the position that his symptoms couldn't be psychological or for seeing the center to which he had been referred as inadequate and untrustworthy. However, he really didn't fight hard for those positions even though he feared being labeled as having a psychological problem. I attempted to meet him where he was and answer his questions without blocking his escape into physical illnesses. In the process of doing it, I was rather matter-of-fact and straightforward in helping him realize that the relationship between tension and somatic symptoms was a very common and natural aspect of our human heritage and had nothing to do with being inferior or weak-willed or odd. I shared my opinion that a year or two of these symptoms was certainly enough and assured him he had taken some very responsible steps toward understanding what might be necessary for dealing with them. So, part of establishing the alliance in this first session included the fact that he wanted some expert opinion about the steps he had taken in attempts to find out about his condition; he found I would not summarily dismiss the possibility they were on a physical basis solely but knew I attached no particular value to whether they were physically or psychologically based, and he sensed I was genuinely interested in supporting him through the process of determining what might be their source. It certainly was not an alliance for any psychotherapy and, in fact, that issue was never raised.

In the next session he makes no reference at all to his meeting with the diagnostic center. He reported feeling good for a while after our last meeting. Then in the past few days he found himself very anxious and tense. He related this to the coming Christmas vacation and being home and started to talk about and explain some of the turmoil and upset that existed in his family. All of this was done rather matter-of-factly, and when I attempted to focus on some of his feelings he pointed out that he has not and doesn't focus on feelings. I indicated that psychotherapy would be a way to do that, and he immediately responded by saying he wanted to start psychotherapy after vacation break. This was the first of many fast movements this man would make in his psychotherapy. At times in his therapy, I would have to tell him to stop while I caught up - i.e. he would forge ahead so rapidly I didn't realize he had made such a big move.

Certainly he had made an intellectual decision to pursue psychotherapy, but I couldn't help wonder what had happened to his fears and concerns about psychotherapy. In the next session he pointed out he had been confused lately and was sick for four days. He was sure this was a physical illness and called his father. He found out that his father was quite able to accept his son's symptoms being on a psychologcial basis and the father reassured him that if that were the case it was OK. The very next day the patient felt fine and then realized his being "sick" was not on a physical basis. In some way or another he had settled for himself the issue of hanging onto finding a physical "cure" for his symptoms and was now ready to pursue his psychotherapy. The therapeutic alliance included setting up the frequency of sessions, times for them, fee, and we had identified a number of issues related to his relationships with his parents upon which he wished to work.

The process of psychotherapy now started to include some transference elements the major one of which included the feeling that he had to please or perform. By the twelveth session there was another shift in the therapeutic alliance. It was signaled by the fact that he moved from his usual place in the therapy office, so that he could sit closer to me; and by the fact that he had written a letter to his father which he feared might alienate him. In this session he is able to feel and experience some of his anger for the first time. The therapeutic alliance now included a need to be close to me and to feel some support from me. They included expressing and sharing some of his anger but also wanting some indications that he wasn't being irresponsible or acting-out neurotic needs. In addition, this shift in the therapeutic alliance finally allowed him to recognize and not fear his dependency needs.

Summary

When all is said and done, what do we mean by this term "therapeutic alliance?" The concept was initially introduced into the psychoanalytic literature by Zetzel (1956) and expanded upon by Greenson (1965). It refers to a specific aspect of the relationship between the patient and the therapist and at the same time is part of the process of psychotherapy. It has its most prominent position at the beginning of psychotherapy. Unless particular attention is paid at that time to the formation of a therapeutic alliance, the effectiveness of psychotherapy to ameliorate psychic distress will be markedly curtailed. But that is not to say that it is a "one-time-event," an off or on toggle switch. One does not establish therapeutic alliance and then move on into psychotherapy. But one doesn't accomplish a great deal in psychotherapy until therapeutic alliance is established to a considerable degree.

Now I have talked about it as a collaboration - therapist and patient working together toward some predefined goal or on some jointly defined task. But therapeutic alliance is more than just being task oriented or collaborating. It is also a bonding together - a working together. It includes mutual trusting. The patient trusts that the therapist will be a constant and stable ally and the therapist trusts that the patient will learn and work at being a diligent self-examiner. Patients trust that therapists will not abandon them or leave them lost in a tunnel of confusion. The process of psychotherapy takes time and often patients have to go down into their own private "pits-of-hell" in order to finally know how to extricate themselves. They need therapists to stay with them in these pits particularly when they feel they can no longer find their own ways out. Therapists trust patients will endure and will risk the fear, anxiety, confusion of ambiguity and uncertainty as well as the pain of examining old unhealed wounds. And both parties risk the changes in their own lives that sincere and honest attempts to alter the shadows of the past may demand.

Therapeutic alliance is a continuum - not a one-time event. It threads its way through the entire course of the psychotherapy and grows and is modified by that process. The "work" of psychotherapy itself (interpretation, material flow, finding psychotherapy useful in understanding oneself and others) all affect therapeutic alliance. As therapy successfully proceeds, therapeutic alliance is strengthened. For as therapy successfully proceeds, the "fox" learns that the therapist's "touch" is nurturing, healing, and freeing. Hopefully, patients also learn how to select others in the world from whom they may get similar "touches," and hopefully patients learn how to ask for those "touches" from others who are capable of giving them. The therapeutic alliance takes on aspects of a realistic hope for growth and development. Both participants may benefit. The patient can experience release and freedom from constricting and damaging beliefs, attitudes, orientations, and perceptions. The therapist can experience the joy and beauty of seeing human beings assume their dignity and become what they in their most deep parts feel themselves to be. For me it is a great honor to be witness to the "becoming" of creation - to see that which has been hurt, abused, constricted, held down take form and come alive, sparkle and fly. No caterpillar comes out of a cocoon without a struggle. Therapists just stand by and encourage that struggle. We cannot break open the cocoon and free the butterfly, for without the butterfly's struggle its wing muscles are undeveloped and it will never fly. Therapists cannot do the breaking through or the flying for their patients. They can help to create therapeutic alliances which encourage and permit breaking through and flying.

And as the therapeutic alliance grows and is modified, patients learn new ways of approaching their feelings, their problems, and their issues in life. And then patients take over from psychotherapists many of the therapeutic functions. Patients learn to step back and take time to see what they feel, believe, think, dream. In a word they develop the skill of introspection and hone it to a fine art. They can stand off and observe themselves without undue anxiety or premature judgment. They are now eager to understand themselves and others. At the point they have learned these lessons well, therapy ends. You see, we psychotherapists are useful only for a period of time. It is our task to teach others they can easily do for themselves what they have hired and expected us to do for them. It is a glorious and sad time when that moment comes. But I leave those feelings to the chapter on termination!

CHAPTER 6

TRANSFERENCE

Close to nine in the morning on a rather blustery, cool spring morning *it* happened. Making my way to the campus office, walking fast with my head bent down against the wind and my mind preoccupied with the morning's work, I came around a corner of a building and almost collided with a young man riding his bicycle. He also was in a hurry, perhaps almost late for a 9 AM class. Momentarily startled by the near collision, but with the fast reflexes and uncanny balance of the young, he adroitly swerved his bike and without missing a stroke in pedaling sped by me. And as he sped by, he turned his head toward me, smiled and said, "Hi, Dad." Now, that is transference! I was presently seeing this young man in psychotherapy. We were very much involved in examining some of his feelings for his father. At that moment when we unexpectedly came upon one another and were engaged in the movements of avoiding a collision, the "important therapeutic essence "of our relationship was blurted out. At that moment I was more his "Dad" than his therapist. And, of course, in the therapy hour I was a confusing mixture of the two for him.

I was walking down a corridor of the psychology building toward a stairway to the second floor. To one side and at the foot of the stairway was a small group of people listening to a woman whose back was toward me and who was describing in a rather boisterous and flamboyant fashion some event seemingly of interest to the group. By the time I recognized her as a woman I'd seen for two sessions and also recognized that she was talking about me, it was much too late to graciously alter my course. I proceeded past this group, my patient's back still toward me and her not knowing I was there, and ascended the steps to the second floor. I couldn't help but overhear her explain to the group that she was upset late last night, had called my home to talk to me, and over the phone heard the noise of a wild and raucous party. She further explained, in a rather joyous mood, that when I got on the phone I was so "bombed" out of my mind either by alcohol or drugs that I really couldn't carry on a "decent" conversation. Now, that is transference! Had she in fact called my home the night before, I'm afraid all she would have found would have been a rather dead silence, since both my wife and I were quietly reading. On the phone I think I would have been rather subdued and pensive - a reflection of how the novel I was reading was affecting me. She was a women with an hysterical personality structure whose therapeutic issues included conflictual feelings about a rather impulsive, seductive father. In her mind, I was fast becoming the kind of person she needed in order to bring into our relationship the "important therapeutic essence" of her therapy.

For a number of months I had been treating a man who had been referred by his physician because of hives which were diagnosed as psychophysiologically based. Our initial therapeutic alliance included the understanding that we could talk about anything during the course of the therapy but never about his hives. Like many others with psychophysiological disorders he could wax eloquent for hours upon his symptoms - giving the proverbial "organ recital" and thus avoid dealing with the psychological issues behind those symptoms. He readily agreed to the restriction in discussing his hives and the psychotherapy was soon underway as he dealt with a great many unresolved feelings and issues he had with his father. About the eighth month of therapy, as this work neared its conclusion, he said he knew he was breaking our initial agreement but he hadn't had any hives now for over three months. I really thought our therapy work probably was at an end and we would be entering a period of termination. But I did not share that thought with him, or probably more precisely I did not verbalize the thought. I'm not sure what I may have shown in my demeanor, attitude, and orientation in that session. The very next session he seemed completely unfocused, complained about therapy not really helping him, and I had a great deal of difficulty following him. Near the end of that session, I told him I simply did not understand what was going on today. His immediate and accurate response was, "Good, that's how I want you now." Then at the very beginning of the next session, he looked at me rather intently for a few seconds and said, "I wish you'd let your hair grow longer." He then began discussing his mother and the

210

therapy shifted so that the transference now was related to earlier unresolved feelings he had with and about his mother. He had learned very well how to utilize psychotherapeutic intervention for his growth and development. While his major symptom, hives, was now gone; he nevertheless recognized that he could gain additional understanding about himself by "working" some of his feelings and issues related to his relationship with his mother as he had done with the relationship with his father. His wanting my hair to be longer, was a way of saying it would be easier for him to transfer feelings for his mother to me if I were a woman.

Now with these introductory examples, let us ask ourselves the question, "What is transference?" Frequently beginning psychotherapists are a bit in awe of this concept - see it as something that is supposed to happen if therapy is successful and yet consider it as rather magical or mysterious. Many schools of psychotherapy completely disregard the concept, see it as archaic or an epiphenomenon, or design their therapeutic interventions in such a manner as to negate the development of strong transference effects. Some schools of psychotherapy incorporate transference phenomena within the rubric of interpersonal relationships between therapist and patient and don't think it necessary to separately identify those feelings, attitudes, and beliefs which the patient may have for the therapist and which have their origins in earlier important and infantile interpersonal relationships. And, society at large tends to find the concept rather confusing and unnatural. The old cliche that "of course you will fall in love with your psychotherapist" or the fear "you'll just become too dependent upon your psychotherapist" bespeaks typical views of what will happen in psychotherapy and are generally assigned to some magical powers the therapist will have over the patient. While transference is very complicated, poorly understood, and multidimensional phenonena it is not mysterious or magical. We shall attempt to present it in as simple a fashion as possible understanding that it is not a concept fully defined or adequately understood. Investigation of these phenomena continue and there are many variations in the way dynamic psychotherapists conceptualize the issues.

History and Definition

Joseph Breuer in his treatment by hypnosis of Anna O originally observed that many of her symptoms were associated with memories from the past which centered around her intense relationship with her father. In addition, in the latter stages of this treatment, Anna O developed intense erotic feelings for Breuer which understandably upset and frightened him. I say "understandably" so since at the time of his work with Anna O no one had any idea of the concept of transference. Instead it appeared that Anna O had fallen deeply "in love" with Breuer, a situation that eventually threatened his marriage and resulted in the termination of Anna O's treatment.

Freud was quite aware of this situation, and it is to his credit that he was still willing to persist with the "talking cure," although I know of no one who has indicated how Frau Freud may have felt about his perseverance. A first reference to this phenomena of "transference" is found in Freud's (1911-15) writings on rapport:

> It remains the first aim of the treatment to attach him [the patient] to it and to the person of the doctor. To ensure this, nothing need be done but to give him time. If one exhibits a serious interest in him, carefully clears away the resistances that crop up at the beginning and avoids making certain mistakes, he will of himself form such an attachment and *link the doctor up with one of the imagos of the people by whom he was accustomed to be treated with affection.* (p. 139 italics added).

The italics are added and indicate that section of the quote pertinent to the concept of "transference." One of Freud's fine contributions was the recognition that symptoms and personality structure are frequently related to intimate interpersonal experiences of early life. While the feelings originally observed as transference phenomena were erotic ones, it soon became evident that any kind of intense feeling one human being can have for another could also develop for the therapist.

Psychoanalysts have given the most attention to the concept of "transference" and the various schools within psychoanalysis have emphasized different aspects of the phenomena. While Freud (1905 [1901], 1912, 1916-1917 [1915-1917]) emphasized that it was infantile

212

feelings and attitudes, frequently disguised in a new form, that were transferred to the therapist; Anna Freud (1936) included "transference of defence" and "externalizations" as transference phenomena. The first term referred to those instances in which the patient would respond to the therapist repeating the same measures he or she used in childhood to defend against wishes and desires which entailed painful consequences. So the child who learned to fear expressing anger may have developed a passive and submissive attitude as a defense against becoming angry. That behavior would then be part of the adult's response to the therapist. By the second term, "externalization," she referred to the phenomena in which patients project onto therapists their own feelings and desires. So the patient's own unconscious sexual desires would be "externalized" and transferred onto the person of the therapist. The patient would then see the therapist as the one wanting to have sex with them instead of recognizing their own sexual desires. An additional expansion of the concept of "transference" occurred with the writings of Strachey (1934), Klein (1952) and Greenson (1965). That expansion started to distinquish transference from the "working alliance" and from the "real" relationship but encompassed all inappropriate thoughts, fantasies, attitudes, emotions which the patient may display in the therapy hour. Rosenfeld (1965) includes *all* aspects of the patient's relationship with the therapist as transference. Obviously such a broad expansion of the concept led others to call for a much more limited view of the concept. Waelder (1956) as well as Loewenstein (1969) suggested the concept should be restricted to the classical psychoanalytic situation alone.

It is obvious that we do not have one definition of "transference" and that this concept will continue to undergo discussion and refinement. But an adequate and useful definition is provided by Greenson (1965):

> Transference is the experiencing of feelings, drives, attitudes, fantasies, and defenses toward a person in the present which are inappropriate to that person and are a repetition, a displacement of reactions originating in regard to significant persons of early childhood. I emphasize that for a reaction to be considered transference it must have two characteristics: it must be a repetition of the past and it must be inappropriate to

213

the present (p. 156).

However, no matter what definition one might use, a basic assumption for the concept of "transference" is that the past influences the present. On that assumption there is very little disagreement among students of human behavior. A second assumption is that those aspects of our past that are still unresolved, or "alive" or actively influencing the mental process of the present, may be revealed in the transference. What is important to remember is that not everything in a person's past remains an active or dynamic or unusually influential part of their present. Much of the past is resolved, laid to rest, integrated as part of a successful and adequate adjustment to external reality. But as Rogers (1951) has suggested, when too many past experiences are denied or distorted we will no longer have an adequate "cognitive map" by which to lead our life and we will experience tension, anxiety, and symptoms of distress. The psychotherapeutic situation is purposefully designed to focus upon and address those aspects of our psychological life that are unrecognized or distorted or "active" in the sense of strongly influencing the present and/or perhaps pressing for resolution. Fenichel (1945) in defining transference makes this point. He wrote:

> The patient misunderstands the present in terms of the past; and, then, instead of remembering the past, he strives, without recognizing the nature of his action, to relive the past and to live it more satisfactorily than he did in childhood (p. 29).

The past leaves scars for every human being. And those scars are the "signs" of both what has happened to us as well as the fact that the wound has healed. But it is the unhealed psychological sores from the past, often activated or made apparent by circumstances and conditions of the present, which become the business of psychotherapy. As patient and therapist start to focus more and more narrowly on those portions of the patient's "life river" which are blocked, filled with debris and effluvium; it should be no surprise that strong feelings from those times in the past when the patient started to block that life flow should emerge. Part of any person's health is a striving for wholeness. At some level we all sense and know our incompleteness and experience some desire to "become."

In the psychotherapeutic situation both patient and therapist have a "mind-set" toward investigating "becoming" which emphasizes a focus upon feelings, desires, wishes, attitudes, fantasies, and defenses. We work to bring them more fully alive and that work is done in an intimate relationship with another human being. It should then be no surprise that the patient would start to have some strong feelings, attitudes, and desires with and about that other person who is involved in discovering the debris and working in the effluvium. Some of those feelings, attitudes, desires, and beliefs will be a function of the "interpersonal relationship," and the "therapeutic relationship." They will be directly related to the here-and-now and to the present relationship between patient and therapist. But some of those feelings, attitudes, desires, and beliefs, while perhaps activated by specific aspects of the present relationship between therapist and patient, are overdetermined by the "active" past - by those lessons of the past still unresolved, still very active in present life. It is *those* feelings, attitudes, desires, and beliefs which the patient has within the context of the psychotherapeutic experience that are the transference phenomena. *Those* feelings, attitudes, desires, and beliefs which the therapist has within the context of the psychotherapeutic experience are the counter-transference phenomena.

Now, admittedly, it is going to be difficult at times to know whether or not the specific feelings, attitudes, beliefs, desires, and patterns of relating we deal with in the psychotherapeutic session are transference phenomena or a result of the "interpersonal relationship," the "therapeutic relationship," or a combination of them all. In any event, I think we can usefully assume that transference responses do not just appear full-blown as if they sprung from the head of Zeus having no relationship at all to the external reality of the here-and-now. In my experience, except perhaps for some very florid psychotic productions, transference responses are a product of the dynamics of both the present circumstances as well as past emotional intimate relationships. In that regard, they are not at all inappropriate, wrong, or pathological. They are very much an important part of the patient's psychic reality and when examined are found to have made "sense" and to have served some adaptive functions.

215

In Everyday Life

At a recent conference on psychotherapy, I met a former student of mine who was also a participant at the conference. It had been some twelve years since we had seen one another and in that time she had obtained her Ph.D. degree, finished her analysis, was a practicing psychotherapist, had married and was the mother of two children. Nevertheless, upon our meeting she initially related to me very much as though she was still the "college student" and I was the "brilliant professor." She felt some hesitation in approaching me, held me in undue awe, and tended to be deferential. It was as though her years of education and experience in psychology since we had last met were of no consequence and didn't exist. Instead, the initial interactions took on the characteristics of professor-student relationships with some exaggerated child-authority elements. These initial interactions seemed to have no characteristics indicative of the fact that the two of us were colleagues. She readily recognized this transference phenomena and we could marvel at how "powerful" it can be at times and talked some about it. Needless to say, such recognition was most helpful in shifting our relationship to that more characteristic of two adults and two colleagues. The experience was for me a poignant example of the occurrence of transference in everyday life.

Now one could argue that her mode of initial response was nothing more than a habitual pattern well associated with me and reinforced during her years as a student. I would have no particular quarrel with that explanation, except to say that is transference, i.e. the imposition of an habitual way of responding to situations and with persons in which such responding is no longer appropriate.

Transference is a common state probably existent to some degree in all our interpersonal relationships. We all have our "history" and the infant, the child, the adolescent is still with and in us. And the values, beliefs, attitudes, feelings and ways of responding that we learned, developed, and were taught in those early years can still be a very active part of our present perceptions of others and of our ways of responding to them. In fact, it seems some of our early learnings are extremely tenacious and overdetermine what we will learn from that point on. They may operate much as does imprinting in some animal species. This may be particularly true for those things we learn concomittant with high emotional states; which, of course, means those things we learn in order to garner parental approval or avoid parental disapproval. Richard Rodgers and Oscar Hammerstein's song *Carefully Taught*, which was part of their wonderful play *South Pacific*, is a touching example of how our early learnings can live with us through our childhood and adolesence only to be indiscriminately and inappropriately applied in our adult life. Here are the lyrics:

> You've got to be taught to hate and fear. You've got to be taught from year to year. It's got to be drummed in your dear little ear. You've got to be carefully taught.

> You've got to be taught to be afraid of people whose eyes are oddly made and people whose skin is a different shade. You've got to be carefully taught.

> You've got to be taught before its too late. Before you are six or seven or eight, to hate all the people your relatives hate. You've got to be carefully taught. You've got to be carefully taught.

These lyrics, written long before the issue of racism was so apparent to white citizens of this country, point to how attitudes, beliefs, feelings can be strongly entrenched in our "child minds" and obviously overdetermine our interactions with "people whose eyes are oddly made, and people whose skin is a different shade, and all the people (our) relatives hate." Those attitudes, beliefs, feelings, and ways of behaving learned early in our life concomittant with strong emotional states are not just erased, forgotten, or changed with the simple passing of time. It takes other experiences and sometimes a great deal of work to modify and change such early learning-experiences. As a good friend of mine put it, "If you think learning is hard, try unlearning!" One might say psychotherapy is a process designed to assist "unlearning."

Since all of us have our past learnings which will be relatively solidified in some fixed patterns of responding to other human beings, we may speak of the universality of transference phenomena. We can be sure that to some extent all human relationships involve some transference phenomena. In our interactions with other human beings we will not just respond on the basis of the "reality of the present" but will invest that other person with qualities from our past, we will judge them and try to make them fit into the world (not according to Garp) but to us! Our transferences come from deeply entrenched forms of perceiving and responding that do not ask to be changed, only to be confirmed.

We all interpret our life experiences in the light of our past and that is particularly true for our interpersonal interactions. We don't exist in emotional isolation and it is hard to meet somebody, work with them, maintain some interest in them for any length of time and not have some emotional responses - stoicism and the art of scientific pragmatism notwithstanding. Also, as human beings we have the capacity to transfer patterns of emotional relationships from one person to another, particularly if we can find some connecting links. These universal aspects of the human condition make transference a common factor in all our interpersonal relationships.

Blanck (1983) has pointed out that persons in positions of authority and nurturing are especially likely objects for our transferences. If you think about it for a moment, how did you feel the last time you were approached by a policemen for some traffic violation or went to a physician for a physical examination? And what are your feelings and ways of responding when you are required to keep an appointment with your child's teacher and the school's principal to discuss some aspects of your child's school work? I submit that in all these situations the personage of the policeman, physician, teacher and principal will be of less importance, at least initially, than your own perceptions of these figures of authority and nurturance. And furthermore, I'd suggest that your "understandings" of authority and nurturing persons will be overdetermined by your early experiences with your own father and mother - the initial persons of authority and nurturance in your life.

If at a cocktail party your hostess indicates she wants to introduce you to her good friend, I submit you will have different feelings, beliefs, attitudes and expectations when she says the person's name is Judge Rosenberg than when she says the person's name is Joe Smith. The issues of authority and semitism are brought to the fore by the first name. The second name sounds like meeting a "regular" person. And if she says she'd now like you to meet Sally White, I submit you will have some notions of what that person will be like. Your feelings about her will change in a hurry once, on the way to meeting her, your hostess explains she is a Federal Court Judge who not only has a degree in law but also the Ph.D. with a major in sociology. In all these circumstances you had expectations and feelings based upon your past experiences with a number of significant and important persons in your life. You were assigning characteristics and orientations to the people to whom you were to be introduced with little or no consideration of their own individual and unique personages. That is transference operating in the realm of everyday life; and admittedly, it is only a small part of the total interactions with those persons. Upon meeting them you may readily change, alter, modify your intitial expectations and impressions.

In everyday life we generally carefully ignore, downplay or disavow transference reactions. How many times have we felt, "Gosh, that person wasn't at all what I expected." Or we have been told, "You aren't at all like I thought you'd be?" At times when someone has told me I'm not at all as they thought I'd be, it is all I can do to refrain from asking, "And how did you think I would be?" Or all of us have had the experience of meeting someone and thinking that person is so like our brother, or sister, aunt or uncle. Generally there are some connecting links activating those thoughts; such as the person's appearance or bearing, demeanor or particular pattern of acting that reminds us of the other. But then we may go further and ascribe attitudes and opinions characteristic of our brother, sister, aunt or uncle to that person. We also find we have some feelings for that person similar to feelings we have for the person of which he or she reminds us. But etiquette requires we ignore these transference phenomena and instead focus upon contemporary reality factors rapidly setting-aside, minimizing and controlling the "distortions" encumbent upon transference.

So while transference reactions may be part of all human relationships, our social structures and amenities help control its influence and emphasize the importance of contemporary reality. In psychotherapy, however, we may choose to focus upon those feelings, attitudes, desires, and patterns of responding that appear to be transference reactions and momentarily pay less attention to the social amenities which overlook or downplay such responses.

In Psychotherapy

Psychotherapy is a process which means that it is ongoing,

changing, dynamic, and fluid. Life in motion is a process. It continues from one point to another is related to and builds upon what has gone before and creates something new in the present. In psychotherapy there are internal and external processes going on simultaneously - or interpersonal and intrapsychic processes. It is the therapist's task to be as aware of those processes as possible. Three elements of those processes are probably more readily available to the therapist, than is the fourth. That is, the therapist's external behavior, the patient's external behavior, and the therapist's intrapsychic processes are all fairly available to the astute, attentive psychotherapist who has not led an unexamined life. Then in addition, therapists have to develop skills for sensing and finding patients' intrapsychic processes. Psychodiagnostic tools as well as some of the techniques of psychotherapy are designed to assist in that task. The transference responses are particularly useful in identifying patients' intrapsychic processes.

As was noted in the former chapter, within the first three sessions the psychotherapist will have some pretty good hypotheses about the important psychodynamics in the case as well as being able to discern the development of a therapeutic alliance. In addition, generally within the first few sessions detectable transference responses will also start to emerge.

In the fourth session a patient reports having had a dream in which I was present and in which he had a great fear that he would drive me mad. Part of that dream came from his own fears that he was, in fact, mad. But the further analysis and working through of those transference feelings led him to his childhood conviction that it was his madness (in the guise of Oedipul desires) that led his father to leave the family, become a rather inadequate and pathetic figure, and his mother to have a "sacchrine sweet" love for him instead of a maternal one. It is not surprising that with those unconscious convictions tied to his sexual desires, he was seriously blocked in all of his attempts to form meaningful heterosexual relationships. In fact the theme of relationships ending in rejection was woven in and out of the therapy for sixty sessions. And then he had a dream in which he is "a criminal type trying to steal something." He fears his feelings of being inherently bad and corrupt are coming to the fore and he feels so responsible for all relationships. He sees the energy in him as corrupt and evil and knows such an interpretation reinforces all his old beliefs. Yet, he can also say, "Im ready to break through and change but it will disrupt everything in my life." I was ill for his very next session and had to cancel. Does fate really have something to say about psychotherapy? Or was I ill because I was afraid of what he might try to *steal* from me? The session after the one I cancelled, he reports having had many mood swings but the strong feeling was that he is so responsible for what happens in relationships - he causes others' upset and decline. And, of course, maybe he *caused* my illness. It was a fine example of how contemporary events also shape the therapy and the transference responses. Transference is not something that *just* comes from the patient but the therapist also may wittingly or unwittingly play a role in its formation. Two more sessions of struggling with the fear his "madness" leads to disaster in relationships and then on the sixty-third session he reports a series of relationships with women that did not end in rejection and were not disastrous. A most significant aspect of this finding was that the evidence for it had always existed. He had assiduously kept a file in which he placed every letter he had ever received from the women he had pursued. Up to this time, he had only "used" those letters which confirmed his convictions of rejection and responsibility and was genuinely amazed to realize there were a whole host of letters referring to good relationships. How marvelous the workings of our minds are to keep us from seeing contradictory evidence until we are able to adequately utilize it.

Malan (1979) provides a number of examples of transference including one in which the phenomenon is manifested in the very first session. A woman complaining of depression created an atmosphere of sullenness and defiance in the first session until finally she is silent. Silence in sessions is not infrequently related to emerging transference responses. When asked what was happening she indicated that she felt some kind of game was being played with her and that the interviewer expected her to say something. That feeling in the context of the other things she had said in the interview (which included the belief she wasn't a good wife and mother, she didn't get on well with her own mother, and that she had a "brainstorm" at age nineteen following an argument with her boyfriend who wanted a sexual relation with no commitment to loving or marrying her) led the interviewer to the conclusion that she had a life problem of giving and receiving. He therefore said to her that it was difficult to give to one's children the kind of love one has

221

not had oneself; and that like the man who wanted sex without commitment, she must have felt the interviewer wanted much from her without giving anything back. Her response to this interpretation confirms its accuracy as she immediately mutters, "Oh I can't bear it" and breaks down into tears. Following that she continued with the interview with out further difficulty.

In the psychotherapy process, transference is a "coming alive" in some substantial way of important emotional issues. If we think of psychotherapy consisting of a couple of detectives (therapist and patient) looking for the causes of feelings, attitudes, behaviors; then transference responses are the clues pointing to the psychic problems. Keeping tract of these various clues, which at times may seem completely unrelated to the case, and following them down frequently leads us to their source. And these transference reponses have an experienced fullness, depth, and richness about them. They are experienced and felt as part of a present reality instead of some abstract intellectual concept or curious vague memory of feelings. In the above example the man's fears of driving me mad, ruining our relationship and some how psychologically adversely affecting me were not just some interesting, odd, unusual kind of thought, idea, feeling - some interesting irrational epiphenomenon; they were a real aspect of his psychic reality with me. And as much as he could recognize they were irrational and inappropriate; there still remained a strong, firm, embedded conviction that they were "true." He could attempt to "put them out of mind" or intellectually rationalize them away, but they would come back with a strong, firm conviction. They were "alive" and had a firmness and depth which could only temporarily be set aside. And the woman in Malan's (1979) example had her conflicts with giving and receiving very much a part of the interaction with her therapist in the very first session - feelings, attitudes, beliefs with a firmness and conviction that could not be denied.

I believe it is in error to consider transference reactions as distortions of reality. They are, in fact, part of the person's present personal reality and this is precisely what gives them so much power and why the identification of and working with transference responses can be such a potent therapeutic force. With transference responses, the experience from the past comes alive in the present with all its emotional accompaniments and without the cluttered full recognition that they are old, past experiences. For example, it is one thing to remember a time when you were very frightened. Perhaps it was an automobile wreck, or finding yourself in a house on fire, or being held-up at gunpoint. The memory of the fear can be recalled and you may even be able to experience some of it. But I submit that memory and recall is quite different than actually "being" that afraid again at the present moment. And in addition to experiencing in the here-and-now some or a great many of those fears and feelings attendant to earlier events, one experiences them in the absence of memory for those past events. Thus, the transference responses are with substance and as such can be therapeutically useful. Then, in addition, we have generally repressed or become unaware of many of the ideas and feelings attendant to those past experiences. This may certainly be true for those experiences which constituted some difficulty, trauma, or conflict. So transference phenomena not only help re-create with some substance those earlier beliefs and feelings but are also able to admit more of the feelings and beliefs and memories we held at that time than has heretofore been possible.

The reader will recall the case example in Chapter 4 from Hokanson (1983) of the woman whose parents were taken by the Nazis when she was six years of age. It provides an excellent example of transference. There we readily see the fact that feelings from the past are existing in the here-and-now relationship with the therapist, have a fullness and richness of affect, are not experienced as memories from the past, and are more complete and on a broader scope than has been possible for her heretofore, except perhaps for the times of their initial occurrences. You will recall this woman's defense against a world which gave her love only to abruptly and unexpectedly withdraw it was to guard against fully giving herself to anyone.

In her sixteenth session she has difficulty getting started. Like silence, difficulty starting a session is not infrequently a sign for emerging transference material.

Therapist: Having a hard time getting started today?

Client: No. I know what I want to say. It's just so hard to say it....I've been waiting to tell you for several days, but now that it's upon me, I don't know how to start [Crying, wringing hands, very upset]. I'm so frightened and guilty, I feel like I'm coming apart.

223

Therapist: Try to talk about it.

Client: Well, you remember that I was depressed and tense at the last session. I tried to shake it, but I couldn't....Herb noticed that something was wrong, and suggested that we go to a play at the theater that night....So we went [Crying]...and I just had a feeling that you would be there....So I looked around, during the intermission, but of course you weren't there [Very agitated]. And then I realized what was the matter with me....I'm in love with you...Need you very badly...completely dependent [Weeping anxiously]. And I'm overwhelmed by fright. I feel completely helpless. I know that disaster will strike, and I'll be left completely alone [Childlike terror in her voice]. It's too much for me to bear. I feel like my whole personality is crumbling....

Therapist: These feelings have really touched on something deep and agonizing within you.

Client: [Almost screaming]: I feel like an infant. So helpless, vulnerable....I just know that I'll be left alone again....These feelings...of closeness and affection for you...I feel completely at their mercy.... I'm at the mercy of the fear...I just can't function...it's as if the feelings are tormenting me, saying...you let down your defenses, thought you could jig around. Okay, now cope with us....I can't stand it. I have to resolve these feelings or I'll crumble [Continues in this way for several minutes, becoming more and more frightened] (pp. 268-269).

A careful reading of the client's words tell us what we already suspected about her dynamics and also tell us what she as a grown woman already "knows" about her situation - although it is an unconscious knowing. She tells us she is a woman who has let down her defenses and now feels like a helpless frightened child knowing that disaster will strike and leave her completely alone. And I submit that her affect in these few lines bespeak the intensity, fullness, richness with which she is experiencing these early feelings of helplessness and fears of disaster. One might say they are irrational and inappropriate which is exactly what society would say. If she expressed such feelings with and for a close friend, a common response would be to comfort her and reassure her and tell her you loved her and wouldn't leave her. And by doing that you'd reduce and abate the transference feelings - you'd be focusing upon contemporary and external realities which is exactly how our social amenities help negate transference. But at another level, her feelings are rational and appropriate - they are real, alive, and powerful forces in her present psychic reality and they are intimately tied with and attached to another human being who is part of her present psychic reality. They are rational and appropriate in the sense that they show us how our present structure of reality is determined by the past. We, of course, understand how rational and appropriate they are when we get to their source. And then we (both therapist and patient) also understand how they are a part of our living which is now past and does not and cannot any longer exist in exactly the same way as it did then.

The working through of the transference experience is so powerfully therapeutic in part because it not only helps us recall and re-experience strong fears, feelings, and beliefs from the past; but it does so in a context which vividly and inescapably teaches us how easily and unconsciously such forces became part of our relationship with another person. Furthermore once we realize how strongly we felt and believed these things about the other person and that they had little or no basis in contemporary reality, that helps identify them even more fully with past experiences. And in addition to all of that, we also have another human being (the therapist) who knows and understands about these feelings and is an ally with us in now working them through. And all of this insight does not just stay in the walls of the psychotherapy office. The patient is now in a position to start to identify transference responses with others in his or her life and thus in a position to enhance opportunities for additional corrective emotional experiences.

The acceptance of the fact that unconscious forces can so overdetermine our behavior remains one of the major obstacles to many psychotherapists' understanding of the concept of transference. People do not like to feel they aren't "masters in their own house."

225

But experiencing transference helps us accept that fact along with giving us the knowledge that there are ways for us to identify and better understand the impact of such forces. Instead of just fearing and/or denying transference responses, we see their inspection and analysis can be specifically profitable to our living.

In order to solve a problem, the problem must exist. Transference might be said to be the patient's way, in collaboration with the therapist's help, to re-create the forceful, active, disturbing ingredients of "the problem." As Wolman (1983) has pointed out, transference serves as a sort of window into the past. I would add that it is like an open window through which can come the unexamined and unresolved childhood attachments and experiences which ultimately brought us to therapy. And in this sense, transference is one of the most powerful connecting links between our present and our past.

Malan (1976) has used the term *successful dynamic interaction* when speaking about the importance of the relationship between patient and therapist and about the transference. That term very much helps convey the vitality and power of transference as well as its benefits. It also recognizes that transference is a product of interaction and not something which is the patient's doing alone. The therapist consciously or unconsciously plays some role in the development of transference. The more the therapist can become aware of transference responses and of his or her part in their development, the more understandable the process of psychotherapy becomes. And also, the more experienced the therapist becomes with transference phenomena the more possible it is to increase, decrease, modify transference for specific psychotherapeutic goals with different patients. In two series of studies, Malan (1976) has presented data which indicates that a thorough interpretation of transference is correlated with good therapeutic outcome as well as with an optimum therapist-patient relationship after termination. Further, those therapies in his study which interpreted transference early and attended to negative transference and patient's feelings about termination tended to be more successful. Lastly, his results suggest that the most important transference phenomena seemed to be ones in which there was a link between the transference feelings and the relation to the parents. Interpretation of these transference/parent links correlated significantly with the psychotherapy outcome scores.

Wolman (1983) noticed transference is related to the nature of the patient's disorder. He finds that patient's with obsessive-compulsive and schizophrenic disorders are likely to exhibit profound positive transference responses. As he put it:

> Some of them worry about the therapist the way they used to worry about their parents. They notice whether he looks pale or suntanned; they worry about his future; they would like to take care of him (p. 183).

On the other hand, he noticed that patients with sociopathic and narcissistic disorders usually develop negative transference responses blaming the analyst for their difficulties, failures and misfortunes.

We now know enough about transference responses to be able to intensify or diminish their strength and the patient's conscious awareness of them. Transference is much more likely to develop when psychotherapy sessions are regularly scheduled, on more than one-time-per-week basis and with the expectation that therapy will be prolonged, than when the patient and therapist are involved in brief, irregularly scheduled and infrequent appointments. If the therapist maintains personal anonymity and refrains as much as possible from revealing his or her self and values and maintains a neutral attitude toward the patient's behavior and session material, transference will be enhanced. Contrariwise, therapists actively expressing their self, values, emotional reactions and interacting in a reality-oriented manner with the patient will help diminsh the development of transference. Then, of course, attending to transference responses with genuine interest and with an acceptance of their distortions without becoming unduly anxious or needing to correct them are techniques for enhancing their development; whereas, ignoring transference manifestations and rapidly and actively correcting them help diminish their intensity.

By now it is obvious that I think therapists have an obligation to recognize and responsibly deal with transference phenomena. Such responses are inevitable in any long-term psychotherapy and may even be detected in the initial sessions. Transference response appropriately handled can become very powerful therapeutic forces. Now after having said all of this, I am also aware of the fact that many systems of psychotherapy do not use the concept of transference *per se*.

Dewald (1976) has pointed out how various systems of psycho-therapy have approached the role of transference. Behavior modification and client-centered therapy have ignored or minimized its role. Supportive and group psychotherapies may make use of transference potentials without exploring them or making them conscious. Transactional analysis, psychodrama, marathon group therapies and some gestalt therapy techniques focus upon the patients behavior in the "here-and-now" indicating when and where that behavior may be inappropriate and detrimental to the patients obtaining desired or wished for results. Such therapies also enhance the opportunities for exploring alternative and perhaps more effective responses the patient may make. Again, there may or may not be focused attempts to identify the transference phenomena in those "inappropriate" responses or to trace them historically. But nevertheless, they are still dealing with transference phenomena, howbeit without so identifying or labeling them. And they are modifying those transference responses when they help patients find "new" ways of responding to persons and situations. In the psychodynamic or psychoanalytically oriented therapies, transference responses are dealt with by verbalizing feelings and fantasies and are used to help make the patient aware of active and unconscious conflicts, feelings, and attitudes which are affecting his or her life. In this fashion, patients come to see and understand how they have responded in a rather rigid and inflexible pattern to so many situations in their lives. Not only are they now able to see, feel, and understand some of those earlier conflicts and hurts; they are also able to put them in a new perspective and to gain some freedom for altering their behavior, attitudes, orientations. Thus they are more open for corrective emotional experiences. All of this, of course, is a way of saying that transference responses are a part of any psychotherapy whether or not the system of psychotherapy directly or indirectly attends to the phenomena. My bias is that it is useful therapeutically and scientifically to identify and address transference responses.

Contributions of Transference to Relationship

I have earlier pointed out that psychotherapy is a whole fabric. Our identification of aspects of its process is an intellectual and academic exercise designed to enable an explication and understanding of that whole fabric. I had also pointed out that the "therapeutic interpersonal relationship" was a compilation of a number of relationship variables in psychotherapy which also included aspects of the transference.

So far, our discussion of transference phenomena has focused upon definitions, examples, and its psychotherapeutic effectiveness. But we cannot leave this chapter on transference without also giving some thought to how the patient's and therapist's experience of transference phenomena affects their relationship. Aspects of the transference phenomena can become part of the therapist-patient relationship and thus helps form the "therapeutic interpersonal relationship."

In the first place, transference and relationship can and do co-exist side by side. We human beings aren't so limited that when we relate in psychotherapy on the basis of transference and make the transference responses a predominant aspect of our interactions, we can't also "remember" or have knowledge (perhaps unconsciously) of our "other" relationship with this person the therapist. It is as though for the purpose of health and growth, the patient elaborates transference (of course, with the therapist's permission and help) and then can feel, sense, explore and see the depths and workings of those transference issues. But the patient and therapist need not be so stupid as to think that is *all* there is in the relationship. In fact, other aspects of the relationship (interpersonal relationship, therapeutic relationship, therapeutic alliance) help maintain a base for relating and a base upon which transference may thrive. So while we, at anyone moment or time of therapy, may view a small "slice" of therapeutic interaction and correctly identify it as transference, that doesn't mean other relationship forces aren't still active and existent in the dyadic relationship. As those other relationship forces affect and enable transference, so transference can also affect and enable the therapeutic interpersonal relationship.

In the section on "Caring, Love, and Souls Meeting" in Chapter 4, I've indicated how transference phenomena eventually affected my feelings in the dyadic relationship. I presume other therapists are equally affected. The transference responses enable me to see with much more focus and clarity the important, hurtful, fearful portions of the patient's life. And those revelations, for that is how they feel, pull me closer to the patient and are part of what helps turn caring

229

into love. For me as therapist, transference responses enable me to understand the patient with both my head and my heart. They provide a rather full empathic experience.

Let us return to the case of the woman who at age six lost her parents to the Nazis. It is one thing to have an understanding of that terror, fear, helplessness she felt at age six; but it is a completely different experience to have her there in your office verbalizing the fear, terror, and vulnerability *along with* the affect appropriate and attendant to those verbalizations and having them focused upon you as though you were/are the parent who will disappear. The first understanding is an intellectual and maybe almost academic one. It minimally involves the person of the therapist. The latter experience is mainly an affective one which very much involves the person of the therapist and takes therapeutic skill to understand and effectively manage.

For me as therapist, the transference leads to those understandings which have a large affective component and that involves both my head and my heart. The transference allows a vital, precious, and more complete understanding of that patient's important world. And in my experience, the more I have come to know the patient, the more I find myself loving that patient. Real understanding seems to negate judgment and dissolve indifference. Those of us who are privileged to see people discover themselves in therapy, repeatedly find that the "real" person is vastly superior to the one that society has permitted and/or insisted they show.

Transference also helps make evident certain aspects of the patient's essence, i.e. soul. And when someone shares their soul with me that helps bring me closer to them and again enhances loving them. The more I understand the other person - their desires, wishes, needs - the easier it is to love them. For then I am in a position to more appropriately and realistically interact with them. As the other person's needs, desires and wants become more obvious; it is easier to respond to them. Loving, after all, is also knowing what the other person needs. Thus transference brings me even closer to the patient. I'm more able to touch, nurture, interact with, and understand part of that patient's essence - an essence which generally has been ignored, avoided, left to lie waste or only received derivative, tangential, indirect or harmful reactions. In these ways transference helps enhance therapists' abilities to care for and love their patients and to make possible souls meeting.

The appropriate handling of transference responses can strengthen and enhance the "therapeutic interpersonal relationship" for the patient. How do you think the patient will feel about the person (therapist) who helped and guided them through these transference responses? How would any of us feel about a person who accepts our feelings and does not object to them or use them to satisfy their own desires but rather patiently waits and gently encourages us and points our eyes and ears in a direction which helps us find the source of those feelings? I think we would be grateful and develop some trust and perhaps even love for that person.

How would any of us feel about the person who helped us find and open a window into our past and did so in such a fashion that it was not too painful or impossibly disruptive and permitted us to see and feel that past and realize its effect upon our present life? Again, probably gratitude and trust and love.

Brow (1980) most descriptively wrote about the process of psychotherapy,

> No easy task, the process requires the unmasking of socially condoned violence to the child. In therapy, the uncovering process requires digging through layers of neglect and indifference, contempt and ridicule, shame and humiliation, criticism and guilt, exploitation and manipulation. Almost without exception, each breakthrough involves breakage and releases costly feelings of outrage, hatred, and murderousness. The reparative process calls for understanding, acceptance, and support, along with a ritualistic observance of the symbolic meanings of the events which come to light (p. 19-20).

And how would any of us feel about the person who involved him or herself (howbeit professionally and for a fee) in a very intimate and emotionally charged alliance with us which not only brought us additional turmoil, anxiety, pain, and discomfort but also an abatement of those "furies" and an insight and experience that placed us on the road to finally putting to rest those old, inevitable, frustrating, and unhappy ways of responding? Again, I submit the feelings would include gratitude, trust, and love.

So, not only does the transference provide clues to important active living hurts as well as create a substance of great therapeutic importance; it also directly effects the "therapeutic interpersonal relationship." And, the adequate handling of the transference is not only therapeutic but also contributes to a positive "therapeutic interpersonal relationship."

Thus, not all love the patient has for the therapist is transference; nor is all love the therapist has for the patient counter-transference. Peck (1978) has made this point very well.

> There is nothing inappropriate about patients coming to love a therapist who truly listens to them hour after hour in a nonjudgmental way, who truly accepts them as they probably have never been accepted before, who totally refrains from using them and who has been helpful in alleviating their suffering. Indeed, the essence of the transference in many cases is that which prevents the patient from developing a loving relationship with the therapist, and the cure consists of working through the transference so that the patient can experience a successful love relationship, often for the first time (p. 174).

> It is no more inappropriate for a psychotherapist to have feelings of love for a patient than it is for a good parent to have feelings of love for a child. To the contrary, it is essential for the therapist to love a patient for the therapy to be successful, and if the therapy does become successful, then the therapeutic relationship will become a mutually loving one (p. 175).

Again, we come to the importance of caring, love, and souls meeting for the process of psychotherapy. Only perhaps this time we start to see more fully how that process is very much a two-way interaction - not controlled by or dependent upon only one member of this dyadic (therapist-patient) relationship. The patient has risked going into his or her fearful, old unresolved feelings and the therapist has encouraged it as well as committed him or herself to living through it with the patient.

Perhaps by now it is obvious that transference is not mythical or magical nor is it a simple phenomenon. It is not always easily or

232

readily identified, and we cannot just assume that certain feelings, like love for the therapist, are always transference responses. And most schools of psychotherapy, other than the psychodynamic or psychoanalytically oriented ones, pay very little or no attention to transference. In the analytic tradition it has been a very important concept, although it is an extremely difficult one to investigate scientifically.

CHAPTER 7

COUNTERTRANSFERENCE

Kohn and Matusow (1980) in a book describing a portion of their life together and entitled *Barry and Alice* provide us with a fine example of countertransference. Barry was an attorney who sought psychotherapy because of his bisexuality. His wife Alice, a psychiatric social worker, was dealing with feminist issues in her therapy. Both of these people were being seen individually by the same therapist. When they took the opportunity to share with one another their thoughts about therapy and their therapist, they both discovered they were having similar arguments with him. Barry's concerns were about the therapist's views on bisexuality and homosexuality and Alice's concerns were about the therapist's views on feminist issues. She had not felt supported by the therapist in returning to work, in not being a full-time mother, and in exploring outside relationships for herself. Barry did not feel supported in exploring and pursuing a bisexual life. As Barry wrote it,

> Although Dr. Green rarely presented his views directly, over four years Alice and I had learned his subtle ways of expressing them. For example, he never commented when I told him I had slept with a man. Instead he sat there with a blank expression on his face. However, if I told him about a satisfying sexual experience with Alice, he would usually smile and make a positive, supportive comment. Whenever I challenged him on his negative attitude toward homosexuality, he would say: "Did I ever say anything negative about homosexuality?" Of course, I had to say: "No." While I knew that his stony silence signaled his disapproval, it was difficult to challenge him about his negative attitudes because he

235

never expressed them directly (p. 110).

Eventually Barry withdrew from therapy and wrote a letter to Dr. Green. It is quoted here not only as part of an example of countertransference phenomena but also to point out how patients can become aware of such phenomena and how they try and help psychotherapists overcome countertransference reactions.

> Dear Dr. Green,
> I'm writing you this letter to tell you where I am regarding my future in therapy. I've always tried to be honest with you not because it was you but because I felt it was the way I would really change and get the most out of therapy. I will try to be honest in this letter too, because in ending my relationship with you I want you to understand how I've come to that decision and what part of it has to do with you and what has to do with me.
> When Alice and I went to Vermont in early July, we shared for the first time our impressions of you on particular issues. I shared mine about homosexuality and she shared hers about feminist ones. We both knew prior to sharing them that your bias was against our point of view and that you professed neutrality in therapy, even though you had strong personal views on both subjects. But what we realized was that your personal views constantly came out in your therapy in subtle or not so subtle ways. When a person is in therapy with another person for four years, he can pick up how that person reacts to other subjects; I know that silence on your part regarding homosexuality is not really neutrality because of your reaction to other behavior which you get excited about or encourage, such as when I have good sex with Alice or a good experience in dealing with the Attorney General.
> I'm sure this comes as no surprise to you because I know I've confronted you on numerous occasions over the past year about your attitude toward homosexuality. However, you always deny that your bias or predisposition is brought into your therapy with me.

236

Well, I disagree and can cite many situations where it has.

I knew in Vermont that I could not return to therapy with you because of your view toward homosexuality. How many times have you told me that I have not changed your mind? Well, I do not see it as my job to change your mind in the therapy relationship. I want someone who at least comes to the relationship with that as a given. When I started my trip, I thought that before I went back into therapy I was going to seek out a non-homophobic analyst (if one exists). I talked to several people about my therapy while on my trip - some psychiatrists, counselors, and just lay people. I was reinforced in my views toward you but also began to question whether I needed or wanted to return to therapy at all. I knew that I was relating easily to people, that I was feeling good about myself, and that I was taking control of situations in a positive way when necessary. I've come to the decision that I don't want to continue therapy at this time. It's not that there isn't more for me to get into and learn about myself, but more that I'm not willing to put energy into it at this time because I'm not feeling the need.

I originally thought I went into therapy because the issue of homosexuality was more than I could handle and it was threatening my relationship with Alice. I know now that there were many other issues and problems that were affecting my life and which you helped me get to involving my childhood. What I'm trying to say here is that you helped me get to many important things that have and will always affect my life. These revelations were real positives that cannot be set aside because of your views on homosexuality. I therefore, will probably always feel mixed about you and our relationship. There were good things and bad and, at this point, I feel the positive far outweigh the bad. But also at this point in my development, I could not continue with you in therapy because of your views on homosexuality.

These are my views right now. I hope they are clear to

you. I intend to see you the day after Labor Day as planned, but will not schedule any appointment thereafter.

Barry (p. 111-113).

It is not unusual that any therapist's strong personal views, biases, prejudices become part of the psychotherapeutic process. Likewise, it is not unusual that the therapist's past as well as present life can also have an impact upon the therapy. The therapist's own conflicts, fears, unresolved issues and unconscious impulse life are not just automatically excluded in the interaction with patients. Furthermore, as Barry points out in his letter, patients who spend a considerable period of time with their therapist not infrequently identify and attempt to help that therapist with his or her counter-transference reactions. For these reasons, a concept like countertransference is important in order to most fully understand and explicate the process of psychotherapy. And a concept like countertransference is important in order for us to learn how to minimize and/or therapeutically use the therapist's personal and emotional responses to the therapy.

The Concept and Its Early Conceptualization

Countertransference has been even more difficult and elusive a concept to define and understand than has been the concept of transference. The entire subject of countertransference is poorly understood and barely explored. The concept originated with Freud and the first reference to it was in 1910.

We have begun to consider the "counter-transference"...arising as a result of the patient's influence on his [the physician's] unconscious feelings, and have nearly come to the point of requiring the physician to recognize and overcome this counter-transference in himself (p. 289).

Freud (1937/1964) later noted that:

238

It would scarcely be surprising if constant pre-occupation with all the repressed impulses which struggle for freedom in the human mind should sometimes cause all the instinctual demands which have hitherto been restrained to be violently awakened in the analyst himself (p. 267).

But Freud never went into any depth defining or explicating countertransference. He considered it to be a therapeutic "error" and for some forty-five years that attitude prevailed. Very little was written about countertransference during that time and with the forbidding attitude toward its existence it is not unusual that there was a great deal of difficulty obtaining any research data. Psychotherapists were understandably reluctant to drop their defenses and expose inner conflicts and feelings which they weren't supposed to have if they were to be excellent therapists. Cutler (1958) pointed out that our lack of clear definition and understanding of the concept was due not only to difficulties in operationally defining the term but also to problems of attaining research data. He wrote:

...most therapists, having training in at least the rudiments of personality theory and psychodiagnosis, do not readily drop their defenses to allow us to examine their conflicts and inner feelings, at least not short of the analytic couch (p. 349).

The prevailing attitude of the day that countertransference was a therapeutic "error" led many therapists to feel guilty about and be afraid of their emotional responses. This could result in therapists becoming completely unfeeling and quite detached from their patients, for the extreme of the position was that the therapist was not to have or at least must resist having any feelings. In some sense, it may have been an abortive attempt to achieve scientific objectivity. The concept of countertransference and the attitude that it was a therapeutic "error" formed much of the argument for requiring analysts to have a personal or didactic analysis in which they would become aware of their own instinctual impulses and their defenses against them.

A great deal more has been written about countertransference in the last thirty years. The term now is used to mean a number of different things and there is no clear consensus for its definition. Some would restrict the term to the therapist's unconscious reactions, others would use it to refer only to the therapist's specific attitudes and defense mechanisms occurring as a result of the patient's transference responses. These definitions are the more classical positions and Fliess (1953), Glover (1955), Reich (1951, 1960), and to some extent Gitelson (1952) are its main proponents. Some would include all of the therapist's feelings (conscious and unconscious) under the heading of countertransference and this is what Kernberg (1965) has called the "totalistic" approach. Its proponents include Cohen (1952), Fromm-Reichmann (1950), Heimann (1950), Racker (1957), Weigert (1952), Winnicott (1949, 1960), and to some extent Thompson (1952). Obviously the most limited definition is that which sees countertransference as therapists' feelings, fantasies, and thoughts specifically related to patients' transference responses. The most general definition is that one which includes all aspects of the therapist's reaction to the patient.

No matter what definition one uses for countertransference; at base there is agreement that the concept refers to the fact that the therapist's own life experiences, attitudes, needs, expectations, wishes, and personality structure can and do influence the psychotherapeutic process. Strupp's (1973) studies indicated that differences in diagnostic formulations, prognostic estimates, therapeutic plans and goals as well as the character of the therapist's communications and the patient's neurotic process itself were all affected by therapists' attitudes. The clinical literature has emphasized that therapists' feelings and behaviors such as shrinking from certain topics, being preoccupied with their own problems and/or concerns, being unable to identify or empathize with the patient, or becoming over-identified with the patient were all instances of countertransference and markedly interfere with the ability to listen to patients, understand them and respond therapeutically. In addition, the person of the patient, coming to represent in varying degrees some person from the therapist's past, can result in the therapist projecting past feelings and wishes upon that patient - simply an example of the therapist's transference - which is countertransference. Two other common examples from the clinical literature include, 1) situations in which the specific content

240

of the patient's material activates unresolved problems or issues in the therapist's life and provokes countertransference responses, such as becoming unduly anxious or fearful of the ideas and feelings aroused in him or her by the material with which the patient is dealing, and 2) therapists using the therapy relationship for narcissistic gratifications and self assurances. So at base there is agreement that the therapist's needs, wishes, conflicts, and personality can effect the therapy process. Much of the experimental and clinical literature supporting that proposition also emphasizes the deleterious effects of countertransference. That literature grew out of an ethos which saw countertransference as therapeutic "errors." That attitude helped foster an ethos in which therapists then suppressed, repressed, became phobic and paranoid about their feelings for and with patients and unrealistically strived for a detached, unfeeling objectivity.

Countertransference: Something to Know But Not Fear or Hide

It was Heimann (1949/1981) who made the first substantive contribution to the idea that countertransference could be constructive and not just an "error" or troublesome facet of the therapy to be analyzed away. She recognized that the prevailing attitude of the day led many therapists to feel guilty about and be afraid of their feelings toward patients, and she did not deny the fact that countertransference reactions could have harmful effects for the psychotherapeutic process. But she advanced the idea that the therapist's emotional responses to the patient could *also* be one of the most important tools for constructive therapeutic work. She saw countertransference as a part of the relationship between patient and therapist which the patient also helped to create - thus it could also reflect a part of the patient's personality. In her view, countertransference was a way in which the therapist could more fully understand the patient's unconscious. For these feelings, which the therapist notices in response to the patient, could be one way in which the therapist's unconscious understood the patient's unconscious. In her words:

> I would suggest that the analyst along with this freely working attention needs a freely roused emotional

241

sensibility so as to follow the patient's emotional movements and unconscious phantasies. Our basic assumption is that the analyst's unconscious understands that of his patient. This rapport on the deep level comes to the surface in the form of feelings which the analyst notices in response to his patient, in his "counter-transference". This is the most dynamic way in which his patient's voice reaches him. In the comparison of feelings roused in himself with his patient's associations and behaviour, the analyst possesses a most valuable means of checking whether he has understood or failed to understand his patient (p. 141).

Heimann's contribution to our eventual understanding of counter-transference and freedom to consider the phenomena was not inconsiderable. As Langs (1981) noted:

The realization that despite their harmful effects there are constructive potentials to countertransference-based responses not only opened the path to more creative investigations of the analyst's experiences and functioning within the analytic interaction, but also served to lessen the morbid anxiety and tendency toward avoidance that was evident in analysts in regard to this aspect of their work - an attitude that has by no means been fully resolved (p. 139).

Since Heimann there has been growing agreement that countertransference is interactional phenomena and that psychotherapists cannot just be "objective" observers of the psychotherapeutic process. Racker (1972) wrote:

The truth is that it [countertransference] is an interaction between two personalities, in both of which the ego is under pressure from the id, the superego, and the external world; each personality has its internal and external dependences, anxieties, and pathological defenses; each is also a child with its internal parents; and each of these whole personalities - that of the

242

analysand and that of the analyst - responds to every
event of the analytic situation (p. 180).

This understanding of countertransference as interactional
phenomena also includes conceptualizing it as having the potential
for both positive as well as negative effects upon the
psychotherapeutic process. Little (1951) was one of the first to write
about countertransference as intensely interactional phenomena.
She pointed out that while the therapist may be seen as a mirror
reflecting the patient's feelings, beliefs, and attitudes; the patient may
also be a mirror reflecting the therapist's feelings, beliefs, and
attitudes. It is not unrealistic to expect that patients come to know a
great deal about their therapists, and her thesis was that therapists
have the task of helping patients make that knowledge conscious.
Obviously this can be a risky and fearful task for the therapist and
thus it is likely to be blocked by great resistance. This is particularly
true when the professional attitude toward countertransference is
that is must be avoided - an attitude that enhances phobic and
paranoid responses to countertransference reactions. She strongly
argued that countertransference cannot be avoided - it is a product
of the combined unconscious work of the patient and the therapist.
Since it cannot be avoided, it becomes important to identify it,
control it to some extent, and where possible use it therapeutically.
In her words:

> The whole patient-analyst relationship includes both
> "normal" and pathological, conscious and unconscious,
> transference and counter-transference, in varying
> proportions; it will always include something which is
> specific to both the individual patient and the individual
> analyst. That is, every counter-transference is different
> from every other, as every transference is different, and
> it varies within itself from day to day, according to
> variations in both patient and analyst and the outside
> world (p. 145).

Psychotherapy being a process where both the head and the heart
are involved and both conscious and unconscious factors at play
cannot help but have an effect upon both participants in the dyad. A
little thought makes it obvious that therapist as well as patient will

243

have an emotional experience as a result of the dyadic interaction. The writings in Chapter 4 on the "therapeutic interpersonal relationship" should help make it obvious that two people working intimately together session after session, sometimes for months or even years, are going to develop numerous feelings, fantasies, thoughts and ideas about and for one another. Furthermore, psychotherapy is a process which requires not only the patient but also the therapist to invest a great deal of interest, concern and psychic energy. Furthermore the therapist must be willing to consider and work with the material the patient brings to the sessions. Not infrequently, that material may touch the therapist's vulnerabilities but the therapist cannot run from such material just for his or her own comfort.

A great deal of attention has been paid to what happens to the patient in psychotherapy, and the literature on outcome therapy almost solely attends to that issue. But there is little doubt that psychotherapy also effects the therapist; howbeit, relatively little attention has been paid to that fact. Kopp's (1972) *The Naked Therapist* is one of the first books devoted to identifying therapists' experiences with the process of psychotherapy, although it is limited to their embarrassing experiences. Very little has been written about therapists' private and personal viewpoints. For the most part, the literature in this area is sparse and little attention has been given to how psychotherapy affects the therapist. Yet all psychotherapists know they have had strong feelings for certain patients. They also all know they haven't always been able to determine if such feelings were productive or destructive to the psychotherapeutic process. And all psychotherapists know of instances in their practice where countertransference reactions were not adequately handled. What experienced therapists would go back to conducting psychotherapy as they did in the first or second or third year of their practice? We all have our failures or as Little (1951) so beautifully put it:

> We all have our private graveyards, and not every grave
> has a headstone (p. 148).

In my own experience, strong emotional responses have involved both me and the patient in almost every long-term intensive psychotherapeutic relationship in which I have taken part. There have been patients whom I knew I could not help and my countertransference reactions to them would take too long to analyze. So, they were best referred to another therapist. There have been patients who made me work hard in attempts to understand them and in that process led me to know more about myself. There have been patients who made me very anxious and whose problems touched deep fears and unresolved conflicts within myself and thus forced me to face another aspect of my own psychology which had been ignored or left unattended. There have been patients for whom my empathic responses certainly seemed to be informed by their unconscious "speaking" to my unconscious - that point at which I deeply felt an understanding with a strong but pure affective component and which I have characterized as souls meeting. And in almost all cases, I have come to realize that the patient is aware of me not only as a therapist but also as a human being with strengths and weaknesses, abilities and limitations. An example is found in a patient referred to me just before I was to take a three month vacation. He was in a fair amount of psychological distress and relatively well motivated for psychotherapy. I found myself feeling anxious for the pain and distress he reported and felt it would be too much to continue to wait three more months to begin psychotherapy. I suggested he see a therapist who could begin work with him immediately. As I continued to encourage him to begin his psychotherapy immediately, it became obvious to him that I was unduly anxious about his distress. He said to me, "Look, I've lived with these problems for thirty years, waiting another three months isn't going to hurt." I, out of my countertransference reactions with him, hadn't looked at the situation that way!

In so very many ways patients help therapists. I think all experienced therapists have "learned" something from almost every patient they have seen. Part of such "learnings" are out of the graciousness and kindness of the patient who forgives the therapist's transgressions and fallibilities. Part of such "learnings" are out of patients' desires to have an even better therapist to help them. Also, such "learnings" can stem from the therapist's desire to better help the patient, to assist in the patient's maturation as well as to experience the joy of intellectually comprehending how countertransference reactions effect the psychotherapeutic process. In such a way does countertransference investigation become exciting - not something to fear or avoid, be phobic or paranoid about - but another facet or way to approach and better understand the

245

complexities involved in the psychotherapy process. As Racker (1972) wrote:

> It is precisely this fusion of present and past, the continuous and intimate connection of reality and fantasy, of external and internal, conscious and unconscious, that demands a concept embracing the totality of the analyst's psychological response, and renders it advisable, at the same time, to keep for this totality of response the accustomed term "countertransference" (p. 181).

Thus, countertransference is not something therapists need fear or of which they should be ashamed. In the first place, to blame oneself or others for unconscious processes is ridiculous. In the second place all therapists by virtue of being human will have feelings for and fantasies about their patients. All of the rational and irrational feelings we have for others in our lives we may at times feel for our patients. And if we are really going to be involved in our patients' therapy, our feelings for and fantasies about those patients are also going to become stronger. As Reich (1951) put it:

> Counter-transference is a necessary prerequisite of analysis. If it does not exist, the necessary talent and interest is lacking (p. 159).

Weimer (1975) has said the same thing:

> In fact, countertransference reactions are so inevitably a part of a meaningful psychotherapy interaction that their absence may indicate insufficient involvement of the therapist with his work (p. 246).

And lastly, our attention to countertransference phenomena not only assists us in continual self-analysis but also provides another exciting and fruitful approach for studying the psychotherapeutic process.

As we have moved away from the notion that countertransference reactions were only the "neurotic" and/or transference projections of therapists onto their patients and were thus therapeutic "errors" and toward the idea that countertransference is an interactional

246

phenomenon, it became possible to better identify the role of countertransference in the psychotherapeutic process. Heimann (1981/1949), Reich (1951), Racker (1972), and Tower (1956) have all indicated that some countertransference responses may be specifically useful in better understanding the patient's dynamics. For Heimann "counter-transference is an instrument of research into the patient's unconscious" (p. 140). As noted, her basic assumption is that the therapist's unconscious understands the patient's unconscious, and therapists comparing their own counter-transference feelings with patients' associations will have a way in which any "patient's voice" will dynamically reach them. Reich (1951) also sees countertransference as having some role in the production of the therapist's empathic insight into the patient. She wrote:

> The act of understanding the patient's productions in analysis and the ability to respond to them skillfully is not based solely on logical conclusions. Frequently the analyst can observe that insight into the material comes suddenly as if from somewhere within his own mind. Suddenly the confusing incomprehensible presentations make sense; suddenly the disconnected elements become a *Gestalt*. Equally suddenly, the analyst gets inner evidence as to what his interpretation should be and how it should be given. This type of understanding impresses one as something which is experienced almost passively; "it happens." It is not the result of an active process of thinking, like the solution of a mathematical problem. It seems obvious that this kind of insight into the patient's problem is achieved *via* the analyst's own unconscious. It is as if a partial and short-lived identification with the patient had taken place. The evidence of what is going on in the patient's unconscious, then, is based on an awareness of what is now going on in the analyst's own mind (p. 25).

Weimer (1975) has an illustrative example. In it the patient tells his therapist about a problem he has of often spilling his drinks when he is talking with a woman. As the patient relates this problem, the therapist has an association about premature ejaculation. He asks

247

the patient if the association is correct and it is. While this interpretation was "intuitive," it was based on the therapist's associations and was a true product of the therapy session as well as a realistic appraisal of the patient's condition. It is, of course, the "intuitive" aspect of the countertransference-insight phenomena that is so unsettling to any scientist and such a problem for persons not accustomed to attending to and flowing with their feelings. It may be of some importance that all the analysts initially talking and writing about this "empathic" or "insight" aspect of countertransference were women. Women are the members of our society to whom we attribute intuitive skills; and, of course, we also devalue intuition.

Tower (1956), also sees transference and countertransference intimately related and believes countertransference phenomena can serve as a tool for further understanding the patient's psychodynamics. For her, countertransference phenomena are *"the vehicle for the analyst's emotional understanding of the transference neurosis"* (p. 165). She limits countertransference only to those phenomena which are transferences of the therapist to the patient, and speculates that countertransference structures are "essential and inevitable counterparts of the transference neurosis" (p. 165). Racker ((1972) also has described the use of countertransference as a tool for better understanding the patient's psychological problems. He believes countertransference can be expressions of the therapist's identification with important psychodynamics in the patient. He wrote,:

> Whatever the analyst experiences emotionally, his reactions always bear some relation to processes in the patient. Even the most neurotic countertransference ideas arise only in response to certain patients and to certain situations of these patients, and they can, in consequence, indicate something about the patient's and their situations (p. 199).

These views of countertransference are certainly a far cry from the earlier positions which saw the phenomena as therapuetic "error" and something to be avoided, controlled, or dispelled. None of these latter writers view their position as being without dangers. And none of them would say that countertransference is *only* a product of the patient's dynamics. The dangers, of course, lie in the fact that countertransference is interactional phenomena and an amalgam of patient and therapist dynamics. Thus, it may be difficult for therapists to identify their own personal contributions to that amalgam. As Heimann (1949/1981) indicates, this approach "does not represent a screen for the analyst's shortcomings" (p. 142). While it may be an easier "world" to see countertransference as all the therapist's doing (the older position) or as all the patient's doing (the ridiculous extreme of this "new" position), clinical experience would suggest that the matter is much more complicated. Two people intimately working together in psychotherapy create psychodynamics reflective of their respective psychologies. Both participants' pasts and presents, as well as their reactions to those pasts and presents, combine to create a new emotional experience involving both of them. The patient's reality and transference as well as the therapist's reality and countertransference are all combined. While the manifestation of the countertransference may have conscious components, it is not unusual that the conditions creating it are unconscious. It thus takes skill and patience, an acceptance of and alertness to one's own countertransference responses, a goodly amount of self-knowledge, and a willingness to continually engage in self-analysis in order to strive toward constructive and therapeutic use of the countertransference phenomena. In this way therapists continue to receive psychotherapy from their patients - in this way therapists continue to "learn" from their patients.

And, of course, therapists like all other human beings are bound to resist many self-learnings. Everyone of us prefers to remain oblivious to certain aspects of our psychic being. As Rogers (1951) pointed out we work to maintain and enhance our self-concept and thus wish to ignore, deny, distort all those facets of our psychic being in conflict with our own particular self-view. Psychotherapists are not immune to psychological defenses and resistances. In a very broad sense countertransference reactions can be seen as manifestations of resistance. Clinical experience has identified a number of signals indicative of countertransference. Menninger (1958) summarized the common signs. They include such things as having difficulty understanding certain material the patient presents, feeling depressed or uneasy during or after sessions with a particular patient, persistent drowsiness or falling asleep during a session, trying to impress the patient or a colleague with the importance of the patient, arguing with the patient, finding yourself needing the patient's praise or affection, and dreaming about the patient. Psychotherapists sensitive to such signals; who accept the fact they will have their own biases and prejudices and conflicts; who work to achieve a deep self-knowledge; who maintain a desire for continual growth and development; and who continue a self-analysis will be in a favorable position for constructively and therapeutically responding to countertransference phenomena.

Countertransference: Sexism and Homophobia

At the beginning of this chapter, an example was given of countertransference related to attitudes and conflicts centering around homosexuality and feminism. I think these are the areas particularly susceptible to the development of countertransference reactions for male psychotherapists. Racism is probably a third important area, but we may be more willing now to admit our racist attitudes and biases. At any rate, in any psychotherapy where the participants are from different races it remains quite difficult to avoid dealing with transference and countertransference issues attendant to racism. I do not think the same can be said when the participants are from different sexes or from different sexual orientations. Sex bias and sex-role stereotyping are relatively well entrenched aspects of the Western world's societies and we now know psychotherapists haven't escaped culture's teachings on these matters. It has been empirically demonstrated that psychologists expect women to be more passive and dependent than men even though it is also acknowledged that these traits are not good for ideal mental health. (Broverman, Broverman, Clarkson, Rosenkrantz, & Vogel, 1970; Broverman, Vogel, Broverman, Clarkson, & Rosenkrantz, 1972; Fabrikant, 1974; Neulinger, Schillinger, Stein, & Welkowitz, 1970; Nowacki & Poe, 1973). A double standard of mental health has been empirically demonstrated in studies by Delk & Ryan (1975,1977) and by Aslin (1977). In their studies, male therapists held more of a double standard paralleling traditional sex-role stereotypes than female therapists and Type A therapists stereotyped more than Type B therapists. And Fabrikant (1974) reported finding that female patients on the average were in therapy more than twice as long as male patients. Our ideas about what men and women should be are established relatively early in life, there are many social rubrics surrounding the nature of male-female interactions, and for the most part we are relatively unaware of what "training" we have received pertinent to those issues.

In addition to the fact psychotherapists do not escape society's sex biases and sex-role stereotyping, professional training had not attended to the issues of sexism and homophobia until just recently. With the advent of feminist therapy, brought on in part by the emerging recognition of sexist attitudes in many psychotherapists, additional insights into sex bias and sex-role stereotyped therapy became more obvious (Barrett, Berg, Eaton, & Pomeroy, 1974; Brodsky, 1973; Kirsch, 1974; Rice & Rice, 1973; Tennov, 1973). And within the past decade, the American Psychological Association's Board of Professional Affairs established a task force to examine sex bias and sex-role stereotyping in psychotherapeutic practice (APA, 1975). The task force concluded that 1) sex bias exists, 2) traditional sex roles are fostered through therapy, and 3) therapists tend to devaluate and have biased expectations for women. Rawlings and Carter (1977) in their book dealing with psychotherapy for women said:

> It must be clear by now that a major consideration in the treatment of women is the countertransference reactions, or as Sullivan (1953) put it, the *selective inattention* of male therapists (p. 107).

Research on these issues of sexism is certainly in its infancy and much more empirical data needs to be amassed. But in addition to the technical problems involved in obtaining such data, investigations in this area and the emergence of feminist therapies has produced rather strong emotional responses and vituperative statements by persons from both sides-of-the-fence. Such defensive responses and resistance to considering the issues is not atypical whenever we confront countertransference phenomena.

The issue of homophobia has received even less attention and consideration than that of sexism. In the first place, homosexuality was considered a mental illness and an illegal behavior in all of the states in the union until relatively recently. With such strong censures against its existence, it is not surprising research on homosexuality was impossible to conduct and not surprising that psychotherapists would develop a strong antipathy to any hint of a homosexual orientation in themselves. In the second place, science has remained quite unaware of the ways in which conventional beliefs distort theory and research. Levenson (1972) helped call our attention to that fact but we are still probably a long way from fully realizing to what extent our biases, prejudices, and conventional views seriously limit our perception of external reality. Kohut (1984) notes how countertransference reactions may not only shape the fields we observe but also seriously limit what we can see.

> In applied analytic work, the analogy with small-particle physics vis-a-vis the immanent role of the observer in shaping the observed field would, with certain exceptions, be misleading. It would be misleading because the difficulties, that at-time well-nigh insurmountable difficulties that the observer faces, are not due to his influence on the field of observation but to his own shortcomings as an observing instrument. These great difficulties, in analogy to the reactions which in the clinical situation we view as countertransferences, are due to the distorting influence of emotional biases on our empathy-based perception. I refer to the fact that prejudicial tendencies deeply ingrained in us will often decisively influence what part of the potentially available data we perceive, which among the perceived items we consider important, and, ultimately, how we choose to explain the data that we selectively perceive (p. 38).

There can be little doubt that the "prejudicial tendencies deeply ingrained in us" affected what we could see about and how we interpreted the data on homosexuality. With Kinsey's (1947) publications it became much harder to deny the prevalance of homosexuality in the society. His statement that fifty percent of the male adults had not had homosexual experiences to the point of orgasm since the onset of puberty implied that fifty-percent had had such experiences. It was his data on homosexual behavior that caused such a furor, deprived him of government and foundation grant monies, and may well have cost him his position except for the support of his department chairman and the president of his university. Hooker (1957, 1965a, 1965b, 1967, 1975) then provided us with some of the most accurate and useful empirical data on male homosexuality - and she did so having to endure the exigencies attendant to doing any research in a taboo area. In December of 1973 the American Psychiatric Association removed homosexuality from the list of mental diseases and in 1975 the American Psychological Association supported that action and adopted a resolution urging mental health professionals to take the lead in removing the stigma of mental illness that had been associated with homosexuality. In addition, the American Psychological Association has now added a division on Gay and Lesbian issues and there is a scientific journal dealing exclusively with issues of homosexuality. A number of professional documents are available to help therapists become more aware of their own biased attitudes toward homosexuality (Chafetz et al., 1974; Gonsiorek, 1982; Hall, 1978; Kingdon, 1979; Martin, 1982; Nuehring et al., 1974; Pendergrass, 1975; Riddle & Sang, 1978; Woodman & Lenna, 1980).

Nevertheless, most psychotherapists no matter how knowledgeable about the literature on homosexuality and no matter how well-intentioned, lack sufficient knowledge and/or experience about the process of "coming out," the psychological experience of being an outcast and oppressed member of society, and the "culture" of gay and lesbians communities to be able to easily and accurately empathize with patients who happen to be homosexual. And added to such limitations is the fact that psychotherapists have received very little accurate information about homosexuality (since so much of the earlier research was seriously contaminated by our conventional biases) and have had little or no opportunity to examine their own homosexual orientations. Chapman and Chapman (1969), Davison and Friedman (1981), Davison and Wilson (1973), Garfinkle and Morin (1978), Kurtz and Garfield (1978), and Levy (1978) all give examples of ways in which prejudices about homosexuality are expressed by therapists.

Making these two issues, sexism and homophobia, even more cogent for countertransference responses in male psychotherapists in this society is the fact that their professional work calls for a stance and orientation opposed to their sex-role stereotyping. Burton (1972) has indicated this most cogently:

I have earlier written that becoming a therapist calls for
a full development of the feminine side of the

253

therapist's personality, and experience shows that those therapists who are overburdened by masculine needs do not remain long in direct treatment with clients. Intuition, sensitivity, affect, feeling, artistry, color, all highly relevant to the work of the therapist, are better realized as feminine qualities, and they are most certainly correlated with success and gratification in work as a therapist (p. 17).

It can be very threatening for some males to approach their "feminine" side. Our sex-role stereotyping has been quite insistent that males not be "soft," "intuitive," or "emotional." Any psychologist should understand Kopp's (1976) statement about homophobics, i.e. "In order to disown the shameful softness in themselves, they sought out and beat up homosexuals in the Village" (p. 22). There is much confusion, conflict, and fear surrounding the very natural phenomenon of homosexuality so it should be no surprise that this part of human existence can lead to serious countertransference responses in psychotherapists. I say "serious" because it is not only physically that one can hurt, injure, and batter another human being but psychologically as well.

I certainly was not immune to my society's teaching regarding sex bias and sex-role stereotyping and my formal education did nothing to contradict or even challenge those conventional biases. If anything, that education helped reinforce them. It was really rather late in my life that I finally was forced to face those aspects of my psychology and I have no doubt but that such confrontation and struggle has resulted in me being a better psychotherapist.

Countertransference: Honesty

At base, countertransference has to do with the therapist's self-honesty. Bruch (1974) has said:

Doing psychotherapy requires the ability to listen to others without letting your personal problems and frustrations, or prejudices and preconceived notions, interfere with being fair, firm, and honest (p. 117).

It is, of course, a way of saying that psychotherapists should know themselves as well as possible and be honest about their problems, frustrations, and prejudices so they may avoid the more troublesome consequences of the countertransference structure. Perlman (1979) has also stressed the importance of therapists' self-honesty for an effective psychotherapy:

> Honesty with oneself, honesty in facing one's own prejudices, biases, attractions, or revulsions, is the first step in attempting to form a working alliance with another. Otherwise one's own resistances arise. And in the often unconscious, skillful strategies of our psychological defense system, we defend ourselves in several ways (p. 103).

Thus, it is not that therapists are going to avoid countertransference reactions. Rather it is that experienced psychotherapists may know and use their own countertransference responses. This means that psychotherapists should as much as possible keep an open mind on all issues and apply the same standards of self-honesty and forthright self-appraisal to themselves as they require of their patients. It means that psychotherapists must be open to and willing to have their feelings, biases and prejudices - so that they may know what they are and thus *who they* are! It is when we lack the courage to face truth about ourselves that we start to take on roles which make us less human than we really are. And as Kopp (1968) has pointed out, all psychotherapists, like the Wizard of Oz, are continually urged to be something other than human. But these urgings to be omnipotent and all wise and totally responsible and completely adjusted are frequently transference inspired traps. They are avoided by remaining human which means that psychotherapists must not be afraid to love and to hate, to feel hopeless and helpless and inadequate. It means that mistakes will be made - for that is part of being human. And some of those mistakes will be harmful to the therapy and an apology will be appropriate. Hopefully it is through such errors that we therapists learn to become even better therapists. The good psychotherapist is not truly perfect, rather truly human.

It is by seeking truth and exercising self-honesty that our conflicts, biases, prejudices become evident and we experience psychological growth. And it is by seeking truth and exercising self-honesty, by being willing to take unto ourselves our own human nature and involve ourselves in continued self-knowledge and personal growth that we serve as models to our patients.

Thus, in at least two ways countertransference responses impinge upon and become part of the "therapeutic interpersonal relationship." Countertransference reponses reveal to our patients the kind of person we are and something of our biases, prejudices, fears, and conflicts. Thus, they "speak" loudly about who we are and reveal to patients much about us as persons. How the psychotherapist handles countertransference responses can say much to patients about commitment to self-scrutiny, self-honesty, personal growth, development and change.

The psychotherapist who works with the patient, listening to his or her wisdom, and willing to learn how to be an even better psychotherapist for that patient and other patients is certainly enhancing the therapeutic alliance. For the patient can then know he or she is working with somebody who truly cares, wants to do his or her very best, and is not uncomfortable with being human.

CHAPTER 8

INTERPRETATION, INSIGHT, CONCEPTUALIZATION

The terms "interpretation," "insight," and "conceptualization" are *not* used interchangeably but rather to denote an interrelated sequence of events which are an important and necessary part of the process of psychotherapy. The sequence generally begins with an interpretation usually made by the therapist. If the interpretation is both accurate and made at an appropriate moment, the patient will gain some "insight" which when "worked through" can result in a new and/or different conscious conceptualization of and emotional response to important life events or experiences.

Interpretation is a technique of psychotherapy as well as part of its process. It is a verbal activity which includes much more than just an intellectual or cognitive understanding on both the therapist's and the patient's part.

Strupp (1973) defined interpretation as:

> ...an attempt to describe by means of verbal symbols an emotional reaction or a behavior pattern exhibited by the patient in relation to the therapist, of whose interpersonal or dynamic significance the patient is unaware or insufficiently aware (p. 49).

Kahn (1969) said:

> Interpretation is that act of verbal and affective intervention, contribution, and evaluation by the analyst which crystallizes two new experiences for the patient: (a) recognition of his *being*, and (b) the *knowing* of his *experiences* (p. 384).

Both definitions help to convey the fact that interpretation is not an

257

explanation! Long ago Fromm-Reichmann pointed out that patients need an experience, not an explanation. Interpretations that are intellectual explanations may serve some purposes in supportive psychotherapy where one is attempting to reduce anxiety and bolster ego-strength by reinforcing an intellectual defense mechanism, but they do not generally lead to insight or to the discovery of some inner truths.

Certainly it has been the insight-seeking therapies that stress the importance of interpretation and its role in helping patients increase their own self-awareness. But the cognitive therapists (Ellis, 1970; Beck, 1976) also emphasize the importance of patients changing their disruptive cognitive patterns and those therapists help patients reconceptualize or restructure their "world views". In the process of doing that, patients also learn a great deal about themselves. Even the strict behavior therapists whose interventions may be aimed directly at behavioral symptoms will have patients knowing more about themselves after therapy than when they began. It is probably fair to say that all psychotherapies lead to increased self-awareness. They do, however, differ markedly in the way they go about increasing self-awareness, as well as the attention they give to and emphases they place upon self-awareness and the technique of interpretation. Certainly not all systems of psychotherapy say self-awareness and interpretation are important or necessary parts of the psychotherapy process.

Interpretation in Psychotherapy: Its History

Freud's well-known statements about making the unconscious conscious and replacing id with ego represents the historical position which held that interpretation leading to cognitive insight into the origin and meaning of the disorder was curative. Thus, for a good many years, interpretation was seen as being a very important aspect of psychoanalytic work and as a very powerful agent ameliorating psychic distress. Interpretation was seen as the procedure which led to insight for the patient and the insight was seen as a curative element. Some of the strong feelings and beliefs about interpretation among the early workers in the field is reflected by Strachey's (1934) comments:

But I believe it would be true in general to say that analysts are inclined to feel interpretation as something extremely powerful whether for good or ill. I am speaking now of our *feelings* about interpretation as distinguished from our reasoned beliefs....we are told that if we interpret too soon or too rashly, we run the risk of losing a patient; that unless we interpret promptly and deeply we run the risk of losing a patient; that interpretation is the only way of enabling a patient to cope with an unmanageable outbreak of anxiety by "resolving" it; that interpretations must always refer to material on the very point of emerging into consciousness; that the most useful interpretations are really deep ones; "Be cautious with your interpretations!" says one voice; "When in doubt, interpret!" says another (p. 141-142).

His comments nicely reflect the fact that the importance placed upon interpretation was more a matter of theoretical positions than of clinical experience or research evidence. But they also indicate the great amount of confusion there was over interpretation's role in the psychotherapeutic process. Certainly some of that confusion remains to this day, although I think we will see that a more considered and systematic approach has now been given in attempts to better understand the function of interpretation.

It was not until the late 1940's and early 1950's that belief in the great importance of interpretation and insight in the psychoanalytic school of thought was challenged (Marmor, 1976). Those therapies concerned primarily with symptom relief and direct behavior change dismissed the therapeutic role of interpretation and insight as secondary at best. And within the entire field of psychotherapy, there was growing awareness that insight did not always lead to behavior change. Salzman (1976) pointed out:

It has long been noted that insight alone is not enough to effect change in a patient's behavior (p. 20).

and Hobbs (1981) attributed his original interest in the issue of insight to the time when he noticed that:

...insight occurred but behavior did not change (p. 633).

Such observations were the focal point of many criticisms of the role of insight in the psychotherapeutic process. Those criticisms eventually threatened the dominant theory of the day which stressed the importance of interpretation and insight as "keys" for unlocking repressed conflicts and freeing afflicted individuals.

One way to approach these criticisms and still keep the dominant theory intact was to differentiate between types of insight. This Alexander and French (1946) did when they made a distinction between intellectual and emotional insight. They emphasized the importance of emotions in psychotherapy and saw emotional insight as the only one that was therapeutic. That differentiation eventually set off a controversy which Bond (1975) saw as

...one of the oldest and most often mentioned conundrums in the history of psychotherapy (p. 13).

The arguments in this conundrum centered on the validity of the distinction that only emotional insight was curative. For an understanding of what goes on in psychotherapy, it may be useful to identify different types of insight. However, it is not necessary to assume only one kind of insight is capable of leading to change. Schonbar (1965) and Rangell (1981) argued that both types of insight could bring about change. And Schonbar (1965) elaborated upon the possibility that insight can be "partial" and cumulative.

During several years of treatment, he had recognized many times over his anger at his psychotic mother's unpredictable shifts between affection and hostility; his relationship with her did indeed change during these years. One day he started to relate his feelings about women to his experience with his mother. "What about your mother?" I asked. This was old hat, and made him angry; he launched into his familiar list of complaints, and then suddenly began to sob; at that moment he was experiencing the feelings we had talked about many times. And I rather doubt that he could have reached this experience without all the previous bits and pieces of partial intellectual and emotional insights he had

260

achieved in a meaningful relationship (p. 81).

Here was the idea that one interpretation and insight might well not have observable effects until a combination of insights helped to produce a whole picture and that it will still not have its full meaning until it is placed within a context larger than that of the psychotherapeutic relationship *per se.*

In addition to postulating different types of insight as well as the possible cumulative effect of a number of interpretations, the observation that interpretation and insight did not always lead to behavior change led to the conclusion that change required additional experiences. Again, it was Alexander and French (1946) who suggested that "corrective emotional experiences" were necessary to effect a "cure." No longer was interpretation and insight considered the most important therapeutic skills available to the psychotherapist. Now much more than just interpretation and insight were necessary.

At the present time there are few who would argue that interpretation and insight are the only important and essential elements in effecting change. However, to consider interpretation and insight as negligible elements in the process of psychotherapy is as much an oversimplification of a very complex process as was the historically dominant position that interpretation and insight were the only necessary elements for change. To expect that a single concept or phenomenon like interpretation or insight will explain psychotherapy's effectiveness is naive in the extreme. Therapists who expect that interpretation and insight will "solve everything" are going to be sorely disappointed. The idea the psychotherapist will tell you what is wrong (the interpretation) and then your problems will be over is simplistic in the extreme and an inaccurate conceptualization of the process of psychotherapy. Nevertheless, many patients still believe that is what psychotherapy is all about and still want and expect their doctors to tell them what's wrong and advise them what to do. We cannot escape our society's preoccupation with pragmatism and with easily observable results.

Our understanding of the role and/or importance or lack thereof of interpretation and insight in the psychotherapeutic process is still far from complete. Much discussion and controversy over these particular aspects of the process of psychotherapy will remain for a considerable period of time.

One of the reasons for such controversy is that we still approach the problems of understanding the process of psychotherapy from a directional or causality metaphysics. We want to know what "causes" the changes we see in psychotherapy and are searching for that variable, element, force, concept, that best accounts for such change. In the case of interpretation and insight, that means some of the discussion and argument about its role in the process of psychotherapy centers upon the issue of whether it produces changes or is a product of that change. Hobbs (1962) is one who has suggested that:

> It [insight] is not a source of therapeutic gain but one
> among a number of possible consequences (p. 742).

He also said that a patient can't really accept an interpretation until there was a sufficient re-organization of the self. It was the re-organization of the self that was important and the interpretation the patient could accept was then irrelevant. Alexander and French (1946) as well as Rogers (1951) are others who have suggested that insight depends upon other changes occurring in the patient first. For Alexander and French (1946) an emotional readjustment was needed before the patient could have insight. For Rogers (1951) a change in self-concept had to precede any insight into denied and or repressed material. In such conceptualizations the acceptance of interpretation and the occurrence of insight may only be indications that some changes have already taken place in the patient's self-structure. And, of course, if the acceptance of an interpretation and the resultant insight are only a product signalling a much more important change or modification in the patient's psyche; interpretation could be considered nothing more than an epiphenomenon and of little value in describing the process of psychotherapy.

But this "directional" orientation overlooks the possibility that interpretation and insight both produce and result from change. Psychotherapists involved in using interpretation know full well that their interpretations must only be given at certain moments and within a complex of relatively identifiable "therapeutic interpersonal relationship," alliance, and transference variables in order to be accepted, or understood, or considered and in order for them to lead to some degree of insight. This, of course, is another way of saying that certain changes in the patient's self-concept, emotional readjustment, or cognitive processes must have already occurred. The accepted or considered interpretation and resultant insight are then certainly "signs" that some change has already taken place. Furthermore, the common rule-of-thumb that one does not make an interpretation until the patient can accept it or is almost ready to make that interpretation for him or her self, might be another way of saying that interpretation and insight are *only* signs of changes that have already occurred. In such an event, one might say "Why even bother with interpretation?" The answer to that question suggests that interpretation and insight also produces change.

In the Western world, it seems examination of the personal inner world is a fearful, scary, threatening, private experience. Sending people to the moon and exploring outer space seems much less risky and frightening than does exploring our own inner worlds. There seem to be powerful forces keeping us from self-exploration. Perhaps we believe we have much more control over the outer, external physical world than we do over our own inner psychology. But in any event, when we are engaged in the exploration of our own personal inner world, we do it with caution and generally only tentatively approach many of our inner "truths." So while during psychotherapy our view of ourselves may be slowly changing to accomodate "new" ideas, experiences, events, or cognitive constructions; and while we may well be almost ready to specify and/or identify and by verbalizing own and "speak" those new conceptualizations or insights, there is still a tentativeness about taking such a step and nagging doubts about the authenticity of our emerging self discoveries. So while it may be true that we are about ready to make the interpretation for ourselves, and the insight resulting from such a conceptualization is almost already formed and available to us, the therapist's stating that insight via the procedure of interpretation may well serve at least two functions. One is that it helps confirm and make less tenuous the conclusions to which we were coming anyway. This is simply another way of saying "two minds are better than one." The therapist, being a person whose judgments and perceptions we have come to trust and being one who is involved with us on our inner journey, also "seeing," "understanding," "comprehending" what we are starting to see helps dissipate the tentativenss or doubts we may hold about our own new discovery. The therapist's interpretation is a way of conceptualizing and/or symbolizing the data and information about ourselves we have been discovering and may provide us a new way of construing our own personal world. While we may be close to coming to the same conceptualization ourself, having another who also "sees" the same things we are seeing and feeling can add authenticity to our insight. Secondly, the open stating of this "new" view by the therapist (which is the interpretation) can markedly reduce the anxiety and fear we have about accepting a conclusion to which we are being drawn by our own experience. Once it is said out-loud in the therapy room in the context of the "therapeutic interpersonal relationship," it may no longer seem such a radical, perverse, terrible, unacceptable conclusion. We now have both support for the view to which we were inexorably drawn as well as acceptance for experiencing, having, being a human being with such desires, wishes, feelings, fears, and ideas.

If nothing else, in these two ways the therapist's interpretation produces additional changes in the patient's experience of and work in psychotherapy. Thus, interpretation and insight are both results of changes that have already occurred in the patient and therapist during the process of psychotherapy as well as actions that can result in further or additional changes.

Now an additional facet of the reinforcing properties of the therapist's interpretation is related to the fact that there are many aspects of ourselves we wish to avoid seeing or feeling. Much too frequently insight is thought to be a joyous, "ah-ha, now I see it, that's what it is" experience. I think that insight is more typically an "Oh shit, not that!" experience. Thus, interpretation more frequently can lead to insights we wished to avoid facing and insights that may require considerable re-organization and change in our lives. The reader will again recall the case in Chapter 4 of the woman whose early life experiences in Nazi Germany were a crucial part of her adult life. The insight she finally obtains pertinent to those early experiences and how they have altered her life and affected her marriage certainly aren't easily construed as a joyous, ah-ha experience. Recall that in the sixteenth session the patient realized (had insight into) the truth that she had for a good many years, and all of her marriage, never once let herself go and have the feelings of love and needing and being needed of which she was capable. Is there not pain and sadness and loss with that insight? Remember her words:

Oh, my God! What a waste!...Ten years of marriage down the drain...And it wasn't Herb's fault - the poor, sweet, tolerant guy - it was mine. I was too scared to give him the feelings that rightfully belong to him....It was safer, the way I made it happen....Oh, my God! Herb, what have I done to you...and the children? (Hokanson [1983] p. 289-290).

At one point, there was probably some joy attendant to the freedom her knowledge and insight gave her - that kind of joy and peace that is part of any complete and accurate understanding. But the insight also required her to face the "true" nature of her marriage and to have to share and deal with her husband on many issues that cannot be anything but difficult and painful for both parties. That, I submit, is an "Oh, shit, not that!" experience attendant to insight and furthermore is an example of how great change may be produced by insight. This "new" understanding of her life now *requires* major changes in her marital relationship. It will be impossible for her to go back to her old ways - at least impossible unless she can sufficiently deny, distort and repress this "new" understanding. There are, of course, a number of ways she can change. The changes could include divorce, or an acceptance of the marriage as it is with the realization that she may never be able to give herself completely to her husband, or a change in their relationship where she comes to more deeply love her husband. This listing certainly does not include the host of possibilities available to her for accomodating the "new" understanding into her total life - and they are all written here in a rather cold, unfeeling, pedantic fashion which doesn't convey the long struggle, pain, hurt, confusion and regret that are probably part of her coming to live with the conscious realization of what she unconsciously knew all along. But at any rate, it is difficult for me to comprehend how her insight couldn't help but produce a rather significant change in her life. An important point, however, is that such change need not be reflected in symptoms or behaviors.

This leads us into a second reason why the controversy over the role and/or importance or lack thereof of interpretation and insight in the psychotherapeutic process will remain for a considerable period of time. Almost all of the research outcome literature in psychotherapy and certainly the major thrust of the criticism of

265

interpretation and insight assumes that symptom and behavioral changes are the aim, goal and *sine qua non* of effective psychotherapy. Again, part of this is most understandable when we realize how externally oriented and pragmatic our society is and how poor its people are at understanding any kind of force other than a physical one. Furthermore, logical positivism seems only able to deal with that which is readily observable and symptoms and people's behaviors are more readily observable than are their thoughts, ideas, feelings, fantasies and internal psychological states. It is understandable that researchers in psychotherapy choose questions for study on the basis of their amenability to statistical measurement and control and thus end up with symptoms and behaviors. Then, add to that the fact that many patients coming for psychotherapy consciously want relief from their symptoms (like depression) so they can go back to being the way they were before they experienced those symptoms. Patients do not have an easy and rapid understanding that their symptoms are a result of the way they were before those symptoms appeared and that there is no way they can go back to how they were before the symptoms appeared. For these and undoubtedly for other reasons, most of the criterion for evaluating the outcome of psychotherapy has focused upon symptom and behavioral changes. The implicit assumption is that behavior change is the most important goal of psychotherapy and should therefore be its end result. But all clinicians are familiar with the fact that patients report self-understandings and self-acceptance as important results of their psychotherapies. Feifel and Ellis (c.f. Schonbar, 1965) as well as Strupp, Fox, and Lessler (1969) provide us important data indicating that patients see self-understanding and other insight-related factors as the major gain of their psychotherapy. As Strupp, Fox, and Lessler (1969) wrote:

> The patients' accounts also revealed that the disappearance of specific symptoms was only a minor aspect of the improvement they experienced. Even in the more limited and abbreviated courses of therapy there were gains which approximated the kinds of far-reaching changes experienced by patients in more intensive therapy. It is important to emphasize this point, frequently lost sight of by the proponents of conditioning therapies, which focus largely on the

amelioration of specific symptoms. The significant gains emphasized by most of our respondents were increased mastery not only over specific symptoms but in many areas of living. Thus they forcefully called attention to the function of psychotherapy as an educational or re-educational process (p. 14).

Their study documents the minor emphasis patients may place on alleviation of symptoms such as anxiety, depression, physical disturbances and the major emphasis they give to improvements in the areas of interpersonal relationships and self-image. Furthermore, these changes were apparent to close associates and occurred relatively rapidly in psychotherapy. A quote from one of the patients they studied nicely summarizes the importance of inner changes even though there may be little overt behavioral change.

I have learned to accept myself as I am, and I find that I rather enjoy being me; the most drastic change, in other words, has been to learn that I can live an enjoyable life without any drastic changes. I do not mean that I now make no effort to improve myself; on the contrary, I think I am more intent on this than before. The difference is in my outlook and attitude more than anything else. As a result of the above, I find that I have more self-confidence, and am willing and able to tackle things that I would not have attempted before, though I may not like it any better (p. 36).

Clear support for what Strupp, Fox, and Lessler (1969) had discovered and what many clinicians already knew is found in the conclusions Smith, Glass, and Miller (1980) reached after a most lengthy and mammoth review and analysis of the psychotherapy outcome literature. In their words:

Psychotherapy is *primus inter pares* for the benefits it bestows upon the inner life of its clients. For whatever contribution psychotherapy may make to its clients' social adjustment (their productivity at work or in school, their dependence on other persons and institutions), its contribution is greater to the

267

improvement of their inner experiences of emotion, feeling, and satisfaction. Of the levers that can move society forward, psychotherapy is only one. It may not educate so well as schools; it may not produce goods and services so well as management science, it may not cure illnesses so well as medicine; but it reaches a part of life that nothing else touches so well (p. 184).

The discussion and eventual understanding of the role of interpretation and insight in the process of psychotherapy has been badly hampered by our reluctance and inability to give systematic attention to changes in persons' inner lives using those changes as outcome criterion for the investigation of psychotherapy. With the clinical knowledge and empirical results now available, there is no longer any excuse to focus solely upon symptomatic and behavioral changes as outcome criteria for evaluating psychotherapy. Bergin and Lambert (1978) indicated the importance of assessing both changes in behavior *and* in internal states of experience. They said:

> ...measuring experiential phenomena with adequacy and precision remains a crucial task for future research in criterion development (p. 173).

They talk about making a distinction between *dynamic* and *symptomatic* criteria and point out that such a distinction has proved valuable in the interpretation of change data. There is little doubt that future studies of psychotherapy should include measures of inner, *dynamic,* experiential elements. Lewis Mumford (1967) had said it forcefully and poetically:

> To dismiss the most central fact of man's being because it is inner and subjective is to make the hugest subjective falsification possible - one that leaves out the really critical half of man's nature. For without that underlying subjective flux, as experienced in floating imagery, dreams, bodily impulses, formative ideas, projections, and symbols, the world that is open to human experience can be neither described nor rationally understood. When our age learns that lesson, it will have made the first move toward redeeming for

268

human use the mechanized and electrified wasteland that is now being bulldozed, at man's expense and to his permanent loss, for the benefit of the Megamachine (p. 75-76).

Accepting the fact that psychotherapy is now the most potent force we have for modifying the inner life of human beings certainly means any investigation of its effects, its process, and its techniques *must* include an assessment of those inner subjective states. After all, it is those inner subjective states which all human beings know exist and which ultimately are the substances of creative, happy, fulfilling existences or of frustrated, conflicted, unhappy and miserable lives. I submit, interpretation and insight (or if one prefers conceptualizations and re-conceptualizations) will play an important and effective role in both signalling (being a result of) as well as in producing changes in the inner life of human beings.

Interpretation: Discovering New Ways Of Looking At One's World And One's Self

Patients' constructions and/or conceptualizations of their worlds and themselves is always an essential part of the problem which brings them to and that they bring to psychotherapy. We need not be overly specific here, but certainly different theorists construe the condition of psychological problems in different ways and their approach to therapy will vary somewhat in accordance with those constructions. The Freudians and those of a classical analytic tradition view these misconstructions as a matter of repressed, unacceptable id impulses of which the patient is presently unaware. Aspects of the patients' unconscious desires need to be brought into conscious awareness where they become subject to secondary process functioning. Milton Erikson, as interpreted by Havens (1985), suggests that it is the conscious mind with its biases and confusions that interfere with the patient being aware of, knowing and realizing the knowledge, experience, truth, and capacities inherent in the unconscious. Peck (1978) also has come to a similar view of the disordered relationship between the conscious and the unconscious where he writes:

269

The problem is not that human beings have such hostile and sexual feelings, but rather that human beings have a conscious view that is so often unwilling to face these feelings and tolerate the pain of dealing with them, and that is so willing to sweep them under the rug (p. 248).

Rogers (1951) sees psychological distress coming from persons denying and distorting too many significant sensory and visceral experiences which relate to the "self," the "me," the "I." And Raimy (1975) has further developed that proposition with his "misconception hypothesis."

If those ideas or conceptions of a client or patient which are relevant to his psychological problems can be changed in the direction of greater accuracy where his reality is concerned, his maladjustments are likely to be eliminated (p. 7).

Certainly Beck in cognitive therapy (Beck, 1976, Beck et al., 1979), Ellis in rational-emotive therapy (Ellis, 1962; Ellis & Grieger, 1977) and other cognitive-behavior therapists such as Arnkoff (1980), Arnkoff & Glass (1982), Goldfried (1979, 1980), Kendall & Hollon (1979), Landau & Goldfried (1981), Mahoney (1974), and Meichenbaum (1977) all describe the development of behavior in terms of cognitive processes and seek to explain change in psychotherapy as a result of changes in the way patients perceive and construe events. These theorists have for the most part adopted an information-processing perspective. While the ideas of an unconscious and of disordered relations between conscious and unconscious is not a part of their theories, they nevertheless construe behavior change as a matter of overcoming cognitive misconstructions or obtaining new information and a new understanding.

Thus, there is a sense in which all systems of psychotherapy can agree that patients' views and beliefs about their worlds and about themselves are important data for the process of psychotherapy.

Since patients' constructions of their worlds and themselves is always an essential part of problems that bring them to and that they bring to psychotherapy, it follows that part of the task of any psychotherapy is to make most explicit what patients believe about themselves and their worlds. This is not an easy task. Furthermore everyone of us realizes that there are experiences, memories, events which we would just as soon forget and which we certainly have not fully accepted and integrated into our own reality. Thus our knowledge about our world and about ourselves is rather incomplete. Only when we start to systematically and purposefully focus upon who we are, what we believe and how we feel about ourselves and our world, do we more intensely realize the incompleteness and contradictory nature of our conceptualizations. Scarlet O'Hara's famous line, "I'll think about that tommorow," is a statement with which we can all identify - there are some things we just do not want to think about, face, or deal with today.

Part of the process of psychotherapy is designed to create an environment in which it is possible to systematically and purposefully focus upon ourselves and upon what we believe as well as to help us face unpleasant realities or problems. Part of the process of psychotherapy is designed, in Don Juan's terms (Castenada, 1968), to stop the patient's world. By that I mean we disrupt or interrupt patients' ways of looking at themselves or their worlds so that they do not continue in their traditional or patterned ways of "seeing" and "understanding" but rather have an opportunity to discover truths, beliefs, experiences they have ignored. Thus patients have the chance to re-construe their worlds. In Kelly's (1955) terms, stopping the world would be helping patients see the cognitive ruts in which they continue to rattle around as well as seeing possibilities for reconceptualizing their life's data.

One of the techniques for helping patients "stop their worlds" and for increasing the possibilities of them discovering new ways of looking at themselves and their worlds is interpretation. And as all psychotherapists know, patients do not want their worlds stopped. Like all of us, they "want to eat their cake and have it too." So they want relief from their symptoms, distress, and unhappiness without having to give up anything or change anything or endure any more pain or discomfort. Thus, stopping the world is a very difficult task that takes a great deal of skill, sensitivity, and knowledge. It requires of the patient an activity of self-inquiry that leads to new discoveries, specific explications, greater understanding and a more full sense of being understood. It requires of the therapist a keen sensitivity and ability to empathize with the patient, an openness to his or her own intuitive and unconscious processes as well as a willingness to be vulnerable by living a life of openness and self-confrontation, and accepting a commitment to discovery and to understanding.

At this point it might seem that interpretation as one aspect of the process of self-discovery is a rather straight forward cognitive, rational, intellectual task much like learning a new subject, foreign language, or mathematical equation. After all, if much of patients' problems are disordered self and world views, then teaching them new ways of looking at themselves and their worlds is the answer. While that statement may be true, it is not accurate. In the first place, no psychotherapist has "answers" for other persons if by answers we mean knowing what those persons should believe about themselves and their worlds. Rather psychotherapists are much more like experienced archeologists who can teach patients (apprentice archeologists) how to look for clues and signs of worthwhile digs and how to go about the process of digging and excavating and "reading-the-signs" that are discovered in the process of doing archeological work. The experienced archeologist will have a great deal of knowledge that helps make fairly accurate guesses about what may or may not be found in any particular dig. But only when one is involved in the process of that dig and systematically working the material discovered does even the experienced archeologist come to an understanding of what has been discovered.

In the second place, no psychotherapist has anywhere near the complete knowledge of the patient that the patient alone possesses. In this sense, the psychotherapist is truly an apprentice archeologist working with a person (the patient) who has complete knowledge of the terrain which is to be investigated. It is only that this other person (the patient) does not know that they already know. So it is not a matter of teaching them something new as much as it is a matter of assisting them in self-discovery. As Paul (1978) so appropriately put it:

> When we offer an interpretation, we seek to share with
> our patient a discovery, not teach him a lesson (p. 16).

And what it is, of course, that we are attempting to discover is the truth about the patient's reality. It is the truth about the patient's present life, past history, inner emotional desires, hopes, fears, joys and shames as well as the truth about the patient's relationship with the therapist which is the task of psychotherapy and thus the content of our interpretations. And, even as it is for the archeologists, these discoveries are not just intellectual, rational understandings. For I presume that archeologists discovering artifacts have considerable emotion attendant to those discoveries - perhaps a disconcerting bafflement, confusion over what is found, what it means, what it is. Maybe they feel great excitement about what is uncovered and an impatience to do even more excavating with a hope and somewhat contained joy about what may be fully revealed.

In psychotherapy, where the subject matter for investigation is our own personal existence, the clues and discoveries we make along the way and which are at times marked by interpretations are filled with and surrounded by a great deal of emotion and feeling. I think the simile of an archeologist breaks down at this point. For in my experience, self-discovery and the final integration of that discovery into self-understanding does not occur without a considerable amount of affect attendant to the process. There are reasons why all of us have distorted and misconstrued our worlds. It does not just happen capriciously. And the good reasons for those distortions include psychic survival and all the strong emotions involved in protecting our own existence. In addition, there seems to be a natural tendency to cling to old ways of perceiving and behaving - a natural resistance to change. So along with any desire and excitement for self-exploration, there is always an additional desire or force working to prevent self-discoveries. Interpretation may be helpful both in enhancing the discoveries of self-exploration as well as in pointing out those desires, forces, reasons for resisting self-understanding.

All of this is to say that our investigations into and integrated understandings of ourselves is an activity which is much more complicated and involves a great many more intense affects than investigations into and learnings of all other subjects. It is both the personal and integrated requirements of self-understanding that make it so different from learnings about and understandings of other subjects. Hammer (1972) found a way to say all of this rather succinctly:

> What does self-understanding or self-integration really mean then? It should be obvious that it does not refer only to an intellectual comprehension. Rather it refers to a state of realization in which one makes real or

273

brings into concrete existence formerly rejected aspects
of self. It is knowing by becoming one with, as the word
"knowing" was used in the scriptures to mean having
intercourse with. One must have a true intercourse with
the rejected aspects of self, by becoming one with it, in
order to really hear, know or understand himself. He
must be in immediate and direct contact with himself.
This is the essence of integration which produces
liberation from conflict (p. 9).

Interpretation is one of the tools which can be used in the process
of psychotherapy to aid in the task of exploration and discovery. It is
mostly a verbal interaction, dependent upon the therapist's skill,
knowledge, ability to empathize and to carefully understand another
human being. It is, in the context of a "therapeutic interpersonal
relationship" and transference constellation, aimed at helping
patients become aware of some aspects of their own psychological
existences. But, of course, it is useless for the therapist to have made
a discovery and then pointed it out to the patient by interpretation if
the patient is unable to "see" or understand the discovery. So no
discoveries in psychotherapy are really valid until the patient makes
the discovery. For this reason, interpretations are made only when
there is some reason to believe the patient is ready or able to hear it.
And for this reason, interpretations are only valid when and if
patients confirm their validity.

When interpretations are valid, in the above sense of being
understood and confirmed by the patient, then we say that an insight
has occurred. Much as serious students of history find that their
studies give them a new perspective for viewing events of the world,
or serious students of art and music find expanded and more
meaningful and fulfilling ways for hearing music or viewing art; so
serious students of self-discovery (patients) find their insights can
take them into new, different, and markedly expanded worlds. And
in addition, the process of psychotherapy also teaches patients ways
of continuing self-discovery, of remaining open to experiences and
feelings and thus of continuing lifelong pursuits of inner truth. Thus,
psychotherapy is not simply a method for treating psychological
disorders and maladjustments, but part of a total educational
enterprise where one's own psychological life is the subject matter.

Interpretation: Primarily Not A Logical, Rational Event

The last section, which dealt with the importance of discovering truths about oneself and integrating them into a re-constructed view, tends to portray interpretation as a rather straight-forward cognitive or intellectual task - one that relies upon the rules of logic and rationality. In my experience the more logical, rational or intellectual the interpretation the more likely it is to miss-the-mark. Logic and rationality do not seem particularly helpful when we are seeking truths of the heart, the imagination, the passions, the sensations, the mind and the soul. Reason does not deal with the intensity of these elements of existence and thus can only give us a distorted picture of them. Reason and logic seem to know little or nothing about feelings.

Our affect is inseparably tied to our memory and indicates the quality of the experience. Feelings have strong powers in their own rights and at times will overwhelm memory, distort what we call reality, and block any further learning. If our feelings or intense beliefs are not included in psychotherapy, there can be no effective change. It is not so much what we think intellectually that results in psychological problems but what we believe affectively. The affect will hold onto the early distortions and denials no matter how adept we become at intellectually and rationally "kidding ourselves."

Rationality addresses only our rational mind plus all our society's teachings about what is related to what. But interpretation needs to include the heart, the imagination, the affections and passions - the unconscious mind. Keats poetically tells us how important sensations are instead of thoughts:

> I am certain of nothing but of the holiness of the Heart's affections and the truth of Imagination - What the imagination seizes as Beauty must be truth - whether it existed before or not - for I have the same Idea of all our Passions as of Love they are all in their sublime, creative of essential Beauty.... I am the more zealous in this affair, because I have never yet been able to perceive how any thing can be known for truth by consequitive reasoning....O for a Life of Sensations rather than of Thoughts! (Abrams, [1979] p. 864).

275

Interpretation in psychotherapy cannot be limited just to logic and rationality or to the life of thoughts. It must also include that which is vitally necessary for giving the lives of human beings' meaning and intensity. Without such inclusiveness, how shall we ever get to accurate truths about ourselves? The artifical intelligence of the computer, the biogenetic engineering of the genetists, and the chemical-electrical impulse analyses of the neuroscientists can only lead to limited- perspective facts devoid of the Heart's truths. This is not to say they aren't important, powerful, and useful findings. It is only to say they lead us further and further from the Heart's truths.

Some preliminary empirical evidence is now available indicating the importance of feelings and personal events in the process of psychotherapy and the importance of avoiding rigidly logical, rational, intellectual discourses. Orlinsky and Howard's (1978) review of studies relating process to outcome suggests that patients who deal with feelings and with personal events are more successful with psychotherapy than patients who focus "objectively" and more generally on external or non-personal events. Those patients who are less integrated, logical, rational, relevant and coherent in their communications tend to improve more than patients who evidence more intellectual self-control. In discussing those studies the authors propose the term *Dramatic Interpretation* and with it suggest that:

> ...therapists are better advised to pursue the logic of feeling than the logic of fact (p. 307).

Summarizing the process-outcome research on therapy as *Dramatic Interpretation* they say:

> ...successful cases are likely to be those in which the patients talk about themselves and their personal lives in a concrete, responsive, and not too "rational" way; in which the therapists direct their comments to their clients' immediate inner experiences, feelings, and operations, in a genuine or self-congruent fashion; and in which a high degree of shared meanings and mutual attunement of symbolic perspectives is attained in the relationship (p. 308).

276

It is the "shared meanings and mutual attunement of symbolic perspectives" which leads to the therapist's deep understanding of the patient and which then permits interpretations of "immediate inner experiences, feelings, and operations." Orlinsky and Howard (1978) call *Dramatic Interpretation* the "soul" of a relationship, and so it is.

Interpretations in the context of the process of psychotherapy are not common, ubiquitous occurrences. Much more common when examining the transcripts of therapy sessions are questions and investigations - askings and wonderings and in that fashion letting the patient produce the data. It is also not uncommon that psychotherapists are led to various intellectual conclusions in psychotherapy - intellectual conclusions which may solve some mysteries but do not attain the "truth." Interpretations in the process of psychotherapy are relatively rare and include a great deal more than an intellectual, logical, or rational understanding of the material and of the patient's life. Interpretations which are an understanding of the patient's soul's truth include a direct empathic understanding and/or identification with the patient's unconscious processes and not just with his or her more contrived conscious mental states. This kind of understanding of the other person's soul does not occur for long periods of time but comes about in inspirational brief moments - in brief moments when the patient's and the therapist's souls are meeting. It is a product of what Kris (1952) called "regression in the service of the ego." The psychotherapist in listening to the patient must use not only the intellect but also feelings and in addition be able to abandon reason and regress to preverbal and prerational levels of existence where reason does not exist but truth lives. The psychotherapist's ego must not prohibit exploratory regressions into the unconscious and into the connections between the patient's and therapist's unconscious.

Such interpretation is also a product of what Schachtel (1959) called the *allocentric attitude*:

> ...this attitude is one of profound interest in the object, and complete openness and receptivity toward it, a full turning toward the object which makes possible the direct encounter with it and not merely a quick registration of its familiar features according to ready labels....the interest concerns the whole object, not

merely a partial aspect of it; and the perceiver turns toward the object with his entire being, his whole personality, i.e. fully, not just with part of himself....The object, the world, reveals itself to the man only according to the degree and quality of the interest he takes in it (p. 151).

Only the sincerely interested and spontaneous mind will hold unconscious intercourse with the beauty that is truth and understanding and will go beyond an intellectual understanding and reach into the depths of the soul where there is truth uncontaminated by conscious thought. The psychotherapist in making an interpretation can transcend the limits imposed by personal identity, ego, the faculties of reasoning, and the fears associated with being intuitive and spontaneous. The understanding must go far beyond where reason and rationality have the capacity to go for it must be filled not only with thoughts but also with affections as well. In psychotherapy, the affective states provide much more reliable information than do the intellectual states. And the psychotherapist must be able to read, feel, and comprehend in much more than an intellectual way those affective states. As Elvin Semrad (Rako and Mazer, 1983) is reported to have said to his students:

When you talk about what's important, the patient will always tear (p. 140).

and:

Once he showed his tears, that was enough for me. I respect the autonomic nervous system to show feelings like I respect few other things (p. 140).

The affective states are frequently undisturbed by verbal and conscious functionings and work on the mind as symbols which while not always explicit are fully felt and understood. Madison Avenue advertising firms seem quite aware of this phenomenon for they produce highly symbolic and creative advertising copy for magazines and the TV media. I think the mind rigidly adhering to logic and rationality can never find truth, only facts. True knowledge is not something that can be forced or planned but rather is something that

278

given the right circumstances comes unforced, uncontrollably. Part of any psychotherapist's task is to know how to help create the conditions in self, patient, and therapeutic environment which will be conducive to discoveries of truth and not just of facts. So many of the truths with which we deal in psychotherapy and which are made evident through the element of interpretation are foreign and alien to logic, rationality, and intellectual understanding. They are in the realm of affections and require the logic of feelings and of the unconscious.

French and Fromm (1964) have called the language of the unconscious an *evocative language*. By that they mean that while the patient cannot describe or explain what is going on in his or her unconscious, and while language cannot express with vividness and accuracy the dreams, free associations and other irrational products of the mind; the patient's words and images are able to evoke in the empathic therapist a sense of what is going on. deRacker (1961) has developed the thesis that the patient will unconsciously place in the therapist those meanings that need to be interpreted back. Langs (1981) has given us a succinct summary of deRacker's position:

> The patient will place into the analyst, in a scattered and disguised form requiring only conscious integration, everything the analyst needs to formulate his intervention (p. 251).

Now before continuing any further with what some may start to think is nothing more than a mythical, mystical mumbo-jumbo of words unnecessarily complicating the already complicated process of psychotherapy and invoking concepts and ideas which have no business being in the lexion of psychology; we might well consider an example of interpretation. Peck's (1978) case of Theodore indicates how an important, effective, very short and one might say "little" interpretation came out of the therapist in the context of a very emotional and moving relationship between therapist and patient and as a result of a juxtaposition of logic, rationality, empathy, and an emotional, tension ridden, hopeful stance on the therapist's part.

Theodore was a thirty year old man who for a period of seven years before beginning therapy led a hermit's existence. His stated problem was an inability to make even minor decisions or to get enthusiastic about anything. His history suggested a rather ordinary

279

childhood in a stable well-to-do home, parents who cared for him, good school grades. A week before he entered college he was rejected by a woman with whom he had a passionate love affair. His freshman year of college he was drunk a good deal of the time, he eventually had several other unsuccessful and halfhearted love affairs and in the middle of his junior year at college a close friend of his was killed in an automobile accident. He stopped drinking that year and his problem making decisions became worse and eventually prevented him from selecting a topic on which to write a senior thesis for his degree. From that time on he really did nothing and at the age of twenty-three went to live in a small cabin in the woods with no one close by and few friends. For the three years prior to entering therapy, he had not dated.

Theodore felt his problems were basically related to his sexuality and for six months therapy focused upon those issues. While such work was unproductive, it did reveal important facets to this man's psychological condition. He had a total lack of enthusiasm, a rather global snobbishness, and an enormous penchant for secrecy. It was in the sixth month of therapy that the first break in his strong defensive structure occurred and he revealed that he had shifted from being a rather religious person quite active in the church to never again going to church after the first unsuccessful love affair. Futhermore, he was enthusiastic in showing his irritation and resistance to discussing and considering this event and rather insistent that the change was rationally understood as coming of age in a time when religion wasn't fashionable anymore.

A month later comes the interpretation which was so important. In that session the patient points out that the last time he was enthusiastic about anything was ten years ago in his junior year of college and it was over a paper he was writing for a course in modern British poetry having to do with one of Gerard Manley Hopkins' poems. His therapist leaves the office during this session and goes to his library to get a volume of British poetry returning to read the poem on which his patient's paper had centered. The next events in this session must be told in Peck's (1981) own words:

> Tears came to my eyes. "It is, itself, a poem about enthusiasm," I said.
> "Yes,"
> "It's also a very religious poem."

"Yes."

"You wrote the paper on it at the end of the fall semester. That would have been January?"

"Yes."

"If I calculate correctly, it was in the next month, February, that your friend Hank died."

"Yes."

I could feel an incredible tension growing. I was not sure what was the right thing to do. Hoping, I ploughed ahead.

"So you were rejected by your first real girl friend at seventeen and you gave up your enthusiasm for the church. Three years later your best friend died and you gave up your enthusiasm for everything."

"I didn't give it up, it was taken from me." Ted was almost shouting now, more emotional than I had ever seen him.

"God rejected you so you rejected God."

"Well, why shouldn't I?" he demanded. "It's a shitty world. It's always been a shitty world."

"I thought your childhood was quite happy."

"No, that was shitty too." (p. 215).

It is worth belaboring this example. In the first place, the therapist leaves his office during a therapy session to go to another room (his library) and get a book. This is generally not common behavior for any therapist, and we can assume he felt some "important" need at that time to examine, be closer to, understand more fully the last moment his patient felt some enthusiasm. Then when the therapist reads the poem, tears come to his eyes. He does not tell us why and we need not speculate. It is enough to know he was truly moved at some rather deep level of his being; and I submit those feelings were a product of himself, the poem, and his knowledge and understanding of, as well as his feelings for his patient. His next statements identify two overarching and predominant elements in this patient's frame-of-reference, i.e. enthusiasm and religion. The patient has consciously verbalized his lack of enthusiasm and lack of interest in religious matters. Nevertheless, he (via his therapist's actions) introduces into the therapy session a poem representing the opposite of his stated and lived beliefs. Then a fact, a product of logic and rationality, is introduced by the therapist, i.e. the patient's work on this poem predated by a short period of time his close friend's death.

It is then that Peck's words indicate so clearly that the interpretation to come is not a product of clear, objective, logic and rationality. He reports an incredible tension, a confusion as to what was the right thing to do and hoping says:

> So you were rejected by your first real girl friend at seventeen and you gave up your enthusiasm for the church. Three years later your best friend died and you gave up your enthusiasm for everything (p. 215).

There certainly is a sense in which this is an interpretation - the therapist is indicating a temporal connection between two important psychological events in the patient's life and his major symptom of lack of enthusiasm. Furthermore, it is important to note that this "interpretation" was not made with words that could indicate the therapist was insisting upon its accuracy, relevance or importance. Such words as "Don't you see that...," or "It is obvious that there is a tie between...," or "Your problem with lack of enthusiasm is related to..." would indicate such insistance. We don't know the therapist's demeanor and tone of voice when these words were said, but they could almost be said tentatively, wonderingly but not insistently. We can assume, from Peck's words, that they were not said with firm conviction as he was not sure what was the right thing to do. It is almost as though the therapist is thinking-feeling-struggling along with the patient to "know" the truth embedded in this material and this life-of-the-moment between these two people. And the therapist is free enough of those defenses which the patient maintains to avoid "seeing" the relevance of this material, as well as free enough of convention and the dictates of the conscious mind, to risk tension and confusion and say what comes to him.

The patient's response to this "interpretation," or I think more accurately this tentative hypothesis about the relationships between lack of enthusiasm and two important losses, indicates its cogency and the "meeting of two souls." The patient says, almost shouting and emotionally, "I didn't give it up, it was taken from me." What an open, honest, fully felt and believed cornerstone in this man's psychological existence. He doesn't argue the accuracy of the therapist's hypothesis or otherwise defensively manuever to avoid its implications. He seems to have been truly touched, perhaps hurt and a bit angry, and forcefully corrects a very important aspect of the therapist's hypothesis. In my experience, we therapists generally only have hypotheses; and the patients' interpretations always take precedence over those hypotheses. For, it is only they who harbor the full truth about themselves. I submit it is a completely different "world" if you feel that you gave something up instead of feeling it was taken from you. This patient, with great feeling insists on being heard - it was taken from him!

The therapist's reponse at this point is then an interpretation. He said, "God rejected you so you rejected God." Now, how in the world can one make any logical, rational sense out of such an interpretation. In the first place, this patient has told us he doesn't even believe in God and has nothing to do with religion. In the second place, where in the psychological literature is there any indication that therapists should be invoking the concept of God into their therapuetic considerations? There is a position from which one could say this is just all too mystical and shaman-like to be part of any psychotherapeutic consideration. But that position has to deny the importance of irrational or illogical minds or of the unconscious or the heart's truths.

The patient's response to this interpretation indicates its accuracy, its importance, and its ruling role in his life. "Well, why shouldn't I?" he says in a demanding manner. There is no arguing the point, he accepts it as the "truth" it is for him and goes on to tell us why he rejected God. I submit that in this vignette we have an example of what Orlinsky and Howard (1978) meant when they wrote about patient and therapist having "...a high degree of shared meanings and mutual attunement of symbolic perspectives" (p. 308). And in this example, that shared meaning and mutual attunement comes about even though the patient's cognitive processes, overt vocalizations, and life-style deny the relevance of the symbolic perspective of God. Furthermore, the therapist's understanding of this patient surpassed any logical, rational process and included a tie, commitment, relationship, and affection which helped allow the *Dramatic Interpretation* or the event of souls meeting. We have in this vignette an example of what French and Fromm (1964) called *evocative language.* The patient did not in words or by some logical process lead us to the point of understanding his belief that God took his enthusiasm from him. But he certainly *evoked* from his therapist a statement or interpretation of that belief. As deRacker (1961) has theorized, it is as though the patient unconsciously placed in the therapist those meanings which needed to be interpreted back. The patient's response to this interpretation suggests his therapist did "understand" the language of the patient's unconscious. This interpretation is a "knowing" beyond a mental reporting of life experiences or a methodical juxtaposition of consciously reported events in terms of some relatively rigidly fixed theoretical position. The therapist's first "interpretation" dealing with the relationship between important losses and lack of enthusiasm is certainly one form of knowing and does have elements of a mental juxtaposition of life events consistent with the theoretical orientation of early experiences affecting later behaviors. But the second interpretation containing only seven words carries a meaning far beyond its few words and deep into the soul of this patient to a *knowing* which is at one and the same time extraordinarily simple and complex. It is the kind of interpretation that leads to the *knowing* of which Kahn (1969) has written and which was quoted at the beginning of this chapter:

> Interpretation is that act of verbal and affective intervention, contribution, and evaluation by the analyst which crystallizes two new experiences for the patient: (a) recognition of his *being*, and (b) the *knowing* of his *experiencing* (p. 384).

Now saying that interpretation includes more than a logical rational presentation of material and needs to reach unconscious, symbolic, meaningful truths of the soul can still sound too much as though it were something mystical or intuitive. Few would hold the position that interpretation is a rigorous scientific procedure. It certainly does not have the kinds of rigorous scientific underpinnings that many procedures in medicine and surgery have for treating different physical diseases and for surgical invasion of body organs. But the anatomy and cells of our bodies have relatively fixed limits and within those limits one person's kidney or liver, or heart or leg have some great similarities to any other person's kidney, liver, heart or leg. However, the billions of cells in the brain and the uniqueness of each individual's psyche - its experiences and ways of viewing the world - make it extremely difficult for us to fix limits or write nomothetic prescriptions which with some slight alteration might be applied to all psyches. As Erickson (1980) has pointed out:

> The variability of subjects, the individuality of their general and immediate needs, their differences in time and situation requirements, the uniqueness of their personalities and capabilities, together with the demands made by the projected work, render impossible any absolutely rigid procedure (p. 144).

Since we lack easily definable terms and any rigorous theoretical system for conceptualizing the procedures of interpretation, recourse has been taken to calling it an intuititive art. There is a sense in which that term is appropriate for it refers to a direct perception of truth independent of any reasoning process. However the term can also be used in a pejorative fashion assuming that only that which is arrived at by a reasoning process is valid. Furthermore, the term frequently serves to stop any further inquiry into how one may obtain intuitions. By using the term, we think we have explained something and think we have agreed that what it is we have explained is not a proper subject matter for any further rigorous or scientific investigation. For these reasons, I do not like to use the term "intuititive art" for explaining or trying to understand the procedure of interpretation in the process of psychotherapy. I think we can go much further in understanding the procedure of interpretation, can better explicate how therapists may help themselves obtain insights into patients' truths, and can start to identify ways in which therapists can help patients show and state their soul's knowledge.

Part of understanding the way in which therapists come to their interpretations is to be found in carefully examining how and to what therapists listen. This is the kind of data that is extremely difficult to obtain since listening occurs silently within the therapist. Furthermore, if we asked the therapist to indicate to what he is listening that would so modify the silent listening process as to effectively negate it. Thus it is only retrospective data we obtain *and* furthermore only that retrospective data available to therapists' awareness or conscious minds. That knowledge available to therapists' unconscious is more likely to be expressed in phrases that begin with "I have a hunch that...," or "I can't help feeling that...," or

"It just seems to me that...."

But, we can start to identify how therapists actively listen. It is not just to the patients' words that therapists are attending. It is to the tone and particular choice of patients' words in the context of their behaviors, demeanors, and affects that therapists listen. It is the sequence and pattern of the material as well as the temporal juxtaposition of topics and the pauses, "slips-and-errors," and omissions in the material to which therapists listen . And it is not just to what patients are doing or saying or not saying that therapists listen. They also listen to their own associations and feelings concomitant with all the other material they are hearing-seeing-feeling. In this task of carefully listening, seeing, feeling therapists are not forcing the material into any logical or rational framework but are open to those symbols, meanings, and understandings that emerge as a result of such active listening. They are open to the camouflage language that is used in attempts to hide the real meaning of what is being said. And when, in this process of active listening, it becomes clearer to the therapist what the patient is saying; some additional information may be asked for or some pertinent question may be raised. This active listening and questioning may well continue until there emerges an understanding which might be tentatively shared with the patient. Eventually by such active listening and questioning and by the willingness to remain unjudgmentally open to all the cues from patient and from self and to refrain from any rigid or predetermined conceptual arrangement of the material presented, the therapist may arrive at an important interpretation - generally just ahead of the point at which the patient arrives at a similar conclusion. As Chessick (1983) has written it:

> If the therapist does not have the capacity to listen with evenly suspended attention or to empathize with the patient - or, in more technical terms, to regress in the service of the ego and oscillate back and forth between such a regression and the secondary-process capacities of putting the information received in this regression into terminology that can then be expressed to the patient - the therapist will fail (p. 204).

Now there is no great mystery to this. It is just that it is much more complex and intricate in the psychotherapeutic framework than

286

it is in our everyday interactions with one another. But, all of us have experienced someone saying to us, "Oh we must get together some time," when we know full well they really don't want to be bothered and have no intention of getting together with us. In such situations we rarely confront the issue by asking, "When?" Instead we are more likely to reply, "Yes, we'll have to," and go our way knowing full well neither one of us has any intention of acting upon the stated but every intention of acting upon the unstated desire. Or most of us have met people who are so obsequious that it makes us uncomfortable, until it dawns upon us that their manner is a camouflage to hide their feelings of being superior to us. In our everyday interactions we are able to identify many of the rationalizations that occur. Without being consciously aware of it, we take into account not only the others' words but also their actions and behaviors related to those words as well as our own associations and feelings generated by those words. But we generally don't purposefully or intently and consciously attend to the numerous cues of which we are aware at any one moment in interacting with others. Without consciously knowing how, we nevertheless sift through all that material to arrive at some conclusion about other people and/or our relationship with them. And also, in everyday interactions we don't purposefully set-aside our own perceptions, biases, and frames-of-reference nor do we attempt to unjudgmentally or with an "evenly suspended attention" listen to others. We are nevertheless involved in the process of interpreting others meanings and we do so rather automatically without conscious awareness of all the varied cues to which we may well be attending in forming our "interpretation."

So I am very reluctant to dismiss interpretation, which is primarily *not* a rational logical event, to the realm of mysticism or intuition. Rather, it seems to me we need to more carefully observe and attend to those skills and abilities which we use in our attempts to understand the language of the unconscious as well as the varied ways in which we human beings communicate with one another. Our interpersonal communications occur on a number of different levels and with a number of different "languages" - each one of which may have its own culture, spirit, and unique meaning. When souls meet they say something to one another. We are capable of understanding that which is said if we will only take the time, energy, and consideration necessary to "listen" to what is being said.

287

Interpretation: The Beginning Of A Process Not The End.

I have pointed out that interpretation and insight will not "solve" everything - they are not the "cure" - and any psychotherapists who thinks they are will be sorely disappointed. Historically theoretical propositions in the psychodynamic schools of psychotherapy strongly emphasized the curative role of interpretation. However, clinical experience has indicated it as only one step in the process of understanding truths about oneself and integrating those truths into a re-organized perspective of one's world. Even with this knowledge, it is not infrequent that beginning psychotherapists make the error of over-interpreting. They may have some interpretation for almost every slip of the tongue, dream, or resistance the patient offers. It is not uncommon for beginning psychotherapists to be anxious about "curing" patients instead of understanding them. With the historical orientation that interpretation is related to cure and with patients' common expectation that the doctor will tell them what is wrong, it is not surprising that beginning psychotherapists feel a need to make many interpretations. By so doing, they hope to impress or assure their patients and themselves that they know what is going on in the psychotherapy. Unfortunately, making lots of interpretations, most of which the patient probably cannot understand and undoubtedly a goodly number of which are only theoretical and intellectual hypotheses, will not do much to convince the patient that the psychotherapist really does understand what is going on.

Instead of "curing" patients, psychotherapists are better advised to be concerned about understanding patients in great detail, with much precision, and with an emotional intensity that helps assure they are connected with this other human being in an unselfishly equal task of inner exploration. Then the therapist may tell the patient what is understood with the knowledge that such understanding is still far from complete and that at some level of existence the patient knows the complete truth. Furthermore, understanding in detail, with precision, and with emotional intensity generally means that you see and feel in a palpable way an active connection between the patient's past experiences, present life situation, and existing transference responses. The affect, memory, and behavior from these three artificial divisions of the patient's existence are relatively congruent and obviously interrelated. It is as

288

though the data for the interpretation is overwhelming and you have a rather clear understanding of what is going on at that moment in the patient as well as indications the patient is ready to receive the interpretation. The fact that the issue for interpretation is not only evident in the patient's past and present life but is also existent and alive in the "therapeutic interpersonal relationship" helps both therapist and patient feel and know its importance. Thus, interpretations need not be elaborate but rather realistic and fairly accurate. They are generally given in clear, simple language and in a matter-of-fact, almost casual, friendly and pleasant manner. It is not with our words or the force of authority that the interpretation leads to insight. It is with simplicity, accuracy, and appropriateness that the interpretation can precipitate the insight into truths the patient already knows but hasn't verbalized.

While interpretation is important it is not the end-all or be-all of psychotherapy, nor is insight. At the same time, both interpretation and insight are necessary and unavoidable aspects of the process of psychotherapy. They must exist at some level or a therapeutic change does not occur. Even classical behavior modification procedures which may pay no attention to the variables of interpretation and insight will nevertheless modify patients' thinking about themselves and thus require patients to re-organize those new ideas into their self-concepts. There is a sense in which that is all interpretation and insight does anyway - provides us new perspectives on old realities - new ways of seeing and being we never thought could exist for ourselves.

Far from being the end-all and be-all of psychotherapy, interpretation and insight are really only marks of progress or change in the psychotherapeutic process. They mark the end of approaching, skirting, avoiding, or trying to figure out the truth or some element of the truth embedded in our thinking-feeling-experiencing. They mark the beginning of a new perspective, a new way of seeing something, an insight if you will. Thus, they mark the beginning of a time when we can start to experience living some of that new perspective which then allows us to start to understand how many and in what ways our old conscious conceptualizations affected our present existence. In this sense, interpretation and insight are the end of approaching some truths and the beginning of working them. Because of this, interpretations and ensuing insights can be experienced by the patient as a death-dying-losing (the end of a way of seeing and being that has gone on so long) as well as being experienced with some excitement, fear and renewed energy for new things - for beginning to incorporate a new way of seeing and being into our existence. In conceptualizing interpretation as both an ending and a beginning, I do not mean to imply that one observes any dramatic marked or rapid change. While I suppose that can happen, more commonly noted are small accomodations indicating the end of one thing and the beginning of another. We human beings do not seem to like too much change all at once. So when something ends, we may well be reluctant to see it go. And when something new begins, it generally grows in small, tentative, and fragile forms at first.

As an end and a beginning, an Alpha and Omega, the interpretation must be made at a time when both participants in the therapeutic endeavor (patient *and* therapist) are prepared to see, accept, and handle the resultant insights. That is, both participants must be ready to accept that ending and the new beginning. Patients have to feel sufficient trust in, acceptance and support from the therapist and have sufficient resources and inner strength in order to be able to "see" that which has governed and directed their life for so long and share that "seeing" with another human being. And the therapist has to be willing to accept the additional commitment to the patient that the new beginning may entail. Far from being an easy, simple, much-to-be-desired event; interpretations and resultant insights can mean further work and struggle and even closer connections and emotional involvements between patient and therapist.

It is not that interpretations are necessarily so accurate as to markedly reconceptualize the patient's world. They are not great earth shaking single pronouncements. Rather they generally are quite incomplete but hopefully accurate enough and sufficiently appropriate to lead to a reconsideration of some of the material, ideas, and emotions the patient is reporting. In combination with alliance and the "therapeutic interpersonal relationship" they help patients to consider something they may not have consciously seen before or may have thought too dangerous or fearful or ridiculous to verbalize. There is a sense in which the interpretation gives the patient permission to consider other thoughts, ideas, experiences, feelings which are related to the material under interpretation and which then lead to ever expanding and probably more precise interpretations. If the interpretation is a sufficient approximation of the truth being psychologically displayed by the patient's life and therapy material at the time and is made when the patient can accept it, then the patient will "work" that approximation so that both patient and therapist can add to and embellish it thereby enhancing its authenticity and cogency and making it even more specific to the truths being sought.

At any rate, therapists can be sure that patients will respond to their interventions and not only to those interventions of interpretation. It is incumbent upon therapists to carefully attend to the nature and form of the patient's response to interventions in order to know what psychological forces are currently active in the patient and what additional interpretations or interventions are appropriate and necessary. And it is not just the immediate reactions that are important, but also the nature of the material that becomes part of the therapy after that intervention - sometimes becomes part of the therapy for a number of sessions. Malan's (1976) term *duration ratio*, which refers to coincidence in time between improvements in disturbance of long duration on the one hand and therapy of brief duration on the other, may be appropriate here. As already indicated, I think it is unrealistic to expect that an interpretation would make an immediate and marked change in the patient. For the most part interpretations do not lead to easy or simple insights like those experienced when we suddenly realize the principles involved in the development of some algebraic equation. We may have been struggling for a while to understand the development of the binomial expansion and then suddenly have an "ah, ha!" experience where things fall into place and we rapidly gain the perspective or understanding necessary to derive that equation and even write it in a number of different ways. But that is a very simple task and usually not directly and intimately related to our personal integrity. Much more complex and of a much more personal nature is our understanding, belief about, and view of ourselves and our world. Understanding how that has come about and how it needs to be re-organized is an extremely complex proposition which probably won't fit the neat categories and fixed laws of mathematics and the physical sciences. We must feel, dream, think about, examine, and work the insights obtained by the process of psychotherapy. It takes time, effort, and energy to examine, modify, and change our lives. Thus, it is not surprising that there

291

would be a *duration ratio* between the time we gained some insight and had started upon the task of considering important elements of our existence and the appearance of changes as a result of that work. And furthermore, the working-out of the full meaning and importance of the insight is a process of which we are generally not fully aware.

An example of this *duration ratio* is found in the case of a nineteen year old man who was discussed in Chapter 3. He came to therapy because he felt he had avoided facing some of his feelings about interpersonal relationships by escaping into binge eating and sex. He was a very bright, handsome, accomplished young man who was fun-loving and had many friends. He had noticed that whenever relationships got serious, he lost interest in them. His history was remarkable in that he never knew his father - a man who was divorced from his mother when the patient was nine months old and with whom this patient never had any contact.

Most remarkable to me was that this man seemed to see no relationship at all between this history of complete lack of relationship with father and his present problems. He simply had no feelings about or for his father at all and had not given the situation much, if any, thought. It was also obvious he had avoided those feelings for years and that the first task would be to see if we could form a therapeutic alliance. While part of his whole attitude, demeanor, and life-style invited a friendly, considerate, and rapid involvement in a relationship with me, the lack of any overt signs of distress, confusion, and unhappiness over his life's experiences told me that neither he nor I really knew what was going on at the moment. So I must wait and let the therapy data accumulate.

In the second session he talks about fearing he is a fraud who wears many masks and feels many demands to "clean up his life." He is aware of feeling clumsy and awkward and breaking things. Then he goes to an early memory of a bird he had as a child, it was very important to him and gave him joy. However, one day it was flying around the bathroom as he was washing-up. He chased it out of the room and slammed the door shut to prevent its re-entry. The bird was caught between the door and the door jam and killed. He relates this incident with little or no affect other than a demeanor which indicates great interest in my reaction and an expectation that I should be horrified. I guess I passed his test, for then he said, "I hurt something I love." That leads to a number of examples of things he has loved that have fallen and broken and then to remembering that he was really angry with the bird and wanted it gone. At the end of the session, he points out that he is really afraid to see himself and he fails to show for the next appointment.

He starts the fourth session showing some anger for a friend by whom he feels "raped" and who he feels is usurping his place and "penetrating" his past. He feels this friend could ruin his relationship with others important and close to to him. I heard this as a statement about our relationship in therapy, his dislike of me penetrating into his past and his fears about how that would modify his relationships with others important to him. Furthermore, it was for me a sign both of the developing therapeutic alliance and of transference. I felt, however, it much too soon to make any interpretation - the "fox" was certainly not tamed and was particularly skittish about close relationships. But I could point out that he seemed particularly concerned about his friend ruining his relationship with the older male teacher. He responds to this by talking about his tendency to put older male figures on pedestals and fears questions from them about his father. He goes on to explain that he has a letter from a lawyer assigning his father's social security and veteran's administration benefits to him and that is all he has related to his father. He points out that he constantly keeps that letter with him. What more must this man do to tell me how very important his father or the idea of having a father and the years of ignoring the reality of his existence and lack of relationship are to him!

In the fifth session, he brings the letter from the attorney in for me to see. He talks about a sexual attraction to a new person and the fact he doesn't like to show he's interested. He's sure people he likes and is attracted to really won't accept him. He says he can't look them in the eye as he fears they really will be sick of him. And then he talks about the fact that he "fucks-up all his relationships." It is then the first interpretation is made. I say to him, "Better to do that than fall-in-love and need someone and have them leave you." I expected that these words would speak to him not only about his present and past relationships with others but also would have some meaning in terms of his lack of relationship with father (where he at a deep level felt some responsibility for it) as well as be directly related to the emerging transference and therapeutic relationship with me. His immediate response to this interpretation indicates he

293

heard it and he quietly and seriously explains that his prayers have shifted since starting psychotherapy. They are now ones that have no joy in them and he is repeatedly asking, "Please don't let me fuck-up." So he needs a father who will love him enough to not let him push him away.

His *duration ratio* response to this interpretration was seen in the material of the next three sessions. For in those sessions he presents a great deal of important material centering around being a sucking, vomiting, insecure infant who only eats, sleeps, and masturbates; and he presents dreams in which he is an infant who causes fighting and great conflict between his mother and her lovers. He talks about how his close-intimate relationships are really strange ones, and how he fears he will really be found out to be a "bad man" instead of the "happy-go-lucky-showtime-image" he conveys. That is, his response is to actively move into the therapy and to share experiences and feelings which he had always kept to himself and which, of course, he feared would cause others to become disgusted and leave him. Then in the ninth session when he talks about how some of his relationships with friends are changing and he has no control over that, he is also able to state his fear that as he starts to depend upon me I won't be around for him. So, two weeks from the time of the first interpretation, he has abandoned "fucking-up" the therapeutic relationship and has risked needing someone. Now obviously, these changes in the material he presents in the therapy session are not *just* the result of the earlier interpretation. The "therapeutic interpersonal relationship" with all of its facets as well as the therapeutic alliance are crucial parts of the whole psychotherapeutic process which along with the variable of interpretation effects these changes.

In the next session he points out how very good the last session was, and within that session and the next two he indicates that he has started to form a close-intimate relationship with someone he really likes and respects. He points out how this is really a different experience for him as he has tended to form relationships only with people who are "needy" - with people whom he can take care of and try to help but doesn't really like and can't love. It is then (in the eleventh session) that a second interpretation is made. I point out to him that he wants others to need him so he won't be left and that he is very skilled at getting people "hooked" on him and avoiding his own dependency needs. His response to that interpretation is seen

294

within the next two sessions where he experiences much affect and deep pain. Both in and out of the therapy session, he feels very sad and cries easily and at length. He faces the painful reality that his father is never coming back. As he describes it, the feelings are as though he were dying but they also contain some kind of freedom or some sort of release.

The partial review presented here helps indicate how interpretation is only one step in the process of understanding oneself, is a relatively infrequent activity in the light of the total kinds of interactions between patient and therapist, and is both an end (or a simple but nevertheless cogent and overarching conclusion from a mass of data) as well as a new beginning (in that it then permits and/or leads to remembering and considering additional pertinent and important information). One can also see in this brief presentation how interpretations build one upon another. It may help emphasize how psychotherapists need not be concerned about "curing" patients but rather about understanding them and doing so in some detail.

Certainly for this last case example, within the first session it seemed obvious there was a relationship between the patient's "difficulties" with interpersonal relationships and the lack of any relationship with his father. However, he gives us no overt indication that he has any awareness of that relationship other than the fact he does tell us about the existence of this "hiatus" in his life. Any interpretation in the first session tying the lack of relationship with his father to his difficulties in interpersonal relationships would have been true but certainly not accurate or specific. Furthermore, for both parties (therapist and patient) such an interpretation would have been an intellectual understanding at best. I say "at best," for I think there are reasons to expect he couldn't have considered the interpretation at all. I think he would have had to avoid the interpretation (even though at an unconscious level he certainly would have heard it and already knows it) and may have even developed a resistance to its consideration. There were just too many other important emotional issues existing in that first session - issues that had to do with beginning therapy, fears of revealing himself to himself let alone to another person, and all the confusion and turmoil involved in starting a relationship with a psychotherapist. You can't expect someone so busily and anxiously dealing with such a *potpourri* of affect to hear something so "foreign" to their present emotional state as well as so inaccurately and inconsiderately aimed at the core of their dilemma as the intellectual interpretation would have been. Thus such an interpretation would only satisfy the therapist's needs to "show-off" and might well come from insecurities about "helping" and "curing" the patient. Much better to wait and let patients tell us what interpretation is to be made and when, and to show us the paths they wish and or need to walk in order to finally arrive at *the* interpretation which is then the end of the therapy - "the agony at the bottom of the pit" - and the beginning of that reorganization and living that represents a life in some important respects quite different from the one they lived prior to psychotherapy.

In the example given here, the patient tells us that first he needs to have it recognized that he "fucks-up" relationships. It is, of course, a way of saying that he fears/believes he ruined the relationship between he and his father as well as a way of recognizing his own role in his interpersonal relationships with others in his present life, *and* of saying that part of him will want to "fuck-up" the relationship with the therapist. The interpretation given is then pregnant with meanings as it is aimed at his past, present, and transference life. In addition it is rooted in the patient's present affect-life. The next step toward moving into his "life without father" passes another important milestone when he tells us how he has arranged his interpersonal relationships with other people. He recognizes and wants us to know that he selects persons who need him and will be dependent upon him and in this way avoids dealing with how he needs others as well as making sure others won't leave him. But he has told us all this only after he had directly indicated his own dependence upon therapy and his fear the therapist might not be there for him. It is after admitting that dependency and hearing the interpretation of how he attempts to keep people from leaving him, that he allows himself to experience some of the pain associated with the lack of relationship with his father and with the realization his father is never coming back.

That, at least, is the way it seems to me interpretation has operated in his case. And I have only used that case as an example of how I see interpretation generally operating in psychotherapy. Obviously none of this has the directness of evidence required by a rigorous science. Interpretations are rarely declarative hypotheses lending themselves readily to scientific investigation. They rarely produce immediate and profound psychological change in the patient or in the patient's behavior. And there is really no good reason why they should. Human beings are not such simple robots or automatons that we immediately or rather dramatically change our psychological functioning or behavior even when we have come-up with rather startling and dramatic new insights and/or information about ourselves. The process of reassessment and reorganization necessary for such change to occur takes time. It takes reflection and consideration. We must have time to sense and feel the accuracy of our new insight as well as time to accept how our old views affected and directed our life. Then we have to develop a growing sensitivity to the precise and useful meanings of our new insight. And while our thoughts, dreams, feelings, and ideas may start to reflect the fact such reassessment and reorganization has begun, it may well be some time before we see or experience the final result of that process. Furthermore, the final result of that process is going to be dependent upon the kinds of experiences we have and information we obtain between the insight into the new information and the working through process it requires in order to change our psychological functioning and our behavior. It is to me fascinating and significant that in the case presented here, once the interpretation was made about "fucking-up" relationships, there was never in the rest of his therapy any mention again of that need. Likewise, once the interpretation about holding relationships by selecting persons dependent upon him was made, he started to seek out new friends in which that dynamic did not operate and to modify and work to drop/end those relationships in which it was so apparent. All this happens without any talk in the therapy hours about its need or desire or importance.

Instead of declarative hypotheses lending themselves to some kind of scientific investigation, interpretations are much more frequently instrumental in their function. They succinctly state a psychological force or dynamic which is presently functioning on a number of different levels in the psychotherapy session and then permit some closure on those issues sufficient to allow additional and further material to be talked about, felt and recognized. In this sense, the validity of an interpretation is to be checked by carefully examining the patient's 1) immediate response to the interpretation, 2) subsequent associations to it in the form of the material presented in immediately subsequent therapy hours, 3) changes in dreams,

297

camouflage language or any other symbols indicating unconscious processes, and 4) changes observed and/or reported in symptoms or behavior in or outside of the therapy hour.

There is a sense in which psychotherapists are involved in a microanalysis of the give and take and ebb and flow of the minutiae of psychotherapeutic material at the same time they are involved in a macroanalysis of the overarching force or dynamic holding together all the minutiae. The interpretation is generally aimed at the overarching force or dynamic. And once made, careful attention must then be given again to the minutiae for that is where we will generally start to see the effect of the interpretation. If the patient talks about potatoes and corn, then about carrots and peas but insists radishes and onions are what is important, it is obvious the patient is talking about vegetables. We would make an interpretation about vegetables and then see what it does to the patient's talk, dreaming about, associations to, and feelings about potatoes or corn, carrots or peas, radishes or onions. And interpretations which are sufficiently accurate and appropriate will start to modify those minutiae and do so in rather dramatic ways. In the case example above, the minutiae of the session immediately following the first interpretation is so markedly different than that of any previous sessions as to be decidedly surprising. For now he is presenting material related to the little child in him - a sucking, vomiting, insecure infant who only eats, sleeps, and masturbates. Hardly the fun-loving, competent, enjoyable, accomplished young man, who has some problems in interpersonal relationships, he presented in the sessions prior to the interpretation.

Interpretation - Summary

Interpretation need not be a mystical process - a concept to be avoided or shunned in our attempts to better understand the process of psychotherapy. Interpretation is certainly not the end-all or be-all of psychotherapy as its early conceptualizations suggested. But it is part of the skill (or technique if you prefer) psychotherapists use in attempts to help patients more completely understand themselves and to help patients re-conceptualize perceptions and experiences vital to their lives. Interpretations help identify misconstructions and unavailable or avoided truths which have contributed to distress and unease. In that regard interpretation plays a role in helping persons modify their beliefs and their lives.

Phenomena vital to our psychological existence are not simply and easily understood or modified. And what is of great significance is that our perceptions, experiences, beliefs and feelings are primarily *not* logical, rational events. Thus, interpretations deal with material not readily amenable to comprehension through the processes of formal logic and the modes of thinking most of us have been taught to use in our formal education.

Nevertheless, there are ways of attending to the enormous inter-connections and inter-relationships of minutiae we have learned during a lifetime and which we have excluded from conscious awareness. The interpretation, then, is a way of stating a simplicity that is hopefully on the other side of complexity and encompasses and identifies important truths of the soul. In that way it permits the beginning of a new process of perceiving, experiencing and understanding. And it is that process, carefully nurtured and attended in combination with corrective emotional experiences, that can result in psychotherapeutic success.

CHAPTER 9

MATERIAL-FLOW

Early in my formal training as a psychotherapist I learned to summarize a therapy session in one or two sentences. During a session I make sparse short-hand notes of material the patient presents as well as any strong or not understandable feelings I have. Making such notes helps me set aside conscious preoccupation with the material and its order and attend most carefully to what the patient is saying-doing in the immediate present. It frees me from consciously having to remember and recall the order of material as well as from "forgetting" just when my own emotional involvement was so confusing. Then after the patient has left, I write a rather detailed progress note which reflects both the order in which material occurred in the session, the important issues the patient was dealing with, as well as the nature of the affect shown and felt by both the patient and myself. I attempt to make these notes as objective and nonjudgmental as possible. After they are made, I summarize the therapy session with one or two sentences by asking myself, "What did this person *say* to me today?" By *say* I mean not only the patient's words but also the affect and the way my hearing it affected me. I write the answer to that question in the first person.

Most frequently this procedure cannot be accomplished in the ten minutes between patients. Thus the notes are made at the end of the morning for the two or three patients I've seen by then and again at the end of the day for patients seen in the afternoon. In addition, I generally audio-tape all therapy sessions for one or two patients. My purpose here is two-fold: 1) to give me an opportunity to examine my therapeutic procedures and skills, and 2) to examine how accurately my progress notes reflect what transpired in the session. Over the years I have found these procedures most helpful in better understanding the process of psychotherapy as well as trusting my abilities to "hear-see-feel" what is going on in the therapy with any particular patient.

I keep these one or two sentence summaries of what the patient has said to me on a sheet separate from the progress notes. What I have observed by attending to these sentence summaries, is a flow of material from one session to the next. It is almost as though the patient has started to think/feel in one area or on one issue and session after session we stay on that course, perhaps with slight detours into areas related to the material and detours which will mark areas for further investigation and/or work in the future. But these are only detours or markings of what may be dealt with eventually. For the most part, the sessions stay in a particular area or on a particular issue. The working and embellishment of the particular issue includes adding more information, ideas and feelings until there comes some settlement - some resolution - or some moving to a next layer of material. At times the material flow is so obvious that it is almost as though there had not been days or a week between one session and the next. At times the patient will start the very next session by picking-up on some issue or event from the last session and continuing right on as though hours of living for both of us had not transpired since our last meeting. Furthermore, it seems to me that what is done in one session frequently gets "lived-upon" in between sessions and the next meeting contains the earlier as well as the now "lived-upon" information. Since much of my therapy work is done in a college setting, where time and existence is marked by an academic year which has more interruptions and hiatuses than is true for the typical eleven-month, one-month vacation year, it has been easier to see how patients unconsciously plan their therapy in order to be ready to do some "living-upon" issues with which they are dealing. Not infrequently I noticed that students in therapy will deal with issues centering around their feelings and conflicts with parents in such a fashion as to be ready to make some changes in their perceptions of and interactions with their parents by the time fall break or spring break or Christmas vacations come - that is at that time when they will leave the campus and return home where they will confront the reality and existence of their parents and where they will now be able to "live-upon" what they have been considering in the therapy sessions.

Neither the flow of material in therapy or the selection of when

302

the material will be "lived-upon" seems to be a matter of conscious selection by either the patient or me. I have always left it to the patient to start the session and set the agendas. I follow their lead. Their unconscious knows where they need to go and my task is to understand them in the "here-and-now" and as skillfully as possible help keep their attention on the path or paths they have chosen. Milton Erickson (Gordon, 1978) has a therapeutic metaphor quite appropriate to that task.

> I was returning from high school one day and a runaway horse with a bridle on sped past a group of us into the farmer's yard...looking for a drink of water. The horse was perspiring heavily and the farmer didn't recognize it, so we cornered it. I hopped on the horse's back...since it had a bridle on. I took hold of the rein and said, "Giddy-up"...headed for the highway. I knew the horse would turn in the right direction...I didn't know what the right direction was. And the horse trotted and galloped along. Now and then he would forget he was on the highway and start into a field. So I would pull on him a bit and call his attention to the fact the highway was where he was supposed to be. And finally about four miles from where I had boarded him he turned into a farm yard and the farmer said, "So that's how that critter came back. Where did you find him?" I said, "About four miles from here." "How did you know he should come here?" I said, "I didn't know...the horse knew. All I did was keep his attention on the road" (p. 205).

Patients seem to have a sense of where they need to go. It is not that they necessarily have a long view of where "they belong." But when placed in the environment of a therapeutic relationship, they seem to wander in some specific direction or assiduously avoid going in a direction they have already pointed out.

Following is the entire transcript of sentence summaries from one case. The patient was a nineteen year old college sophomore who sought therapy because of an insomnia which she had suffered for a number of years. She was seen two times a week until the twenty-sixth session and then once a week for a total of thirty-seven sessions. Also during this therapy there were a number of "breaks" for vacations and for time with her family. She came from a very wealthy family, was one of three children (all female) and her developmental history was unremarkable except for the divorce of her parents when she was fourteen years of age. Prior to the divorce, she felt the family had lived comfortably and happily in the family home in the Boston area. In fact she felt life had really been rather idyllic. She remembered no fighting, bickering or any reason for the divorce, and as far as she could see it was mutually agreed upon and accomplished with little or no rancour. Since the divorce, both parents had subsequently remarried and the patient kept contact with both of them taking turns living in one part of the country with her mother and than at other times in another part of the country with her father. This was the same pattern her sisters followed. The home in Boston had been sold and she reported having very little memory of the time before the divorce, in fact she said, "Boston's a fog." Clinically she presented as a very warm, emotional, intelligent woman who evidenced considerable strained sadness when speaking of her parent's divorce.

Here then, are the sentence summaries from her therapy sessions:

#1 I'm so alone, without warmth and support. The divorce was very upsetting in my life.

#2 My mother is not capable of real warmth and doesn't put people at ease. I'm afraid to be angry with people.

#3 Do you really want to listen to me? I've had so many material things without feeling anything except feeling empty. I've not had strong sexual feelings.

As is so often my experience, in the first sessions patients talk not only of what are important issues and feelings in their lives and for their therapy but do so in a context of the emerging therapeutic relationship and transference. I initially listen more carefully to this material in terms of what it is saying-indicating about the emerging therapeutic relationship and do little work with it in terms of how it may relate to the patient's developmental dynamics. I do that because I think establishing the therapeutic interpersonal relationship and the therapeutic alliance are the first and most important tasks. Secondly, the developmental dynamics generally are only vaguely outlined in these initial sessions - she is really only pointing to some "paths" that may be important. By the third session she can specifically respond to the therapeutic relationship. She knows she has been listened to and it is a bit of a surprise for her as well as somewhat disconcerting. She has said she is so alone and without warmth and support and now she is starting to experience some of that and it is anxiety producing. So she can't really believe I'd want to listen, and she has to tell me she can't reciprocate with feelings. Again, as is so common in my experience, once patients have made some resolution of the therapeutic alliance (generally within three sessions) they move to more significantly dynamic material in the next session or so. Such was the case for her.

#4 As a child I had repetitive dreams of doom and I think they may be related to my insomnia symptom. Because my mother never came to me when I was ill and I needed her, I'm a person who is not worth coming to.

#5 I've been into my hopeless-doom feelings which scare me. I've held back my anger at mother because I fear my wish she were dead will turn into a reality.

#6 I put on pretensions and cover over my desires in establishing interpersonal interactions. Having you sleepy and confused today is important.

#7 I don't think my father and I really interact. I have trouble relating with adults and I put adult males on pedestals.

(At this point there is a hiatus in our sessions as she leaves for Spring break and spends a week with her mother in which she was able to have some rather open and good talks.)

#8 I'm feeling better now and don't have so much insomnia. I need to get back to things we discussed three or four sessions ago and my fear of lack of control.

#9 I have a real sense of optimism, I'm working better and making friends. I think my mother is so mechanical and can't show her feelings except sadness and loneliness.

#10 I don't know what to talk about, tell me. I talk about father in a monotone voice and without feeling and tire and hypnotize you.

#11 I want to know about you and your family. I want to know what you think and feel about the world.

305

#12 I've really had no adult guidance. But, I'm starting to do things in the world and it feels good.

In sessions #4 through #7 she has started to work with some of the feelings and issues relating to her mother as well as started to make forays into what is for her a very scary world of relationship-feelings for father. I think the time with her mother certainly helped her work the issues with her and when she returns there are a couple of sessions which I see as plateaus. Session #8 and #9 are ones of enjoying, marking, and solidifying some gains already made as well as saying more needs to be done, i.e. I need to get back to things we discussed three or four sessions ago and my fear of lack of control. Then in session #10, #11, & #12 she attempts to more directly approach the issues with father and males and, of course, is doing so in the context of our relationship and the transference. But this frontal or more direct attack is extremely fearful and my own counter-transference issues also inhibited the work - for I did feel very tired and mesmerized.

#13 I wonder if I'm like my mother and can't love and am selfish. I have lots of money behind me and I don't know how I feel about that.

#14 I dislike other aspects of myself that are like mother. I dislike me, am a bad person and am angry with mother because she screwed me over royally.

#15 It was a good weekend where I cried and remembered the divorce. I can't look my new step-father in the eye and I never did deal with the issue of my parents' sexuality.

(She has a long weekend where she visits her father and step-mother in the West.)

#16 I can see I really do have a family in the West. My father is warm but bland and I don't know what really interests him.

#17 I really don't know or understand men. My peers are a sexual threat to me.

#18 Ultimately I fear losing touch with people I'm making contact with and it will be irreparable and your included in that. My nanny was really my mother and with the divorce and her illness I've lost her.

In these session (#13-#18) she is in different ways and from different angles working some of her issues with men and sexuality as well as casting about for some sense of what it would mean for her to be a mother and mothered. The material of the eigthteen session is effected by the fact that I will be on vacation for three weeks and that she plans to spend some of the time visiting her old nanny.

#19 I can feel love for my Nanny and know how deep it was. I feel better about seeing my family now.

#20 I was able to be more assertive with mother. My younger sister was very resentful of me.

#21 I feel my life is so futile. I've detached from the family and can't seem to get anyplace.

#22 My relationship with mother is important. I want to get to know her better.

#23 I am starting to accept the divorce and to realize I was badly hurt by it.

In these sessions she seems to be resolving some of the issues from the past related to being able to love, to her relationship with her mother, and to the hurt and pain of the divorce. And as she works through these issues she 1) starts to see her life as having been futile ("a series of symptoms of neurosis and no progress"), 2) begins to form a relationship with a male student on campus, and 3) is able to move into more directly dealing with her feelings about men and sexuality.

#24 I'm ready now to start dealing with my sexuality. I dream about my step-brother and maybe guilt and sex are tied together for me.

#25 Close, intimate talks are good and I have more freedom for them now but it is still hard and scary.

#26 Guilt is related to mother laying guilt-trips on me and I never could express anger at her without feeling very guilty.

#27 I'm not sure what my mother's values are. I'm not sure mother would like or help me if she knew me.

#28 I do avoid facing guilt. My early memories seem to exclude the relationship with my father and I did not show him any

307

affection. I did at the time of the divorce but then I pushed him out of my life. He's coming back in now.

#29 Guilt and my father and my view of men may be all interrelated. I've never let a man know me. I don't see them as having a capacity to understand emotional needs.

#30 I am more aware of feminism and sexism and am trying to accomodate that and not just be overpowered by males.

#31 I had two dreams which were fun and are working through 1) my divided loyalties to mother and nanny, 2) my tendency to dissociate myself from endings, and 3) accepting my sexuality.

#32 I'm feeling better and I think I'm getting out of my depression. But I'm not ready to face an ending yet. Father's loyalty is still an issue. Why didn't he love me?

#33 I've found I can be open and risk being me and get wonderful love feelings and it's so good. Can Joe (the college man she has been establishing a relationship with) feed me like that?

#34 I am moving out of my family for my emotional involvement. I realize the divorce was mutual and theirs.

#35 I'm ready to end. There is some scariness with it related to my desires to be dependent and taken care of vs. being independent and my own person. Lets take time to say goodbye.

#36 I'm ready to end. Therapy has been good. I got more out of it than I thought and other things in my life helped too.

#37 We end. Goodbye. Thank you.

In these last sessions she is now dealing with her own life, free of the ties that kept her from moving away from the family, and she works the issues related to father, males, and sexuality. As she so correctly points out in session #36 not only the therapy but other aspects of her living and life during the therapy were beneficial. In particular her contacts with family members and her nanny, at times when she was ready and able to deal with them as persons in their own rights, as well as the relationship with Joe were "other" aspects of her living that proved therapeutically beneficial. She started to form the relationship with Joe around session #21-#23. That was when she started to make a transition in the therapy material from the earlier work of allowing herself to remember the divorce and some of her feelings about and issues with mother to focusing more on the feelings related to father, men and sexuality. Then by session #35 being left and leavings no longer had so many over-determined and confused feelings associated with it and we could take the time necessary to see what being left felt like.

Tracing the development of her therapy in these sentence summaries indicates that she started by focusing upon therapeutic alliance issues in the form of stating she was alone, without warmth and support, had a mother unable to feel and by pointing out she also can't feel even though the therapist may really want to listen to her. But then she does feel. In sessions #4 and #5 she is living her feelings of hopelessness and doom - feelings undoubtedly reminiscent of her life at age fourteen when the divorce occurred. And her attention in therapy goes from focusing upon her feelings about and relationship with her mother (#2-#5) to tentative moves into the confusion about older males and father (#6-#12) to finally working issues that include the entire family (#13-#20). She seems then more free to have and focus upon her own life (#21-#23) and to deal with her own feelings about sexuality, guilt, and close intimate relationships (#24-#29) including dealing more directly with her feelings about men (#28-#31). She is then ready to end and can handle a leaving-goodbye (#34-#37).

Certainly within the first few sessions it was possible to identify definite areas of her life which contained the important repressed and denied material. Her insomnia, while not exactly identified as beginning during the time of the divorce, seems highly related to her attempts to avoid facing the implications of the divorce. And those implications theoretically included her emerging sexuality and unresolved oedipul conflicts. Her solution was to withdraw and shut down all feelings - feelings of course that would not leave her alone when she slept so she had to avoid relaxing and dreaming. Now it doesn't matter whether or not such a theoretical and intellectual conceptualization is accurate or not. What is of much greater significance and a great deal more fun is to "see" what "roads" this patient takes to get back to where she "belongs" - back to her family (now expanded into families) and back to her own feelings and life. By carefully attending to the variables involved in a "therapeutic interpersonal relationship" and the process of psychotherapy, we can be reasonably certain that patients will go where they know they need to go and get back where they belong. It is again the importance of therapists knowing that they do not cure anyone. We simply create situations in which it is possible for patients to start moving and then we follow along with them making sure we continue to follow them and protect the space that has been created in the therapeutic relationship which allows them to continue moving. Kopp (1976) has said it this way:

> Perhaps the most important thing that any healer must learn is the fact that he cannot heal anyone. It is possible to learn various procedures that may contribute to healing and growth, but in so doing it is essential to know how to *let be*. In the final analysis it seems that the healer is, at best, a participating witness to an unfolding process of which he is a part. I inevitably run into trouble whenever I lose sight of this principle and somehow believe I'm doing it. (p. 168).

Generally systematic attention to material flow of therapy will help therapists know which road they are on, what is coming up further down the road, and when the patient has successfully navigated and seen the road already traversed. By attention to the material flow we can identify 1) the working-through process, 2) important, anxiety producing, and fearful areas that lie ahead, 3) the different layers of material involved in the problem, 4) what is being "lived-upon", and 5) what changes have occurred.

Working Through

There is a sense in which what I call "material flow" is the entire "working through" process. The term "working through" was originally introduced by Freud (1913) and expanded upon by Fenichel (1945). It denotes the process by which patients having obtained some insight into a previously unconscious impulse or desire start to identify its effect and connection in varied and manifold dimensions of their lives. The new insight has to be re-established and tested time and again within different aspects of life and within new connections and experiences. In their use of the term, Freud and Fenichel saw it as a process that followed a correct interpretation which made the patient aware of an unconscious impulse. That theoretical conceptualization is too limiting and narrow from my perspective. Patients can "work through" material even without explicit interpretations or completely conscious

310

realization of the unconscious dynamics.

In the present case example, the patient intially reports a lack of connectedness or closeness with others as well as an inability to feel anything except to feel empty. Of course it is not that she is unable to feel but rather that she has defended herself against having her feelings. She does not need to be told this nor does she need to have any particular insight into the fact she defends herself against feelings. At some level of her being she already knows that anyway, and pointing it out to her is really only to complain about it and set her the task of overcoming her defense without really having any appreciation for the importance of maintaining it. At any rate, the first task in psychotherapy is to establish a therapeutic alliance; and, of course, that means establishing some connnectedness and feelings with/for another person. So as she starts to establish a relationship with the therapist, she will start to experience some feelings including transference responses. By the third session, some of that has been accomplished. She asks, "Do you really want to listen to me?" Now, the psychotherapeutic situation is such that it helps to neutralize defenses against feelings. In the first place, patients can more easily risk having feelings for the therapist because they only see and deal with that person in very isolated and circumscribed conditions. In her case, she only had to interact with me for some fifty minutes twice a week. Furthermore, the nature of that interaction was markedly limited - we would only meet for fifty minutes, always in the same place, and we would only talk. The atmosphere of the therapy office also helps neutralize defenses. It is generally a warm, comfortable, relaxing place, quiet and away from the hub-bub and harrassments of life. It is an environment that has few if any connections with other "living spaces" in the world. Then, of course, the variables and procedures embodied in establishing a therapeutic relationship help to reinforce an accepting, non-judgmental atmosphere. Lastly, the therapist's own verbal and non-verbal reactions based upon and tied to what Nacht (1962, 1963) has called *the deep inner attitude* helps to recondition the patient and/or extinquish some of their fears of closeness. Marmor (1966) succinctly highlights the therapist's learning function with these words:

> A host of experimental studies seem to indicate that the non-verbal as well as the verbal reactions of the

therapist act as positive and negative reinforcing stimuli to the patient, encouraging certain kinds of responses and discouraging others. According to these investigators, what seems to be going on in the working-through process is a kind of conditioned-learning, in which the therapist's *overt* or *covert* approval and disapproval - expressed in his nonverbal reactions as well as in his verbal confrontations, and in what he interprets as neurotic or healthy - act as reward-punishment cues or conditioning stimuli (p. 364).

The therapist's opportunity for having such an effect upon the patient is probably related to emerging transference responses. Marmor's "conditioned-learning" is similar to what Freud (1938) called "aftereducation." Part of the "working through" process is an intellectual understanding. But another aspect of its importance is more emotional and related to "aftereducation." If patients at some level of their being start to perceive therapists as their parent, then therapists takes on some of the "power" any parent has over a child, i.e. the power to effect the child's values, beliefs, attitudes, and world views.

And so as the patient in this case experiences the development of some tie and closeness with and to me - some agreement for working together on rather important, scary, difficult and personal issues - she allows herself to begin having some feelings. The first strong feelings she has (#4 & #5) are those of hopeless-doom along with some feelings of anger for mother. The working through of some of her feelings about mother starts in session #2 and continues through sessions #3 to #9 and then again in #13 and #14. At points throughout those sessions, a major theme of her feelings about father and males emerges (#6, #7, #10, #11). Her verbalizations about that theme as well as her demeanor and my emotional response suggests how very tentatively she wishes to approach that area. And in this "working through" she also modifies her life outside the therapy office. She has allowed herself to have feelings of doom and hopelessness which scared her. She goes to see, be with and talk with her mother. And she starts to make new friends. By session #15 she can permit herself to remember and have feelings about the divorce - and has sufficient resolution of issues surrounding her relationship with mother to allow her to now move

312

closer to her feelings about father and momentarily about the woman who raised her and in that regard served as her "mother." Session #19 through #23 are a further working and reconsidering of where she is vis a vis mother, the divorce, loving, and her own life. Interestingly enough at this point she is starting to form a close relationship with a male peer. And in session #24 she starts to deal with father, males and her own sexuality and that theme continues through session #33. And by session #31 her dreams summarize for her the issues she has worked through: 1) her divided loyalties to mother and nanny, 2) her tendency to disassociate herself from endings, and 3) accepting her own sexuality. Then sessions #32-36 are mainly devoted to "working through" ending the psychotherapeutic relationship.

Important, Anxiety Producing, And Fearful Areas That Lie Ahead

It is not unusual that in the course of "working through" one aspect of the problem, patients will identify and/or alert us to another perhaps even more important and crucial aspect of the problem. But they commonly do so while indicating they aren't yet fully ready to deal with a conscious and systematic attention to those "other" aspects of the problem. Furthermore, as they resolve some of the immediate and present issues in the therapy sessions, it provides positive reinforcement helping them to risk working on more and more anxiety producing issues. In addition, the "therapeutic interpersonal relationship" has a better chance over time and with positive experiences in therapy to serve as a firmer platform upon which both patient and therapist may stand to investigate and deal with more and more difficult and anxiety producing problems.

In the present case example, within the first few sessions she identifies three crucial aspects of her problem. She tells us, "the divorce was very upsetting in my life," "I am angry with my mother," and "I have problems with my sexual feelings." She chooses to start to work on her feelings of hoplessness and doom which are also related to issues with her mother. But mid-way in the process of doing that, she also again raises issues of father and hiding her desires (#6 & #7). She continues the "working through" process of issues with her mother (#8, #9,, #13, #14,) but takes time also to more openly show her confusion about men and father (#10, #11,

313

#12) and to remain with that theme in some consistent fashion for three sessions. This theme emerges most consistently in therapy after she has achieved some positive gains with the work in earlier sessions. She is feeling better, has less insomnia, and a real sense of optimism. There are then a number of sessions (#15-#23) which are a continual working of her relationships with mother and now father and her nanny as well as some solidification in accepting the divorce and seeing its effect upon her. By session #24 she tells us she is now ready to start dealing with her sexuality. And in session #32 she lets us know that "ending" will be the next issue. She tells us, "But I'm not ready to face an ending yet." Who mentioned ending? Three sessions later she lets us know she is ready to end the therapy.

Different Layers Of Material Involved In The Problem.

In reviewing the sentence summaries I have also noticed how they tend to reveal the various layers of material involved in the problem. As already noted, first are issues related to the problem but imbedded in establishing a therapeutic alliance. For the present case those were session #1-#3. Next come her feelings of hoplessness and doom, session #4 & #5 and through sessions #2-#13 she is working issues with mother as well as moving into issues with father. Session #13-#20 focus upon her entire family, her feelings about them and her relationships with them. Then in Session #21 she starts to accept her own life separate and apart from the family and in session #24 starts to work on and deal with her own sexuality, guilt, and close, intimate relationships. By session #28 she can deal more directly with her feelings about father and in session #29 & #30 with her feelings about relating to men. Then by session #32 she is ready to start ending therapy.

In viewing the case this way, it becomes apparent how important it is for the therapist to take a lead from the patient. The divorce was a very important and upsetting experience for her which helped solidify her fears of not being wanted and her fears of not being able to love or give or have any feelings. In addition, her own developmental history was made more confusing by having two "mothers" - one of whom she felt she must be loyal to and the other from whom she felt much love, support, and nurturing. She chose to deal with the issues and feelings about mother first and then moved into seeing and

314

accepting the fact she was now a member of a much larger and extended family (mother, father, step-mother, step-father, sibs and step-sibs). Then she had the freedom to be her own person and, at that point, returned to dealing with her own sexuality in the context of her feelings about mother and father and then in the context of men in general. She "knew" the route she had to take to get back to that place where she would have freedom to feel and try to find and give love. I believe she "knew" that route much better than any therapist. Besides it is most enjoyable to "see" how patients work out their solutions to their problems.

What Is Being "Lived-Upon"

As patients go through psychotherapy they not infrequently start to make changes in their lives outside of the therapy hour. Historically for classical analysis it was feared patients would "act out" their problems by making changes in their lives outside of the therapy hour. So sometimes patients were required to forgo any major changes until analysis was complete. Now it is more common to analyse and interpret any changes the patient may make that are indicative of "acting-out" problems. But what has not received any great deal of attention are those changes patients may make in their lives indicative of progress on their problems. Part of the reason they receive little attention is undoubtedly related to the fact that they need not be dealt with in the therapy session. Nor do patients generally present such material for therapy work. But in one way or another they generally let us know that they have started to "live upon" some of what has started to happen to them and change them in the therapy. I think it is important to note these kinds of "living-upon" experiences for they 1) indicate what changes have occurred in the therapy, and 2) they will be an important part of the "aftereducation" or the "corrective emotional experiences" the patient receives. Thus, what happens in these "lived-upon" experiences will, in some measure, determine what material will be important to deal with in the therapy sessions and what kind of progress the patient will continue to make.

In the present case, between sessions #4 and #5 she "lived-upon" her feelings of hopelessness and doom. In the fourth session, she remembers some repetitive dreams she had as a child and also is able

315

to express her feelings that she may be a person unworthy of any attention. After that session, she was able to feel/experience some of her hopelessness and doom. Even though those feelings scared her, she found herself able to stay with them for the days between sessions. Then between sessions #7 and #8 she "lived-upon" some of the work she had done in psychotherapy around her feelings about and relationship with mother. She went to see and talk with her mother. That evidently was a positive experience, for she comes back feeling much better and ready to return to a further working through of some of these issues. The next obviously "lived-upon" event occurs between session #15 and #16 when she visits her father. That experience seemed to help her realize she did have a family and also seemed to reduce her anxiety about males to the point where she could start to more directly express and deal with her feelings about men in the therapy sessions. Then between session #18 and #19 there is another "lived-upon" event where her conflicts around loyalty to mother and love for her nanny seem to be finally resolved. She chooses to visit her nanny, who was then no longer with the family, and re-remembers how deep her love was for that person. Then around session #21 and #22 she has developed a relationship with a boyfriend and by session #24 is moving much more directly into dealing with her own sexuality and her feelings and fears about men. This relationship was a positive one and by session #33 she can state her amazement at how being open and risking has led to good love feelings.

Now, undoubtedly this woman did many other things during her thirty-seven sessions of psychotherapy and a goodly number of them might well have also been "living-upon" some of the insights and understandings and perspectives she obtained by her work in psychotherapy. I have listed only those of which I was aware and which she had mentioned. Furthermore, three of them were consciously planned by her, i.e. she decided to use her time during school breaks to visit specific persons - persons who coincided with the work she was doing in psychotherapy. There is in my mind little doubt that all of these experiences greatly contributed to her progress in psychotherapy. She started to relate to and deal with important persons in her life at those points where she was now able to gain some perspective unencumbered by overwhelming anxiety and in a relationship (psychotherapy) where she could gain support for openly examining and facing herself vis a vis the other members of her family. She also started to form a close relationship with a male peer at a time and place in her life where she had the space to consider and examine her feelings and experiences in and with such a relationship.

Life is of one fabric and it seems to me that issues worked upon and worked out in psychotherapy have to effect or be "lived-upon" in our life outside the therapy office. It is, in fact, in this fashion that we obtain "corrective emotional experiences" in addition to those which may be available to us within the therapeutic interpersonal relationship. And those "corrective emotional experiences" outside of the therapy office are very important in helping persons accurately sense the validity of the perspectives and understandings they obtain within the psychotherapuetic process.

Near the end of her therapy (session #36) she acknowledges that she got out of psychotherapy more than she thought she would *and* that other things in her life helped too. There is no doubt in my mind that is true, and I think that the five identified "lived-upon" elements are a large part of those other things that helped too.

What Changes Have Occurred

By attending to the session sentence summaries, it seems possible to identify what changes occurred. In session #5 she tells us she has been able to feel - perhaps not what she wanted to feel but they are strong feelings - hopelessness and doom. Then in sessions #8 and #9 she reports feeling better, abatement of some symptoms, and having a real sense of optimism. By session #19 she knows she can love and do so deeply and by session #32 and #33 she reports feeling better and brings up the issue of ending therapy. Those are all explicit indications of change. Certainly all the material she started to "live-upon" are indices of change as well, as are the various layers of material she systematically progresses through. Signs of change are found in session #22 where she recognizes that her relationship with her mother is important and wishes to get to know her better. Her ability to feel and desire this improved relationship is related to the fact she has accepted and worked-through some of her anger and hostility for her mother. In Session #23 she acknowledges being able to accept the divorce as well as knowing it was harmful to her. These are not just intellectual understandings. She can "feel" their validity

317

as well as recognize the divorce had unfortunate but not irreversible consequences for her. In session #28 she is starting to "take" father back into her life after having pushed him out a few years earlier, and in session #30 she indicates how she is consciously working to not be overpowered by males.

Summary

Attention to the material flow of psychotherapy may have the potential of adding a great deal to our analysis of the process of psychotherapy. Certainly no therapist believes that it is only the material within the fifty-minute hour that is therapeutic. Patients can and do work and live upon the insights and experiences obtained within the psychotherapeutic sessions. And that work and living may be reflected in the next and future sessions of therapy. About all we psychotherapists have to go on is that small portion of the patient's life reported within the therapy session. We must not make that material represent more than it is, but we also should not "waste" any of what is said there. For by taking the psychotherapeutic sessions as a totality - instead of attending only to one session at a time - we are much more able to see the working through process, expand upon the complexities or different layers of the problem being worked, hear about anxiety producing, fearful areas yet to be faced, and get a better understanding of the ways in which patients do "live upon" their experiences and insights in order to resist any change or to more fully work through and incorporate into their psychological beings the changes they seek for health.

CHAPTER 10

CORRECTIVE EMOTIONAL EXPERIENCE

Introduction

The words "corrective emotional experience" encompass the very essence of what psychotherapy is all about. For, hopefully, psychotherapy provides experiences that might modify, alter, or change our maladaptive, no longer useful, perhaps even destructive feelings, beliefs, and convictions. It seems impossible to talk or write about psychotherapy without also giving attention to those events or experiences which patients have in or out of the psychotherapy hour that seem to be particularly significant in their helpful, healing, meaningful and corrective nature.

There is a sense in which corrective emotional experiences encompass all that the patient "learns" as a result of his or her psychotherapy. These experiences mark points along the therapy path where significant elements have coalesced in such a fashion as to provide an affective-cognitive experience which has intensity, passion, and an overwhelming and undeniable accuracy. It is almost never an "ah ha!" experience (as insight might be). Rather, it is a powerful, but relatively quiet and most importantly "unspoken" experience. It is almost as though dwelling upon the experience and attempting to put it into words would destroy its curative power and its undeniable importance. That is, by placing the experience totally in the conscious realm we cheat ourselves of its full significance as we don't have the ability with words to fully describe what we have experienced. But it also seems to be an experience that we must momentarily savor - that is, it requires a silent, sacred place in which to rest.

Before beginning our discussion of corrective emotional

319

experiences and as a way of inviting the reader to feel some of what it may mean, I wish to share a portion of a letter recently received from a former student and patient. In that letter he writes,

> Well, I know, John, that you are writing a book. You realize of course that you are taking your three dimensional self and putting it into something so far removed as language. Good luck. You can never put your twinkling eyes nor your infectious laugh on paper. At least, not to people who don't know you. You have to be there.

> And like Peter Sellers, I was there, so let me see if I can conjure up what was important to me, and what I learned. I like to watch. Well, watching you, I learned to laugh again. To burp and enjoy it. And years later, to enjoy my bodily functions. (No, I'm not shitting you.) Some seeds mature quickly, others take longer. (I told you I had developed a complete command of the obvious.) I learned to trust. I learned to discriminate between different kinds of feelings, and to discriminate objects of a particular feeling, i.e. men/women. I learned that I was limiting my choices. I learned that I had been very unhappy for a long time and didn't know it. I learned that I could express my hostility without the other person's attacking. (That was a biggie, and I still don't believe it.) I found that someone could take a pile of garbage and find the good. I learned to play some games with the cards face up. (Kopp's phrase, which for a card player like me was the perfect verbiage.)

> I discovered I could let down my guard and not be killed or annihilated. As unusual as it was for me at the time, I had a close encounter with someone who really had almost no desire to compete or put me down. I found someone who spoke his mind freely, said how he felt, and then shut up. Honesty. (Geez, no wonder you have no friends.)

> As hard as it was, and is, I asked for help. Nobody pushed it on me. I was ashamed of being weak. And helpless. And I found out everybody feels this way. (Some help you are.) And one of the answers is that nobody knows all the

320

answers. What a relief. (You were starting to annoy me there for awhile.) So I don't have to be perfect or OK or even get cured in order to reassure you. Or please you. I have to do it because I want to do it. You're just along for the ride and you can't and don't even care to believe that you can control what I do, what I think, or how I feel. (But then, if not narcissism, this would require at least some competence.) You kept me on track when I avoided noxious subjects. Take my mother. Please. And you defused yourself from her: you stopped being my mother, (you mother.) And I mean shit, you bastard, if YOU could do it, certainly I could do it. Goddam caught me in my own game.

I know there's more, and you probably know a lot of it. I wish I could clearly say that look, here's something you didn't know that I learned, or here's something that you never thought about this way, but maybe that is also beside the point, as Eastern religions suggest; that the process of looking is the answer, and the content really doesn't matter as much.

Here I am, an old man in a dry season, being talked to by the boy inside. And I can listen now. And see. And feel. And think. And touch. And be touched. And wonder of all the stars beyond the mountain where bare-ruined choirs echo the sweet birds song. And Lady McBeth washes in a mountain stream, scrambling with the wash down corridors of time to see the mermaids singing to me, each to each. And in the field, the lunes are silent with majestic awe to tremble to and fro, shifting weight from one foot to the other, rooted in the soft mud, free to fly. So am I.

Learnings, intertwined with interpersonal relationship, infused with feelings and meanings --- basic concepts of TRUST and RISK and most importantly ENCOUNTER all tied together with living and being with struggles and pains and eventually with BECOMING and being one's own "old man in a dry season" who can listen to the "boy inside."

And now, let us attempt to write about one aspect of the process of psychotherapy that is related to much of what this man reports as his "learnings."

The Concept

So far, we have discussed the contributions of relationship (which included alliance, transference, countertransference) and of interpretation and insight as well as material flow in the process of psychotherapy. We have also pointed out how these variables are interdependent upon one another and interact to form the whole fabric of psychotherapy. Now with the term "corrective emotional experience" we are attempting to identify an event of frequent occurrence in psychotherapy. The corrective emotional experience provides the patient with an experience which in and of itself, in view of all the other interrelated elements of the psychotherapeutic process, results in affective and cognitive modifications of the well-established, rigid neurotic beliefs and feelings which are part of the patient's problems. It is with this term, "corrective emotional experience," that we go beyond insight and understanding and move to experience. And that "experience" is best identified by observing both the way the therapist is understanding of and skilled in participating in the patient's world and the way the patient feels and understands and experiences the intimate personal relationship with the therapist. The term "corrective emotional experience" as part of the process of psychotherapy represents the proposition that learning, insight, and understanding by themselves are not enough. We need to take any "new" perspective and live it - live it in and/or out of the psychotherapy hour. For it is by living the "new" perspective that we experience it. And in experiencing it we are able to assess its accuracy and cogency as well as to embellish, hone, and perfect it. For it is in living the "new" perspective that we truly learn it. The "corrective emotional experiences" in psychotherapy are then experiences well imbedded in the active and total intimate, personal relationship between therapist and patient.

Almost all psychotherapists would agree psychotherapy rests upon the assumption that new and different emotional, intimate, personal experiences with other human beings are capable of correcting earlier damaging, confusing, and hurtful interpersonal experiences. There is a sense in which that is all we are talking about when we talk about "corrective emotional experiences" - we talk about those experiences the patient has with the therapist and with other persons in his or her life which help "correct" those earlier confusing, hurtful, judgmental, rejecting interpersonal experiences. By the term "corrective emotional experiences," we simply wish to identify as many of those experiences the patient has within and without psychotherapy that are corrective of early emotional confusion, trauma, distortion, or fixation.

Admittedly this goes beyond the classical definition advanced by Alexander and French (1946). They were the ones who gave us the term and had it deeply imbedded within the psychoanalytic framework. Alexander (1961) was very specific about his use of the term. In accordance with psychoanalytic theory, he recognized that patients would transfer significant feelings held for important figures in their early lives to the therapist. But, in addition, he also reasoned that patients could recognize that part of those feelings were not suited to the therapist's reactions - i.e. were really not suited to the person the therapist was. And also, and most importantly, patients would start to recognize and experience this discrepancy between their feelings/expectations and the therapist's reactions. Recognizing and experiencing this discrepancy would constitute the "corrective emotional experience." In Alexander's (1961) words:

> Simultaneously recognizing and experiencing this discrepancy between the transference feelings directed toward the original objects in the past, and the reactions of the therapist, who is a distinct personality and is experienced as such by the patient, is what I called the corrective emotional experience (pg. 327).

So, Alexander and French helped to point out that patients do not perceive therapists as abstract intellects but as distinct persons. Furthermore, they hypothesized that once the therapist had some knowledge of the client's neurosis and how that person expected the therapist to respond, then the therapist was in a position to assume a role which could provide a discrepancy between patients' feelings/expectations and therapists' responses. That is, then the therapist was in a position to effect a "corrective emotional experience." While it certainly was an interesting idea and an important part of the rationale for explaining the efficacy and

323

usefulness of a short-term or psychoanalytically oriented psychotherapy, clinical experience soon indicated that "playing a role" was not particularly valuable. Psychotherapy is not that simple and few, if any, therapists would advocate "playing a role" with patients. As Eagle (1984) has pointed out:

> In general, Alexander and French tended to reduce many complex processes to the simple factor of "corrective emotional experience" and tended to ignore or not sufficiently emphasize other factors involving determining whether tests have been passed or failed, judging whether or not conditions of safety obtain, and deciding whether or not to bring forth warded off contents (p. 221).

While I see "corrective emotional experiences" as part of the essence of psychotherapy, I don't want to give the impression that they are any more important or crucial to the psychotherapeutic process than the other variables covered by and discussed in this book. In fact, I think it a rather useless task to set priorities of importance for the various variables constituting the process of psychotherapy. They all have a place and are all interrelated. And for "corrective emotional experiences" to occur relationship, alliance, transference, countertransference, interpretation and material flow all have to be there for they are varied and essential aspects of the whole process. In a way, a "corrective emotional experience" is a creative act. And as Rollo May (1975) has pointed out:

> *Creativity occurs in an act of encounter and is to be understood with this encounter as its center* (p. 77).

The "corrective emotional experience" cannot occur within or without the therapy hour unless there is an "act of encounter" - a meeting of two persons who feel, sense, and encounter one another. "Corrective emotional experiences" do not happen in a vacuum. As Greben (1981) has stated:

> Patients in psychotherapy do not improve in a vacuum: they require a relationship with a strong and known person, with whom to share themselves and against whom to measure themselves (p. 452).

324

"Corrective emotional experiences" are dependent upon a relationship - upon two people involved with one another. Unfortunately, it is not unusual that patients have been exposed during their development, to confusing communications and hurtful relationships that have left them mistrustful of any new involvement. In that sense, they are in no great rush to form a relationship with a therapist. Furthermore, most of us chose as friends only those persons who agree with our way of seeing reality. Thus, we nicely protect ourselves from new ideas, challenges, or experiences and have friends who help us maintain our neuroses. On both counts (fear of involvement, and relating only to those who help maintain the pathology) the therapist has some obstacles to overcome in forming an involvement with the patient. We have already discussed, in the chapter on relationship, the necessity for the therapist to help create an interpersonal climate appropriate for the work of psychotherapy and one that would help the patient take the risk of involvement. Hopefully, at its base, the relationship that develops is experienced by the patient as safe, secure, free from undue threat, and supportive; and the therapist is perceived as dependable, trustworthy, and consistent. And, hopefully, the therapist does not have the same maladaptive views as does the patient.

It is then this involvement between patient and therapist that can lead to an "act of encounter" - a meeting of the two persons which can result in a "corrective emotional experience." Again quoting Greben (1981):

> There is an intensity and immediacy which will be missing from the therapeutic experience if the scrutiny of the two participants is not turned upon what happens and is felt between them. The more candid and inclusive the exploration of this area can be, the more likely is the therapy to have marked effect upon the patient (p. 454).

Cognitive and emotional events are organically connected when we deal with what is happening and felt between the two persons intimately involved in the therapy. Many times in our living and thinking we artificially separate cognitive and emotional events. They cannot become separated when we focus upon what is happening and felt between us. We then have an emotional experience, very difficult

325

to deny because of its intensity, that can have some corrective functions.

It is time for an example. Following is a transcript from a portion of a therapy session with a young man who was really quite confused and who used his fine intellect to contain and rationalize his strong feelings.

P: I called my girlfriend...and now she called me and was upset because she had lost her job. You know, I sort of felt that was okay. Because she had wanted to practice harp more and she couldn't do that with going to school and holding a job. So, I, you know...she was very upset about it and I later realized that I was upset all summer about money because of my mother being upset. We both failed our life in that one. But I didn't know this when she got upset and I said, she's upset because of me. (long pause) I guess something along...and then I said, I just felt like this and then I felt like this again and I said it's all my fault and hit myself on the head and groaned. Then I learned she was upset because she felt it would matter to me whether I had money or not. And then I said, no, that was just that way for someone that I should have been.

T: Well, you make me wonder, will I be upset because of you?

C: What?

T: You make me wonder, will I be upset because of you?

C: It doesn't register.

T: It doesn't register? How do you feel about the fact that you've shared much information with me, subconscious information you've called it. How do you feel about me knowing those things about you?

C: Part of me was considering before I came in here, asking you is it all right if I say that I hate you. And that I wanted to kill you by not coming in here. That's what in effect I

326

did. [He had missed the session before this one] I wanted to say that because I was afraid concomitant with my father punishing me for expressing myself...if I said that would it really be asking Daddy, could I say something you won't like and you won't punish me?

T: Right. Absolutely!

C: So I can say that. (surprised) Just went ahead and said it!

T: Right! Am I punishing you?

C: No.

T: No. I have no desire to punish you. Any other feelings about the fact that you've shared much of this very important information about your life with me?

C: (Said with anger and strong feeling) I felt like you were trying to kill me, that whenever I'm in a group situation you're always trying to get me, that whenever I say anything you hate me. That you're trying to force me to be things I don't want to be. I wish that I could just kill you dead and that you are dead. You've just been pushing me too hard. And I can't take any more and you're just using those tapes to confound me and laugh at me afterwards. You pull me along like you care about me but you really don't.

T: I really just use you and laugh at you.

C: Um-hmmm.

T: And have none of your real interest and the importance of your whole life in my heart.

C:(said tenderly, softly, and thoughtfully) And at the same time I feel a great attraction to you and I feel this attraction is...I don't know....it isn't sexual unless you want to redefine sexual in some way. It would be more social and although I

327

feel you try to do it a good way that you don't.

T: But there's something there that you talk about in terms of attraction.

C: Um-hummm

T: But you can't be sure whether I really do want to help you or not.

C: Um-hmmm

T: And at times you're confused, very much. Like you're just a toy. At other times it sounds like you have the feeling that maybe that's not the case.

C: And then I also have the feeling that you're a very good therapist who's working with Psychological Services.

In this short space of a few interchanges, the patient has the experience of feeling angry, showing and expressing it to some extent to and for the person with whom he is angry, and realizing that his anger and its expression does not bring the expected reaction. Not only does it not bring the expected reaction from his therapist, (i.e. anger at missing a session and chastisement for saying "I hate you.") but there is also present in this experience active feelings about and for his own father - feelings tranferred onto the therapist. It is those feelings also for which he is now having a "corrective emotional experience." That is, while heretofore his father may well have not tolerated any display of anger or rebellion from his son, in this particular example that part of the patient which sees the therapist as his father is now also learning that "father" accepts his anger and his statements of hate. He learns "father" will not abandon or attack him for having such feelings. That is, on many counts, he is learning that someone upon whom he depends for support and help will not deny that support and help just because he is angry with him. And all of it is a learning that is not just intellectual or cognitive. It is not simply rational, logical learning but one that is also organically connected to emotion - the emotion of anger, fear, as well as acceptance, understanding, and consideration. Initially, the patient

328

doesn't really want to focus upon the feelings between himself and the therapist - he doesn't want to deal with the therapist's statement, "...will I be upset because of you?" He tries to avoid it, i.e. "It doesn't register." But the avoidance isn't insisted upon and the patient seems to feel enough acceptance, safety, alliance, and relationship to take the risk of saying "I hate you." Of course, it is initally couched in the framework of not saying it but asking if it would be OK to say it. Nevertheless, as soon as a modicum of true acceptance is given, the patient can readily move into words and feelings which clearly show his anger.

Perhaps this is a "first" for the patient. There may have been no other time in his life when he could openly express this kind of anger and realize that it was heard, considered, and didn't lead to rejection, retaliation, punishment. So he takes this risk of saying his hate which means that, along with the words and the cognitive activity of verbalizing his condition, he also has currently active some of his angry feelings and a decent amount of fear and anxiety. That is to say, the affective state of which he speaks is presently active and alive in the space of the relationship between patient and therapist. In this instance, we are not speaking of anger-toward-father in the abstract. We are not engaged in an intellectual discussion of anger for father. The feelings of anger, the fear of expressing them, the expectations that such expression will have an unsatisfactory or punishing outcome, and the risk of alienating and losing emotional support because of such feelings all exist in that space between therapist and patient. They are not in the abstract, they exist in actuality. And it is then in that therapeutic space that a "corrective emotional experience" may occur. For as the therapist responds with acceptance and understanding, and not in the very way the patient expects others would respond to this sharing, the patient learns something "new." He has at least learned that not every human being responds to his anger with rejection, retaliation, and punishment. But what may be more, he may have learned that he is accepted with angry feelings - that he does not have to hide or deny or distort them in this relationship.

Now I submit that "corrective emotional experiences" within the therapy hour are not at all unusual events. Rather, I think they are probably quite frequent and are part of what gives patients more and more courage to be the persons they are. Almost any psychotherapist can recall instances of patients saying something to the effect that they were surprised they weren't put down or degraded for what they thought and felt and believed. Patients say, "I really expected and feared you'd say I'm crazy," or "I was afraid that you'd say what I did was a really stupid, childish thing," or "I really thought you'd think I was a terrible, uncaring person for having such feelings." It seems not unusual for patients to expect censure, lack of support, maybe pity and hidden ridicule when they first come for psychotherapy. After all, a goodly number of our patients' problems come from the fact that they have been reared and existed in an environment which in various ways may have been unsupportive or hostile to the development of their own individualities, perspectives, and feelings. There may well be no *a prior* reason for them to believe any other situation or personal relationships will be any different from what they have already experienced. In fact, they have every reason to expect the wider world to be exactly like their own worlds - and in fact may even insist on that wider world meeting the expectations they have developed on the basis of their limited world experiences. It is this insistence which frequently gives psychotherapists difficulty. For some patients become very adept at drawing from therapists the very responses they expect. Levenson (1972), Epstein and Feiner (1979), and Marguilies and Havens (1981) have all stressed the importance of therapists being aware of participating in patients' maladaptive expectations. For if therapists take part in the patients' maladjustments, then very little if any "corrective emotional experiences" can occur. For then patients are being "told" and/or experience what they already know. While that may seem to assure a safe, predictable, and consistent world; it can only succeed in repeating its own nonsense *ad nauseum*. Such a condition, of course, results in no symptom or psychological change.

But fortunately, patients generally experience acceptance by their therapists and learn to develop feelings of trust for them. Common "corrective emotional experiences" are those in which the patient realizes the therapist does not condemn nor think less of him just because he believes one thing or another or feels one way or another. It is such experiences that give any human being the courage *to be* who they are. Rollo May (1983) quotes a patient as saying:

> I remember walking that day under the elevated tracks in a slum area, feeling the thought, "I am an illegitimate child."

330

I recall the sweat pouring forth in my anguish in trying to accept that fact. Then I understood what it must feel like to accept, "I am a Negro in the midst of privileged whites," or "I am blind in the midst of people who see." Later on that night I woke up and it came to me this way, "I accept the fact that I am an illegitimate child." But "I am not a child anymore." So it is, "I am illegitimate." That is not so either: "I was born illegitimate." Then what is left? What is left is this, "*I am.*" This act of contact and acceptance with "I am," once gotten hold of, gave me (what I think was for me the first time) the experience "Since I am, I have the right to be" (p. 99).

This "I am, and have the right to be" realization is not an uncommon experience for a person in psychotherapy and can certainly be related to the "corrective emotional experiences" the patient has with the therapist. For as the patient perceives acceptance by the therapist, it becomes obvious that another significant person of some repute and importance and standing in the community thinks this patient has the right *to be* even if the patient him or herself doesn't think they have that right. Again, quoting May (1983):

It may well be true that for any human being the possibility of acceptance by and trust for another human being is a necessary condition for the "I am" experience (p. 101).

The therapeutic relationship *per se* (see Chapter 4) undoubtedly helps to establish the acceptance patients feel and the trust they place in therapists. After all, the very qualities of nonpossessive warmth, empathy, and genuineness invite acceptance and trust. Furthermore, the therapeutic relationship is instrumental in forming a "space" in which patients may risk without fear of ridicule or censure. In that risking of being the "I am" in the relationship with the therapist can come a "corrective emotional experience."

So far, all of what we have said about "corrective emotional experiences" indicates they require an involved, intimate, personal relationship between at least two people. Furthermore, they require genuineness - that is no therapist manufactures "corrective emotional experiences."

While Alexander and French (1946) initially thought one might

331

markedly reduce the time necessary for an effective therapy by having therapists assume roles which would help counter maladaptive reactions and expectations in patients, it soon became apparent that therapists playing roles counters some of the very attitudes and postures necessary for establishing and maintaining therapeutic relationships and effecting "corrective emotional experiences." That is, in psychotherapy we are not "playing." It is not a "mind-game." It is among many other things an emotional relationship between two people. And both of the participants are emotionally involved. So, we cannot manufacture involvement. We do know some of the things necessary for building relationship and developing involvement and those things we can attend to and do. But we cannot manufacture that involvement nor the "corrective emotional experience."

However, the therapist and patient together may happen to come upon circumstances and situations in their psychotherapeutic relating that provide the opportunitites for "corrective emotional experiences." It is obviously the psychotherapist's responsibility to be aware of such events and hopefully to be able to honestly respond in such a fashion as to help accomplish a "corrective emotional experience."

Now this may need some elaboration. I do not think it is enough for the psychotherapists to understand the patient's psychodynamics and to have in addition to that an understanding of what kinds of experiences and/or responses would be therapeutic for the patient and then to give those responses. The therapist's feelings, attitudes, beliefs, postures must also be in harmony with the responses made to the patient's statement. So while intellectually the therapist may know the patient needs experiences where he or she is not completely rejected or alienated if anger is expressed, that intellectual knowledge is of no use whatsoever if when the patient expresses anger toward the therapist it results in the therapist's wanting to reject and pull away from that patient. That is, the *person* of the therapist is of considerable importance. The therapist is a real person and the patient, as noted in the chapter on relationship, is quite capable of distinquishing that real person of the therapist from the transference image of the therapist. As Franz Alexander (1961) pointed out it is the patient's emotionally experiencing the discrepancy between transference reactions and the therapist's actual behavior and personality that is required for the "corrective emotional experience."

The essence of the corrective influence is then found in a series of experiences with this person of the therapist - experiences which teach patients they can and may behave and feel differently than they have heretofore. Patients learn that, if it were not for the distorting results of transference, they would be responding to the person of the therapist differently. So, for "corrective emotional experiences," the therapists' *person* must also be part of the relationship with the patient - i.e. there must be an intimate, personal relationship.

An observational study at Mount Sinai hospital in Los Angeles conducted by Alexander (1980) attempted to assess the efficacy of therapists using "corrective emotional experience" techniques. Following Alexander's original formulation for "corrective emotional experience," these therapists set-out to discover the salient conflict for their patients in the first few interview sessions. They then proceeded to react to these patients in a manner the patients least expected - i.e. differently from how the patients' parents reacted. Thus, the therapists were deliberately directing the therapeutic interaction and attempting to manufacture a "corrective emotional experience." The therapy sessions were both observed, taped and reviewed by a panel of therapists.

The results were not what Alexander expected. Although the therapists did their best to direct therapy in specific ways, the patients did not react to the therapists as parental-type figures only. Elements of personality, idiosyncratic to the individuals involved and particularly to those of the therapist, were not eliminated. Therapists could not help but convey their personal quirks and their values to the patients whether any attempt to commmunicate such values was made or not. As a result, the effectiveness of the "corrective emotional experience" was mitigated by the therapists' own personalities. As Alexander wrote it:

> The patient reacts to the therapist's overt, but also to his nonverbal, hidden intentions and the therapist reacts to the patient's reaction to him (p. 12).

So, when dealing with the matter of a "corrective emotional experience," it would seem to be crucial that the therapist maintain those aspects of a therapeutic relationship well identified by Carl Rogers, i.e. a warm, empathic, *congruent* therapist as part of a "corrective emotional experience." The results of Alexander's observational study are really rather heartening, for they seem to indicate that we human beings are quite capable of subtle discriminations (at an unconscious if not a conscious level) and that the "truth" of a matter is rather readily apparent to us as is the falseness of role playing. For "corrective emotional experiences," we need the "truth."

The Literature and Research

Now having said all of this about "corrective emotional experiences," it might be important to point out that the term itself is not at all a part of the common denominator of terms in the psychological literature relevant to psychotherapies. In fact, it is hardly found at all. One can examine the index of book after book on psychotherapy and never find any reference to "corrective emotional experience." And the term is also virtually nonexistent in the research literature. I certainly cannot account for these facts. It seems to me the words accurately convey what is happening in one part of the process of psychotherapy. But, perhaps the terms have been too identified with Alexander and French and with psychoanalytic theory. Those who disagree with psychoanalytic theory may wish a different term. Those who are orthodox analysts, may still find Alexander and French's ideas too heretical. And yet, almost all psychotherapists will testify to the importance of "new experiences" as being a very important if not crucial part of the change process in psychotherapy. And all systems of psychotherapy recognize the importance of new experiences to counter existing maladptive feelings and beliefs.

As already noted in Chapter 3, Brady, Davison, Dewald, Egan, Fadiman, Frank, Gill, Hoffman, Kempler, Lazarus, Raimy, Rotter, and Strupp (1980) all identify "new experiences" as being very important if not crucial for the therapeutic change process. The importance of patients having some experiences in or out of the psychotherapeutic hour which help to modify, change, dissolve and/or reformulate their "old" or "neurotic" ways of feeling and behaving is common to all therapies - be they psychoanalytic, humanistic, or behavioral. In this sense, all theories of psychotherapy view the phenomena (here identified as "corrective emotional experience") as an important part of the psychotherapeutic process.

334

It is just that the different schools have different words or terms to identify that phenomena or part of the phenomena of "corrective emotional experience." Terms such as "extinction of a generalized response," "role playing," "risk taking," "behavioral rehearsal," "reparenting," "homework," "directed behavior" may all be examples of procedures that could result in "corrective emotional experiences."

One of the overriding themes in all therapies is that "neurotic" or maladaptive behaviors are learned. Furthermore, nobody would argue with the concept of generalization. As Hilgard and Marquis (1961) put it:

> When an organism has been conditioned to respond to a particular stimulus it can be shown that other similar stimuli will also elicit the response, even though these other stimuli have not been used in training (p. 328).

So if the first stimulus is the parent, the individual has learned to respond to that stimulus (parent) in a certain way. That response can easily be generalized to the therapist, another authority figure. The "corrective emotional experience" of therapy may then be construed as an extinguishing of the previous training.

> If the conditioned stimulus is repeatedly presented unaccompained by the usual reinforcer, the conditioned response undergoes a progressive decrement (called extinction) and finally fails to occur (p. 281).

So, if the patient repeatedly meets with the therapist and the therapist does not respond as the patient expects, the patient will find no need for the maladaptive behavior, i.e. the conditioned reponse. And this extinction itself can also be generalized to other authority figures.

A further principle of classical conditioning is that the degree of generalization is in proportion to the degree of severity and intensiveness of the previous training. That is, the more severe the early trauma, training, learned maladaptive behavior; the harder it will be to teach the patient new behaviors, i.e. to provide a "corrective emotional experience."

Certainly the techniques in Gestalt therapy of "the experiment," "directed behavior," and "homework" are all designed to provide the patient with experiences aimed at modifying their feelings, expectations, fears, and anxieties related to behaving, acting, or feeling certain ways. As the Polsters (1973) put it:

> Through experiment, the individual is mobilized to confront the emergencies of his life by playing out his aborted feelings in relative safety (p. 234).

In various ways, patients in psychotherapy are given opportunities for relevant practice in behaviors they may be avoiding - and, of course, those behaviors also include feelings. Behavioral rehearsal or role playing are documented and effective methods of implementing change (Galvin, 1981; Kazdin & Mascitelli, 1982; Keane, Black, Collins, and Vinson, 1982; Sarup, 1981). It's just that we've labeled it "behavioral rehearsal" or "role playing" and not "corrective emotional experiences."

So, it would seem that all systems of psychotherapy are in agreement as to the importance of "new experiences" which help to counter, modify, change, and extinquish the old feelings, beliefs, or behaviors. It is just that each system of psychotherapy has its own term for identifying this facet of the process of psychotherapy. Obviously we need to better identify, refine, and define the nature of the "new experiences" or "corrective emotional experiences" which are beneficial, healing, and curative of maladjustments. But, it certainly appears as though all systems of psychotherapy include in their formulations conditions which can be called "corrective emotional experiences."

To further identify, define, and refine "corrective emotional experiences," it will become increasingly important to include patients' descriptions of what they experience as "happening" to them in the therapy hour. That is, we will have to ask patients what they see and feel taking place. One way I have attempted to accomplish this is to make part of the therapy "contract" the requirement that both the patient *and* I keep a journal of our experience together in psychotherapy. The journals are to be kept confidential; although if both of us near the end of the psychotherapy feel it would be possible to share our journals, that could be done. But, in any event, at the end of psychotherapy each of us would write-up what we thought were the significant and important parts of the psychotherapeutic experience. We would share those write-ups with one another and have time to discuss with one another our reactions to those write-ups. In a sense, we are both attempting to identify the significant aspects of the psychotherapeutic experience. And we do that by including both the patient's and therapist's perspectives.

In order to focus upon the variable of "corrective emotional experiences" in psychotherapy, it will also become increasingly important to develop some research methodology to handle this very complex and emotional process. Elliot (1983, 1984), Horowitz, (1982), and Rice & Greenberg (1984) have all written about an approach which would focus upon an intensive analysis of the significant therapy events related to the change process. As Rice and Greenberg (1984) state:

> Our conviction is that a new style of research paradigm is called for, one that will make use of intensive analysis for discovering the internal structure of the interactions of therapy while using some more extensive method for verification of some of the basic processes of therapeutic change (p. 8).

The old research methodologies of aggregating process and procedures summarized ratings across samples and sessions assumed that all process in psychotherapy was the same. It paid little or no attention to what the patient and the therapist may have been *feeling* or may have been *attempting* to do.

So instead of grouping people together on some individual difference variable, Rice and Greenberg (1984) are suggesting that we start to form our samples for study on the basis of

> ...episodes of therapeutic interaction in which clients are engaged in person-situation interactions that have important commonalities (p. 13).

Their book is a presentation of a number of new paradigms for researching change phenomena and the client mechanisms underlying the change. Their approach permits us to more fully examine person-situation interactions and take as our N for study the number of such episodes.

Eliott's (1984) discovery-oriented approach is one of those new paradigms. It places importance upon the experiences and perceptions of both persons participating in the psychotherapy, and does not summarily dismiss phenomenological data. As Eliott writes:

> In more specific terms, the discovery-oriented approach to significant change events in psychotherapy asks a number of basic questions: What would we find out if we asked clients and therapists to point to significant moments of psychological change in psychotherapy? What would they tell us if we provided them with the means of describing in close detail just what was happening during particular moments of significant change? How could we combine this kind of information with other sorts of information on change episodes, in order to tell therapists how to conduct psychotherapy more effectively (p. 249)?

Using the interpersonal process recall (IPR), developed by Kagan (1975) and the comprehensive process analysis, which is an integration of the methodological and conceptual work of Horowitz (1979), Kiesler (1973), Labov and Fanshel (1977), Orlinsky and Howard (1978), and Russell and Stiles (1979); Eliott illustrates the use of his discovery-oriented approach for researching changes in psychotherapy as a result of insight. As far as I can see, there is no reason the same methodology could not be used for researching the effect of "corrective emotional experiences" in psychotherapy change. As Eliott writes in conclusion:

> In particular, the method opened the door for phenomenological analyses of the events, most strikingly exemplified by the rich detail of client descriptions of the impact phases of these episodes and therapist descriptions of the context of the intervention.

> ...As developed here, this discovery-oriented approach has much in common with Greenberg's (1977) task analytic approach, in that it selects specific therapeutic events for study on the basis of potency and recurrence, subjects them to analyses whose result is the identification of common features, and uses these common features as the basis for constructing models of the change process in psychotherapy

338

(p. 283).

It, of course, remains to be seen whether or not these particular research paradigms will prove useful in investigating the very complex phenomena of interpersonal dynamics involved in "corrective emotional experiences." But these paradigms are at least a definite improvement over what we have had up to this time.

Outside of Psychotherapy

Now there is a last aspect of the variable of "corrective emotional experience" left to discuss. And that aspect is one which no research paradigm has yet approached. I refer to the fact that once patients have a "corrective emotional experience" within the psychotherapy hour, it is not at all unlikely that they will then start to experience similar and/or additional "corrective emotional experiences" outside of psychotherapy. Karen Horney (1937) pointed out that life itself remained a very effective therapy. So once patients have significant experiences within the psychotherapy hour teaching them they will not be rejected, alienated, or degraded for being and feeling who they are; it is not unlikely that they then might start to wonder if other persons in the world would not also accept them for their beliefs, feelings, and behaviors.

In my experience, as this process of "corrective emotional experience" happens, patients start to report changes in their behavior and changes they have made in regard to significant persons in their environment. In a much earlier chapter, there was the example of the man who in therapy was able to show and state some of his anger, and then who in a subsequent session pointed out he was able to show his girlfriend some of the anger he really had within him. That is an example of what I am talking about. Patients, without any therapist prompting (although one could assign homework) are trying out their new found "insight," "perspective" and expanding their range of interactions from the therapist outward. This is an example of the healing power in every human being. There is something about us that strives for health and given the right circumstances that healthful striving will naturally occur. As we hit upon a perspective and experience that is freeing and releasing for us, we will start to change our lives with others around us. I take the

339

patient moving out into the environment and relating with other people in significantly different ways as evidence that the therapy work is significant.

Of course, the fashion in which the patient goes about "trying out" new insights, perspectives, orientations in the "outside world" may become very important for the therapy work. For, patients certainly have the ability to take the "corrective emotional experience" and so mistrust it and be so upset by it that they *must* reconstitute their old defenses. Thus, they can go out and interact with some significant others in such a fashion as to "resist" the implications and meanings of the "corrective emotional experience." After all, most human beings know how to go about getting rejected, or go about getting people to respond to them in expected ways, i.e. we can be reassurred that our "old beliefs" are still accurate. Even if it happens that the patient resists the "corrective emotional experience," we should not make the mistake of thinking it had no effect. For the very act of having to deny and work to overcome it suggests it had a rather powerful effect. In my experience, patients working to deny the experience is more common when that "corrective emotional experience" occurred very early in psycho-therapy before sufficient alliance, trust, and "therapeutic inter-personal relationships" had developed. That is, patients' denial responses to "corrective emotional experiences" are similar to patients' responses to pre-mature interpretations. But, for the most part, patients do not resist "corrective emotional experiences." Rather, they quietly integrate them into their lives and start to act on the "new" perspective.

Therapists must listen carefully for indications "corrective emotional experiences" are being acted upon outside of the therapy hour. For it is unlikely patients will come back the next session and tell us, "I had this corrective emotional experience last time and I tried it out on a number of people this week." No, if their outside work has been to resist the "corrective emotional experience" then patients will be pretty definite and point out how what the therapist told them as well as what they experienced with the therapist last time just isn't so. Patients will say something to the effect that the therapist may be able to accept them but others can't. Patients may add something like, "besides, you are paid to accept me." But, if their out-of-therapy "corrective emotional experiences" were extensions of their in-therapy experiences, it is almost in passing that they may mention anything about such experiences. After all, it would be a waste of therapy time to review what has already been accomplished. What *is* accomplished is done. Patients don't care to dwell on that but to go onto the next thing of concern, confusion, and import.

I don't want to discount the possible importance of "corrective emotional experiences" occurring outside of the psychotherapy hour. There is, as far as I can see, no good reason not to expect that to happen. Furthermore, if the "corrective emotional experience" is to be reinforced and become part of the patient's life, it must be generalized beyond the therapist. The therapist is not the one-and-only person the patient has a relationship with and there is no reason at all why what the patient is learning and feeling within psychotherapy doesn't also become an important part of his or her life outside of therapy. Certainly, Alexander and French (1946) in their initial formulation of the "corrective emotional experience" had no problem with viewing its existence outside of the therapy hour. They wrote:

> It is of secondary importance whether this corrective experience takes place during treatment in the transference relationship, or parallel with the treatment in the daily life of the patient (p. 66).

And there are many advantages to "corrective emotional experiences" taking place outside the therapy hour. For it is in this way that we get additional positive reinforcement for being the person we are, it is in this way that we broaden our base of support and satisfaction - that we learn to reach out and be ourselves with other human beings and further expand our possibilities for growth enhancing and person building relationships with other people. It is, of course, in this way that therapists begin to play less and less of an active role and that patients start to know they can expand the processes that were begun in psychotherapy and do so on their own.

When these "corrective emotional experiences" have occurred in enough significant areas of the patient's life, and when the patient is on the way to expanding the processes that were begun in psychotherapy and making them part of life outside of therapy, then termination becomes important.

341

CHAPTER 11

TERMINATION

There comes a time when the process of psychotherapy must end. And while that ending may have elements common to other endings, separations, or losses in life; its nature is also rather highly determined by the extent, ramifications, developments in and particular nuances of the process which is now coming to an end or being terminated. I like to use the word "terminated" to identify the point of and process by which we end the psychotherapy. My liking of the term, beyond the fact it is a traditional term for this process, is that it implies a finality - it has a "death-like" quality. Separations and deaths (ultimate, final separations) are part of the very nature of life. And as Becker (1973) has pointed out, we human beings vacillate between denying and fearing death. In any event, we know psychotherapy can offer no cure to separations and deaths. Psychotherapy can only help us understand and accept our feelings about these events. And so, when psychotherapy ends, both patient and therapist will have some feelings about this ending - this termination.

The End Of A Process

So termination is, simply put, the end of a process! But, termination is *not* simple, it *is* a process in and of itself, and it *is* an extremely important part of the entire psychotherapeutic process and one which requires effective handling by the psychotherapist. For, most importantly, termination is not just the end of the psychotherapeutic process. It is also the end of a unique and important interpersonal relationship. And in many respects (as noted throughout this book) the relationship has been a healing, growth producing one closely associated with the patient's "becoming." In these respects, the relationship has characteristics similar to the one between a nurturing, reliable parent and his or her child. Bowlby's (1980) studies have significantly highlighted the importance of attachment and subsequent loss on children and the relationship of these experiences to subsequent personality development. Those studies are not inappropriately recalled by any therapist attempting to be sensitive to the various feelings and fears patients can have attendant to the process of termination.

In addition, it would seem important for any therapist to remember that "endings" for any of us human beings are powerful events. Some of the most difficult stresses humans experience are in response to separations. Separations and losses (whether from the death of a significant person, changing of jobs, moving away from parents, or graduating from college) almost universally provoke increased anxiety and other emotions. This seems to be a natural response. And our responses to present separations and losses are undoubtedly complicated by the activation of repressed emotions coming from earlier unresolved experiences of separation and/or loss. As Maholick and Turner (1979) so aptly put it:

... there is a recurrent cyclical phenomenon of goodbyes encompassing the entire life of man from birth to death (p. 584).

Our earlier experiences with goodbyes are certainly going to play some role and have some say at the time we terminate the psychotherapeutic process. Our goodbyes in life generally have not been without emotion and feeling - and sometimes feelings so strong and/or ego alien we cannot face or recognize them. As Fromme (1956) has pointed out:

The awareness of human separation, without reunion by love - is the source of shame. It is at the same time the source of guilt and anxiety (p.9).

Feelings of regret, sadness, anger, and guilt are commonly associated with unresolved separations. Thus, when the event of termination comes in the process of psychotherapy; it is likely that the ending of

344

the psychotherapeutic relationship will also be a painful reminder of other leave-takings, separations, and losses in the patient's and therapist's lives. Again, I quote Maholick and Turner (1979):

> Termination of therapy can be thought of as a recapitulation of the multiple preceding goodbyes of living. At the same time, it is a preparation for being able to deal more adequately and openly with future goodbyes (p. 584).

So, part of the process of termination can activate earlier unresolved issues and feelings about goodbyes, separations, and losses in our lives. In this sense, it is not just the therapy we are terminating - but also working-through our feelings of separation and loss from earlier times in our history. Mann (1973) in discussing time-limited psychotherapy, also points out the importance of attending to these common feelings related to separation.

> Since anger, rage, guilt, and their accompaniments of frustration and fear are the potent factors that prevent positive internalization and mature separation, it is these that must not be over-looked in this phase [termination] of the time-limited therapy (p. 36).

So it is important for therapists to keep in mind that termination can be a powerful event in and of itself, complicated by the patient's earlier experiences with endings, and reminiscent of the loss of a nurturing, reliable parent. Then, in addition, it is important to remember that the termination is *also* the end of a process - the process of psychotherapy. And the importance that process and the nature its its "therapeutic interpersonal relationship" has upon the issues and feelings present at termination must not be discounted. Remember, for a moment, some things we have said about the nature of the process of psychotherapy and the therapeutic interpersonal relationship. It is a process which has made great demands upon patient and therapist alike. Those demands have included not only time and money, but personal involvements and commitments. It has required unsparing honesty from both patient and therapist as well as an ability on both persons' parts to face unpleasant and ego threatening facts. As has been pointed out in a number of ways through this book, the process of psychotherapy has required of both patient and therapist much emotional involvement and struggle. The term "therapeutic alliance" was used in an attempt to convey some of the nature of the commitment necessary on both the patient's and therapist's part. The words "love" and "souls-meeting" were used in attempts to convey some of the intensity and force of the emotional involvement between the two persons of the psychotherapeutic dyad. Commitment and love are not easily dissolved or lost. It takes a divorce. And so the process of psychotherapy *per se* has generated, as a matter of its being, issues of considerable importance that must be felt, faced, and dealt with at the point of termination. As Mendel (1966) has pointed out:

> In fact, if we look at the constant process of beginning and ending these intimate relationships, the process with which we are involved all of our lives as psychotherapists, it is difficult to understand how any one of us can manage to function in a profession which is taxing and dangerous to our own psychic. Each time we have completed work with a patient, we have to give up a relationship with a fellow human being with whom we have lived intimately and in considerable detail for a number of years, and in whom we have invested a great deal of interest, concern, and psychic energy (p.35).

And as Edelson (1963) has pointed out:

> The client mourns the loss of a person with whom he has been able to be unreservedly himself, to say anything, to be completely frank, to come to know himself and feel his identity most fully (p. 58).

Both therapist and patient suffer specific separation and losses at the end of psychotherapy. After all, in one sense the entire task of psychotherapy is to help bring people to their love and to their own understanding. That is the ultimate purpose or goal of psychotherapy. And in the process of that occurring, both parties in the dyad develop ties, needs, dependencies and gratefulnesses. After all, both parties in the psychotherapeutic dyad have had a very unique, close, intimate, involved, and growing experience. When that comes to an end, there are bound to be plenty of feelings on both

346

sides of the relationship - feelings that will include sadness and a sense of being cheated - feelings that are related to and important in light of what the two have been through together.

The term "termination" then is used to refer to all of those feelings the patient and therapist have about ending their work together as well as those feelings and concerns either member of this dyad may bring from their own life of "goodbyes." In addition, it identifies a stage in the "therapeutic interpersonal relationship" where transference, countertransference, corrective emotional experience relationship(s) factors have less and less play. Alliance factors are almost taken for granted now but the collaborative goal seems to be to end the psychotherapy. Interpersonal relationship variables seem to come more and more to the fore now. Issues of resistance, transference, countertransference, therapeutic relationship, insight, corrective emotional experience are more and more behind us - or probably more correctly said, now start to take a realistic place in the interpersonal relationship between therapist and patient. The therapist and patient work out ways to come down from and leave the "platform-of-relationships" upon which both have stood and from which the significant work of psychotherapy was done.

As a patient, I no longer feel the need for my therapist (this other human being with whom I'm working) to be a source upon which I may transfer feelings, conflicts, confusions. I'm feeling better and better and start to realize there really isn't much to work on right now. And, I also start to wonder and want to know more about this other person - this person who has been my therapist, who has patiently and in a way mysteriously helped bring me to my present place. I realize I don't really "know" this person - all I've known is my therapist.

And as a therapist I've started to "hear" the patient's camouflage language indicating a move toward termination. I start to listen to my own feelings and opinions about termination with this specific patient, and start to experience some anxiety about "losing" this patient as well as about adequately handling the termination.

So both patient and therapist start to leave the "platform" upon which so much psychotherapeutic work has been done. And the feelings that both persons in this dyadic interaction have about leaving the platform and about the work they have done and the psychological places they have been together constitute part of this

347

"termination" process. The other part of it is the working through to a place where the two parties can separate and are relatively clear about the nature of their relationship with one another now that therapy has ended. That is, the realities of the relationship between these two persons (therapist and patient) have become clearer and are explicated. And those realities may certainly include the fact that they could at some future time and with some future need remount the "platform" and recreate the conditions for the building of another psychotherapeutic process.

Termination: Its Meaning and Importance To The Process of Psychotherapy

A number of persons have called attention to the importance of handling the termination stage of psychotherapy well. Beck, Rush, Shaw, Emery (1979) are of the opinion that a well handled termination enhances the patient's ability to consolidate the gains made in psychotherapy and to generalize them to future problems. Freud (1937, [1964]) certainly saw the therapist as having a responsibility for helping the patient work through the meaning of termination. Janis (1982) as well as Cavanagh (1982) take similar positions. In fact, I think one would be hard pressed to find anyone writing in the area of psychotherapy who saw the termination of the process as relatively unimportant or insignificant.

A) Premature Termination

The fact that workers in the area of psychotherapy see termination as important is demonstrated by the amount of attention given to what has been called "premature termination." And the attention given is often such as to suggest that premature termination is "bad." It is "bad" either because the therapist really missed the meaning of the patient's request or suggestion to end treatment; or it is "bad" because the patient really stopped coming for treatment which the therapist saw as needed.

I think these are really two separate issues, and the profession is ill served when we lump them together. In the first instance (where the patient is coming to the session but also verbalizing a desire to end or verbalizing dissatisfaction with the therapy) there still remains

348

some contact between therapist and patient - i.e. the patient has not unilaterally acted upon terminating the psychotherapeutic relationship. Furthermore, generally in these situations, there have been a number of therapy sessions prior to the request to end or the complaint about therapy. That is, generally some therapeutic alliance has been established. Thus, in this situation the entire issue of termination becomes a topic for discussion and analysis. In the second instance the patient has generally failed to return for a scheduled appointment after the first or second interview. Generally very few sessions have been held, little or no therapeutic alliance established, and the patient has unilaterally broken contact with the therapist. I am inclined to reserve the term "premature termination" only for patients in the first instance who do, in fact, then end the therapy without working-through the reasons for the termination. I think we need a different term for those patients who fail to "get-into-therapy."

1. Patient Requests Termination.

In those instances where the patient is already involved in the psychotherapeutic process and then indicates a desire (or even a demand) to end the therapy; that request, desire, demand, and its accompanying feelings become the topic for consideration and analysis and thus part of the present process of psychotherapy. For it is within the present process of psychotherapy (wherever that process is - alliance, transference, countertransference, etc.) that the request for ending the psychotherapy is embedded and must be examined and discussed.

Now, I do not want to suggest that whenever the patient mentions termination or ending, it is inappropriate or premature. There certainly are times when the patient's mentioning the possibility of ending psychotherapy is very much in harmony with their emerging readiness to terminate as well as with the therapist's expectation that the end of the psychotherapeutic relationship is nearing. In fact, in my experience those times are in the majority.

But there are also instances when patients quite unexpectedly bring up the issue of termination. Not infrequently unexpected requests for termination may well signify issues quite different than and apart from ending the psychotherapy. I stress that it is the unexpected requests or those couched in such a manner that they

349

lack authenticity or genuineness that are inclined to signify issues other than termination. Or, the patient's words and affect are not congruent and bespeak a confusion that clearly indicates more than termination as the issue. It is not uncommon that patients' unexpected requests for ending psychotherapy can be ways patients try to bring-up or point-to other issues important for the continued process of psychotherapy.

Psychotherapists might well remember patients always possess the power to terminate psychotherapy. So the time and manner in which they chose to terminate is of some significance. And patients do not need therapists' approval to terminate. If patients are really quite unhappy about or dissatisfied with their psychotherapy, they are certainly free to end treatment. The fact patients keep their therapy appointment and present as a topic for discussion their desire to terminate gives the therapist an opportunity to understand and examine the unexpected request to terminate.

Beier and Young (1984) give a nice example of how a patient's unexpected announcement for ending psychotherapy was probably more of an attempt to force the therapist into accepting and/or rejecting her and to force the therapist to take responsibility for her than it was any real attempt to end the psychotherapy. Here are the patient's words:

> I am through. (pause) Instead of getting better I am getting worse. I think that therapy has not helped me at all. I am sick and tired of giving up the little money I have and wasting hour after hour coming to your lousy office. There is no sense to it. I still can't live with myself any more easily than before I came here. It's gotten worse. I don't know what I am going to do, but one thing I am sure, this is the last time I will see you (p. 121).

As Beier and Young (1984) indicate, with such strong feelings about the therapy, it is highly unlikely that she would have come in for this session at all if she really had given up on the idea of any further treatment. As these authors state:

> In fact, in our experience many patients who come in to the hour with a request for termination may be more concerned with the therapist's consent than with leaving.

The patient may not really wish to break off treatment, but sometimes wish to obtain the therapist's refusal, or try to arouse the therapist's anxiety by threatening to quit, or just get the therapist to commit himself about the patient's progress (p. 120-121).

In that quote, Beier and Young (1984) suggest some of the reasons patients may make unexpected termination requests. Cavanagh (1982) also suggests possible reasons patients make unexpected termination requests. Those reasons include attempts to see if the therapist really cares for them, to get the therapist to express positive feelings for them, to hurt or punish the therapist. He also points out patients may want to terminate psychotherapy because of the increased anxiety it is generating for them, because of uncomfortable and/or ego alien feelings they may be having for the therapist, or out of the fear some "new" and frightening material may emerge from the process of psychotherapy. He also includes the possibilities patients may feel the therapist is incompetent, not the kind of person with whom they want to work, really not understanding them, or is attempting to "lay some trip" on them.

Garfield (1980) also recognizes that patients' threats of termination can be related to issues other than ending. He suggests such threats could be attempts to get the therapist to recommit to the therapy, to get the therapy to change, to get the therapist to reassure the patient that progress can be made. And, of course, there also remains the possibility that such threats are indications of real dissatisfaction with and loss of faith in the therapy and or therapist.

Thus, where patients unexpectedly raise the issue of termination; it seems important to explore and attempt to understand that request. One can work with it as one would work with any other issue in the process of psychotherapy. Only by such exploration can an adequate decision be made about continuing or not continuing the therapy. If, however, the patient or the therapist is unwilling or unable to do that work and the therapy relationship abruptly ends, I would call that a "premature termination."

2. Patient Unilaterally Terminates.

There are times when patients fail to return for a scheduled appointment after one or two sessions. Studies indicate that between 37% to 45% of people seeking psychotherapy in urban mental health centers fail to show up for appointments after the first or second interview (Garfield, 1980). I don't know of any empirical data giving rates for patients seen by private practicioners. But my own experience would suggest such rates in private practice would be much lower. There could be motivational differences between patients seeking psychotherapy through private practicioners and those seeking psychotherapy in urban mental health centers. Patients who seek appointments with private practicioners have not only had to go through the process of considering their need and desire for psychotherapy, they have also had to consider how to finance the treatment and have had to go through the task of selecting a therapist. Those seeking appointments in local or community mental health centers may not need to engage in the latter two tasks.

At any rate, I am not inclined to see patients who fail to keep appointments after the first or second session as "premature terminators." For if we say they have terminated prematurely we are also assuming they had made a psychotherapuetic alliance. For in order to terminate psychotherapy you must have been "in" the therapy. Rather, these patients who fail to keep appointments after the first one or two sessions may well be persons who for any number of reasons have not formed or established any therapeutic alliance.

Hartley and Strupp (1983) reported some research results with persons who dropout after one or two sessions. i.e. those who unilaterally terminate. They found patients in the dropout group tended to be less involved in the therapy than patients who continued their therapy. The dropouts also were more highly defensive, and were less willing to assume responsibility for their behavior and their therapy. These authors suggest the possibility that therapists' sensing such attitudes may even try harder to establish alliance and a therapeutic relationship. It is possible in trying even harder to "help" that a therapist could add to the patient's fear of and reluctance to become involved in psychotherapy. For in trying hard "to help," one could avoid dealing with the reality of the patient's defensiveness and unwillingness to assume responsibility.

We have no definitive information on the number of patients

coming to mental health centers and/or seeking psychotherapy who are responding out of some need to placate a third party or meet some imposed obligation. Any therapist is leery of the patient whose appointment has been made by a third party - a spouse, friend, parent, attorney. The questions which inevitably arise under such circumstances have to do with wondering who really wants the therapy - the patient for whom the appointment was made or the person who made the appointment. Of course, even if the patient calls for the appointment, we don't know if she or he is doing it with a spouse, parent, attorney standing right there and insisting upon it. As already noted it might be informative to see patients the moment they make the appointment. They would not have had time to prepare what they want to say in the first session. And with that vulnerability we might learn a great deal more about their motivations for seeking psychotherapy and perhaps more rapidly identify their fears, problems, and ambivalences with the psychotherapeutic process.

It is important for therapists to be sensitive to patients' "reasons" for coming to therapy at the time they do come; and it is important to set reasonable goals in light of patients' fears, problems, and ambivalences with the psychotherapeutic process. It seems that psychotherapists may be too inclined to think they must "help" anyone who seeks their services. This seems to be particularly true for those who work in the public sector. There therapists may feel less freedom to refuse to see a patient than do therapists in private practice.

But in recognizing patients' fears, problems and ambivalences with psychotherapy and their lack of motivation and/or ability to form a therapeutic alliance; we may well be able to set goals to work upon which prove much more realistic than the goal of getting the patient to continue with therapy sessions.

I have not found it uncommon to have patients come to the college's Psychological Services and present rather difficult and serious problems as though they were rather inconsequential - something they will probably grow out of and need not deal with. These patients frequently are urged by others who have gotten tired of their litany of symptoms and complaints to come to the Services and "get" psychotherapy . And it is not that these students who present themselves don't want treatment. Rather, it is that they are seriously conflicted and generally poorly informed about the nature

353

of psychotherapy. They obviously are unwilling to consider any kind of long-term psychotherapy. But, they have come for a session and they are generally willing to spend two or three sessions "considering/discussing" their problems. That is, their goal seems to be one of spending some time with a psychotherapist and finding out a little bit about what that process-experience is like. My goal for these sessions is to provide the patient with as rewarding a therapy experience as possible under the circumstances and within the time limits imposed. The idea is that we can start to dissipate the patients' anxiety and fear of their own "insanity" as well as some of the fears they have of relating to a therapist. With this goal, they may well move to a place where they want and desire to establish a therapeutic relationship which would permit more systematic work on their problems. At the present time they will not move into a long-term psychotherapeutic relationship. But, my experience has been that such patients having had a rewarding initial experience with a psychotherapist frequently return - either to me or to other therapists in the Service - and eventually get to the place where they are ready for and accepting of long-term psychotherapy. I have not seen them as "premature terminators." Rather, they are patients for whom a series of short-term goals must be set and worked on before they are at the place where they are willing and able to tolerate and accept the necessary processes involved in long-term or even intensive short-term psychotherapy. One could say we are doing nothing but working on developing the opportunity to form a therapeutic alliance.

Lastly, there certainly may be instances in which patients do not wish to work on their problems - do not really want psychotherapy. Any therapist has seen persons who in their opinion were definitely in need of psychotherapy but who refuse to seek treatment. Now, the judgment that the patient is in need of psychotherapy may be an accurate one. But, the belief that persons in need of psychotherapy *should* avail themselves of that therapy is a value judgment. In making such a judgment we give patients no say or part in deciding whether or not they want therapy. And, of course, it is really they who have the decision to make anyway. Therapists only delude themselves if they think it is their decision. After all, if patients wish to deny the existence of some difficulty, or to take the position of "let sleeping dogs lie;" isn't that their right?

Therapists have to be able to identify patients' abilities and desires to form a psychotherapeutic alliance. If the desire is not there, why can't we simply accept that reality and the patient's freedom to make such a choice? If the ability to form alliance is not there, that then becomes the first goal. It is not a "premature termination" until some therapeutic alliance is formed. And it is obvious that some patients lack the capacity to meet the demands of therapeutic alliance. Probably the best examples of such situations are persons with borderline disorders. In such situations the first attempts and goals for therapy are to help the patient move toward alliance. That task is quite difficult and we frequently fail at it. But, nevertheless it is a necessary one - one of securing patients' alliance in working with them on their problems.

B) Indices for Termination

In the majority of cases, patients do not verbally initiate the process of termination. But they do give various indications that the end of the psychotherapy is approaching. As psychotherapy proceeds, both therapist and patient should have some sense of how they are succeeding in meeting the goals of the therapy and/or developing new goals. Therapists attending to the material flow of the therapy and keeping a sensitive ear tuned toward hearing how patients are relating to significant others in their environment, can obtain some measure of the extent to which patients are making progress in resolving conflict areas and in reaching some of the goals of the psychotherapy. Toward the end of psychotherapy, patients have generally achieved improvement in the complaints (which include symptoms) they initially identified and stated as well as in feelings of self-esteem, self-acceptance and ease with interpersonal relationships (Luborsky, 1984).

Now, the therapist must not be in too much of a hurry to suggest termination upon "hearing" that the patient has satisfactorily achieved the initial treatment goals. I say this because it is not unusual that once patients have resolved the problem and/or issue with which they entered therapy, they then present another issue or conflictual problem area upon which they wish to work. I am repeatedly impressed with the human mind. It seems to have an ability to know which issues to approach, and how much work to do on them before calling it quits. And the mind seems to be able to do this without verbalizing or even fully recognizing what needs to be worked on. As noted in Chapter 9, patients seem to have a sense of where they need to go. And as further noted in that chapter, frequently the material flow will give us clues as to what material is coming-up next and will need to be worked on.

Of course, we shouldn't be surprised by any of this. With very little thought each one of us recognizes the fact that if we wish to do some important "self-work" with another human being we will involve ourselves in "testing" that person to see whether or not we are accepted and can work well together. We will not share our deepest fears and secrets and shames until we have some sign the other person will honor and value our position and predicament. As we experience acceptance and benefit from the psychotherapy and as we obtain some resolution of and improvement in our personal situation, we are then more inclined to take a next step with the therapist and present another "problem" upon which to work. Furthermore, as the work of therapy reduces some of our anxiety, helps us recognize the use of our defense system and thus reduce its impact; then more feelings and perspectives may become available to us enabling us to see additional areas of difficulty and conflict and areas upon which we then wish to work further in therapy.

So, it is not enough to say that a sign of termination is when the patient has arrived at a satisfactory resolution of the presenting complaint. Certainly patient and therapist should recognize that the symptoms and suffering are lessened or absent. But before the therapist suggests termination, it is probably wise to wait and "hear" if the patient presents any new goal or goals upon which he or she may wish to work psychotherapeutically.

Typically as the termination phase of psychotherapy approaches, the opening of new problem areas ceases and the patient has fewer complaints to share. In fact, the patient may even struggle to find something to talk about. This "struggling" is quite unlike that observed when patients are resisting dealing with an area. In the latter instance, the struggle has more a quality of struggling *against* something - attempting not to talk about something in therapy. In the former instance, the struggle has more a quality of struggling *toward* something - of attempting to find something to talk about in the therapy. The patient has difficulty finding conflict/problem areas of real concern. In essence, things are really going rather well for the patient and the few conflict/problem issues mentioned are frequently ones the patient has already dealt with or solved in one way or another. That is, these issues are not brought up in therapy necessarily as material upon which to work, or from which to gain more understanding or insight. Rather, they really are examples of how well the patient is applying many of the skills, tools, insights, new perspectives developed during the course of the psychotherapy. They may intially be presented almost as a conflict/problem area but within a few minutes it becomes obvious they are really examples of how the patient has already dealt with the problem. At the same time, one may also notice a shift in the way the patient talks about "other" significant persons in his or her life. Whereas early talk about "others" in the patient's life focused upon them as a source of frustration, difficulty, conflict and hurt; now the patient starts to talk about "others" as a source of support, enjoyment, and satisfaction.

Now along with these obvious (but also perhaps somewhat subtle) changes, the therapist may note a tendency to pull back as a source of support. The therapist will start to recognize that therapeutic skills are needed less and less now, and will start to recognize that the patient is requiring much less "work" from the therapist. I initially enjoy that feeling - that point where I recognize my "work" with this patient is so much easier. I then realize it is *too* much easier. The patient is not really presenting anything to work on. I start to sense the "ending" may be coming.

It is at that point I will start to carefully listen for camouflage language indicating that the patient is preparing to end the psychotherapy. Perhaps it will present itself in one of their dreams reported in the therapy hour, or in finding themselves focusing upon "leavings" and not understanding at all why they are on that topic. Or the patient may even make a passing statement such as "I wonder what it will be like when we end."

With the above indices for termination, I will generally initiate its possibility. I do it by saying something like, "It seems as though we may be coming to the end of the therapy." It is said with a tenuousness. I also most carefully listen to the patient's response as it may be quite telling. Generally there is confirmation of the fact the patient, too, has been wondering about it. But generally there is also the expression of some fears about ending - fears they aren't really "cured" or fears their improved state won't last.

To go ahead with termination, the patient must give indications of being ready to deal with separation from the therapist. For it is in this stage of the process of psychotherapy that we deal with universal

357

issues surrounding leavings as well as the very specific feelings and issues about ending the present psychotherapeutic relationship. Once it is clear both patient and therapist agree psychotherapy is coming to an end, then a specific date is set for the "last" session. The date by which the psychotherapy will end is set by attempting to estimate how much time is needed in the specific case to deal with the issues of termination. But in addition, a major purpose for clearly specifying the date of the last session is so that both patient and therapist will know *exactly* by what time they need to have their "psychological work" about ending completed. Once the decision to terminate is made, it is most unwise to keep it open-ended, i.e. I would not say something like, "We will see how much time we need in which to end." That could only invite procrastination. For the ending is not necessarily a particularly enjoyable prospect. Remember it does entail separation and loss. And, when we are clear about how much time we do have left together, then we are much more inclined to spend time focusing upon the issues psychologically important to that ending. Thus, I think it important to be definite about the ending date - setting it in consultation with the patient who will also have some sense of how much time is needed to terminate - and then holding to that date.

C) Feelings About Ending

A common fear and concern expressed by patients once termination is suggested is that they are not completely "cured." While this could be an attempt to prolong the therapy indefinitely, more often I find it a legitimate confusion on patients' part. That is, they know they are ready to end psychotherapy - really don't need to continue therapy any longer at this time - but they also realize that they still do have some confusions, conflicts, uncertainties, and anxieties.

In the first place the concept of "cure" is really (or should be) foreign to the concept of psychotherapy. As Dr. Murray Banks is reported to have said when a patient told him he wanted to be permanently adjusted, "Go to the cemetery. That's the only place people are permanently adjusted." There is no "cure" to living except to continue learning and do the living. And that means all of us will have confusions, conflicts, uncertainties and anxieties from time to time. But it is not unusual for people to associate psychotherapy to a medical procedure and expect that once the "treatment" is over they should be "cured." In addition, the early history of psychoanalysis was such that people were led to believe that a complete and successful analysis was all that was needed and they were then permanently well adjusted.

In the second place, psychotherapy should be terminated prior to the "cure" anyway. By that I mean, we may terminate the psychotherapy at that point where it is obvious patients are well on their way to resolving the issues which brought them into psychotherapy *and* have learned ways of self-analysis, introspection, dream interpretation, and of attending to and honoring their feelings. That is, we end the psychotherapy at that point where patients have developed methods for continuing to learn about and know themselves and by so doing do in fact modify symptoms and resolve conflicts and problem areas. We end the psychotherapy at that point where patients have developed methods for being and interacting with other human beings in such a fashion as to resolve difficulties, learn about themselves and the others, and maintain mutually enjoyable relationships. We terminate at that point where patients no longer need the psychotherapy as it is evident they will continue to effectively deal with their issues, be involved in their own growing and becoming which will carry them further in the direction of their goals. We end at that point when patients are telling us they no longer need us to assist them in their process of becoming. As Cavanagh (1982) writes:

> When people have a clear picture of their ultimate goals
> and good momentum in the right direction, they are ready
> to finish the job on their own (p. 134).

Even though patients frequently are concerned upon ending psychotherapy that they aren't completely "cured," my experience suggests that at some level they do know they are ready to end and can "finish the job" on their own. I say that because their concern about not being completely cured is generally easily handled by the above explanations. It is almost as though they are reassured that they don't have to be a paradigm of adjustment now that they have had psychotherapy.

The second concern patients have - one which I find almost universal - is the fear that they can't handle their problems without

359

the therapist's help. In fact, this fear coupled with the above concern about being "cured" operate in such a fashion as to almost assure patients will experience a return of some of the symptoms which initiated their psychotherapy. This phenomenon of patients experiencing a slight recurrence of symptoms as termination approaches has been noted by many (Beck, Rush, Shaw, Emery, 1979; Klerman, Weissman, Rounsaville, Chevron, 1984; Luborsky, 1984). It is as though the patient believes that without the continued presence of the therapist, the symptoms will return. In part, this belief may come from the fact that the reasons for the abatement of the symptoms in the first place are not all that obvious. And then, of course, it was in the presence of the therapist that those symptoms started to go away. Also, the return of symptoms is a way for patients to express ambivalence about ending. And the return of the patient's symptoms can also affect the therapist - for if inexperienced in these matters, the therapist may start to question the wisdom of the decision to terminate and question his or her ability to really help anyone.

But all of these feelings on both the patient's and therapist's part are typical of an infant's magical thinking about Wizards of Oz and helpless little girls or boys or men or lions (Kopp, 1968). Such feelings ignore the realities of the signs which have indicated that termination time has come. It ignores the reality that the therapist has been involved in a systematic process called psychotherapy designed specifically to attend to the presenting complaints and that those symtoms and complaints have abated. And most importantly, it ignores the reality that the patient has been intimately involved with and an active participant in changing his or her own perceptions, cognitions, feelings, behaviors. Psychotherapy is not something one person (a therapist) has *done* to another person (a patient). As Kopp(1968) has so nicely pointed out, the Wizard of Oz admitted he wasn't a very good wizard but he was a good man and he only told Dorothy how she could help herself. If she wanted to get back to Kansas, all she had to do was use her feet and will it - not rely upon some magical wizard. But, in Kopp's wisdom, he also pointed out that Dorothy had to accept the responsibility for her decision as well as the consequences of making it. And he points out that therapists have to remember they aren't wizards, a hard task when patients insist we must be. What we are attempting to escape with our infantile-magical thinking is accepting the responsibility for and consequence of our decision. Mann (1978) is one who sees the patient's reluctance to separate from the therapist as being grounded in infantile wishes. He writes:

...the struggle around the refusal to relinquish infantile and childhood wishes in favor of the uncertain pleasure of adult reality. Adult reality means accepting the end of time, the end of one's self (p. 58).

But most importantly, the slight recurrence of symptoms at termination (or what patients fear as a relapse) is a way patients have of finding out they can handle their feeling-symptoms on their own. I frequently tell patients to expect a return of some of their original symptoms and I explain their purpose; i.e., it is a way of letting themselves know they are quite capable of handling the issues which brought them to psychotherapy and which we have spent so much time, effort, energy, and money investigating. I notice that Beck, Rush, Shaw, and Emery (1979) are of a similar opinon. For they write:

The patient's experience of a relapse near the end of treatment may indicate that he is engaged in a form of reality-testing; that is, the patient is testing his ability to cope with depression (p. 320).

Klerman, Weissman, Rounsaville, Chevron (1984) also noticed this return of symptoms and the importance of attending to them. They write:

If they find themselves already missing the relationship or experiencing a slight recurrence of symptoms as termination approaches, they may interpret their feelings as a relapse. To prevent this misunderstanding, such patients should be told that toward the end it is usual for patients to have feelings of apprehension, anger, or sadness about ending the treatment, but that the appearance of these feelings does not portend a return of depression (p. 140).

Now while the fears of not being "cured" and those surrounding the issue of recurrence of symptoms and thus a complete return of the problem for which they sought psychotherapy are common, they are not based in reality and are generally handled quite easily. There are other feelings commonly associated with termination that are directly related to the fact that termination also means the end of the "therapeutic interpersonal relationship." That is, termination means that there will now be a separation between the two persons of the therapeutic dyad. Thus it portends the loss of a very important and meaningful interpersonal relationship. The realization that this separation and loss are upon us can freqently result in some feelings of apprehension, anger, and sadness. For patients, the ending means they will no longer have a "special" time in which they meet with someone who gives them total attention and acceptance, who truly helps them see things they were unable to perceive heretofore about themselves and about others, and who has walked with them a sometimes stormy, tumultuous, frequently scary and difficult path. That is not an easy thing to lose. Patients can well wonder what will happen when they no longer have this "safe harbor," this *true* ally in their fight against the slings and arrows of outrageous fortune. And it is understandable that patients might be angry about having to lose this person/ally so important in their becoming.

We have not yet talked about the feelings the therapist may have upon ending. There is no doubt that endings also can be difficult for therapists and they also can feel sad and angry upon the ending. We will consider those feelings in a moment. But at this point it needs to be noted that the therapist still has "work" to do - i.e. still has a task which includes attending to both the unrealistic and realistic feelings of the patient - a task which includes seeing the patient through the termination phase of the process of psychotherapy.

It becomes important for psychotherapists to help patients differentiate between these feelings of sadness at the ending of meeting with someone who has been such an ally and such a help to them and the feelings that it is the therapist who maintains the benefits accrued by psychotherapy and his or her loss means the loss of those benefits. Luborsky (1984) has given us words to express what patients need to hear at termination:

> You believe that the gains you have made are not part of you but depend on my presence. You fear that you will lose the gains when we stop our regular schedule of sessions and your initial symptoms will come back, as they

have recently begun to in anticipation of termination (p. 28).

The belief the symptoms will come back without the therapist are not realistic ones. The fact that there has been a consensual decision to terminate suggests that both therapist and patient are in agreement and confident in the patient's ability to maintain the gains already made.

But, it is realistic that the patient may well feel sad or angry about the ending, not know why, and realize it may relate to the therapist in some way. That is, it is realistic that the patient (as well as the therapist) may experience some mourning at the loss of the therapy. One need not really worry about this - nor does it take or necessitate psychotherapeutic work. It is not depression, it is mourning. It takes accepting and living through. Patients can be reassured of their abilities to resolve those feelings of sadness and mourning and of the fact it is normal they should have such feelings. As one therapist put it:

> Barbara, I'm your whole world right now, everyone who ever loved you, everyone who ever scorned you. In the past you've cut off forever the people who have hurt you. But I'm not trying to hurt you. I'm urging you to go to love, go to life, and enjoy it with all the wonderful intensity you used to have (Gordon [1979] p. 263).

And this kind of request is not a "whistling in the dark" - i.e. it is not made out of countertransference problems urging the patient to "get well." Rather, it is a statement containing "truths" made at a time when the patient is able to hear it and able to act upon it. That is, it is not an unrealistic request.

As Klerman, et. al (1984) indicate, the last three to four sessions should contain a) an explicit discussion of the end of therapy, b) an acknowledgment that it can be a time of grieving, and c) indications that the patient recognizes his or her independent competence.

In many respects, a good termination acts as a corrective emotional experience. For through the positive separation from the therapist, patients learn they can sustain a loss and can endure through it and can in fact thrive.

D) After Termination

It is not uncommon that patients wonder about and have interest in keeping up some form of contact with their therapist after psychotherapy is over. If it has been a helpful relationship with a good termination, it is not unlikely there will be positive feelings on both patient's and therapist's part. Furthermore, part of the process of termination includes a dissolving transference, a shift on the therapist's part into a more neutral position, the therapist expressing more personal opinions and even when appropriate sharing more of his or her life - i.e. becoming less a therapist and more like a friend. Of course, such a stance also helps to erode the transference even more.

There is debate among psychotherapists as to whether or not patients once terminated can ever re-establish effective psychotherapeutic relationships with the therapists with whom they had terminated. Paul (1978) is one who claims that once the unique nature of the bond between patient and therapist is severed, the patient couldn't resume therapy again with that therapist. I'm not at all sure I share that opinion. Rather, it seems to me that some past positive experiences with another person as a therapist as well as positive feelings about the kind of person the therapist is (i.e. as a result of seeing and knowing more that real person) would provide some decent building blocks for re-establishing a psychotherapeutic relationship if needed. There is debate as to whether or not the door should be left open at the end of therapy. Some therapists suggest leaving the lines of communication open, others stress no further contact whatsoever, and still others suggest a weaning period where the frequency of sessions is diminshed little by little.

I have in different cases and under different circumstances used each one of these positions. But generally, I leave the door open and reassure patients that future contact is possible should they so desire. In cases where the patient will not be living in the same town as I do, I'm inclined to let them know that if they'd like to write I'd be glad to respond and would enjoy knowing how they are doing. I have never found such correspondence a burden nor do patients attempt to continue their therapy via correspondence. Rather, the fact they can still maintain contact seems more to be a matter of knowing I'm still "there" and serves to contribute to the post-treatment maintenance of their therapeutic gains.

In the cases where the patient is still in the same town, I generally reassure the person that I think they have made excellent progress with their therapy and if at any future time there are any issues they'd care to work on, I'd certainly be glad to make time for them.

Then there are a few patients for whom terminating the therapy became necessary not because they were done but because they were moving to another part of the country. That termination included dealing with the fact that they were still in need of continuing psychotherapy and with helping them establish a tie with a psychotherapist elsewhere. In such cases, no "door" was left open other than that necessary to make a referral to a different psychotherapist, nor was any writing encouraged. Rather, such cases required dealing with the fact a) they will not have to start all over with another psychotherapist as the gains they have made to this point will remain with them; b) that we both feel sad at our work together having to come to an end but understand life is frequently not as we would have it; and c) that they know how to choose a psychotherapist and realize it will take a few sessions to get re-established in their psychotherapy.

Most psychotherapists, however, agree that it would be extremely difficult to establish a social relationship after terminating psychotherapy. Reasons for wanting a social relationship could come from some of the positive feelings both patient and therapist have for one another as a result of the psychotherapeutic process. But that could provide a very poor base upon which to build a social relationship. For, the psychotherapy relationship has been constructed to focus upon and help one of the persons in the dyad specifically. It has had an unequal distribution of power. And part of the process of the psychotherapy has required one member to share a great deal more about himself or herself than has the other member of the dyad. The process has also required one member of the dyad to permit and encourage transference of both negative and positive feelings. The discussion in Chapter 6 on transference indicated that we behave in such a fashion in our social relationships so as to negate the development of transference. For the above reasons alone it is difficult for either party in a later social relationship to feel that the relationship is on a level of equality.

But most importantly, therapist and patient don't really *know* one another. That is, they don't really know what that other person is like on a day in and day out basis. Most people probably have little trouble understanding that the patient certainly wouldn't know much about the kind of person the therapist is. But, likewise, the therapist only really knows that part of the patient which has been involved in the psychotherapeutic work. In psychotherapy we are only concerned with the conflictual and problematic areas of the patient's life. We really do not know much at all about those aspects of the patient's life which are going well or are of no problem or concern. Furthermore, the relationship between the two persons is a highly circumscribed one for the purpose of psychotherapy. The meeting time is set and limited, and the meeting place is quite restricted. How these two people will interact with one another during the therapy is fairly well established. Being with one another for an hour a day for even two or three or four days a week under these circumstances and in the psychotherapeutic office is quite different than being with one another as friends - day in and day out on some occasions. And the psychotherapeutic process has little if anything in it to help either party know whether they would even like one another as friends. Certainly, as a result of a successful and positive experience in psychotherapy, both participants generally feel they do like one another and both can have some strong feelings of love and affection for one another. And those feelings are genuine. But they are based on and stem from the very circumscribed and working relationship the members of the dyad have had up to that point. And that working relationship was one in which the therapist was very much "in charge of" and thus in control of the psychotherapy. Change the circumstances of the psychotherapeutic relationship and you *may* change the feelings the members of the dyad have for one another. Once therapists start to see how very much they are "in charge of" and thus in control of the psychotherapy, they begin to understand a bit more fully what great changes would be needed to shift a psychotherapeutic relationship with a patient to a social relationship. It would be a complex and complicated endeavor fraught with some dangers. And I have found that patients have not been particularly interested in nor pursued the issue of making a social relationship out of what had been a psychotherapeutic one.

Therapists' Feelings

As already noted, termination is also an emotional experience for therapists. After all, therapists have risked and invested much of themselves in the work with patients. In addition, therapists may well have been through some very difficult and tumultuous times with their patients. Furthermore, it is not unlikely that the patient has "taught" the therapist many things too - certainly more about the workings of psychopathology and psychotherapy. And it is not unusual when work with patients teaches therapists things about themselves. Any therapist can tell you things they have learned from their patients.

All therapists have had patients whom they found to be quite stimulating and most professionally rewarding. It is hard to realize work with them has come to an end - that we must begin over again with someone new - that we will no longer have the joy of "working with" this patient. As already noted in the chapter on relationships in therapy, therapists develop affection and love for their patients. It is hard to "lose" contact with persons with whom we've worked so closely and so intensely. It is hardly surprising then that therapists could be reluctant to see their patients terminate.

And the process of termination requires that the therapist assume some responsibilities for working through the patient's feelings about ending. Thus, there is a challenge for the therapist. Therapists must focus the expression of their own feelings at termination in light of what implications those feelings may or may not have for the patient and for the patient's process of termination as well as maintenance of the gains of psychotherapy.

Martin and Schurtman (1985), writing about therapists' expressions of anxiety at the termination of psychotherapy point out they may: 1) act as though termination is insignificant and thus not take the patient's concerns about termination seriously, or 2) project their own concerns/emotions upon the patient and see the patient as having feelings/problems with the termination that are legitimately the therapist's, or 3) over-intellectualize the entire process and relationship with the patient and see termination as only something the patient must deal with. Such therapists focus intently upon the technique of termination and in this way avoid the emotion and significance of the termination for themselves. Martin and Schurtman (1985) call this defense *principalization.*

What I am trying to say here is that in addition to attending to the importance of termination for the patient, it is essential that therapists *also* work to understand their own feelings of loss, to recognize the transference and countertransference issues involved, and to face up to the fact that termination is an "issue" for them as well as for patients. Therapists should be free to seek out support through supervision, their colleagues or their own therapists. Termination can help shape the patient's perception of the entire course of psychotherapy. Ideally, during termination, the therapist might also be a role model for the patient showing how it is possible to positively and honestly end a relationship.

As a way of highlighting some of the feelings involved in the termination phase of psychotherapy, I share the following experience. It took place on a day in which I terminated psychotherapy with two patients as well as experienced the death of a friend. In addition all of this occurred at the end of the school year - a time when I also "experience" the loss of students and with moving to our summer home a loss of my usual work/living routine. It all happened to me a few years back, although in telling it I start to relate it to you in the present tense.

I, my wife Nona, and three of our children had gotten up early in the morning to drive back to the college from our summer house. I was to see my patients - and to do some other things not at all well explicated or thought about. I knew it was to be a goodbye to a couple of patients. One was an easy ending - his work had been minimal, short but probably of some significance. The other was to be like a divorce - and I knew that at some level of my being. But, nevertheless, I didn't give myself any conscious thought of what faced me for the day as we drove back to town.

It was a beautiful morning, full sun shining brightly behind as we drove West through lush green countryside. A variety of green reached our eyes, rolling hills covered with trees and broad, wide pastures and meadows glistening in the morning sun. The car was smooth and quiet and not even the radio to make "noise." Each of us must have been in our own thoughts; two asleep and the three of us in the front seat not talking. My thoughts were away from me, not centered in my being or on anything in particular except the beautiful morning. I wasn't even thinking about being in town or my day's work. How I consciously resisted thinking about Bruce and our last session. Then Nona drove for a while and I sat taking in the beauty of the morning. Did I need some beauty in the universe? Still no thought about the day's work, except for a fleeting thought about the eleven o'clock appointment with my research assistant. My involvement in that research is certainly minimal now, I don't care to attend to it one little bit. It doesn't turn me on anymore.

Into the driveway and into the house. A look at the little mail we have and a cup of coffee while we plan the day. It is 10:30 AM and we all start on the various day's tasks - Nona to the bank and town and shopping, the kids on getting together things we need to take back to the cottage, and me to the office to meet with my research assistant. The day commences to turn and the "work" is worked-out: those things we human beings do in the belief that this is what makes the universe turn, or holds it all together, or keeps us happy, or is our "thing" or what?

At 10:45 AM Lewis dies - quietly, at home in the hospital bed in his own living room - eons away from his birth in Connecticut and his life's pilgrimage through China and the rest of God's creation. There he leaves us to face alone what every creature must face alone. And at his "passing" the sadness and the joy and the meaning of all creation spoken in one soft word - "hallelujah!"

I'm busy now - going over computer results in which I'm really not interested and which I probably really don't understand anyway, figuring out what more we need to do to get the data out of the computer. At least it doesn't take long and I'm finished with that task in good time. Across the campus and back home. Still not conscious of the fact that divorce is getting closer to me - still not thinking of the day's therapy work.

There is a bike in front of the house. Who is there? Someone is on the porch. It is my first patient for the day. He forgot I'd changed the time from 11:30 AM to 1:30 PM for today. No problem. I'm here and we can meet now. That will give me more time later on. That's OK. Good to get some of the work out of the way. In a sense the session goes easily. I'm not really close to him. I don't know why. Does his intelligence threaten me? I don't think so. Does his cynicism and anger threaten me? Maybe! In a way it is as though he presents no problem on which to work, but that is not true. He is symptomatic, but I don't seem to attend to those symptoms. I'm not sure why, except I do think he himself is reluctant to "get involved." Of course getting involved is going to open-up many issues - and is there time for them all? Of course not, he leaves mid-summer for someplace else. But his therapy is going OK and it was good to see him early, giving me more time later on.

During the session Nona and the kids return. I hear them in the house calling me. They don't know of my "earlier-than-expected-appointment," but they soon shall. It quiets down again. They know I'm busy!

The session is over and I start my charting. My daughter tells me Lewis has died. He was dying as we drove back to Oberlin. He died as we arrived. Of course it was expected. Expected or not, makes no difference, it is a loss - a weird sense of "of course" but still a wondering what my world will be like without Lewis' quiet strength and great example, his real interest in other people and his great ability to empathize. Nona is down with his wife, Jo, now. I go back to my desk to finish the charting and to spend time preparing for Bruce's last session. It is a hurried, rather frantic, mechanical attempt in which I don't really let myself feel or think. Nona comes in and tells me how things are down at Lewis' house. The body will be taken very shortly now. Do I want to go down and see the body before it is taken away? Yes, very much - but also no. No, I don't want to face that fact yet.

Now my feelings are more frantic, confused, and I can't really concentrate or focus on what I want to do. I vacillate between trying to summarize my sessions with Bruce and going to see Lewis' body and Jo. The vacillation doesn't last long, for to end the tension I must act. The first act is toward Lewis.

The day remains beautiful, quiet, green, warm, peaceful as I walk the short block to Lewis' house. My memories and sadnesses come upon me and they feel good. I start to accept that he is gone. I now must live my liturgy - live it knowing there is no way I can "touch" the dead. My communications there will be all one way and any answers I hear will be fragments of my own projections. Or are they? I don't know. How can I know?

Jo is still herself - a bit slower and sadder and certainly holding on to being and only gradually letting herself fully know he is gone; without letting herself yet know the full meaning of that loss. Lewis looks peaceful - much whiter now that the blood has ceased its endless pursuit of body tissue - its long long journey encased in the space of our little bodies. A grandson, Lewis Jr. is there - just came in on the plane from Florida. We all talk some. Of things in general, of Lewis, of events taking place this day, of Lewis, of pleasantries, of the fact Lewis Jr. lost his mother the same way (by cancer) almost two years ago to the day - six days different to be precise. We wait for the undertaker to come and remove the body. It is a long wait, for it is something we want in a strange crazy way and something we don't want to have happen at all. At least his body is still here.

Jo's tenderness shows in small, familiar, tender moments. She stops at his bed, pulls the covers up to cover his shoulders, as though he may be cold (which he certainly is but not as she would wish). She tenderly feels his forehead and cheeks, stating the terrible reality she knows she has to face and yet with all her being doesn't want to. "He's cold now." She realizes there are moments when she thinks she sees him breathing, and yet knows he's not. God is doing his work with us as God takes Lewis to Himself. A good work God does even though we mortals don't comprehend the meaning-significance of all of this. We do comprehend our love for Lewis - lots of different kinds of love in that room (wife, grandson, friend); and we do comprehend our love for one another - our wanting to comfort and be for one another.

The station wagon to take his body comes. A young man anxious and unsure of how to proceed attempts to play the role of the understanding funeral director. I remain with Lewis Jr. and another friend goes with Jo to answer all those questions our society necessitates be asked upon the death of one of us humans. Questions that seem to me to have nothing to do with death or God or suffering or pathos or hallelujah! They are Caesar's questions: where born, social security number, where to be buried. They go on and on and on and Jo makes herself busy quietly and graciously getting the answers. Her love, her husband, is dead. He lies in this living room where so much joy and peace and love has been poured out. And Jo, with patience and graciousness, answers Caesar's questions.

I don't think the young man can really understand it all. He doesn't know us and he must be conflicted about what we are all feeling. What is Jo feeling? What is this all about? But in typical business fashion, he takes no moment to hear his feelings or ask us about ours. He takes no moment to relax and become human - although human he certainly is. But he attends to his "papers" and remains anxious.

I want to go, I want to stay! My time is running short! Now I am attending to my "papers." I have another patient coming to the house. This young undertaker is taking forever to fill out Caesar's papers. Jo, I really need to leave, but I don't want to leave. Can the friend stay until the body is taken? No, he has a doctor's appointment. It may be a valid excuse, but it is obvious he is leaving.

371

I guess it is not all right for the patient to be late for the doctor, but all right for the doctor to be late for the patient. He offers to put a note on my door at the house so my patient will not think I have simply forgotten him. I know there is no one home at the house to tell him we are back from the lake. I don't want to miss the last appointment with him. If the therapy as short as it has been means anything, I think it means he can start to develop trust relationships with others. My not being there for him would only add to his not involving his emotional life in anything. I really should go, Jo. I'm worried about that patient. Of course I could call him at home later and explain what happened. What am I going to do? I stay, the friend delivers the note. The decision is made, I start to relax a little. I join Jo in the living room - trying with my presence to hurry along this paper-filler-outer.

The time comes. Lewis' body is to be taken out of the house. Another young man joins him with a litter carrier. We go to the bed, the litter carrier is made ready with a rubber bag and sheet. The young men do their job well - not too mechanical or unfeeling, but also with no disgust or hesitation. Lewis' body is uncovered - frail, small and as he is moved Jo says "He doesn't feel any pain anymore." The body is handled tenderly and slowly wheeled out the door, onto the porch, down the steps. Jo following slowly, myself and Lewis Jr. We are the cortege as the last remains of Lewis leave his home. We realize this is the last leave-taking. There is such a finality about it all for us. We are so materially oriented. We need the body to see and hear his spirit. Now it goes away from us never ever to return.

Jo turns to me - with the look of being so lost and the question of what do we do now in her eyes. The love - deep deep love she has for Lewis - wells up in her and the terrible pain of losing that love, of realizing the finality of it, overcomes her. We embrace and she quietly cries. This woman who quietly does everything - who always quietly has been so strong and effective - so gentle and tender about doing her and God's work in God's kingdom quietly cries over the loss of the man she loved. Jo quietly cries. It is the still small voice of God. Lewis Jr., Jo, and I embrace. Three souls hurting in the summer sun, on a porch filled with plants. And Jo says, "It is a beautiful day." The still, small voice of God!

I now know why I stayed. I needed to stay. I needed to see his body leave this lovely home. I needed to be there for Jo and Lewis Jr., and for myself. Thank God I stayed!

And now to the living tasks. Jo wants to do some laundry - to now clean up the bed in which her husband lay for so many months - to do that last task she can for him. To clean-up and put away that bed. To start to order her life without him, but still always with him. Jo and Lewis Jr. turn into the house and I go to the street - to hurriedly walk back and take up the practice of psychotherapy. My patient is waiting - my reason for being late momentarily bothers him. He doesn't comprehend what kind of being I am! But then maybe I don't either.

The session goes well. I really have no time to feel what Lewis' going has meant to me or to prepare for my next patient, Bruce. I momentarily realize that and realize that I haven't really had any time to think how I feel about this being the last session - maybe time - I see Bruce.

Our therapy together has been intense, we have gone through so much in such a short period of time. His openness has been remarkable and so has mine. He has found himself and in the process of it, loves me. I so admire and respect him and am drawn to his beauty and creativity. It is a heartache so close now on top of another heartache. I can't contain them all. He looks me right in the eyes, and there is so much love in it and it bares my soul and I'm uncomfortable but also want it. Bruce had become an important part of my life. He reaffirmed my knowledge in the power of psychotherapy to change feelings and behavior - my responsibility to understand the elements of the process and be responsible in implementing them and attending to the conceptualization of problems. But more, he also awakens again the fact that closeness and intimacy in therapy is histological. Only one small slice of the persons life is attended to in the therapy session. We psychotherapists are cheated from the fullness of the client's life - from all its joys and pains. We focus intensely upon the hurt, complex, conflict, frustration, block, pathology, fixation. We are working in a stream of life but see only fully and completely the accumulated debris that is blocking the flow of that stream. And in that intense work, we don't have much time to look around and see all the rest of that stream of life - the flora, fauna, clear water, smooth flowing that surrounds the debris.

It is at this ending with Bruce, that I wish to see the rest of his life - to see and feel it as intensely as what we have worked-on up to this point. And yet, I realize it is over. He to his life now and I to mine!

373

Never again will I know so closely his existence - his growth and joy and fright! I have to say good-bye. He has to say good-bye. He pays me a great compliment - I have given him his life. I start to refuse it and he calls me on my unwillingness to accept this compliment. I'm humbled and know he's right in terms of me being a bit unwilling to accept his praise and thankfulness.

It is so hard to say "good-bye." We hug and kiss and I walk him to the door. I say "adios" as he walks slowly away, head downcast in his own thoughts and feelings and knowing he can't turn around and look back. That's how it is sometimes. Best not to look back - and be stuck in one place that is no longer where we are - but to move onto the next thing in creation that is us. Growing is saying good-bye. But it also is forward looking, it is becoming. Bruce is becoming, I am becoming, and Lewis in death, the final stage of growth, is becoming. Do seeds and caterpillars and tadpoles hurt in their becoming?

Back to my study with only a moment to chart - how in the hell do you chart becoming? And then the next and last patient for the day. He makes me work and I forget my pain of the day.

We are going back to the lake this evening. That is good. I don't want to stay around here. Nona and I return to Jo's. She is doing fine. Still gracious, patient, and thankful for our help and love. Lewis Jr. will walk alone for a while. I can't do much to help him in his grief. I'm bushed for this day. I want to be with my family and soak up their love. I need to be held.

Once in the car and on the way back home to the lake, I realize how very emotionally drained I am. Thank goodness others will drive. It is a real help to me. I sleep, rest, have my thoughts as the evening of the day of the death and the divorce comes to us all as we speed East. The car is smooth and quiet. We all take a break for a coke. There is good love and caring coming from my kids. And once back, Nona holds me close, covering me with her body and making me feel I won't fly into a lot of little pieces. Making me know there is a living and a life to do - joys and more greatness to come and pain and sorrow and good-byes can be endured and in fact may be like the rain which gently nourishes the land.

Good-bye Lewis! Good-bye Bruce!

And so we come to the end of this book which attempts to make explicit and meaningful my experiences with and views of the process of psychotherapy. I always enjoy my participation in the difficult, complex, at times frustrating, but also very gratifying process we call psychotherapy. Furthermore, I'm confident the continued study and application of that process will lead us to a much more expanded, fuller, exciting and extraordinarily useful view of the psychology of human behavior. Within the process of psychotherapy are the seeds for a greatly expanded consciousness - for finding new ways of viewing ourselves and our world. Within the process of psychotherapy are the seeds for better understanding how to release and enjoy the enormous power and ability of the human mind.

REFERENCES

Abrams, M.H. (Ed.), (1979). *The Norton anthology of English literature*. Vol. 2. NY: Norton.

Alexander, F. (1961). *The scope of psychoanalysis: Selected papers of Franz Alexander*. NY: Basic Books.

Alexander, F. (1961). *The scope of psychoanalysis: Selected papers of Franz Alexander*. NY: Basic Books.

Alexander, F. (1980). Learning theory and psychoanalysis. In J. Marmor & S.M. Woods (Eds.), *The interface between the psychodynamic and behavioral therapies*. NY: Plenum.

Alexander, F., & French, T.M. (1946). *Psychoanalytic therapy: Principles and application*. NY: Ronald.

Alexander, J.F., Barton, C., Schiavpo, R.S., & Parsons, B.V. (1976). Systems-behavioral intervention with families of delinquents: Therapist characteristics, family behavior, and outcome. *Journal of Consulting and Clinical Psychology*, 44, 656-664.

American Psychological Association (1975). Report of the task force on sex bias and sex role stereotyping in psychotherapeutic practice. *American Psychologist*, 30, 1169-1175.

Appelbaum, S.A. (1978). Pathways to change in psychoanalytic therapy. *Bulletin of the Menninger Clinic*, 42, 239-251.

Applebaum, S.A. (1980). Pathways to change in psychoanalytic therapy. In M.R. Goldfried (Ed.), *Converging themes in psychotherapy: Trends in psychodynamic, humanistic, and behavioral practice*. NY: Springer.

Applebaum, S.A. (1982). Challenges to traditional psychotherapy from the "new therapies." *American Psychologist*, 36, 9, pp.1002-1008.

Arnkoff, D.B. (1980). Psychotherapy from the perspective of cognitive theory. In M.J. Mahoney (Ed.), *Psychotherapy process: Current issues and future directions*. NY: Plenum.

Arnkoff, D.B. (1983). Common and specific factors in cognitive therapy. In M.J. Lambert (Ed.). *A guide to psychotherapy and patient relationships*. Homewood, ILL: Dow Jones-Irwin.

Arnkoff, D.B., & Glass, C.R. (1982). Clinical cognitive constructs:

377

Examination, evaluation, and elaboration. In P.C. Kendall (Ed.), *Advances in cognitive-behavioral research and therapy.* Vol.1. NY: Academic Press.

Aslin, A.L. (1977). Feminist and community mental health center psychotherapists' expectancies of mental health for women. *Sex Roles*, 3, 537-544.

Baekeland, F., & Lundwall, L. (1975). Dropping out of treatment: A critical review. *Psychological Bulletin*, 82, 738-783.

Barlow, D.H. (1980). Behavior therapy: the next decade. *Behavior Therapy*. 11, 315-328.

Barlow, D.M. (1981). On the relation of clinical research to clinical practice: Current issues, new direction. *Journal Consulting and Clinical Psychology*, 49, 147-155.

Barrett, C., Berg, P., Eaton, E., & Pomeroy, E.L. (1974). Implications of women's liberation and the future of psychotherapy. *Psychotherapy: Theory, Research and Practice*, 11, 11-15.

Baum, O.E., Felzer, S.B., D'Zmura, T.L., & Shumaker, E. (1966). Psychotherapy dropouts and lower socioeconomic patients. *American Journal of Orthopsychiatry*, 36, 629-635.

Bebout, J. (1974). It takes one to know one: Existential-Rogerian concepts in encounter groups. In D.A. Wexler & L.N. Rice (Eds.), *Innovations in client-centered therapy.* (pp. 367-420). NY: Wiley.

Beck, A.T. (1976). *Cognitive therapy and the emotional disorders.* NY: International Universities Press.

Beck, A.T., Rush, A.J., Shaw, B.F., & Emery, G. (1979). *Cognitive therapy of depression: A treatment manual.* NY: Guilford.

Becker, E. (1973). *The denial of death.* NY: The Free Press.

Beers, C.W. (1921). *A mind that found itself: An autobiography.* NY: Longmons, Green.

Beier, E.G., & Young, D.M. (1984). *The silent language of psychotherapy.* (2nd ed.) NY: Aldine.

Benjamin, L.S. (1984). No shortcuts. *The Clinical Psychologist*, 37, 1, 24.

Bergin, A.E. (1971). The evaluation of therapeutic outcomes. In A.E. Bergin & S.L. Garfield (Eds.), *Handbook of psychotherapy and behavior change.* NY: Wiley.

Bergin, A.E., & Lambert, M.J. (1978). The evaluation of therapeutic outcomes. In S.L. Garfield & A.E. Bergin (Eds.), *Handbook of psychotherapy and behavior change: An empirical analysis*, (2nd ed.). (pp.139-189). NY: Wiley.

378

Bergin, A.E., & Strupp, H.H. (1972). *Changing frontiers in the science of psychotherapy*. NY: Aldine-Atherton.

Bernstein, D.A., & Nietzel, M.T. (1977). Demand characteristics in behavior modification: The natural history of a "nusiance." In M. Hersen, R.M. Eisler & P.M. Miller (Eds.), *Progress in behavior modification*. Vol. 4. (pp. 119-162). NY: Academic Press.

Bettelheim, B. (1983). *Freud & man's soul*. NY: Alfred A. Knopf.

Bhaskar, R. (1975). *A realist theory of science*. Leeds, England: Leeds Books.

Bhaskar, R. (1979) *The possibility of naturalism*. Brighton, Great Britain: Harvester Press.

Bishop, J.B., Sharf, R.S., & Adkins, D.M. (1975). Counselor intake judgments, client characteristics, and number of sessions at a university counseling center. *Journal of Counseling Psychology*, 22, 557-559.

Blanck, G. (1983). Psychoanalytic Technique. In B.B. Wolman (Ed.), *The Therapist's Handbook*, (2nd. ed.). (pp 91-120). NY: Van Nostrand Reinhold Co.

Blanck, G., & Blanck, R. (1974). *Ego psychology: Theory and practice*. NY: Columbia University Press.

Blanton, R. (1962). Science and art in the training of psychologists. *Journal of Clinical Psychology*, 18, 10-14.

Bond, J. (1975). Behavior therapy, learning theory and scientific method. In Aldine Annual *Behavior change*, Vol. 4. Chicago: Aldine Publishing.

Bowlby, J. (1980). *Attachment and loss: Loss, sadness, and depression*. Vol 3. NY: Basic Books.

Brady, J.P., Davison, G.C., Dewald, P.A., Egan, G., Fadiman, J., Frank, J.D., Gill, M.M., Hoffman, I., Kempler, W., Lazarus, A.A., Raimy, V., Rotter, J.B., & Strupp, H.H. (1980). Some views on effective principles of psychotherapy. *Cognitive Therapy and Research*, 4, 269-306.

Breuer, J., & Freud, S. (1893-95/1955). Studies on hysteria. In S. Freud, *Standard Edition*. Vol. 2. London: Hogarth Press.

Brodsky, A. (1973). The consciousness-raising group as a model for therapy with women. *Psychotherapy: Theory, Research and Practice*, 10, 24-29.

Broverman, I.K., Broverman, D.M., Clarkson, F.E., Rosenkrantz, P.S., & Vogel, S.R. (1970). Sex-role stereotypes and clinical judgments of mental health. *Journal of Consulting and Clinical*

Psychology, 34, 1-7.

Broverman, I.K., Vogel, S.R., Broverman, D.M., Clarkson, F.E., & Rosenkrantz, P.S. (1972). Sex-role stereotypes: A current appraisal. *Journal of Social Issues*, 298, 2, 58-78.

Brow, E.C. (1980). The joys of being a psychotherapist. *Voices: The art and science of psychotherapy*, 16, 1, 17-20.

Brown, R.D. (1970). Experienced and inexperienced counselors' first impressions of clients and case outcomes: Are first impressions lasting? *Journal of Counseling Psychology*, 17, 550-558.

Bruch, Hilde (1976). *Learning Psychotherapy: Rationale and ground rules*. Cambridge, MA: Harvard University Press.

Burton, A., & Associates. (1972). *Twelve therapists*. San Francisco: Jossey-Bass.

Carkhuff, R.R., Pierce, R.M., & Cannon, J.R. (1977). *The art of helping*. Amherst, MA: Human Resource Development Press.

Carmen, E., Rieker, P., & Mills, T. (1984). Victims of violence and psychiatric illness. *American Journal of Psychiatry*, 141, 3, 378-383.

Carson, R.C., & Heine, R.W. (1962). Similarity and success in therapeutic dyads. *Journal of Consulting Psychology*, 26, 1, 38-43.

Castaneda, C. (1973). *A separate reality: Further conversations with don Juan*. NY: Simon & Schuster.

Cavanagh, M.E. (1982). *The counseling experience: A theoretical and practical approach*. Monetery, CA: Brooks/Cole.

Chafetz, J.S., Sampson, P., Beck, P., & West, J. (1974). A study of homosexual women. *Social Work*, 19, 714-723.

Chapman, L.J., & Chapman, J.P. (1969). Illusory correlation as an obstacle to the use of valid psychodiangostic signs. *Journal of Abnormal Psychology*, 74, 271-280.

Chessick, R.D. (1983). *The technique and practice of intensive psychotherapy*. NY: Jason Aronson.

Cohen, M.B. (1952). Countertransference and anxiety. *Psychiatry*, 15, 231-242.

Colby, K.M. (1962). Discussion of papers on therapist's contribution. In H.H. Strupp & L. Luborsky (Eds.), *Research in psychotherapy*. Vol.2.(pp. 95-101). Washington, DC: American Psychological Association.

Cummings, N., & Follette, W.T. (1976). Brief psychotherapy and medical utilization. In H. Dorken (Ed.), *The professional psychologist today: New developments in law, health insurance and health practice*. San Francisco: Jossey-Bass.

Cutler, R.L. (1958). Countertransference effects in psychotherapy. *Journal of Consulting Psychology*, 22, 349-356.

Davison, G.C., & Wilson, T.G. (1973). Attitudes of behavior therapists toward homosexuality. *Behavior Therapy*, 4, 686-696.

Davison, G.D., & Friedman, S. (1981). Sexual orientation stereotype in the distortion of clinical judgment. *Journal of Homosexuality*, 6, 37-44.

Delk, J.L., & Ryan, T.T. (1975). Sex role stereotyping and A-B therapist status: Who is more chauvinistic? *Journal of Consulting and Clinical Psychology*, 43, 589.

Delk, J.L., & Ryan, T.T. (1977). A-B status and sex stereotyping among psychotherapists and patients. *Journal of Nervous and Mental Disease*, 164, 253-262.

deRacker, G.I. (1961). On the formulation of the interpretation. *International Journal of Psycho-Analysis*, 42, 49-54.

Devoge, J.T., & Beck, S. (1978). The therapist-client relationship in behavior therapy. In M. Hersen, R.M. Eisler & P.M. Miller (Eds.), *Progress in behavior modification* Vol. 6. NY: Academic Press.

Dewald, P.A. (1976). Toward a general concept of the therapeutic process. *International Journal of Psychoanalytic Psychotherapy*, 5, 283-299.

Dewey, J. (1934). *Art as experience*. NY: Minton, Balch & Co.

Doherty, E.G. (1971). Social attraction and choice among psychiatric patients and staff: A review. *Journal of Health and Social Behavior*, 12, 279-290.

Dollard, J., & Miller, N. (1950). *Personality and psychotherapy*. NY: McGraw-Hill.

Dymond, R.F. (1949). A scale for the measurement of empathic ability. *Journal of Consulting Psychology*, 13, 127-133.

Eagle, M. N. (1984). *Recent developments in psychoanalysis: A critical evaluation*. NY: McGraw-Hill.

Edelson, M. (1963). *The termination of intensive psychotherapy*. Springfield: Thomas.

Egan, G. (1975). *The skilled helper*. Monterey, CA: Brooks/Cole.

Elliot, R. (1983). Fitting process research to the practicing psychotherapist. *Psychotherapy: Theory, Research and Practice*, 20, 47-55.

Elliot, R. (1984). A discovery-oriented approach to significant events in psychotherapy. Interpersonal process recall and comprehensive process analysis. In L. Rice & L. Greenberg (Eds.), *Patterns of*

381

change. (pp.249-286). NY: Guilford.

Ellis, A. (1962). *Reason and emotion in psychotherapy.* NY: Lyle Stuart.

Ellis, A. (1970). *The essence of rational psyuchotherapy: A comprehensive approach to treatment.* NY: Institute for Rational Living.

Ellis, A. (1983). The origins of rational-emotive therapy (RET). *Voices: The art and science of psychotherapy,* 18, 4, 29-33.

Ellis, A., & Grieger, R. (Eds.), (1977). *Handbook of rational-emotive therapy.* NY: Springer.

Epstein, L, and Feiner, A.H. (Eds.). (1979). *Countertransference.* NY: Jason Aronson.

Erickson, M.H. (1980). *The collected papers of Milton H. Erickson on hypnosis.* Vol I. (Edited by E. L. Rossi). NY: Irvington Publishers.

Eysenck, H.J. (1952). The effects of psychotherapy: an evaluation. *Journal of Consulting Psychology* 16, 319-324.

Fabrikant, B. (1974). The psychotherapist and the female patient: Perceptions and change. In V. Franks & V. Burtle (Eds.), *Women in therapy.* NY: Brunner/Mazel.

Fabrikant, B., Barron, J., & Krasner, J. (1977). *To enjoy is to live: psychotherapy explained.* Chicago: Nelson-Hall.

Fagan, J. (1971). The task of the therapist. In F.Fagan & I. Shepherd (Eds.), *Gestalt Therapy Now.* NY: Harper.

Fagan, J., & Greaves, G. (1983). Joen Fagan: Psychic explorer. *Voices: The art and science of psychotherapy,* 18, 4, 73-83.

Fehrenback, P.A., & O'Leary, M.R. (1982). Interpersonal attraction and treament decisions in inpatient and outpatient psychiatric settings. In T.A. Wills (Ed.), *Basic processes in helping relationships.* (pp. 13-36). NY: Academic Press.

Fenichel, O. (1945). *The psychoanalytic theory of neurosis.* NY: Norton.

Fey, W.F. (1955). Acceptance by others and its relation to acceptance of self and others: A reevaluation. *Journal of Abnormal and Social Psychology,* 50, 274-276.

Fisher, D., Nadler, A., & Whitcher-Alagna, S. (1982). Recipient reactions to aid: A conceptual review. *Psychological Bulletin,* 9l, 27-54.

Fisher, J.D., & Nadler, A. (1982). Determinants of recipient reactions to aid: Donor-recipient similarity and perceived dimensions of problems. In T.A. Wills (Ed.), *Basic processes in helping relationships.* (pp. 131-153). NY: Academic Press.

Fliess, R. (1953). Countertransferences and counteridentification. *Journal American Psychoanalytic Association*, 1, 268-284.

Ford, D.H., & Urban, H.B. (1963). *Systems of Psychotherapy.* NY: Wiley.

Ford, J.D. (1978). Therapeutic relationship in behavior therapy: An empirical analysis. *Journal of Consulting and Clinical Psychology*, 46, 1302-1314.

Frank, J.D. (1961). *Persuasion and healing.* Baltimore, MD: Johns Hopkins.

Frank, J.D. (1963). Immediate and long-term symptomatic course of psychiatric outpatients. *American Journal of Psychiatry*, 120, 429-439.

Frank, J.D. (1974). *Persuasion and healing: A comparative study of psychotherapy.* (Rev. ed.) NY: Shocken Books.

Frank, J.D. (1976). Restoration of morale and behavior change. In A. Burton (Ed.), *What makes behavior change possible?* NY: Brunner/Mazel.

Frank, J.D. (1979). The present status of outcome studies. *Journal of Consulting and Clinical Psychology*, 47, 310-316.

Frankl, V.E. (1963). *Man's search for meaning: An introduction to logotherapy.* Boston: Beacon Press.

French, T., & Fromm, E. (1964). *Dream Interpretation.* NY: Basic Books.

Freud, A. (1936/1954). *The Ego and the Mechanisms of Defence.* London: Hogarth Press.

Freud, A. (1954). The widening scope of indications for psycho-analysis: discussion. *Journal American Psychoanalytic Association*, 2, 607-620.

Freud, S. (1893). Charcot. *Standard edition.* Vol. 3. London: Hogarth Press.

Freud, S.(1905 [1901]). Fragment of an Analysis of a Case of Hysteria. *Standard Edition.* Vol.7. (pp. 116-117). London: Hogarth Press.

Freud, S. (1910/1946). The future prospects of psychoanalytic therapy. *Collected Papers.* Vol. 2. London: Hogarth Press.

Freud, S. (1911-15). Papers on Technique. *Standard Edition.* Vol. 12. London: Hogarth Press.

Freud, S. (1912/1964). The Dynamics of Transference. *Standard Edition.* Vol. 12. London: Hogarth Press.

Freud, S. (1914/1964). Remembering, repeating and working through. *Standard Edition*. Vol.12. (pp. 145-156). London: Hogarth Press.

Freud, S. (1916-1917 [1915-1917]). Introductory Lectures on Psychoanalysis. *Standard Edition*. Vol. 15-16. London: Hogarth Press.

Freud, S. (1924/1960). *Collected Papers*. Vol. 2. (J. Riviere, Trans.) London: Hogarth.

Freud, S. (1937/1964). Analysis terminable and interminable. *Standard Edition*. Vol. 23. (pp. 211-253). London: Hogarth Press.

Fromm, E. (1956). *The art of loving*. NY: Harper.

Fromm-Reichmann, F. (1950). *Principles of intensive psychotherapy*. Chicago: University of Chicago Press.

Galvin, K. (1981). Sociometric approaches with the family communication course. *Journal of Group Psychotherapy, Psychodrama, and Sociometry*, 34, 18-23.

Garfield, S.L. (1973). What are the therapeutic variables in psychotherapy? In Proceedings of the Ninth International Congress of Psychotherapy, Oslo, *Psychotherapy and Psychosomatics*, 24, 372-378.

Garfield, S.L. (1957). *Introductory clinical psychology*. NY: Macmillan.

Garfield, S.L. (1980). *Psychotherapy: An eclectic approach*. NY: Wiley.

Garfield, S.L. & Bergin, A.E. (1971). Personal therapy, outcome and some therapist variables. *Psychotherapy: Theory, Research and Practice*, 8, 251-253.

Garfield, S.L., & Kurtz, R. (1976). Clinical psychologists in the 1970's. *American Psychologist*, 31, 1-9.

Garfinkle, E., & Morin, S. (1978). Psychotherapists' attitudes toward homosexual psychotherapy clients. *Journal of Social Issues*, 34, 101-112.

Gergen, K.J., & Gergen, M. (1974). Understanding foreign assistance through public opinion. *1974 Yearbook of World Affairs*. Vol. 27. London: Institute of World Affairs.

Ginott, A. (1980). No shortcut to mourning. *Voices: The art and science of psychotherapy*, 16, 2, 77-79.

Gitelson, M. (1952). The emotional position of the analyst in the psycho-analytic situation. *International Journal Psychoanalysis*, 33, 1-10.

Glover, E. (1955). *The technique of psycho-analysis*. NY: International Universities Press.

Goldfried, M.R. (1971). Systematic desensitization as training in self-control. *Journal of Counsulting and Clinical Psychology*, 37, 228-234.

Goldfried, M.R., & Davison, G.C. (1976). *Clinical behavior therapy.* NY: Holt, Rinehart & Winston.

Goldfried, M.R. (1979). Anxiety reduction through cognitive-behavioral intervention. In P.C. Kendall & S.D. Hollon (Eds.), *Cognitive-behavioral interventions: Theory, research, and procedures.* NY: Academic Press.

Goldfried, M.R. (1980). Toward the delineation of therapeutic change principles. *American Psychologist*, 35, 991-999.

Goldfried, M.R. (1982). *Converging themes in psychotherapy: Trends in pyschodynamic, humanistic, and behavioral practice.* NY: Springer Publishing Co.

Goldfried, M.R., & Padawer, W. (1982). Current status and future directions in psychotherapy. In M.R. Goldfried (Ed.), *Converging themes in psychotherapy.* NY: Springer Publishing Co.

Goldstein, A.P. (1968). Psychotherapy research and psychotherapy practice: Independence or equivalence? In S. Lesser (Ed.), *An evaluation of the results of psychotherapies.* Springfield, ILL: Charles C. Thomas.

Gonsiorek, J. (1982). *Homosexuality and psychotherapy.* NY: Haworth Press.

Gordon, B. (1979). *I'm dancing as fast as I can.* NY: Harper.

Greben, S.E. (1981). The essence of psychotherapy. *British Journal of Psychiatry*, 138, 449-455.

Greenberg, J. (1964). *I never promised you a rose garden.* NY: Holt, Rinehart and Winston.

Greenson, R.R. (1965). The working alliance and the transference neurosis. *Psychoanalytic Quarterly*, 34, 155-181.

Greenson, R.R. (1971). The "real" relationship between the patient and the psychoanalyst. In M. Kanzer (Ed.). *The unconscious today.* (pp. 213-232). NY: International Universities Press.

Greenson, R.R. (1972). Beyond transference and interpretation. *International Journal of Psycho-Analysis*, 53, 213-217.

Gross, M.L. (1978). *The psychological society.* NY: Random House.

Gurman, A.S. (1977). The patient's perception of the therapeutic relationship. In A.S. Gurman & A.M. Razin (Eds.), *Effective psychotherapy: A handbook of research.* NY: Pergamon.

Hall, M. (1978). Lesbian families: Cultural and clinical issues. *Social*

Work, 23, 380-385.

Halleck, S.L. (1971). *The politics of therapy*. NY: Science.

Hammer, M. (1972). *The theory and practice of psychotherapy with specific disorders*. Springfield, ILL: Charles C. Thomas.

Hartley, D.E., & Strupp, H.H. (1983). The therapeutic alliance: Its relationship to outcome in brief psychotherapy. In J. Masling (Ed.), *Empirical studies of psychoanalytical theories*. Vol. 1. New Jersey: The Analytic Press.

Hayek, F.A. (1952). *The counter-revolution of science*. Glencoe, ILL: Free Press.

Hayek, F.A. (1978). *New studies in philosophy, politics, economics, and the history of ideas*. Chicago: University of Chicago Press.

Heimann, P. (1949/1981) Countertransference. In R. Langs (Ed.), *Classics in psycho-analytic technique*. NY: Jason Aronson.

Heimann, P. (1950). On counter-transference. *International Journal of Psycho-Analysis*, 31, 81-84.

Henry, B. (1984). The future of clinical training: forward into the past. *The Clinical Psychologist*, 37, 1, 25-26.

Hiler, E.W. (1958). An analysis of patient-therapist compatibility. *Journal of Consulting Psychology*, 22, 341-347.

Hilgard, E.R., & Marquis, D.G. (1961). *Conditioning and learning*. (2nd. ed.) NY: Appleton-Century Crofts.

Hobbs, N. (1962). Sources of gain in psychotherapy. *American Psychologist*, 17, 10, 741-747.

Hokanson, J.E. (1983). *Introduction to the therapeutic process*. Reading, MA: Addison-Wesley Publishing Co.

Hooker, E. (1957). The adjustment of the male overt homosexual. *Journal of Projective Techniques*, 21, 1, 18-31.

Hooker, E. (1965a). An empirical study of some relations between sexual patterns and gender identity in male homosexuals. In John Money (Ed.), *Sex research: New developments*. (pp. 24-52). NY: Holt, Rinehart & Winston.

Hooker, E. (1965b). Male homosexuals and their worlds. In J. Marmor (Ed.), *Sexual inversion: The multiple roots of homosexuality*. (pp. 83-107). NY: Basic Books.

Hooker, E. (1967). The homosexual community. In J.H. Gagnon & W. Simon (Eds.), *Sexual deviance*. (pp. 167-184). NY: Harper & Row.

Hooker, E. (1975). The adjustment of the male overt homosexual. *Journal of Projective Techniques*, 21, 1, 18-31.

Horney, K. (1937). *The collected works of Karen Horney.* Vol. I & II. NY: Norton.

Horowitz, M.J. (1979). *States of mind: Analysis of change in psychotherapy.* NY: Plenum.

Horwoitz, M.J. (1982). Strategic dilemmas and the socialization of psychotherapy researchers. *British Journal of Clinical Psychology, 21,* 119-127.

Horwitz, L. (1974). *Clinical prediction in psychotherapy.* NY: Jason Aronson.

Jackson, D.M. (1975). *Implications of empathy research for speech communication.* Ann Arbor, Michigan: Xerox University Microfilms.

Jacobs, L. (1978). *I-Thou relation in Gestalt therapy.* Unpublished doctoral dissertation, California School of Professional Psychology.

Jacobson, N.S., & Margolin, G. (1979). *Marital therapy: Strategies based on social learning and behavior exchange principles.* NY: Brunner/Mazel.

Janis, I. (Ed.), (1982). *Counseling on personal decisions: Theory and research on short-term helping relationships.* New Haven: Yale University Press.

Johnson, D.W., & Matross, R. (1977). Interpersonal influence in psychotherapy: A social psychological view. In A.S. Gurman & A.M. Razin (Eds.), *Effective psychotherapy: A handbook of research.* NY: Pergamon.

Jones, M.C. (1924). The elimination of children's fears. *Journal of Experimental Psychology, 7,* 382-390.

Kagan, N. (1975). *Interpersonal process recall: A method of influencing human interaction.* Unpublished manuscript. (Available from N. Kagan, 434 Erickson hall, College of Education, Michigan State Univeristy, East Lansing, Michigan 48824.)

Kahn, M.M.R. (1969). Vicissitudes of being, knowing and experiencing in the therapeutic situation. *British Journal of Medical Psychology, 42,* 383-393.

Kanfer, F.H., & Marston, A.R. (1963). Conditioning of self-reinforcement responses: An analogue to self-confidence training. *Psychological Reports, 13,* 63-70.

Kapelovitz, L. H. (1976). *To love and to work: A demonstration and discussion of psychotherapy.* NY: Grune & Stratton.

Katz, R.L. (1963). *Empathy: Its nature and uses.* NY: Free Press.

Kazdin, A.E., & Wilcoxon, L.A. (1976). Systematic desensitization and nonspecific treatment effects: A methodological evaluation. *Psychological Bulletin*, 83, 729-758.

Kazdin, A., & Mascitelli, S. (1982). Covert and overt rehearsal and homework practice on developing assertiveness. *Journal of Consulting and Clinical Psychology*, 50, 2, 250-258.

Keane, T., Black, J., Collins, F., & Vinson, M. (1982). A skills training program for teaching the behavioral interview. *Behavioral assessment*, 4, 1, 53-62.

Kelley, E.L. (1961). Clinical Psychology-1960: Report of survey findings. *American Psychological Association, Division of Clinical Psychology Newsletter*, 14, 1, 1-11.

Kelley, E.L., Goldberg, L.R., Fiske, D.W., & Kikowski, J.M. (1978). Twenty-five years later: A follow-up study of the graduate students in clinical psychology assessed in the V.A. selection research project. *American Psychologist*, 33, 746-755.

Kelly, G.A. (1955). *The psychology of personal constructs*. Vol. I & II. NY: Norton.

Kempler, W. (1980). The process of therapy. *Cognitive Therapy and Research*, 4, 344-353.

Kendall, P.C., & Hollon, S.D. (Eds.), (1979). *Cognitive-behavioral interventions: Theory, research, and procedures*. NY: Academic Press.

Kernberg, O.F. (1965). Countertransference. *Journal of the American Psychoanalytic Association*, 13, 38-56.

Kernberg, O.F. (1975). *Borderline conditions and pathological narcissism*. NY: Jason Aronson.

Kiesler, D.J. (1973). *The process of psychotherapy*. Chicago: Aldine.

Kingdon, M.A. (1979). Lesbians. *The Counseling Psychologist*, 8 1, 44-45.

Kinsey, A.C., Pomeroy, W.B., & Martin, C.E. (1948). *Sexual behavior in the human male*. Philadelphia: Saunders.

Kinsey, A.C., Pomeroy, W.B., Martin, C.E., & Gebhard, P.H. (1953). *Sexual behavior in the human female*. Philadelphia: Saunders.

Kirsch, B. (1974). Consciousness-raising groups as therapy for women. In V. Franks & V. Burtle (Eds.), *Women in therapy*. NY: Brunner/Mazel.

Klein, M., Dittmann, A.T., Parloff, M.B., & Gill, M.M. (1969). Behavior therapy: Observations and reflections. *Journal of Consulting and Clinical Psychology*, 33, 259-266.

Klein, M.H., & Gruman, A.S. (1981). Ritual and reality: Some clinical implications of experimental designs. In L. Rehm (Ed.),

Behavior therapy for depression. NY: Academic Press.

Klein, M. (1952). The origins of transference. *International Journal of Psycho-Analysis,* 33, 433-438.

Klerman, G.L., Weissman, M.M., Rounsaville, B.J., Chevron, E.S. (1984). *Interpersonal psychotherapy of depression.* NY: Basic Books.

Kohlberg, L. (1981). *Essays on moral development, The philosophy of moral development.* Vol. 1. San Francisco: Harper.

Kohn, B., & Matusow, A. (1980). *Barry and Alice: Portrait of a bisexual marriage.* New Jersey: Prentice-Hall.

Kohut, H. (1971). *Analysis of the self.* NY: International Universities Press.

Kohut, H. (1977). *The restoration of the self.* NY: International Universities Press.

Kohut, H. (1984). *How does analysis cure?* Chicago: Univiversity of Chicago Press.

Kopp, S.B. (1968). The wonderful wizard. *Voices: The art and science of psychotherapy,* 4, 1, 77-81.

Kopp, S.B. (1971). *Guru.* Ben Lomand, CA: Science and Behavior Books.

Kopp, S.B. (1972a). *The naked therapist: A collection of embarassments.* Ben Lomand, CA: Science and Behavior Books.

Kopp, S.B. (1972b). *If you meet the Buddha on the road, kill him! The pilgrimage of psychotherapy patients.* Ben Lomand, CA: Science and Behavior Books.

Kopp, S.B. (1974). *The hanged man: Psychotherapy and the forces of darkness.* Ben Lomand, CA: Science and Behavior Books.

Kris, E. (1952). *Psychoanalytic explorations in art.* NY: International Universities Press.

Kurtz, R.M., & Garfield, S.L. (1978). Illusory correlation: A further exploration of Chapman's paradigm. *Journal of Counsulting and Clinical Psychology,* 46, 1009-1015.

Labov, W., & Fanshel, D. (1977). *Therapeutic discourse.* NY: Academic Press.

Lambert, M.J., DeJulio, S.S., & Stein, D.M. (1978). Therapist interpersonal skills: Process, outcome, methodological considerations, and recommendations for future research. *Psychological Bulletin,* 85, 467-489.

Lambert, M.J. (1983). *A guide to psychotherapy and patient relationships.* Homewood, ILL: Dow Jones-Irwin.

Landau, R.J., & Goldfried, M.R. (1981). The assessment of

schemata: A unifying framework for cognitive, behavioral, and traditional assessment. In P.C. Kendall & S.D. Hollon (Eds.), *Assessment strategies for cognitive-behavioral interventions*. NY: Academic Press.

Langs, R. (1976). *The therapeutic interaction*. NY: Jason Aronson.

Langs, R. (Ed.). (1981). *Classics in psycho-analytic technique*. NY: Jason Aronson.

Lazarus, A.A., & Davison, G.C. (1971). Clinical innovation in research and practice. In A.E. Bergin & S.L. Garfield (Eds.), *Handbook of psychotherapy and behavior change*. NY: Wiley.

Lazarus, A.A. (1977). Has behavior therapy outlived its usefulness? *American Psychologist*, 32, 550-554.

Levenson, E.A. (1972). *The fallacy of understanding: An inquiry into the changing structure of psychoanalysis*. NY: Basic Books.

Levy, T. (1978). *The lesbian: As perceived by mental health workers*. Unpublished doctoral dissertation, California School of Professional Psychology.

Lewin, K. (1951). *Field theory in social science*. NY: Harper.

Lewis, C.S. (1956). *Till we have faces*. NY: Harcourt, Brace & World.

Lewis, H.B. (1981). *Freud and modern psychology: The emotional basis of mental illness*. Vol. 1. NY: Plenum Press.

Little, M. (1951). Counter-transference and the patient's response to it. *International Journal of Psycho-Analysis*, 32, 32-40.

Loewenstein, R.M. (1969). Developments in the theory of transference in the last fifty years. *International Journal of Psych-Analysis*, 50, 583-588.

Lowen, A., & Koltuv, M. (1983). Reich and beyond Reich to bioenergetic analysis. *Voices: The art and science of psychotherapy*, 18, 4, 42-47.

Luborsky, L. (1984). *Principles of psychoanalytic psychotherapy: A manual for supportive-expressive treatment*. NY: Basic Books.

Luborsky, I., Singer, B., & Luborsky, L. (1975). Comparative studies of psychotherapies: Is it true that "Everyone has won and all must have prizes?" *Archives of General Psychiatry*, 32, 995-1008.

Maholick, L.T., & Turner, D.W. (1979). Termination: That difficult farewell. *American Journal of Psychotherapy*, 33, 583-591.

Mahoney, M.J. (1974). *Cognition and behavior modification*. Cambridge: Ballinger.

Malan, D.H. (1976a). *The frontier of brief psychotherapy*. NY: Plenum.

Malan, D.H. (1976b). *Toward the validation of dynamic psychotherapy: A replication*. NY: Plenum.

Malan, D.H. (1979). *Individual psychotherapy and the science of psychodynamics*. London: Butterworths.

Malone, R.P. (1981). Psychopathology as non-experience. *Voices: The art and science of psychotherapy*, 17, 2, 83-91.

Manicas, P.T., & Secord, P.F. (1983). Implications for psychology of the new philosophy of science. *American Psychologist*, 38, 4, 399-413.

Mann, J. (1973). *Time-limited psychotherapy*. Cambridge: Harvard University Press.

Margulies, A., and Havens, L. (1981). The initial encounter: What to do first. *American Journal of Psychiatry*, 138,421-428.

Marmor, J. (1966). Theories of learning and the psychotherapeutic process. *British Journal of Psychiatry*, 112, 363-366.

Marmor, J. (1976). Common operational factors in diverse approaches to behavior change. In A. Burton (Ed.), *What makes behavior change possible?* NY: Brunner/Mazel.

Martin, A. (1982). Some issues in the treatment of gay and lesbian patients. *Psychotherapy: Theory, Research and Practice*, 19, 341-348.

Martin, E.S., & Schurtman, R. (1985). Termination anxiety as it affects the therapist. *Psychotherapy*, 22, 1, 92-96.

Maslow, A.H. (1966). Abstracting and theorizing. In A.H. Maslow (Ed.), *The psychology of science: A reconnaissance*. (pp. 66-71). NY: Harper.

Maxwell, M.L., & Maxwell, G. (1980). Psychotherapy and science: Impurely rhetorical. In M.M. Mahoney (Ed.), *Psychotherapy process: current issues and future directions*. NY: Plenum.

May, R. (1975). *The courage to create*. NY: Norton.

May, R. (1983). *The discovery of being: Writings in existential psychology*. NY: Norton.

Meehl, P.E. (1960). The cognitive activity of the clinician. *American Psychologist*, 15, 19-27.

Meichenbaum, D. (1977). *Cognitive-behavior modification: An integrative approach*. NY: Plenum.

Meichenbaum, D.H. (1980). Nature of conscious and unconscious processes: Issues in cognitive assessment. Invited address presented at the Meetings of the Eastern Psychological Association, Harford, Conn., April.

Meltzoff, J., & Kornreich, M. (1970). *Research in Psychotherapy*.

Chicago: Aldine.

Mendel, W.M. (1966). The problem of existing as a psychotherapist. *Voices: The art and science of psychotherapy*, 2, 2, 35-38.

Menninger, K. (1958). *Theory of psychoanalytic technique*. NY: Basic Books.

Mitchell, K.M., Bozarth, J.D., & Krauft, C.C. (1977). A reappraisal of the therapeutic effectiveness of accurate empathy, nonpossessive warmth, and genuineness. In A.S. Gurman and A.M. Razin (Eds.), *Effective psychotherapy: A handbook of research*. NY: Pergamon.

Morris, R.J., & Magrath, K.H. (1983). The therapeutic relationship in behavior therapy. In M.J. Lambert (Ed.), *A guide to psychotherapy and patient relationships*. Homewood, ILL: Dow Jones-Irwin.

Mowrer, O.H., & Mowrer, W. (1938). Enuresis: A method for its study and treatment. *American Journal of Orthopsychiatry*. 8, 436-459.

Mumford, L. (1967). *The myth of the machine; technics and human development*. NY: Harcourt, Brace and World.

Nacht, N. (1962). Curative factors in psychoanalysis. *International Journal Psycho-Analysis*, 43, 206-211.

Nacht, N. (1963). The non-verbal relationship in psychoanalytic treatment. *International Journal Psycho-Analysis*, 44, 328-333.

Neulinger, J., Stein, M.I., Schillinger, M., & Welkowitz, J. (1970). Perceptions of the optimally integrated person as a function of therapists' characteristics. *Perceptual and Motor Skills*, 30, 375-384.

Nowacki, C.M., & Poe, C.A. (1973). The concept of mental health as related to sex of person perceived. *Journal of Consulting and Clinical Psychology*, 40, 160.

Nuehring, E.M., Fein, S.B., & Tyler, M. (1974). The gay college student: Perspectives for mental health professionals. *The Counseling Psychologist*, 4, 4, 64-72.

Oppenheimer, R. (1956). Analogy in science. *American Psychologist*, 11, 3, 127-135.

Orlinsky, D.E., & Howard, K.E. (1978). The relation of process to outcome in psychotherapy. In S.L. Garfield & A.I. Bergin (Eds.), *Handbook of psychotherapy and behavior change: An empirical analysis*, (2nd ed.) (pp. 283-329). NY: Wiley.

Palmer, J.O. (1980). *A primer of eclectic psychotherapy*. Monterey, CA: Brooks/Cole.

Parloff, M.B. (1976). Shopping for the right therapy. *Saturday Review*, February 21, pp.14-16.

Parloff, M.B., Waskow, I.E., & Wolfe, B.E. (1978). Research on therapist variables in relation to process and outcome. In S.L. Garfield and A.E. Bergin (Eds.), *Handbook of psychotherapy and behavior change: An empirical analysis.* (2nd ed.) NY: Wiley.

Patterson, C.H. (1967). Divergence and convergence in psychotherapy. *American Journal of Psychotherapy,* 21, 4-17.

Paul, G.L. (1967). Strategy of outcome research in psychotherapy. *Journal of Consulting Psychology,* 31, 109-118.

Paul, I.H. (1978). *The form and technique of psychotherapy.* Chicago: University of Chicago Press.

Peck, M.S. (1978). *The road less traveled: A new psychology of love, traditional values and spiritual growth.* NY: Simon & Schuster.

Pendergrass, V.E. (1975). Marriage counseling with lesbian couples. *Psychotherapy: Theory, Research and Practice,* 12, 93-96.

Perlman, H.H. (1979). *Relationship: The heart of helping people.* Chicago: University of Chicago Press.

Polster, E., & Polster, M. (1973). *Gestalt therapy integrated: contours of theory and practice.* NY: Brunner/Mazel.

Prochaska, J.O. (1979). *Systems of psychotherapy: A transtheoretical analysis.* Homewood, ILL: Dorsey Press.

Racker, H. (1957). The meaning and uses of countertransference. *Psychoanalytic Quarterly,* 26, 303-357.

Racker, H. (1972). The meanings and uses of countertransference. *Psychoanalytic Quarterly,* 41, 487-506.

Raimy, V. (1975). *Misunderstandings of the self: Cognitive psychotherapy and the misconception hypothesis.* San Francisco: Jossey-Bass.

Rako, S., & Mazer, H. (1983). *Semrad: The heart of a therapist.* NY: Jason Aronson.

Rangell, L. (1981). From insight to change. *Journal of the American Psychoanalytic Association,* 29, 1, 119-141.

Raush, H.L., & Bordin, E.S. (1957). Warmth in personality development and in psychotherapy. *Psychiatry,* 20, 351-363.

Rawlings, E., & Carter, D. (Eds.), (1977). *Psychotherapy for women: Treatment toward equality.* Springfield, ILL: Thomas.

Reich, A. (1951). On counter-transference. *International Journal of Psycho-Analysis,* 32, 25-31.

Reich, A. (1960). Further remarks on countertransference. *International Journal of Psychoanalysis,* 41, 389-395.

Reik, T. (1949). *Listening with the third ear.* NY: Farrar, Straus & Co.

Rice, J., & Rice, D. (1973). Implications of the women's liberation movement for psychotherapy. *American Journal of Psychiatry*, 130, 191-196.

Rice, L.N., & Greenberg, L.S. (1984). The new research paradigm. In L.N. Rice & L.S. Greenberg (Eds.), *Patterns of change*. (pp.7-29). NY: Guilford.

Ricks, D.F., Wandersman, A., & Popper, P.J. (1976). Humanism and behaviorism: toward a new syntheses. In A. Wandersman, P.J. Poppen, & D.F. Ricks (Eds.), *Humanism and behaviorism: Dialogue and growth*. NY: Pergamon.

Riddle, D.I., & Sang, B. (1978). Psychotherapy with lesbians. *Journal of Social Issues*, 34, 84-100.

Rilke, R.M. (1980). A poem. *Voices: The art and science of psychotherapy*, 16, 2, 54.

Rogers, C.R. (1951). *Client-centered therapy*. NY: Houghton-Mifflin.

Rogers, C.R. (1957). The necessary and sufficient conditions of therapeutic personality change. *Journal of Consulting Psychology*, 21, 95-103.

Rogers, C.R. (1959). A theory of therapy, personality, and interpersonal relationships as developed in the client-centered framework. In S. Koch (Ed.), *Psychology: A study of a science*. Vol. 3. NY: McGraw-Hill.

Rogers, C.R. (1961). The characteristics of a helping relationships. In M.I. Stein (Ed.), *Contemporary psychotherapies*. Glencoe, ILL: Free Press of Glencoe.

Rogers, C.R. (1961a). *On becoming a person*. Boston: Houghton Mifflin.

Rogers, C.R. (Ed.), (1967). *The therapeutic relationship and its impact: A study of psychotherapy with schizophrenics*. Madison, Wis: University of Wisconsin Press.

Rogers, C.R. (1968). This is me. In W.G. Bennis, et al. (Eds.), *Interpersonal dynamics: Essays and readings of human interaction*. Springfield, ILL: Dorsey Press.

Rogers, C.R., & Dymond, R. (1964). *Psychotherapy and personality change*. Chicago: University of Chicago Press.

Rose, A.P. (1954). *The gentle house*. Boston: Houghton Mifflin.

Rosen, J., & Stern, E.M. (1983). Direct to the schizophrenic. *Voices: The art and science of psychotherapy*, 18, 4, 23-28.

Rosenfeld, H.A. (1965). *Psychotic states: A psychoanalytic approach*. NY: International Universities Press.

Rosenthal, D., & Frank, J.S. (1958). The fate of psychiatric clinic outpatients assigned to psychotherapy. *Journal of Nervous and Mental Disease*, 127, 330-343.

Rosenzweig, S. (1936). Some implicit common factors in diverse methods in psychotherapy. *American Journal of Orthopsychiatry*, 6, 412-415.

Rosenzweig, S.P., & Folman, R. (1974). Patient and therapist variables affecting premature termination in group psychotherapy. *Psychotherapy: Theory, Research, and Practice*, 11, 76-79.

Rosenzweig, S.P., & Hartford, T. (1972). Correlates of therapists' initial impressions of patients in a psychatric day center. *Psychotherapy: Theory, Research and Practice*, 9, 126-129.

Runkel, P.R. (1970). *The law unto themselves*. Ann Arbor, MI: Planorian.

Russell, R.L., & Stiles, W.B. (1979). Categories for classifying language in psychotherapy. *Psychological Bulletin*, 86, 404-419.

Ryan, V.L., & Gizynski, M.N. (1971). Behavior therapy in retrospect: Patients' feelings about their behavior therapists. *Journal of Consulting and Clinical Psychology*, 37, 1-9.

Ryan, W. (1971). *Blaming the victim*. NY: Random House.

Saint-Exupery, A.D. (1943). *The Little Prince*. NY: Harcourt, Brace & World.

Salter, A. (1949). *Conditioned reflex therapy*. NY: Farrar, Straus.

Saltzman, C., Luetgert, M.J., Roth, C.H., Creaser, J., & Howard, L. (1976). Formation of a therapeutic relationship: Experiences during the initial phase of psychotherapy as predictors of treatment duration and outcome. *Journal of Consulting and Clinical Psychology*, 44, 546-555.

Salzman, L. (1976). The will to change. In A. Burton (Ed.), *What makes behavior change possible?* (pp.13-33). NY: Brunner/Mazel.

Sarup, G. (1981). Role playing, issue importance, and attitude change. *Social Behavior and Personality*, 9, 2, 191-202.

Satir, V., & Brothers, B.J. (1983). Virginia Satir: Past to present. *Voices: The art and science of psychotherapy*, 18, 4, 48-56.

Schachtel, E.G. (1959). *Metamorphosis; on the development of affect, perception, attention, and memory*. NY: Basic Books.

Schofield, W. (1964). *Psychotherapy: The purchase of friendship*. NY: Prentice-Hall.

Schonbar, R. (1965). Interpretation and insight in psychotherapy. *Psychotherapy: Theory, Research and Practice*, 2, 78-84.

Secord, P.F. (1983). *Explanation in the social sciences and in life situations*. Prepared for the conference on potentialities of knowledge in the social sciences, University of Chicago, September, 1983.

Shader, R.I., Kellam, S.G., & Durell, J. (1967). Social field events during the first week of hospitalization as predictors of treatment outcome for psychotic patients. *Journal of Nervous and Mental Disease*, 145, 142-153.

Shaffer, G.W., & Lazarus, R.S. (1952). *Fundamental concepts in clinical psychology*. NY: McGraw Hill.

Shaffer, P. (1974). *Equus*. NY: Atheneum.

Shapiro, A.K., Struening, E., Shapiro, E., & Barten, H. (1976). Prognostic correlates of psychotherapy in psychiatric outpatients. *American Journal of Psychiatry*, 133, 802-808.

Shapiro, R.J. (1974). Therapist attitudes and premature termination in family and individual therapy. *Journal of Nervous and Mental Disease*, 159, 101-107.

Shaw, F.J. (1949). Some postulates concerning psychotherapy. *Journal of Consulting Psychology*, 12, 426-431.

Shaw, F.J. (1946). A stimulus-response analysis of repression and insight in psychotherapy. *Psychological Review*, 53, 36-42.

Shoben E.J.,Jr. (1949). Psychotherapy as a problem in learning theory. *Psychological Bulletin*, 46, 366-392.

Sloane, R.B. (1969). The converging paths of behavior therapy and psychotherapy. *American Journal of Psychiatry*, 125, 877-883.

Sloane, R.B., Staples, F.R., Cristol, A.H., Yorkston, N.J., & Whipple, K. (1975). *Psychotherapy vs. behavior therapy*. Cambridge: Harvard University Press.

Sloane, R., Staples, F., Whipple, K., and Cristol, A. (1977). Patients' attitudes toward behavior therapy and psychotherapy. *American Journal of Psychiatry*, 134, 134-137.

Smith, M.L., & Glass, G.V. (1977). Meta-analysis of psychotherapy outcome studies. *American Psychologist*, 32, 752-760.

Smith, M.L., Glass, G.V., & Miller, T.I. (1980). *The benefits of psychotherapy*. Baltimore: The Johns Hopkins University Press.

Stotland, E., Mathews, K.E., Sherman, S.E., Hansson, R.O., & Richardson, B.Z. (1978). *Empathy, fantasy, and helping*. Beverly Hills, CA: Sage Publications.

Stotland, E., Sherman, S.E., & Shaver, K.G. (1971). *Empathy and birth order*. Lincoln: University of Nebraska Press.

396

Strachey, J. (1934). The nature of the therapeutic action of psychoanalysis. *International Journal of Psycho-Analysis*, 15, 117-126.

Strupp, H.H. (1968). Psychotherapists and (or versus?) researchers. *Voices, The art and science of psychotherapy*, 4, 3, 28-32.

Strupp, H.H. (1969). Toward a specification of teaching and learning in psychotherapy. *Archives of General Psychiatry*, 21, 203-212.

Strupp, H.H. (1973a). *Psychotherapy: Clinical, research, and theoretical issues*. NY: Jason Aronson.

Strupp, H.H. (1973b). On the basic ingredients of psychotherapy. *Journal of Consulting and Clinical Psychology*, 41, 1-8.

Strupp, H.H. (1976). The nature of the therapeutic influence and its basic ingredients. In A. Burton (Ed.), *What makes behavior change possible?* NY: Brunner/Mazel.

Strupp, H.H. (1982). Foreward in M.R. Goldfried (Ed.), *Converging themes in psychotherapy: Trends in psychodynamic, humanistic, and behavioral practice*. NY: Springer Publishing Co.

Strupp, H.H., Fox, R.E., & Lessler, K. (1969). *Patients view their psychotherapy*. Baltimore: Johns Hopkins Press.

Strupp, H.H., & Hadley, S.W. (1979). Specific vs. nonspecific factors in psychotherapy: A controlled study of outcome. *Archives of General Psychiatry*, 36, 1125-1136.

Szasz, T.S. (1960). The myth of mental illness. *American Psychologist*, 15, 113-118.

Tennov, D. (1973). Feminism, psychotherapy and professionalism. *Journal of Contemporary Psychotherapy*, 5, 107-116.

Thompson, C.M. (1952). Countertransference. *Samiksa*, 6, 205-211.

Tower, L.E. (1956). Countertransference. *Journal of the American Psychoanalytic Association*, 4, 224-255.

Truax, C.B., & Carkhuff, R.R. (1976). *Toward effective counseling and psychotherapy: Training and practice*. Chicago: Aldine.

Truax, C.B., & Mitchell, K.M. (1971). Research on certain therapist interpersonal skills in relation to process and outcome. In A.E. Bergin & S.L. Garfield (Eds.), *Handbook of psychotherapy and behavior change: An empirical analysis*. (pp. 299-344). NY: Wiley.

Truax, C.B. (1962). A tentative scale for the measurement of unconditional positive regard. *Psychiatric Institute Bulletin*, Wisconsin Psychiatric Institute, University of Wisconsin, 2, 1.

Turkington, C. (1984). National survey points to mental services gap. *APA Monitor*, 15, 12, 34.

Uhlenhuth, E.H., & Duncan, D.B. (1968). Subjective change with medical students therapists: II. Some determinants of change in psychoneurotic outpatients. *Archives of General Psychiatry*, 18, 532-540.

Vandenbos, G.R., & Karon, B.P. (1971). Pathogenesis: A new therapist personality dimension related to therapeutic effectiveness. *Journal of Personality Assessment*, 35, 252-260.

Waelder, R. (1956). Introduction to the discussion on problems of transference. *International Journal of Psycho-Analysis*, 37, 367-368.

Watson, J.B., & Rayner, R. (1920). Conditioned emotional reactions. *Journal of Experimental Psychology*, 3,1-14.

Weigert, E. (1952). Contribution to the problem of terminating psychoanalyses. *Psychoanalytic Quarterly*, 21, 465-480.

Weimer, W.B. (1980). Psychotherapy and philosophy of science. In M.M. Mahoney (Ed.), *Psychotherapy process: Current issues and future directions*. NY: Plenum.

Whitehorn, J.C., & Betz, B.J. (1954). A study of psychotherapeutic relationships between physicians and schizophrenic patients. *American Journal of Psychiatry*, 111, 321-331.

Wills, T.A. (1982a). Nonspecific factors in helping relationships. In T.A. Wills (Ed.), *Basic processes in helping relationships*. (pp. 381-404). NY: Academic Press.

Wills, T.A. (1982b). *Basic processes in helping relationships*. NY: Academic Press.

Winnicott, D.W. (1949). Hate in the countertransference. *International Journal of Psychoanalysis*, 30, 69-75.

Winnicott, D.W. (1960). Countertransference. *British Journal of Medical Psychology*, 33, 17-21.

Wolman, B.B. (1983). Interactional psychotherapy. In B.B. Wolman (Ed.), *The therapist's handbook: Treatment methods of mental disorders*. (2nd ed.) NY: Van Nostrand Reinhold Co.

Wolman, B.B. (Ed.), (1972). *Success and failure in psychoanalysis and psychotherapy*. NY: Macmillan.

Wolpe, J. (1958). *Psychotherapy by reciprocal inhibition*. Stanford, CA: Stanford University Press.

Woodman, N.J., & Lenna, H.R. (1980). *Counseling with gay men and women: A guide for facilitating positive life-styles*. San Francisco: Jossey-Bass.

Yontef, G. (1976). Gestalt therapy: Clinical phenomenology. In V. Binder, A. Binder & B. Rimland (Eds.), *Modern therapies*. (pp. 65-

398

79). New Jersey: Prentice-Hall.

Zajonc, R. (1980). Feeling and thinking. *American Psychologist*, 35, 151-175.

Zetzel, E. (1965). Current concepts of transference. *International Journal of Psychoanalysis*, 37, 369-376.

Zimbardo, P.G., Ebbesen, E.B., & Malach, C. (1977). *Influencing attitudes and changing behavior*. (2nd ed.) Reading, MA: Addison-Wesley.

Zinker, J. (1977). *Creative process in Gestalt therapy*. NY: Brunner/Mazel.

AUTHOR INDEX

Abrams, M.H., 275
Adkins, D.M., 180
Alexander, F., 7, 87,
260, 261, 262, 323,
324, 331, 333, 334, 341
Alexander, J.F., 78
Appelbaum, S.A., 44, 45,
46, 51, 80
Arnkoff, D.B., 78, 270
Aslin, A.L., 250

Baekeland, F., 112
Barlow, D. H., 33
Barrett, C., 251
Baum, O.E., 108
Bebout, J., 130
Beck, A.T., 3, 130, 258,
348, 360, 361
Beck, S., 78, 270
Becker, E., 39, 343
Beers, C.W., 75
Beier, E.G., 350, 351
Benjamin, L.S., 2
Berg, P., 251
Bergin, A.E., 9, 11, 22,
33, 109, 118, 140, 268
Bettelheim, B., 24, 26,
27, 134, 157, 159
Betz, B.J., 108
Bhaskar, R., 29
Bishop, J.B., 180
Black, J., 336
Blanck, G., 36, 218
Blanck, R., 36

Blanton, R., 21
Bond, J., 260
Bordin, E.S., 111
Bowlby, J., 334
Bozarth, J.D., 81, 108,
143
Brady, J.P., 46, 47, 51,
80, 334
Breuer, J., 87, 212
Brodsky, A., 251
Brothers, B.J., 42
Broverman, D.M., 250
Broverman, I.K., 250
Brow, E.C., 231
Brown, R.D., 180
Bruch, Hilde, 19, 76, 254
Burton, A., 253

Cannon, J.R., 130
Carkhuff, R.R., 10, 43,
50, 108, 130,
Carmen, E., 192
Carson, R.C., 108
Carter, D., 251
Castenada, C., 271
Cavanagh, M.E., 348, 351,
359
Chafetz, J.S., 253
Chapman, J.P., 253
Chapman, L.J., 253
Chessick, R.D., 286
Chevron, E.S., 360, 361
Clarkson, F.E., 250
Cohen, M.B., 240

401

Fromm-Reichmann, F., 75, 76, 77, 240, 258

Galvin, K., 336
Garfield, S.L., 6, 42, 43, 44, 45, 50, 51, 80, 140, 253, 351, 352
Garfinkle, E., 253
Gergen, K.J., 188
Gergen, M., 188
Gill, M.M., 46, 47, 48, 334
Ginott, A., 134, 135
Gitelson, M., 240
Gizynski, M.N., 111
Glass, C.R., 270
Glass, G.V., 12, 13, 14, 184, 190, 267
Glover, E., 240
Goldfried, M.R., 3, 7, 16, 17, 33, 80, 270
Goldstein, A.P., 33
Gonsiorek, J., 253
Gordon, B., 303, 363
Greaves, G., 42
Greben, S.E., 324
Greenberg, J., 75
Greenson, R.R., 105, 183, 206, 213
Grieger, R., 270
Gross, M.L., 19
Gurman, A.S., 33, 81

Hadley, S.W., 112
Hall, M., 253
Halleck, S.L., 104
Hammer, M., 273
Hartford, T., 180

Hartley, D.E., 352
Havens, L., 269, 330
Hayek, F.A., 31
Heimann, P., 240, 241, 242, 247, 249
Heine, R.W., 108
Henry, B., 20, 21, 33
Hiler, E.W., 108
Hilgard, E.R., 335
Hobbs, N., 259, 262
Hoffman, I., 46, 47, 334
Hokanson, J.E., 79, 120, 135, 136, 160, 223, 265
Hollon, S.D., 270
Hooker, E., 252
Horney, K., 38, 338
Horowitz, M.J., 337, 338
Horwitz, L., 80
Howard, K.E., 139, 276, 277, 283, 338
Howard, K.I., 163, 165
Howard, L., 180

Jackson, D.M., 129, 130, 131
Jacobs, L., 80
Jacobson, N.S., 79
Janis, I., 348
Johnson, D.W., 80
Jones, M.C., 3

Kagan, N., 338
Kahn, M.M.R., 257, 284
Kanfer, F.H., 118
Kapelovitz, L.H., 19
Karon, B.P., 140
Katz, R.L., 129, 130
Kazdin, A.E., 788, 336

403

405

SUBJECT INDEX

Acceptance, 147, 164, 290, 329, 330, 331, 356, 362
Allocentric attitude, 277
Altered states of consciousness, 45-46
Anonymity, 147, 164, 194-198
Art of psychotherapy, 22, 59, 145
Behavior therapy, 2, 3, 6-8, 25-27, 32, 37, 78, 79, 228, 289, 334
Benefits of psychotherapy, 9, 10, 13-15
Biofeedback, 25, 45
Bonding, 73-75, 147
Care, 58, 59, 65, 67-68, 106, 110, 143-145, 148-159, 162-163, 165, 229, 232
Change, 8, 11, 15, 33, 47-48, 65, 261, 289, 290, 297, 315, 317-318, 334, 336-340, 373
  and altered states of consciousness, 39, 45-46
  and new experiences, 47-48
  mediating, 8, 15, 47
  pathways to, 37
  variables of 15, 42, 48
Client-centered, 2, 35-36, 228
Clinical practice, 6, 8, 15, 78
Clinical strategies, 16-17
Clinicians, 16-22
  contributions, 33-40, 46
  scientists, and 16-21, 29, 30, 32

theoretical orientation, 5
Cognitive behavior therapy, 7-8, 32, 37, 78, 258, 270
Common factors
  in psychotherapy, 6-8, 10-11, 16, 17, 41-49, 64, 65
  interrelatedness of, 53, 58-65, 86, 257, 324
Conceptualization, 8-9, 24, 30, 36, 41, 45, 52, 257, 263, 269, 309, 373
Congruence, 43, 106, 136, 138, 141, 334
Consciousness, 24, 25, 27-28, altered states of, 45-46
Corrective emotional experience, 7, 44-50, 53-54, 56, 67, 86-89, 144, 165, 225, 228, 261, 299, 315, 317, 319-341, 347, 363
  literature and research, 334-339
  outside of psychotherapy, 339-341
Countertransference, 51-53, 57, 67, 83, 86-87, 114, 140, 144, 155, 232, 235-256, 322, 324, 247, 363, 367
  early conceptualization, 238-241
  homophobia, 250-254
  honesty, and, 254-256
  not fear, 241-150
  sexism, 250-254

409